# TRADITION and REVOLUTION
## The Jewish Renaissance
in Russian Avant-Garde Art
1912-1928

The exhibition and catalog have been made possible
by Salome and Eric E. Estorick.

# TRADITION and REVOLUTION
## The Jewish Renaissance in Russian Avant-Garde Art 1912-1928

Edited by Ruth Apter-Gabriel

The Israel Museum, Jerusalem

Cover: El Lissitzky, detail of illustration for "Shifs Karta" (cat. 105).


This catalog has been published in conjunction with the exhibition
"Tradition and Revolution: The Jewish Renaissance in Russian
Avant-Garde Art, 1912-1928," June, 1987, organized by the Israel
Museum, Jerusalem.


Curator-in-Charge: Meira Perry-Lehmann
Curator of the Exhibition: Ruth Apter-Gabriel
Assistants to the Curator: Amir Azoulai, Shoshana Nomberg,
                           Michal Sofer

Catalog Design: Nirit Zur
Exhibition Design: Halina Hamou
English Editing: Malka Jagendorf
Copy Editing: Judy Lee, Felice Ziskin
Managing Editor: Felicia G. Eisenberg

Photography: Yoram Tamir, Yoram Lehmann, Nahum Slapak,
             Zev Radovan, David Harris
Typesetting: Graph Press, Jerusalem
The text of this book has been set in Geneva Light
Color Separations: Art Plus Ltd., Jerusalem
Plates: Tafsar Ltd., Jerusalem
Printed by: Hamakor Press Ltd., Jerusalem

Israel Museum Catalog No. 285
ISBN 965 278 0715

N
6988
T7
1987

Dedicated to the memory of
Regina and Henry Dessau and
Sarah and Morris Estorick

# Contents

## Lenders to the Exhibition

Sam and Ayala Zacks Collection
Chimen Abramsky, London
Uzi Agassi, Raanana
Boris and Lisa Aronson Collection
Sheine Miriam Broderzon, Holon
Zusia Efron, Jerusalem
Salome and Eric E. Estorick
Marianna and Walter Griessmann, London
Michail Grobman, Tel Aviv
Feige and Levia Hofstein, Ramat Aviv
Esther Markish, Kiron
Natalia Mikhoels-Vovsi, Tel Aviv
The Moldovan Family Collection, New York
Ala Perlman-Zuskin, Neve Monoson
Elaine and Arthur Cohen Collection, New York

Central Library for Music and Dance, Tel Aviv
Institute of Modern Russian Culture, Texas
Collection of Nahum Zemach, founder of the Habimah
Theatre, Israel Goor Theatre Archives and Museum,
Jerusalem
Jewish National and University Library, Jerusalem
Habimah Theatre, Tel Aviv
Ethnography and Folklore Pavilion, Haaretz Museum,
Tel Aviv
The Theater Museum, Haaretz Museum, Tel Aviv
Mishkan Le'omanut, Museum of Art, Ein Harod
Museum of Jewish Art, Jerusalem
Ryback Museum, Bat Yam
Tel Aviv Museum, Tel Aviv

## Acknowledgements

The contributing authors have extended most valuable
help, for which I am deeply grateful. Beyond their written studies, they have shared with me their time, ideas,
and professional expertise, without which this publication would never have been possible.

I am also indebted to Michal Sofer, Mirjam Rajner and
Zusia Efron for their valuable assistance. My thanks
also to those who have patiently advised me through
repeated phone calls, personal visits, correspon-
dence, and translations:
Jacob Aronson; Rita Bachner; Nitza Behrouzi; Galia
Bar-Or; K. Bar-Gera; Mark Barschatsky; Judge David
Bartov; Israel Becker; Malachi Beit-Arié; Shmuel-Mula
Ben-Haim; Merrill Berman; Ruth Blumert; Rachel
Boimvol; Lea Broides; George Costakis; Mordechai
Djerbi; Anna Eiges; Ruth and Gideon Elad; Abraham
Elinson; Sue Fox; Luba Freedman; Haia Friedberg;
Yehuda Gabbai; Naomi Givon; Robert H. Glauber;
Antonina Gmurzynska; Reuven Goldberg; Aliza
Greenberg; Michail Grobman; Lisa and Bill Gross;
Meir Harats; Annely Juda; Jeanette Kaufman; Ada
Kasarnovsky; Ella Leizerovsky; Esther Levinger;
Yitzak Luden; Gitl Maizel; Dov Maizel; Edna
Moshenson; Esther Markish; Jean Jacques Newman;
Zvi Noam; Dov Noy; Hirsh Osherovitch; Rabbi
Shlomo Pappenheim; Lisl Patai; Eliezer Podriatschik;
Ruth Porter; Jacob Raphael; M. Reis; Louis
Schuffman; Paul Schwartz; Leon Shalit; Meir Stern;
Jacob Tversky; Benjamin Ventura; Eva Waintraub;
Moshe Waldman; Israel Wasserman; Rachel
Wischnitzer; Yeshayahu Yariv; Victor Zalkind; Prof.
Benjamin Zemach; Aza Zwi.

Finally, my warmest thanks to my colleagues at the
Israel Museum, especially Izzika Gaon, Meira Perry-
Lehmann, Amir Azoulai, Shoshana Nomberg, Nirit Zur,
Halina Hamou, and Yoram Tamir for their deep involve-
ment in this project.

R. A-G.

# Preface

*Tradition and Revolution: The Jewish Renaissance in Russian Avant-Garde Art* with its accompanying publication unfolds a new chapter in the history of Jewish art. It celebrates and explores the phenomenon of Jewish participation in the Russian Avant-Garde movement at the time of the Bolshevik Revolution.

Through five years of research, persistence and a measure of good fortune, this exhibition of 174 items gradually took shape. The sheer number of works is a clear affirmation of the existence of a Jewish Modernist Art during that turbulent period, and the subjects and content point to the enormous complexity and tensions of Jewish life in Russia at the time.

This show – which begins in Jerusalem and travels on to New York – has been an enormous undertaking, requiring the efforts of many people, in all kinds of capacities, whose enthusiasm has moved the project from an idea to its realization.

Above all, my gratitude is extended to Salome and Eric E. Estorick, whose generous support from the start made the exhibition and publication possible.

Warmest thanks are due to our longtime friends, Marianna and Walter Griessmann of London, who provided the impetus from which this project was born, through their gift of El Lissitzky's hand-colored scroll, *Legend of Prague*, in honor of Teddy Kollek's seventieth birthday. In addition, they have most kindly supported the cultural events held at the museum in conjunction with the exhibition.

I am deeply grateful to Lisa Aronson, who so graciously lent us the extraordinary Boris and Lisa Aronson Collection, which forms the backbone of the show.

This exhibition would not have been possible without the generosity of all the lenders, to whom I extend my heartfelt thanks.

Martin Weyl
Director

# Foreword

The opening of "Tradition and Revolution: The Jewish Renaissance in Russian Avant-Garde Art" at the Israel Museum in June, 1987 corresponds to a number of historic dates. First, this year was the 70th anniversary of the Russian Revolution, which, for the arts, briefly fostered the illusion of freedom in general, and among Jewish artists in particular.

Berlin, which after World War I became the spiritual hub and intellectual meeting point for all Europe and notably for Russia, celebrates its 750th birthday this year. Most of the artists in the exhibition were active in Berlin in addition to Russia, or after leaving Russia. Many of the books displayed in the exhibition were created in Russia and published in Berlin.

A third milestone this year is the 100th birthday of Marc Chagall, perhaps the most outstanding and certainly the most famous of the artists in the exhibition.

The first step towards the realization of this exhibition and the catalog accompanying it was made in 1982, when Marianna and Walter Griessman, long-time faithful friends of the museum, presented the Department of Prints and Drawings with El Lissitzky's *Sikhes Kholin* (Legend of Prague), in honor of the 70th birthday of, Teddy Kollek, Mayor of Jerusalem and Chairman of the Board of Directors of the Israel Museum. The previous owner of the scroll was George Costakis.

Our quest for a suitable framework for displaying this important work, and our study of the cultural climate that surrounded it, led us to a group of Russian Jewish, artists whose activity between the years 1912 and 1928 was a unique fusion of the traditional Jewish and the modernist European. The works of these artists presented us with a brief and unique chapter in the history of Jewish art — brief yet resonating to this day in the ongoing quest of Jewish artists in general and Israeli artists in particular for the expression of a national identity.

The main channels of expression for the group were in the areas of book illustration and theatre design, favorites also of the Cubo-Futurists, whose vocabulary of forms was widely used by the Jewish group. Yet it is hard to dissociate the Jewish artists' concern with the Hebrew alphabet from their belonging to "The People of the Book."

Our main efforts were geared to tracking down suitable works for an exhibition on this elusive subject, and this bordered very closely on detective work. Most of our information came by word of mouth. The main public source of illustrated books was the Jewish National and University Library in Jerusalem, but the most exciting moments were the finding, in Israel, of books that were like brands saved from the fire, owned by venerable surviving Jewish intellectuals from Russia. Relatives of Jewish writers, poets, and actors murdered in Stalin's terror in 1948-1952 were forced to leave the country with little more than the clothes on their backs. The few thin volumes, printed on cheap newsprint, and transferred to Israel, sometimes in roundabout ways, are often the only surviving testimony of the creativity of the artist, cherished by a widow or offspring. We deeply honor the memory of Peretz Markish, David Hofstein, Solomon Mikhoels and Binyamin Zuskin, and are grateful to their relatives, for the trust and generosity that impelled them to lend us, for the duration of the exhibition, these precious documents.

The discovery of the Boris and Lisa Aronson Collection, of which only individual items were displayed in the past, and its identification, completed in preparation for the exhibition, enriched immeasurably both the exhibition and the museum itself, which gained the valuable friendship of Lisa Aronson, life and work partner, and widow of Boris Aronson. The trust and cooperation that characterized our relations made the dialogue and friendship with her into a rare pleasure.

Salome and Eric E. Estorick, whose generosity enabled us to embark on this uncharted journey, have further cemented their partnership with the Israel Museum in recent years. It is not mere chance that bound them to an exhibition of Russian Jewish art. Eric E. Estorick was the first art dealer to visit the USSR after World War II, bringing works by its artists for exhibition at his Grosvenor Gallery in London, and contributing much to its prestige in the West.

For their abiding and generous patronage of the Museum's Department of Prints and Drawings and its projects in recent years, we are deeply grateful to them and are happy to honor their request to dedicate this catalog to their late Russian- and Polish-born parents, Regina and Henry Dessau, and Sarah and Morris Estorick.

Meira Perry-Lehmann,
The Michael Bromberg Curator of
Prints and Drawings

# Introduction

The avant-garde art that sprang up in Russia in the period of the Revolution has been well researched, and its contribution to modern art is undisputed. What has been largely overlooked, however, is that simultaneously, a number of Russian Jewish artists were actively seeking to revitalize Jewish art.

> end of Tsarist rule not only kindled hopes of free-
> n the Jewish masses but also served as a stimu-
> an unprecedented Jewish cultural renaissance.
> literature, poetry, music, theatre, and the plas-
> flourished during this time, as Jews explored
> venues through which to express their national
> ultural identity.

In the field of art, leading figures such as El Lissitzky, Nathan Altman, Issachar Ryback, Joseph Tchaikov, Boris Aronson, and even Marc Chagall[1] attempted to create a new, modern, Jewish art. This was largely achieved by fusing the folk sources of the Jews with the modern artistic languages of the day. If, however, their attempts were often less experimental than those of their Russian avant-garde colleagues, they were nevertheless strikingly innovative when compared to the traditional renderings of Jewish themes.[2]

The search for their ancient folk art led several of these artists deep into the Pale of Settlement, into the world of the shtetl, and to traditional lore. This exhibit and catalog focus specifically on their Jewish works – drawings, prints, and book illustrations – inspired by this quest. Throughout the project, our aim has been to retrace the steps of the Russian Jewish avant-garde during the short period of the Jewish cultural renaissance, from around 1915 to the mid-1920s.

The important Boris and Lisa Aronson Collection is at the core of this exhibition. In addition to drawings by the artists mentioned above, it includes a large body of Jewish folk art[3] – examples similar to those copied and collected during the ethnographic expedition, headed by An-Sky (S. A. Rapoport) in 1912-14, through the Jewish rural areas of Volynia and Podolia, in the Ukraine. As An-Sky's collection is presently sealed off in Leningrad's Ethnographic Museum of the Peoples of the USSR and is inaccessible to researchers, the Boris and Lisa Aronson Collection, published now for the first time, offers a truly unique opportunity to study this rare type of folk art.

Through other works in "Tradition and Revolution," one can trace these Jewish artists' transition from the figur-ative to the abstract, as is most vividly expressed in the works of Lissitzky (compare for example cat. 79 to cat. 104) and Altman (compare cats. 19-26 to cat. 27). Also included are examples of the Jewish artistic contribution in support of the Bolshevik cause, e.g., Lissitzky's 1919 *Had Gadya* illustrations (cat. 190), touching evidence of the Jewish expression of zeal for the Revolution, and Ryback's poster (cat. 139), an example of Soviet propaganda.

The heyday of artistic experimentation drew to a close as political repression set in. For Jewish artists, the newly founded Jewish theatres (such as the Hebrew-speaking Habimah and the Jewish Chamber Theatre in Moscow) became the last refuge of avant-garde activity. Thus we have included many works which exemplify the Jewish avant-garde contribution to theatre design; for instance, Altman's sets for *The Dybbuk* (cats. 19-26), that most celebrated of Habimah productions, and Robert Falk's designs (cats. 112, 113) for *Jacob's Dream.*

The light of artistic freedom began to dim just as the Russian Jewish avant-garde artists were experimenting with a truly international artistic language in support of the Revolution, yet, stripped of subject matter and Jewish content. If the attempts of these artists influenced other Jewish modernists to combine their national identity with an abstract "international" style – these attempts have yet to be assessed. As cultural freedom was extinguished, Chagall, Ryback, and Aronson left for the West around 1922, each going his own way. By and large, their Jewish colleagues remained in Russia, where the new political dogma and the rigid arm of Social Realism strangled the Jewish cultural renaissance, and indeed, all further experimentation in the arts.

Piecing together the far-flung parts of the puzzle that comprise this project – the first of its magnitude on the subject – clearly demanded the mobilization of interdisciplinary areas of research. The editor turned to international specialists in various fields: Professor John E. Bowlt from the University of Texas at Austin, and Professor Nicoletta Misler from the Istituto Universitario Orientale, Naples, specialists on Russian Art; Professor Ziva Amishai-Maisels of the Hebrew University in Jerusalem and Professor Avram Kampf of Montclair College, New Jersey and Haifa University, Israel, specialists on Jewish and Western Art; and Chimen Abramsky, Professor Emeritus of the London University, and Professor Seth L. Wolitz of the University of Texas at Austin, specialists in the area of Jewish studies. It is their insightful work that forms the essence of this catalog.

From its conception, we envisaged this publication as a vehicle for establishing an international dialogue between various disciplines. Widely diverse expertise is clearly needed when we attempt to cut across time, distance, language, and political and cultural barriers in an attempt to reveal all the complexities of this elusive, fascinating period in Jewish art.

By its nature, the conjoining of scholars from such varied fields – and the use of background material, so varied in language, source, and circumstance – results not only in different opinions, but sometimes also in different interpretations of the same information.

It is to be hoped that this very atmosphere of exploration and diversity will spur further investigation which will in turn uncover not only additional artists and works of art but also documentary sources, throwing more light on this brief, golden age of Jewish creativity.

Ruth Apter-Gabriel
Curator of the Exhibition

1  Our research has focused on the artists engaged in the effort to create a modernist Jewish art, and on them, only as long as their interest lasted. Thus the non-Jewish works of these artists, including their later creations in the accepted Social Realist style, have been omitted, as have works by Russian Jewish artists such as Leonid Pasternak and Ben Zion Zuckerman, who largely remained traditionalists. Other works, created outside of Russia but relevant to the subject, have been included: e.g., a few surviving copies of *Makhmadim*, possibly the first Jewish art journal (Paris, 1912), organ of the eponymous movement founded by Tchaikov, among others. *Makhmadim* forged a direct link to the slightly later development in Russia. (For more information on *Makhmadim*, see Avram Kampf, *Jewish Experience in the Art of the Twentieth Century*. Massachusetts: Bergin & Garvey. 1984, p. 34.) However, works by Marc Chagall and Issachar Ryback done in Berlin in the early 1920s, which appear to be a direct continuation of their earlier Russian Jewish trend (see e.g., Ryback's book illustrations [cat. 129-138; 140] and Chagall's illustrations for *My Life* [cat. 152-155]) have been included.
2  For a comparison, see the Simhat Torah flag (cat. 158); Leonid Pasternak's sheet music design (cat. 163) as well as his portrait of An-Sky (cat. 168); and M. Maimon's design (cat. 165).
3  Several of the drawings (cat. 67-70) were done in the synagogue of Mohilev during Lissitzky's and Ryback's joint ethnographic tour in 1916. A few others were reproduced in Boris Aronson's *Contemporary Jewish Graphics* (Berlin, 1924). Alexander Tyshler's "Ruth" cycle of drawings (cat. 41-44) was included in the Kultur Lige's "Jewish Art Exhibition" in Kiev, 1920, at which Boris Aronson served as administrator of the exhibition committee.

# Notes to the Reader

**Transliteration**   Yiddish transliteration is rendered according to *Encyclopaedia Judaica* (Jerusalem: Keter Publishing House Ltd., 1972) based on the U. Weinreich, *Modern English-Yiddish Yiddish-English Dictionary*.

Hebrew words in Yiddish are usually transliterated according to standard Yiddish pronunciation, e.g. חזנות *khazones*.

Russian transliteration is rendered according to the system of the United States Board on Geographic Names and the Library of Congress.

Names have been transliterated from either Russian or Yiddish as follows: if the name appears in the aforementioned *Encyclopaedia Judaica*, the transliteration has been derived from Yiddish; accordingly, if the name does not appear there, the transliteration is taken from the Russian.

**Catalog and Figure Numbers**   "Cat." refers to the number in the illustrated catalog. "Fig." refers to illustrations in the texts.

**Terms**   A distinction has been made between artist associations and groups and periodicals. Associations and groups are set in Roman type. Sponsoring periodicals are italicized, i.e., Makhmadim/*Makhmadim*.

**Alphabetical order**   The Catalog and Biographies of Artists are arranged according to the Hebrew/Yiddish alphabet.

**St. Petersburg**   The city of St. Petersburg underwent a series of name changes: until 1914 it was St. Petersburg; in August 1914 it was renamed Petrograd and following Lenin's death on January 21, 1924, it received its present name, Leningrad.

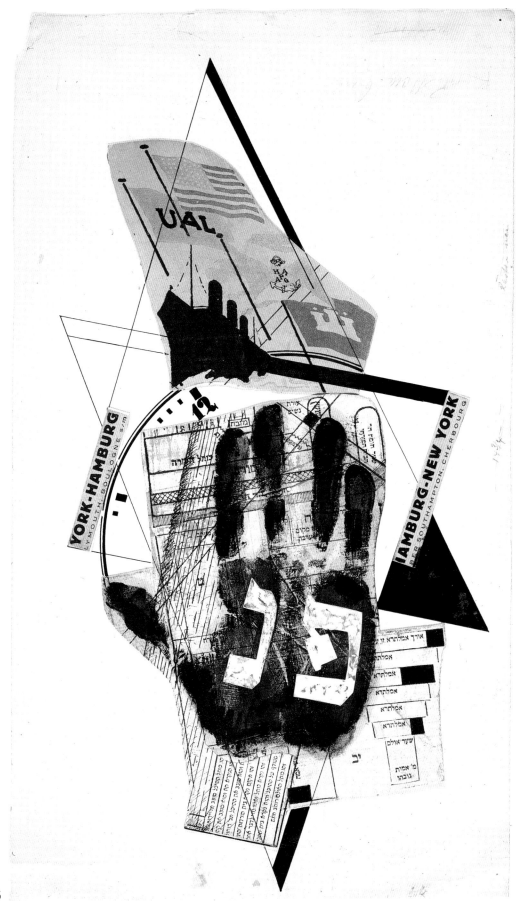

cat. 105

cat. 72₁

cat. 86

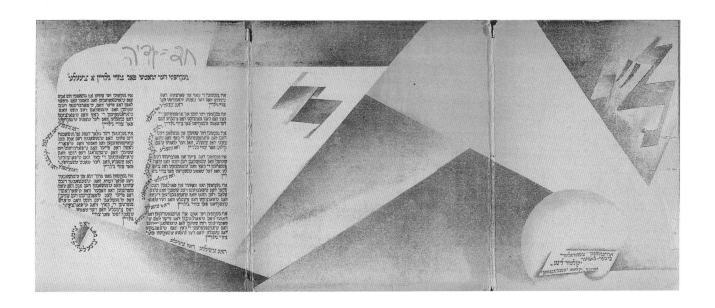

fig. 75

cat. 145

cat. 139

# The Jewish National Art Renaissance in Russia

Seth L. Wolitz

Dedicated to: Shimon Davidson, Yiddish activist and Bundist (Vitebsk, Lodz, Mexico City and San Antonio, Texas), and Sophia Gutentag-Davidson (the last living artist of the *Yung-Yidish* circle of Lodz *en hommage.*)

In the last few years we have experienced a type of national renaissance; a national idea has been brought to life . . . upon which one can build beautiful, new art compositions.
*Di Yidishe Velt* (no. 1, 1912)
St. Petersburg

## The Emergence of the Jewish Plastic Artist

The need for a Jewish national art at the beginning of the twentieth century was an inevitable outgrowth of the emerging political and cultural consciousness among Central and Eastern European Jews committed to the creation of a Jewish secular culture. In order to hasten the metamorphosis of a traditional Jewish identity, with its rich heritage, into a modern one, conformity to modern European national norms was necessary. These included the unique language, folk culture, and artistic monuments which lend weight to historical legitimacy and creative continuity. By 1900 the Jewish renaissance in Tsarist Russia was taking institutional shape. The formation of the Bund in 1897 and in the same year the creation of political Zionism gave Jewry a modern political presence – albeit Janus-faced. Modern Jewish cultural life was even more advanced, complex, and contradictory. The revival of Hebrew for secular artistic expression in the nineteenth century was no small achievement. Just as remarkable was the conscious effort to mold the common language of the Eastern European Jewish masses, Yiddish, into an instrument of aesthetic expression. The rapid growth of Yiddish literature and theatre throughout the Pale of Settlement, in spite of both internal and external opposition, provided the strongest proof of a national renaissance-in-the-making. The emergence of a Jewish press and literature in Russian offered yet another perspective in the shaping of a modern Jewish nation and culture. The necessity of a Jewish art, therefore, was part of a conscious program to provide Jewry with yet another attribute of a modern people.

The Jewish artist in Western and even Central Europe in the second half of the nineteenth century functioned in a milieu of cultural enlightenment. He could enter the plastic arts professionally because he had comparatively easy access to an art academy. He was already part of the majority national-state culture; its language was his own as were its educational perspectives. None of the above could be taken for granted within the Tsarist Empire.

The phenomenon of a Jew as a plastic artist in late nineteenth century Russia was, at best, an anomaly. He had to have immense talent, a steely will, protectors, and a family background at least grazed by the *Haskalah* (the Jewish enlightenment movement) in order to aspire to the status of a professional artist. The case of Mark Antokolski (1843-1902) is instructive, for he was the first Eastern European Jew to achieve fame as a sculptor. His talent as a wood carver in Vilna earned him admission to the Academy of Art in St. Petersburg in 1862, made possible by Tsar Alexander II's (1856-1881) policy to encourage the Jews' assimilation into the motherland. Typically, Antokolski first sculpted Jewish historical subjects, but soon turned to the more profitable historical Russian ones. He associated with the *Peredvizhniki* (Wanderers), a group of Russian artists who rejected academic art and sought in the 1870s and 1880s to express their populist social humanism and to depict only contemporary Russian subjects. Antokolski was a success, but it was his undoing.[1] Embittered by the anti-Semitic scorn of his accomplishment, he withdrew to France. To this day, ironically, Antokolski is considered the best "Russian" sculptor of the nineteenth century. The Russian Jewish artist had to breach one social obstacle after the other, including the Russian language, its culture, its prejudices and imperial restrictions. Antokolski's traditional Jewish background is actually closer to the sculptor Ilya Ginzburg (1860?-1939), to the painter Yehuda Pen (1870-1937), and to the generation of La Ruche (1900-1940) than to the other Jewish artists born in the 1860s: Isaac Levitan (1861-1900), Leonid Pasternak (1862-1945) and Leon Bakst (née Rosenberg, 1866-1924), who were from more comfortable and assimilated backgrounds. And yet Bakst, with all his international success as a designer of costumes and sets for the Ballet Russes, had difficulty obtaining a residence permit in St. Petersburg because of his origin.[2] For a young Marc Chagall (1887-1985) to remain in St. Petersburg while he studied in 1908 with Bakst at the Zvantseva school of art, he needed the fiction of being a house servant of the lawyer Goldberg![3] Nor were the significant art schools open to a Jew with talent, particularly the state-supported ones. Academic anti-Semitism, prodded by the state, severely limited the access of talented Jews to the prestigious Imperial Academy of Art in St. Petersburg. Chagall stumbled at its gates; its doors were barred to Eliezer Lissitzky (1890-1941). Nathan Altman (1889-1970), typical of most young Jewish artists, decided it was hopeless to apply.[4]

When we consider Russian Jewish artists born in the 1860s, such as Levitan, Pasternak, and Bakst, the first generation of Russian Jews to become professional artists, it is striking that they did not deny their origins

1

but, conversely, revealed little artistic inclination to exploit Jewish themes. They were and are considered very "Russian." Levitan and Pasternak certainly associated with and appeared in photographs of the Wanderers. A Levitan Russian landscape, with its lessons gleaned from the Barbizon School and early French Impressionism, is to this day considered synonymous with the spirit of "Mother Russia" which so excited the *fin de siècle* art lover. Pasternak's portraitures (fig. 1, cat. 168), surely his strongest talent, and his other works show little inspiration from the Jewish background in which he took pride, in spite of a few portraits of Jewish writers. Bakst, the most modern of these painters and a member of *Mir iskusstva* (World of Art), provided the *frisson* of the new by fusing Jugendstil with the Russian Oriental motifs so in mode. One would be hard-pressed to discern a "Jewish" motif in *Scheherazade*, his most sumptuous work. These artists were part of Russian culture, and participated in it as "Russian" universalist artists, as did Valentin Serov, Vrubel, or Alexander Benois. What distinguished them from their purely Russian colleagues besides their national (ethnic) origin was the fact that they functioned in Russian culture, both as Europeans and as peers. Although they recognized in their careers the emergence of Jewish national culture in both Hebrew and Yiddish, they belonged to a world which had distanced itself from the shtetl. That Antokolski was a good friend of Vladimir Stasov (1824-1906), and Levitan of Chekhov (the seagull motif was based on a Levitan-Chekhov experience), and Pasternak of Tolstoy, and Bakst of Diaghilev, speaks not only of their social integration, but of the distances they and their parents had traversed from the milieu so cherished and painted by Chagall and the future Jewish avant-garde. The Jewish world left behind was backward, a sad world of yellow and black, as the Russian Jewish poet Osip Mandelstam was to describe it. For them, there was no Jewish tradition in art, no Jewish folklore to stir their artistic imagination. Their parents and they themselves, in their art, had wholeheartedly heeded Alexander II's invitation to enter Russian life. They were not seeking to be "Russian" artists per se, but artists transcending even their Russian space and time. They were universalists when that meant being thoroughly European.

For the young Jewish artists born in the 1880s and 1890s, Europe was the great temptation. Russian art education was recognized as too academic, passé, and even provincial. They were aware of all the *fin de siècle* art movements in Europe, from Post-Impressionism, Symbolism, and the Viennese Secessionists to the Belgian Art Nouveau and Jugendstil. Like their advanced Russian counterparts, they knew that they could find fresh inspiration in Germany, and particularly in Paris. The Jewish Ecole de Paris would be formed by the many young Eastern European Jews who, forbidden to enter the Imperial Academy of Art in St. Petersburg, but having gained basic technical training in the provincial art academies of Moscow, Odessa, Minsk, Vilna, Warsaw, and Vitebsk, hastened towards Paris at the first opportunity.

One fascinating figure overlooked at this time was Pen, one of the first of the many Vitebsk Jews to become an artist. He was lucky enough to have been accepted to the Imperial Academy of Art and after his classical training, returned to Vitebsk and opened his own art school in 1892. He painted traditional Jewish genre scenes such as *The Old Lady with the "Tsene Urene"* (women's devotional book), *The Marriage-Maker*, *The Divorce*, etc., in the style of the Wanderers. His presence as a professional Jewish artist with a viable art school stimulated local Jewish youth to enter the world of art. Pen's nod to Chagall's mother that her son had talent may be apocryphal but not the fact that Chagall did attend the art school for a short time. And so did Solomon Yudovin (1894-1954), Abel Pann (1883-1963), Benjamin Kopman (1887-1966), Ilya

Chasnik (1902-1929), Lissitzky, and Yitzhak Lichtenstein (1883-197?), who noted how many "hundreds of youth" passed through the school.[5] Ossip Zadkine (1890-1967) and Oscar Mietschaninoff (1886-1956) of the Ecole de Paris also seem to have been in contact with Pen in their Vitebsk days. When Chagall returned to Vitebsk in 1914, he renewed his relations with Pen and in 1918 organized a local show in his honor which included works by Yudovin and Viktor Mekler. As Commissar of the Arts in Vitebsk and head of the art school, Chagall also celebrated the October Revolution anniversary (1918) in grand style and even managed to design sets for the local Revolutionary Theatre for the 1919/1920 season.[6] Yudovin and others of the Y. L. Peretz Society, a Yiddishist art and culture center in Vitebsk, would soon oppose Chagall, in the spring of 1919, for acting dictatorially as Commissar of the Arts and not giving the Jewish "traditionalist" artists a greater role in the revolutionary festivities.[7] Nevertheless, ironically, Chagall hired Pen in the summer of 1919 to teach alongside Kasimir Malevich in his new state art school. Chagall also drew Lissitzky back to Vitebsk and invited such Jewish-born artists as Alexander Rom and Moise Kogan to teach at the art school. Pen soon witnessed Chagall's discomfiture when his students turned to the Suprematist Malevich to lead the school, and Chagall, in defeat, departed finally in May 1920 for Moscow, completing his last works in the Soviet Union at the Moscow Jewish State Theatre. Chagall's school was transformed into a "Suprematist school" of pure abstraction whence would emerge Jewish-born artists such as Chasnik, Nina Kogan, Lazar Khidekel, Lev Yudin, M. Wechsler and Evgenia Margaril, the major figures of Unovis (Affirmation of the New in Art).[8] Pen, in short, both saw and participated more than any other Jewish artist in the birth, rise, and waning of the Jewish art renaissance. Vitebsk, far from being an insignificant shtetl, was a unique little city that spawned not only An-Sky (S. A. Rapoport, 1863-1920) and Chaim Zhitlowsky, the great Yiddish intellectual leaders, but a stream of Jewish artists from Pen's and Chagall's schools, whose works would achieve world renown. Obscure Vitebsk, paradoxically, served as the incubator of both modern Jewish secular thought and modern Jewish plastic art, as well as hosting Jewish participation in Suprematist abstraction.

## St. Petersburg: The Legitimation of the Jewish Artistic Folk Heritage

"Hot der kritiker Stasov zey dermont vegn zeyer khoyv tsu dinen dem eygenem folk" (The critic Stasov reminded them of their duty to serve their own people) – I. Ryback and B. Aronson (1919).

By 1900, Warsaw was the Jewish literary and cultural capital of the Jewish renaissance in Tsarist Russia. Vilna and Odessa were, of course, keen competitors, and within the decade Kiev and other provincial cities of the Pale would join in the general fermentation. But St. Petersburg, the capital of all the Russias, a forbidden city to Jews except for those of the highest rank (guilds), played a central role by supplying the status, validation and confirmation of the entire Jewish secular cultural endeavor.[9] St. Petersburg might have been forbidden, but it was the political, social, economic, and cultural center of Russia and with that posture, the Jews could not ignore it.

Mid-nineteenth-century cultural life in St. Petersburg was distinctly cosmopolitan. The rise of Russian literature had infused the native literary culture with honor and vibrant life but this was not the case for the Russian plastic arts and Russian music. The European examples – the French academic tradition in the Imperial Academy of Art and the dominant presence of German and French music in the Imperial Opera and Orchestral Hall – revealed a Russian cultural lacuna which a new generation of Russian artists sought to fill. The critical voice which articulated the yearning for a Russian national art and music was Stasov, who embraced a liberal Russian nationalist position which fused realism and the *narodnost'* (the folkish strain) in the plastic arts and music. He believed that by reflecting Russia's past and present through well-chosen images and themes, the plastic arts and music (using folk themes) would project the essence of "Russianness" with a strong social humanism. This led in the 1860s to Stasov's intense support of the nationalist composers, the Mighty Five, who depicted Russia's past in Borodin's *Prince Igor* and Mussorgsky's *Boris Godunov*, etc. In the 1870s, Stasov actively associated with the *Peredvizhniki* (Repin, Perov, Vasnetsov, etc.), whose canvasses depicted Russia's past and present with a strong emphasis on folk life. Stasov's nationalist vision, however, was not imperialistic. On the contrary, his nationalism was based on the belief that Russia's cultural inheritance was as valid as any other in Europe and therefore needed to be exploited in order to bring Russian cultural life to full fruition. It was this perspective that would have direct bearing on the encouragement of a Jewish national secular cultural expression.

Stasov provided both a theoretical grid and an exemplar that legitimized the national and folk plastic accomplishment as depicted in his studies, *Russian Folk Ornament* (1860-72) and *The Slavic and Oriental Ornament According to Manuscripts of the Fourth to Nineteenth Century* (1886), both published in St. Petersburg. These efforts paved the way to the discovery of the Jewish artistic past, which would parallel the Russian/Slavic national cultural restoration. Stasov's relations with the Jewish artistic and economic elite of Russia were therefore crucial in helping them recognize and appreciate Jewish artistic efforts of the past and – even more – of the present.[10]

Stasov welcomed – and indeed singled out – Jewish artists as part of his dream of seeing all the Russias bursting with national cultural expression. He lauded Antokolski, Ginzburg, and the composer Joel Engel as significant artists who should develop their Jewish artistic heritage. Stasov's liberal cultural nationalism, in short, opposed the unitary Russian cultural state with an alternative concept of multi-cultural Russia, an idea later dear to the historian and theorist Simon M. Dubnow, who conceived of Jewish "cultural autonomy." Stasov induced the erudite and vastly wealthy Baron David Guenzburg (1857-1910) to help him undertake the artistic resuscitation of Jewish plastic traditions by collecting, editing, and publishing the old, original works of Jewish manuscript art. Baron Guenzburg, in the preface to the *L'Ornement Hébreu* edition of 1905 (fig. 2, cat. 159), which was actually prepared by 1886, underlines the overwhelming role of Stasov in legitimizing the existence and study of Jewish art.

> He reproached the Jewish nation for its complete indifference regarding the products of its national genius, he sought out, he discussed, he commented, he stirred minds and resolved to prove his fertile thought by publishing these plates and exposing his theory.[11]

And to reinforce Stasov's opinion, Baron Guenzburg adds: "Russian artists who have become aware of it [Jewish illumination] have been struck by the seal of originality which has been stamped by the unknown artists on their beautiful and unique work."[12] Stasov's interpretations today may no longer carry any authority, but the fact that he, the celebrated Russian critic, embraced them so passionately one hundred years ago when he was a figure of consequence in Russian culture deeply impressed the Russian Jewish intelligentsia.

Stasov was proposing to the Jews the same cultural evolution which he was encouraging among his own Russians: that traditional native art forms could be modernized and brought up to the "European level."[13]

2

It is not accidental that Baron Guenzburg, Samuel Marshak (a Russian Jewish poet), Antokolski, and Engel esteemed Stasov, for he restored their pride and dignity in their Jewish cultural inheritance.[14] What they were more likely to denigrate or simply ignore as a desuet past, Stasov legitimized and made worthy of study and renewed creativity; the Jews were a people of cultural distinction. Engel named Stasov as "the Russian" who opened his eyes to Jewish music (1897). Rimski-Korsakov also played a central role in restoring prestige to the Jewish cultural inheritance. Lazare Saminsky (a Jewish composer) quotes the Russian master: "How strange it is that my Jewish students are so little concerned with their own music. Jewish music exists – this is beautiful music and it awaits its Glinka."[15] For the newly secularized Jewish artists and intelligentsia, Stasov and Rimski-Korsakov served as catalysts in the development of Jewish music and art at the very time that Jewish literature and politics were in full expression.[16]

Following the example of their compatriots, the Jewish intelligentsia in St. Petersburg began to collect and publish Eastern European Jewish folksongs, Jewish religious artifacts, and Jewish illuminations, and to prepare studies on "Jewish antiquities." The study of Judaica stretched from Biblical times to their own times. With the first publication of Yiddish folksongs in St. Petersburg by Saul Ginsburg and P. Marek in 1901, the desire to collect the eastern European Jewish folk tra-

ditions grew rapidly. While the western European artists were discovering the masks and fetishes of Africa and Oceania, the Russians, followed by the Jews, found their need for the "primitive" and their search for pure form led to their own unexplored past. Ethnology, anthropology, folklore, and aesthetics went hand in hand in exalting the artifact which a few short years earlier would have been discounted as unworthy of artistic or cultural attention. By 1908 the Tsarist government had granted the Jewish music students permission to establish the St. Petersburg Society for Jewish Folk Music, which by 1912 had 389 active members and had sponsored 150 concerts. By 1917, it had published eighty-five pieces of Jewish music.[17]

At the same time, members of the Jewish intelligentsia and economic elite of St. Petersburg were becoming active, like their Russian counterparts, in collecting art and performing the role of Maecenas to young Jewish artists. Maxim Vinaver (1862-1926), a deputy in the Duma, gave Chagall a stipend so that he could travel to Paris in 1910.[18] Important families like the Wissotskys and the Guenzburgs purchased Jewish art, as did all the editors of the Jewish Russian-language monthly *Voskhod* (Renascence, 1881-1906), which provided the latest information on Jewish cultural life in Russia and in Europe.

In 1908 the St. Petersburg Jewish Historical and Ethnographic Society was inaugurated by Vinaver in the presence of S. M. Dubnow, S. Goldstein (archivist), M. Kulisher (historian), M. Wischnitzer (historian), etc.; Dubnow originally conceived of such a circle to explore and record the history of Jewish life in Russia.[19] Its role was central in documenting the experiences of the Jewish people and studying Jewish folk practices. Under An-Sky, underwritten by Baron Horace Guenzburg, the society launched a major anthropological expedition into the Pale of Settlement, through the Ukraine, Podolia, and Volynia, from 1912 to 1914, collecting Jewish folk and religious materials (for details see John Bowlt's article in this publication). The Jewish artist Yudovin accompanied the expedition and photographed or copied the folk motifs (for related material, see cat. 1-17).

In addition to the St. Petersburg Jewish magnates, An-Sky invited and received support from every major Russian Jewish cultural figure: Y. Dineson (Yiddish writer), Y. L. Peretz (Hebrew-Yiddish writer), N. Prilutsk (writer, politician), and Hillel Zeitlin (religious writer) in Warsaw; Mendele Mokher Seforim (S. J. Abramowitsch, Hebrew-Yiddish writer), C. N. Bialik (Hebrew poet), I. Klausner (writer) and I. Ravnitzky (Hebrew writer) in Odessa; J. Engel (composer), P. Marek (historian), Y. Maze (educator) and S. Vermel (historian) in

Moscow; G. Brauda (writer), S. Ginsburg (historian), S. M. Dubnow (historian), A. Harkavy (linguist), Y. Viner (lawyer), M. Vinaver (lawyer), V. Yokhelson (ethnologist), H. Shliozberg (lawyer), L. Sev (editor), M. Sirkin (lawyer), S. Izinberg (literary historian), M. Kulisher (historian), and L. Shterenberg (ethnologist) in St. Petersburg, and more.[20] It was the last major Jewish cultural undertaking before and during the catastrophe of World War I. The collection was brought to Petrograd and formed the basis of the Jewish Ethnographic Museum, opened in 1916 and closed by the Bolsheviks in 1918. In that brief time, Jewish artists were able to study the collection, e.g., Chagall, who was astonished when he "saw them [the wood carvings] in An-Sky's collection."[21] In 1916, Ginzburg and Altman joined other Jewish artists in Petrograd to create the Society for the Encouragement of Jewish Art, the first formulation in Tsarist Russia of the quest for a new Jewish art, the intention of which was the creation of a national Jewish artistic expression through the re-working and renewal of older Jewish art.[22] The artifacts of the expedition were the models and sources of inspiration.

In St. Petersburg, Jewish scholarship was joined with Jewish art in the Society's first show. Altman reworked his 1914 drawings, based on tombstone rubbings, Passover *Haggadot* and other Jewish folk art motifs, for *Jewish Graphics* (cat. 30) in a modernist idiom highly influenced by Lyrical Cubism and Neo-Primitivism in usually playful double symmetry and decorative elements with a shallow background.[23] It was the first clear expression of the Jewish graphic style which would soon become part of the modern Russian Jewish national art school. As An-Sky noted already in 1913 to his friend Dineson (1856-1919), "Petersburg is now, thank God, a Jewish town. Even the gentile 'Evreiskii mir' has converted into a 'Yidishe velt' [Jewish World]."[24] Within a decade of Stasov's and Rimski-Korsakov's appeals to recover the Jewish national cultural inheritance, the St. Petersburg Jewish elite had its own established cultural institutions and had legitimized the study and creation of a modern Jewish art and music drawn on its own folk inheritance. If cultural assimilation was not entirely stemmed, at least a worthy modern Jewish alternative was available.

## Paris: La Ruche and the Makhmadim

Paris of 1910 was the hub of modern European culture, and the Jewish artists of Russia hastened to join the international bohemia in Montparnasse. The café La Rotonde was packed cheek-to-jowl with the future leaders of the Russian Revolution in art and politics: the Russians, Lenin and Lunacharsky (Commissar of Public Enlightenment, Narkompros); the Jews, David Shterenberg (1881-1948, head of the Visual Arts Section of Narkompros), Altman (head of Narkompros in Petrograd and future professor of art at the Petrograd Free Art Studios), and Chagall (Commissar of Art in Vitebsk);[25] and many other aspiring artists, revolutionaries in their own way. The atmosphere of Montparnasse was charged with the New.

Not far from the café on Passage Danzig was La Ruche, an octagonal building where artists lived and painted in the studios provided cheaply by the benevolent French artist Alfred Boucher, who had inaugurated it in 1902 as an artists' residence.[26] At La Ruche, Archipenko (Ukrainian), Fernand Léger (French), Diego Rivera (Mexican), Amedeo Modigliani (Italian Jew), etc., met the new Jewish arrivals from Imperial Russia: Jacques Lipchitz (1891-1973) and Zadkine in 1909; Chagall, Moise Kisling (1891-1953), and Joseph Tchaikov (1888-1986) in 1910; Léon Indenbaum (1892-1981) and Altman in 1911; and Pinkas Krémègne (1890-1981), Lichtenstein, Chaim Soutine (1893-1943), Marek Schwarz (1892-1962), Leo Koenig (1889-1970), Michel Kikoine (1892-1968) and Henri Epstein (1891-1944) in 1912. And not far away lived other more acculturated Russian Jews, Anton Pevsner, Naum Aronson, Naum Gabo, D. Baranov-Rossiné, etc.

La Ruche offered the intimacy of an artists' colony, but few of the artists sought to remain strictly in its confines. Chagall, for one, stated: "I went straight into the circles of the French poets and artists."[27] And he found full support from Guillaume Apollinaire, Blaise Cendrars, and Sonya Terk Delaunay, and profited from exchanges with the Section d'Or Cubist painters. Chagall, in the years between 1910 and 1914, occupied an interesting middle ground in Paris in regard to Jewish artistic expression. Whereas Soutine and Zadkine, for example, rejected any ties to "Jewishness," Chagall accepted his Jewish identity, drew on its past as source material but always – almost categorically – denied the idea of Jewish art or of being a "Jewish artist."[28] He considered himself simply an artist without need of epithets. His St. Petersburg art experience – that "smell of Europe" – was a better preparation for Paris than the provincial art worlds of most of his Jewish compatriots. He was

3

4

more receptive to the New: Neo-Primitivism, Cubism, and color theory. He was also aware of the creative thrusts in Russia and even sent canvasses to exhibitions in St. Petersburg and Moscow (1912).[29] His artistic concerns, in short, did not interfere with his Jewish identity. Such was not the case with Zadkine or Soutine, who held a negative view of their origins and used art as a way to a preferable life. Opposed to the assimilationist positions of Zadkine and to the neutralist attitude of Chagall, there developed in 1912 at La Ruche a very strong nationalist posture among a portion of the recent Jewish arrivals. They would adopt the name of Makhmadim (Precious Ones), supposedly coined by the Hebrew essayist and short-story writer Shlomo Zemach.[30] They had no manifesto to publish but Koenig years later (about 1955) captured the spirit of the group in an unpublished manuscript:

> It was a time when young Jewish painters – the greater part from the Pale of Settlement – used to dream of Jewish forms, of inaugurating new Jewish schools . . . and should I be ashamed with my former naiveté? – when I used to run about the Boulevard Saint-Michel with the wonderful idea that we modern Jewish youth would wear little silk prayer shawls instead of scarves and capes like the French youth.[31]

Schwarz, writing some twelve years after the Makhmadim, provides another perspective in his article "The National Element in Jewish Art."[32] For Schwarz, the Jewish artists experienced a sense of cultural inferiority and wished to rectify the situation: "The idea of a Jewish art belongs to Stasov." The problem was that Jewish artists were unaware of their past and when they did look inward, they only "wanted to orientalize" in the style of the Bezalel School (founded in 1906 in Jerusalem by Boris Schatz, 1867-1932) and E. Lilien (1874-1925). Luckily "the interest of our time

in problems of form on the one hand and in folklore on the other, both together, brought us closer to the truth."[33] The discovery of Jewish goldsmiths, artists, and illuminators, back to the thirteenth century, offered in their works, "according to the spirit of their time, Jewish specificity." In short, Jews did have an artistic history and Schwarz, Tchaikov and Lichtenstein decided to create the first Jewish art journal, Makhmadim (fig. 3, cat. 160-162). Koenig adds himself and Krémègne as founders, and perhaps the obscure B. Ravitzky.

Of the supposed seven issues (according to Schwarz) or "perhaps three or four issues" (according to Koenig), only one copy each of numbers 2, 4, and 5 survive in the Israel Museum. Their poverty was so great that they could not afford to print the journal, so they used a hectograph (an old-fashioned duplicator) to make the copies, and mainly Lichtenstein and Tchaikov stitched the pages together (fig. 4, cat. $160_1$). Koenig argued that they had no manifesto because it was time to "show, not speak. We will show the world our new Jewish motifs and forms." Schwarz maintains that the last issue covered eleven artists: "We were convinced that our concept [of a Jewish art] was successfully planted." But he admits that Jewish intellectuals were not very interested in their artistic efforts.

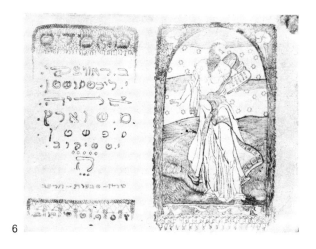

6

The existence of this first consciously Jewish national art group should not be underestimated. They saw themselves – Tchaikov, Schwarz, Lichtenstein, Epstein, and Koenig – as the "cutting edge" of the new Jewish art generation. They were going to express the national and folk aspirations by discovering new art forms "not in costumes and customs of the older Jewish painters." Their enthusiasm, alas, outstripped their art, for they appear as epigones of Lilien: pure Jugendstil. The training at Bezalel and Munich is everywhere evident: the ornamental frames replete with symbolic Jewish objects, citrons, grapes, candelabra, etc.; heavily sentimental and stylized drawings of Biblical scenes: Adam and Eve (fig. 5, cat. $162_4$), Cain and Abel, Moses the Lawgiver (fig. 6, cat. $162_2$), etc.; Semitic faces against shallow, patterned backgrounds and distinctly Art Nouveau Hebrew lettering. In retrospect it seems incredible that in the next studio Chagall, as Koenig states, "was not a part of the first Jewish art journal which was prepared right under his nose. . . ."[34] But as Koenig himself naively admits, at that very same time in Chagall's atelier "his *Jew in Green*, *Jew Flying over the House*, and his futuristic *Eiffel Tower*, painted in sensational colors, were already hanging 'on the walls'." Koenig hints, interestingly, that there was an element of envy of Chagall's growing fame among the French avant-garde and "they, fresh out of the various academies," scorned his "primitiveness."[35]

5

Chagall's comments on the La Ruche period are: "I happily snickered at the idle thoughts of my neighbors concerning the fate of Jewish art: all right, talk away – and I will work."[36] The incongruity of painterly styles between the Makhmadim and Chagall, Modigliani, and Soutine leaves no doubt that the Makhmadim belonged to the artistic rear guard in Paris of 1912. The next few years would produce a metamorphosis in their style. Tchaikov would return to Kiev and become a Cubo-Futurist and an Abstract Constructivist. Schwarz would become an Expressionist and convert to Catholicism. Lichtenstein would become a wandering Jewish artist and remember Makhmadim by using it as the name of his Yiddish publishing house in New York before moving to Safed in Israel. Koenig in 1914 remained an active art and culture critic ever loyal to the building of a secular modern Jewish culture. He died in Israel. Only Epstein remained in France and was "resettled" by the Germans. Their average age was twenty-three in 1912. The year 1914 brought the Paris idyll to a close. The beginning of the new Russian Jewish art was at hand.

## The Revolution and Jewish National Art

World War I, the Revolution, and the Civil War isolated Russia from the West for almost six years. During 1914-20, Russian avant-garde art and Russian Jewish modern art both came to full fruition. Jewish artists, for the most part, moved back and forth between Russian and Jewish artistic and intellectual circles, enjoying the liberty of their condition and hastening the artistic ferment. While Altman and Chagall were taking part in the "Modern Russian Art" shows in N. J. Dobychina's avant-garde gallery in Petrograd, or were participating in the Moscow art shows "Year 1915" and "Jack of Diamonds" (1916), Lissitzky and Ryback (1897-1935) in 1915, in the footsteps of Yudovin and the Jewish Ethnographic Society, were studying Jewish folk art *in situ*. The painted eighteenth-century synagogue of Mohilev (fig. 7, cat. 119) came as a major revelation to both of them, and both its murals and architecture influenced Ryback's 1917 paintings and later lithographs as well as Lissitsky's Jewish book illustrations. Altman had already spent the long summer of 1913 in his home province of Volynia and particularly studied the tombstones of Shepetovke, which served as models for his *Jewish Graphics*, first shown in 1916 in Petrograd (at the Society for the Encouragement of Jewish Art).[37] These central figures of Russian Jewish modern art were seeking old Jewish forms of plastic expression, and as time went on, specifically Eastern European Jewish folk art forms, in order to fuse both personal and national uniqueness with the most contemporary artistic techniques, in a bid to create a modern, national, secular art and culture. By 1910-11 Russian artists like Natalia Goncharova, Mikhail Larionov, Vladimir Tatlin, and Malevich were already producing paintings fusing elements of the "folk-primitive" (folk art, folk ornaments, and folklore) with the latest techniques of Cubism, Futurism, and Orphism. Russian Jewish artists like Chagall and Altman were equally contemporaneous, using Jewish folk sources, but Lissitzky, Ryback and Tchaikov, during the war years, were both mastering the new plastic methods and further absorbing Jewish folk crafts.

The first fully conscious Jewish art exhibition in Tsarist Russia in 1916 was sponsored by the Society for the Encouragement of Jewish Art in Petrograd. It represented the culmination of the various national and cultural forces at work to concretize Jewish art during the preceding fifteen years. It was not an avant-garde show but rather a retrospective from the Jewish Wanderers to Altman. Jewish themes and content provided the central focus. That Altman in the same year could appear as a Jewish artist in the latter exhibit and also be a "Russian" artist in Dobychina's show of contemporary Russian painting (March 1916) underlines the first allegiance of most Jewish artists at that time: to art. This Jewish art exhibition, nevertheless, represents a turning point in Eastern European Jewish art history, for it confirmed and validated the existence of Jewish art and Jewish artists to a Jewish public prepared to accept and encourage secular Jewish art. It was concomitant with this exhibition that Chagall received the commission to paint holiday scenes in the Petrograd synagogue and a considerable number of Jewish artists were being invited to illustrate Jewish children's books.[38] The integration of the plastic arts in Jewish cultural life was now a fact which, with the favorable political conditions of 1917, would precipitate a short but unique burst of Russian Jewish if not Yiddish art.

In Moscow of 1917 Moshe Broderzon (1890-1956), having fled Poland in 1914 as the war front collapsed, shared in the general exhilaration of the first Revolution. Shmuel Niger, the Yiddish critic, remembers the poet in the Moscow days "caught up in the half-refined, half-wild Russian 'Futurism'." His new Yiddish verse was a "mix of old, folkloric Jewishness with the 'latest word' from the Moscow poetic Bohemia."[39] It was in this bohemia that Broderzon met Lissitzky. Their collaboration begat the first modernist Yiddish art and literary text, *Sikhes Kholin* (Small Talk), a slightly erotic and irreverent Ovidian verse tale set in old Prague, "judaized" by making the randy protagonist a rabbi (cat. 72,74).[40] The unique illustrations express the shared aesthetic of these two artists. Each page of scribal lettering of the text is surrounded by a formal architectural design which derives from two sources, the traditional Scrolls of Esther and Art Nouveau. The superb drawing makes use of all the old Jewish motifs, ornaments and symbolic creatures found in old texts, synagogue paintings, and stone carvings. The title page captures the entire intent of the work (fig. 8). The golden peacock, symbol of Jewish artistic expression, draws a Hasid upward: art replaces faith as the source of spiritual uplift. The scribe on the right looking downward to his scroll is the symbol of the old; opposite him stands the new, the artist with his palette boldly facing the golden peacock. (The subtext must surely be the *topos* of the blindfolded Synagogue and the triumphant Church in which secular art replaces Christianity as modern salvation.) At the bottom of the page, a scroll lies flat upon the desk above which the poet's head is turned upward – while the lamp glows with its halo – looking up to the peacock/muse (in its halo) for inspiration. The play between two and three dimensions, the sheer delight in arabesques, and the integration of the Hebrew lettering into the general design underscore a new aesthetic experience – a secular Yiddish culture harmonizing with modern Western aesthetics (further details in Ruth Apter-Gabriel's article in

למפרט זה לי ימים רבים.
שהלכתי באר צרו' התיים. כי צאתי
ידי חובתי להשלמת עצור הליפה אשר
נצב לצבות בריס. אא אלף הבריב
נמילותך. לפנות את הרב. וא יצ
הריס יצילנו מכל צריס
לדור דוריס אגיד

ПОТОЛОКЪ СИНАГОГИ
въ
Могилевѣ

על ידי הפועל
היטם במלאכת
הקודש אלהים בהלל.
יצחק אייזק קגל זציל
טקל סלוצק הבירה

this publication). Around 20 of the 110 copies were made into a scroll, painted in watercolors of high saturation and placed in a wooden casket shaped as if to bear a *megillah* (scroll) (fig. 9).[41] Here, at least, was a Jewish artistic expression which proudly exploited its religious and cultural origins but transformed them through a secular aesthetic perspective: the old and new regenerated.[42] By contrast, the 1917 editions of Chagall's drawings for Peretz's *The Magician* or Der Nister's *A Mayse mit a Hon* (A Story about a Rooster) and *Dos Tsigele* (The Little Kid) (cat. 144), printed in Petrograd (by the Vilna Kletzkin House), are either emblematic or open-Cubistic sketchy designs which eschew the rich Jewish ethnographic sources of Lissitzky's inspiration. Chagall's reduced shapes and short lines in the children's books of 1917 leave their mark more on Lissitzky's modern treatment of *Had Gadya* (1917) (figs. 58-61), in which the linear arabesques of *Sikhes Kholin* (cat. 74) are sharply reduced to essential linearity for representational depiction. But contrary to Chagall, Lissitzky always maintains the integration of text, typography and page design taken as a whole. Broderzon also turned to Tchaikov as the illustrator of his children's tale, *Temerl* (1917) (cat. 45). The Jugendstil of Makhmadim was still evident in Tchaikov's style, but hints of Cubo-Futurism are discernible too. These efforts cannot be stressed sufficiently, for in 1917 they were the first tangible proof to the Jewish elite that a secular autonomous culture of Jews was not just a possibility but was imminent now that Tsarist restrictions on Jews and Jewish publications were removed. One Jewish collector, Kagan-Shabshai, an electrical engineer who had a private Jewish art gallery, began to plan a Jewish museum in Moscow and avidly bought Chagall paintings. He owned Chagall's *The Beggar* (1914) and the nude *Mother and Child* (1914).[43] Chagall, Altman, and Lissitzky announced the organization of an exhibition by the Union of Moscow Jews in the Moscow newspaper *Utro Rossii* on 25 January 1917, to be held at Galerie Lemercier in April.[44] The fact that Chagall was to join Altman and Lissitzky to participate in the Jewish artistic renaissance underscores the rapid growth of Jewish cultural self-esteem on his part from the Paris days to Moscow 1917.

The Bolshevik Revolution of October 1917 and the Balfour Declaration of November of the same year spurred the Jews in Moscow to proceed with their cultural renaissance. Broderzon had a major hand in organizing Shamir, "A Circle of Jewish National Aesthetics," in January 1918.[45] It was to publish a journal of the same name,

> . . . which would publicize the aesthetic renaissance of Jewry on the basis of Jewish creativity and by an organic rapprochement to general European

art. Space will be given to art, literature, music, and articles about Jewish cultural questions. The language of the organ is Yiddish. It also plans to publish, in all three languages of the Russian Jews, various works of young poets, composers, graphic artists, etc. All copies will be published in a beautiful format with ornaments.[46]

Although no journal seems to have been edited, Shamir's shadowy presence appears as the new publisher of the Lissitzky-Broderzon text of 1917, having replaced Nashe iskusstvo. It also sponsored the first critical study of Chagall by Abram Efros and Yakov Tugendkhold.[47] And even with the arrival of the new Bolshevik government in Moscow in March 1918, plans were still being made by the Moscow Jewish community to establish a Jewish museum. It was even reported that "material has already been collected," and that the museum would include old Jewish folk traditions, Jewish social activities, statistics, "participation in the Revolution," etc.[48] The great Jewish fortunes of collectors like the Wissotskys, Zlotopolskys, and Naeyditskes were soon confiscated, bringing this dream to naught.[49]

A new cultural organization, "The Moscow Circle of Jewish Men of Letters and Artists," emerged in the first months of 1918, seeking a broad base of supporters. The organization was able to mount an exhibition of 233 works by 41 artists, including a catalog in Russian and Yiddish. This took place in July and August of 1918.[50] It was its first exhibition, significantly "without Jewish millionaire patrons." In the new Yiddish government-sponsored journal *Kultur un Bildung* (Culture and Education), edited by Niger, a member of the Circle noted the large representation:

> Moscow: Antokolski, Basenko, Gabovitch, Tepper, Tchaikov, Lissitzky, Milman, Zuckerman, Itkind, and others.
> Petrograd: Brazer, Brodsky, Chagall, Yudovin, Kratko, Shekhtol, and others.
> Kiev: Goldfein, Ryback, Epstein, and others.

The official catalog lists the artists in the following Russian alphabetic order:

> N. Altman, Antokolski, Baranov (Rossiné), L. E. Basenko, M. F. Brokh, A. M. Brazer, I. I. Brodsky, I. G. Gabovich, P. I. Geller, I. Ya. Gintsburg, G. Glikman, Grinberg, S. Gruzenberg, I. I. Gurvich, S.M. Zeidenberg, I. Ya Itkind, E. A. Katzman, B. Kh. Kratko, A. B. Lakhovsky, L. M. Lissitzky, A. A. Manievich, Ya. Milkin, L. I. Milman, Ya. Pain, A. L. Pyatigorsky, C. B. Ryback, S. Simkhovich, Z. I. Strazh, I. N. Tepper, Ya. A. Troupyansky, L. E. Feinberg, B. Ch. Fridman, P. A. Kentova, B. Ya. Zuckerman, I. M. Tchaikov, Shekhtel, I. S. Shkolnik,

V. I. Shlesinger, D. P. Shterenberg, M. I. Epstein, S. B. Yudovin.[51]

The new Yiddish Communist newspaper *Der Emes* (*Pravda*, The Truth) on 11 August 1918 expressed enormous enthusiasm: "If only it were possible for this exhibition to be seen in the melancholy Jewish provinces where they perhaps never even dreamed that there could be Jewish artists and that a true Jewish art would be born!"[52] But the critic praises either the old Wanderer Antokolski or the portraits of Mendele by Zuckerman and Strazh. The real innovators, Altman, Chagall, Lissitzky, etc., go unmentioned. Even the more sophisticated critic of *Kultur un Bildung* makes little distinction between the traditionalists (Realists and Impressionists) and the innovators. That Shterenberg, Altman, and Chagall, now all figures of the Narkompros, supported and participated in the exhibit underlines the easy movement of Jewish artists amidst the various art groupings. This exhibit was conservative but could be mounted because the new government needed supporters. It was the largest Jewish artists' show ever to be held and provides a glimpse of what might have been possible. That 41 artists and sculptors of various qualities could be presented in such a difficult time reveals the sponsor's intensity, the organizational skills, and the commitment to building a modern Jewish culture. Nevertheless, the critic of *Kultur un Bildung* was not happy with the attendance. Yet over one thousand people attended the exhibition, "including the literary and musical evenings," and "over half became 'friends' of the Circle," and the works of Antokolski, Strazh, Feinberg, and Zuckerman were sold, adding up to "sixteen or seventeen thousand rubles," but the *balebatishe oylem* (respectable society) did not attend, only the *driter element* (the lower part of the third estate). By noting what sold and who attended, it becomes clear that the sophisticated Jewish collectors did not attend or at least did not purchase the art they collected earlier, and the art purchased was bought by people with very conservative tastes, who chose works by the most popular artists: i.e., those appreciated by *Der Emes*. The nascent schism in art would repeat the same problem encountered in modern Yiddish poetry: the Modernist Jewish artists were too far ahead of their natural constituency, who were just entering the secular world of art.[53] The Jewish artist, of course, with a more universal medium displayed his works wherever he could participate, whether at the "1918 Petrograd Exhibition of Contemporary Paintings" or at Moscow's "24th Exhibition of Paintings and Sculpture" (23 February–17 March 1918).

The collaboration of Jewish artists and writers in book publishing continued to expand in 1918, and not only

9

in Moscow. D. L. Ziv, head of the Jewish Society for the Promotion of Art in Petrograd, at a general meeting underlined the importance of "helping nationalize Jewish art" by inviting "artists to illustrate Jewish publications, textbooks, etc."[54] Kiev, Kharkov, and Odessa in 1918 were also active in publishing and encouraging Jewish secular culture. A large Jewish art show was put on in Odessa with works from "young artists and old Jewish artists like Levitan and Ginzburg . . . and young Odessa artists, Bershadski, Kishayevski, Hirshenfeld."[55] In Kharkov, Lissitzky designed the opening page for their art and literature journal *Kunst-Ring Almanakh* (Art Circle) (cat. 78). In Moscow, in 1918, the journal *Kultur un Bildung* was organizing art courses "under the direction of Jewish artists." In Kiev, Lissitzky, for example, published his finest collaborative effort in Yiddish by illustrating Mani Leib's (1884-1953) *Yingl Tsingl Khvat* (1918) (cat. 79).[56] Each page is conceived as an integrated whole, including even the page number! The page is treated as a canvas upon which are elaborated lyric Cubistic stylizations around the text. Even the initial Hebrew letters are given an illusory third dimension and are almost animated. The rich scroll work of 1917 (cat. 74) has yielded to short strokes, Cubo-Futuristic fragmentation of form, typographic play and rapid Cubistic passage from dark or shading to light. Volume is reduced almost to outline and the background is shallow if not foreshortened as in a stage set. Only the 1919 Kiev edition of *Had Gadya* (cat. 90) offers further proof of Lissitzky's conception of the page of Yiddish book illustration as canvas. His later Yiddish illustrations are basically retreats from the total integration of art and verse as first conceived in his collaboration with Broderzon. The 1918 Russian edition of Gauguin's *Noa Noa*, with the title page by Lissitzky, is surely less

8

advanced than his Yiddish efforts. By 1919, however, the Russian poster *Beat the Whites* revealed his passage into Suprematism and his emergence as an abstract master.[57]

At the beginning of 1919, the Yiddishist movement (not to mention the Hebrew revival) in Moscow came to an end, with the increasing Bolshevik control of Jewish cultural expression. Indeed Niger, Broderzon, and An-Sky had already left the Soviet Union for Poland and Lithuania by December 1918. Meanwhile, Chagall was organizing his art school in Vitebsk and Lissitzky left Moscow to join him. Tchaikov went to Kiev and Altman remained in Petrograd. Yudovin organized in

1919 a special exhibit of Jewish folk art in Vitebsk at the Y. L. Peretz Society and published exemplars in 1920 with S. Malkin in the *Yidisher Folks Ornament* (cat. 170), the last published echo of the Jewish Ethnographic Society expeditions. The main event in Vitebsk, however, was the "First State Exhibition of Local and Moscow Artists" (1919),[58] with the participation of 41 artists, Jewish and non-Jewish. Moscow would only again become the center of Yiddish cultural life – albeit Bolshevized – when the Moscow State Jewish Theatre, founded in 1919 in Petrograd by Alexander Granovsky (1890-1937), would move to Moscow at the end of 1920, where it began performing in 1921 in a theatre decorated by Chagall.

## From Kiev: Blossom and Gloom

"Tjazko nevoli spivaty."
(It is difficult to sing in prison.)
M. Semenko (1892-1939).

Kiev held the greatest hope for a full-blown, modern, secular Jewish culture. Even before World War I, the city was home to the most modern and sophisticated prose masters in Yiddish, David Bergelson (1884-1952) and Der Nister (1884-1950). The Yiddish intelligentsia often gathered at Nahman Mayzel's (1887-1970) for intensive discussions about these directions of modern secular Jewish culture. Mayzel was a central figure in the development of Yiddish secular culture, a founder of the Kultur Lige (Culture League) in Kiev and Warsaw and head of *YKUF* in New York. The future Soviet Yiddish critic Yehezkiel Dobrushin (1883-1952) and the future "tsar" of Soviet Yiddish letters, Moshe Litvakov (1875-1937), both recently returned from Paris, joined in these discussions, where the Dubnowian dream of cultural autonomy was debated alongside the latest currents in Russian and European culture. Kiev, in fact, housed every position a pre-World War I Jew might espouse: assimilationist, acculturationist, Socialist, Zionist, Bundist, Yiddishist and orthodox traditionalist. Nor were lines definitively drawn. Secularism had made significant inroads in the Kiev milieu as Bergelson's masterpiece, *Nokh Alemen* (After All) (1913), so aptly showed. Whereas in Lithuania, Soutine was tormented by his family and village for his interest in art, the enlightened Chief Rabbi of Kiev could permit his son, Boris Aronson (1898-1980), to take art lessons! Indeed painters like Abraham Manievich (1881-1942), Abraham Mintchine (1898-1931) and Ryback (1897-1935) studied art in Kiev both before and during the war.

Kiev, like Odessa, was a flourishing city to which Jews had access. During and after the war the Jews accounted for over 25 percent of the population. Unlike Petrograd and Moscow, where only rich Jews in business and the liberal professions could live, Kiev with its Jewish suburb, Podol, encompassed a complete and large cross-section of Jewry, from the cobbler to the bank president. In the three crucial years of 1917-20, the Jewish cultural leadership in Kiev fought a valiant and then desperate battle to create a unique, modern, secular, autonomous culture for its constituents, Ukrainian and Eastern European Jews.

The first impact of the February Revolution of 1917 in Kiev was a surge of nationalism which found immediate expression in the ability to publish in formerly forbidden languages: Ukrainian and Yiddish. The Ukrainian nationalists quickly organized a democratic national government which made room for minorities and recognized Jewish national autonomy. By July 1917, Jewish parties were represented in the *RADA*, then Grand Council (Parliament) and general name of the first Ukrainian democratic government. Yiddish was recognized as one of the official languages and Moshe Zilberfarb was made first Vice-Secretary of Jewish Affairs and eventually elevated to Minister in the newly formed Ministry of Jewish Affairs. By 8 January 1918, the *RADA* established the law of national-personal autonomy which in simple terms legitimized and legalized Jewish national rights and cultural autonomy. Jews in the Ukraine were legally able to form their own Jewish national *RADA*, whose members were elected from the local *kahals*. In short, by the end of 1917, in spite of the savage haggling between Zionists and Bundists over Yiddish and/or Hebrew as the language of instruction, the massive legal improvement of the Jewish condition – at least on paper – had taken place. Indeed the Ministry of Education gave a decent amount of money to establish a Jewish printing house and to publish Yiddish school texts.[59]

With the October Revolution, relations between the Bolsheviks and the Ukrainian *RADA* grew strained and led to the Bolshevik occupation of Kiev in February 1918, followed in March by the German army, which helped install General Skoropadrky as hetman (Ukrainian leader), but by November, rule had passed to another regime, the Ukrainian Directorate under Petliura, an intense nationalist. With the return to Kiev of the Bolsheviks in February 1919, the Civil War with its horrible pogroms swept through the Ukraine. The Denikins (White Russians) took Kiev in August but the Bolsheviks returned by the beginning of 1920, only to abandon Kiev to the Poles for a short while in May before returning permanently. Amidst all this violence, Jewish secular culture and art managed to blossom, particularly during the February to August 1919 occupation by the Bolsheviks and on their return in 1920 until the Yevsektsiya (Jewish section of Communist party structure) took over the entire running of the Kultur Lige by December 1920.

The Kultur Lige was at the heart of the Jewish cultural renaissance in Kiev. It was organized at the end of 1917 and rapidly became active. It had to. The collapse of the *RADA* made the Kultur Lige the only institution to provide education and culture for the Jewish population. Although conceived as a non-partisan, non-political, cultural organization, it soon came to represent the broadest Yiddishist-Socialist perspective.

The Kultur Lige stands on three pillars: 1) Jewish folk education; 2) Yiddish literature; and 3) Jewish art. Make our masses thinkers. Make our thinkers Jewish. This is the purpose of the Kultur Lige.

(Motto, *Kultur Lige Zamlung*, November 1919, Kiev.)

The Central Committee consisted of Mayzel, Bergelson, Litvakov, Yakov Leshtschinsky and Yosef Leshtschinsky, A. Litvak, L. Etkin, et al. This devoted leadership of old friends and intellectual foes fully understood the import of its duty and within a year had established throughout the Ukraine "four evening folk universities, twelve grammar schools, twenty large libraries with reading rooms, seventy kindergartens and orphanages, forty evening course programs, ten playing fields, three gymnasiums [high schools], twenty dramatic circles, choruses, and troupes."[60] In fact, art studios were opened, an art museum and opera house were planned, and a teachers' seminary was established. The Kultur Lige had its own press, which published vast amounts of teaching material, children's illustrated books, literary and historical studies, and literary journals with graphic work.[61] It served as the central clearinghouse for all publications in Yiddish throughout the Ukraine and Russia. The Kultur Lige was carefully organized into different sections. The art section reported in 1919 that it "has drawn the most accomplished Jewish painters and sculptors who feel that the direction of Jewish art is their route, that their creative possibilities are closely bound to the fate of the national creativity, and they will be fruitful only where the awakened Jewish democratic consciousness forges its distinct Jewish secular culture and artistic point of view."[62] Among the more significant names were Ryback, Isaac Pailes, Tchaikov, B. Aronson, Epstein, Lissitzky, Alexander Tyshler (1898-1980), and I. Rabitchev,[63] who "create the artistic atmosphere about the Kultur Lige." The art section managed to establish studios and "art homes" for artists and their students, including a summer (1918) in the Crimea and winter 1918-19 in Pushtse and Kiev.[64] It was also collecting paintings and sculpture of the associated artists for an exhibition and it had published the following graphic works by November 1919: Lissitzky's *Had Gadya*, and Ryback's *Vinter-Mayses* (Winter Tales), besides publishing children's texts illustrated by the artists. It planned to publish Tchaikov's drawings for *Shir ha-Shirim* (Song of Songs) and Tyshler's Book of Ruth (cat. 41-44), but civil war realities intervened. The art section felt itself duty-bound to "draw the printed Yiddish *belles lettres* closer to modern pure plastic investigations."[65,66]

The Kultur Lige art section was committed to a fusion of Jewish folk traditions with contemporary art concerns in order "to create a modern Jewish plastic art which seeks its own organic national form, color and rhythm."[67] This is the vision of Ryback which was shared at least up to 1919 by Lissitzky, Tchaikov, Aronson, and Dobrushin. Its fullest expression appeared in the Kultur Lige publication *Oyfgang* (1919) by Ryback and Aronson in "Paths of Jewish Painting."[68] Rejecting all previous "Jewish art," particularly the Russian Jewish Wanderers, for failing to create a "specific-national point of view,"[69] the authors underlined the importance of Eastern European folk art, particularly its form as opposed to national subject matter (Jewish genre scenes). Hidden in this proposition are not only pure plastic concerns as opposed to theme and subject, but a battle of perspective which also plagued the contemporary Jewish composers Engel and Saminsky and ultimately the Yiddishist Socialists and the Hebraist Zionists, namely, the validation of the specific Eastern European folk traditions as opposed to the traditional high, all-encompassing Hebrew culture "from Moses to Moses" to Bialik. (This true Kulturkampf would have, alas, terrible political consequences!) Ryback and B. Aronson clearly line up on the Yiddishist-Socialist side. In terms of plastic art, it meant an acceptance of Western European contemporary "elements," Cubism and Futurism.[70] Significantly, they rejected pure abstraction for "the modern Jewish artist . . . in such an art painting cannot reveal living emotions."[71] This position, of course, rejects Suprematism and Constructivism. It was necessary inevitably for Lissitzky, Tchaikov, and even Altman to reject the limitation to abstraction. Chagall would assert these premises as an artist but not as a Jewish artist. Yudovin in Vitebsk, however, would give his assent. The Gabo brothers (Antoine and Naum) would not even deign to consider such a proposition. Nevertheless, it would remain the position of Ryback, B. Aronson, and certainly all the Jewish Ecole de Paris artists.

The West provided another element which was intellectually and emotionally seductive but disturbingly evasive: race. Ryback and B. Aronson believed that by avoiding the extra-plastic concerns and errors of the previous generation by grounding their Jewish national art in purely painterly concerns and by a reworking of the old folk ornaments – color, rhythm, two-dimensionalism, etc., "the modern Jewish artists [would] discover their racial traits."[72] Ryback and Aronson never doubted that pure form was abstract. All painterly concerns start in abstraction. It is at the moment of "incarnation" (*farkerperung*) that "the national [i.e., racial ethnic] element in art expressed itself." At that moment, abstract painterly feelings work over "specific conceptual-material" (*spetsifishe oyffasung-material*) (read: theme, image or subject) so that the art that emerges ("the incarnated art") "mirrors the racial traits, i.e., the national form."[73] For them, "even if the artist wishes to be purely international in his work, it would still reveal the specific, spiritual construction and emotions of his milieu."[74] What is this "national element" if not simply a specific style, the organization and structure of the work, and ultimately, if not inevitably, content? Ryback and Aronson can, in fact, be quite prescriptive: Jewish artists prefer "analytic-synthesized grayness of pigment in deep-dark polychromaticism."[75] Such insights today are recognized as self-reflecting comments upon the aesthetics of Ryback and Aronson and their own "specific . . . milieu" (see Ryback's *The Old Synagogue*, Tel Aviv Museum; for related work, see cat. 136₂).

In the August 1919 issue of the Kultur Lige's critical journal *Bikher-Velt* (Book World), no. 4-5 (Kiev), Dobrushin is in full agreement with the Ryback-Aronson position and also agrees with them that Chagall is the truest expression of their ideal of a modern secular Jewish artist. "Chagall, the great child of our people, absorbed the Jewish artistic primitives, he drew from them the form, color and content of his radiant works based on legends [*The Fiddler on the Roof, Over Vitebsk*]."[76] *The Praying Rabbi* (1914) (at the Art Institute in Chicago) might satisfy the "analytic-synthesized grayness of pigment" but Chagall's other works reflect less the colors of Simhat Torah flags (a Jewish *lubok* for Dobrushin which Kampf and Compton accept uncritically) than Russian icons, *lubki*, works by Bakst and French Post-Impressionists, and *Section d'Or* Cubists. What Ryback, B. Aronson, and Dobrushin really admired in his work that was "Jewish," but never overtly stated, was his effective ability to give everyday Jewish life universal import, just as a local Greek tale in Euripides' words becomes a world treasure.

Tchaikov, who taught sculpture in the Kultur Lige studios in Kiev with Ryback (who taught painting), was no newcomer to the Jewish national art renaissance. In comparing the title of *Bikher-Velt* (1919) on its cover page to the cover of the fifth issue of *Makhmadim*, the Tchaikov hand is easily recognizable. He was one of the founders and most enthusiastic supporters of the modern Jewish art movement. It is distressing, however, to find the same Jugendstil influence seven long years later. But in 1919 Tchaikov, like Lissitzky, was living two artistic existences. Tchaikov used Jugendstil for children's books, as in *Temerl* (1917) (cat. 45) or *Far Kleyne Kinder* (For Little Children) (1918), or worked as a Cubo-Futurist in Reuveni's *Kinder* (Children) (1918) (cat. 46) or in Kvitko's *Lemel Nasher* (Lemel the Nosher) (1919) (cat. 47), or even mixed styles in *Finf Arbeslakh* (Five Chick Peas) (1919) (fig. 10, cat. 48). His most mature Cubo-Futurist style can be best seen in his illustrations of the journal *Baginen* (Beginning) (June 1919, Kiev) (fig. 11, cat. 50), in which sly eroticism commingles with still lifes of Sab-

bath loaves and kerosene lamps. At the same time, his real work as an artist was in sculpture. By 1919 he was sculpting some of the most advanced works in Russia and the Ukraine. Although he never admitted to pure abstract sculpture, his Cubo-Futurist experiments led him to pure abstraction in all but name. At the same time, Lissitzky, who would publish *Had Gadya* (1919) (cat. 90) in Kiev (the design of which Tchaikov would borrow in a 1921 edition of Seforim's *Dos Kelbel* [The Calf] [cat. 58]) and illustrate Ben Zion Raskin's 1919 *Der Ber* (The Bear) (cat. 94), in his lyric Cubist style, would be creating in the same year the first set of Proun abstractions in Vitebsk which would gain him international fame.

10

The year 1919 was a turning point aesthetically for Jewish artists and Jewish culture in general. Although every "modern" Jewish artist and critic believed in the "modern," the problem was what did it mean? The literary battle between Bergelson and Litvakov concerning the modern in the journal *Bikher-Velt I* (February 1919) and *Bikher-Velt 4-5* (August 1919) reflected the disquiet among the plastic artists as well. Bergelson, like Ryback, represented the position that traditional shtetl life was atrophied and a modern, secular, national culture should replace it. The role of art was to give aesthetic definition to the new national and cultural longings. Modern Jewish art then would attain the universal by defining first the new Jewish condition. Litvakov, who had once adhered to the same posture, was shifting to the Bolshevik reality. Modern art and literature were to be *engagé*. A modern creator should function in form and content devoid of any clinging

national or cultural identity beyond the fact of language. This logic in the plastic arts would lead to a non-ethnic "universalistic" art: abstraction. Once again the aesthetic perspective ultimately affected one's political and ideological commitments and vice versa. The Bergelson/Ryback aesthetic reflected the national and personal autonomy passed into law by the defunct *RADA*. The Litvakov/Lissitzky/ (and willy-nilly) Tchaikov perspective represented an abandonment of the national cultural autonomy and its aesthetic based on national secular humanism. This does not mean that the latter denied their Jewish nationality but rather that the national question was no longer their central concern.

For Lissitzky or Tchaikov, and certainly Altman, the quest for the Jewish style may well have reached its term by the end of 1919. Their talents and efforts had brought them up to the cutting edge of Russian avant-garde art, in which their participation was welcomed. Their devotion to purely artistic concerns was always a basic premise in their national artistic experiments; therefore, it was natural that they should abandon ethnic concerns in the face of such exciting abstract challenges when their national identity was no longer a hindrance. Furthermore, they still continued to create Yiddish book illustrations – and significantly in the "style" they had left behind, before their abstractions.

Did they also feel the steadily growing confinement that Jewish art imposed both from within and from without? Bergelson complained that his style of Yiddish writing since the Revolution was too sophisticated for his new readers and that the old bourgeois consumer of his art was now functioning in Russian. This problem was also affecting the plastic artist even more by 1919. In *Kultur un Bildung* (Moscow, 1920), Lissitzky could read this philistine review of his remarkable *Had Gadya*:

> The following album, both in theme and in its artistic expression, is too schematic and generally too 'artificial.' It will hold no special value for children, except, perhaps, as a lovely gift from a child to . . . an adult.[77]

Tchaikov, by 1921, as certainly Lissitzky, had lost his belief in establishing a Jewish artistic style by a renewal of the past:

> We also hold as untrue the approach of the young leftist artist who wishes to resolve this problem according to the archives of our past history and folkloric accomplishment. This only leads to stylization and stylization is aestheticism; i.e., a lie concerning our present day and a caprice of individualism which functions in the service of beauty.[78]

Another reality was the conscious effort by the Bolsheviks to shatter national "bourgeois" autonomy and force an adherence within the party structures. In *Baginen* (July 1919), an ominous announcement appeared. This journal was not a Kultur Lige production. Rather it was the expression of the new adherence of Litvakov, Litvak, and Noah Lurie, responsible leaders of Yiddish Socialist parties, to the Bolshevik party line. The key phrase is: published by the "All-Ukrainian Literary Committee, *Yiddish Section*" (my italics). And to make clear that national autonomy institutions were coming to an end, a small note was inserted on page 95 in the art section:

> From the third of July on, the art studio of the Kultur Lige has been placed under the direction of the All-Ukrainian Committee for Plastic Arts and will be maintained by it. . . . The art section of the Kultur Lige has presented the All-Ukrainian Art Committee with a detailed memorandum about the necessity of organizing a Jewish section in the Art Committee. One must hope that this very important question will be resolved positively.

The arrival of the White Russians in August 1919 stayed the hand of the Bolsheviks, and the Kultur Lige had one last breath of life – i.e., the dream of Jewish national cultural autonomy.

From the end of February to 15 April 1920, the art section of the Kultur Lige sponsored the first (and last) Jewish art exhibition in Kiev. The chairman was Ryback; the secretary was a student of his, Yosef Elman. B. Aronson was the general manager and the "honored members" were Tchaikov, *Bal-Makhshoves* (I. I. Eliashev, the leading Yiddish literary critic), and Dobrushin. The catalog essay (translated in the Appendix) was a last ringing affirmation of Jewish national art:

> The first source of our graphics is the Hebrew letter and the ornaments of old Jewish prayer books and religious articles.
> Modern Jewish artists who self-consciously seek specifically national graphic art forms, like Altman, Lissitzky, Chagall, and others, find in fact a rich selection in our ancient symbols. . . .
> Modern Jewish art seeks to recreate our artistic inheritance in national forms, in which it expresses the accomplishments of modern art.
> The collected primitive folk effort becomes the basis of a higher Jewish art which joins the latest universalist quests with the creative skills of the folk masses.[79]

The eleven participants were B. Aronson, Yudl Yafe, Mordechai Kaganovich, M. I. Epstein, Elman, Lissitzky, Tchaikov, Pailes, Tyshler, Nisson Shifrin and

Rabitchev. No oil paintings by Chagall, Altman and Falk were obtainable for showing because Kiev was isolated due to the civil war. The show therefore was mainly an exhibit of young Kiev artists.[80] (Lissitzky was the only "outsider.") Most were barely twenty. Some of them had studied with Alexandra Exter, the great Russian Modernist, in her studio during 1918-19: B. Aronson, Rabinovich (1894-1961), Shifrin and Tyshler. Her influence upon them, particularly her Cubist conceptions, would lead to Aronson's original Cubo-Expressionist stage designs in the United States, and the stage designs of Rabinovich and Tyshler in Jewish and Russian theatres in Moscow. (In fact, there were steady contacts among Jewish, Ukrainian, and Russian artists in Kiev throughout 1917-20.) When the exhibition closed, over four thousand people had visited it:

> Various educational institutions (gymnasiums, evening schools, folk-universities) organized special excursions to the exhibit. On these occasions, the artists would give a presentation about the new universal art and especially explain the tasks of the young Jewish modern artists who were striving to give their new work a specifically national character.[81]

The Kultur Lige art section organized a series of discussions with the Yiddish writers and poets (David Hofstein, Kvitko, Peretz Markish, etc.) about the plastic arts and their shared ideals of building a secular national art with distinct characteristics. Little did Kvitko or Ryback (or their cohorts) expect that two years later they would be collaborating on a Yiddish children's book, *In Vald* (In the Forest), in Berlin!

With the exhibit completed at Vladimirskaya 61 (Kultur Lige Art Studio Exhibition Hall), the art section began the final stages of organizing the first Jewish art museum in the Ukraine. It was to contain three sections: 1) Jewish folk art; 2) works of modern Jewish painters; and 3) universal artworks.

A chill was in the air. The lead article of the *Kultur Lige Bulletin 2* (June-July 1920), entitled "Mir un di Melukhe" (We and the Regime), defended the valuable work of the Kultur Lige and its existence. Was it not working to "build the new Socialist culture?" Its independence was suspect and unacceptable. By December 1920, the Yevsektsia took over the Kultur Lige, keeping its name and maintaining its press for a few more years while harnessing it into the state cultural apparatus.

The significant end of the Kiev Jewish autonomous cultural experiment was the flight of the Kultur Lige executive at the end of December 1920 when Mayzel, Zilberfarb, Leshtschinsky, Z. Melamed, Kh. Sh. Kazdan, and B. Oysurovitsh arrived in Warsaw with the printing plates intact and set up a new Kultur Lige press. But that is another chapter. Everyone knew the end of an era had come. Bergelson and Kvitko left for Berlin, soon to be joined by Der Nister and Ryback. Hofstein, Dobrushin and Litvakov cast their lot with the Bolsheviks and went to Moscow, where Lissitzky would soon arrive. Tchaikov stayed another year in Kiev before passing through Moscow to Berlin for a while. Tyshler and Rabinovich would soon be in Moscow.[82] Of the Executive Committee of the 1920 Art Exhibit, none was in Kiev by the end of 1921, and the secretary, Elman, had died. Indeed, by 1921 Kiev, grove of Jewish cultural activity, had become a grave of Jewish hopes.

In March and April 1922, the Bolshevik-dominated Moscow Kultur Lige (established in 1918 in imitation of the Kiev one) sponsored an exhibition of the works of Altman, Chagall and Shterenberg (cat. 172).[83] The painters were not only the most distinguished of Jewish-born artists, but all three were absolutely safe and acceptable, being present or former officials of the Soviet government. This was the last Jewish-based art exhibition in the Soviet Union.

Only in the theatre, in "make-believe," could "Jewish art" still thrive, albeit by lacerating itself in cruel, grotesque laughter until the government eventually brought down the curtain on this Jewish Potemkin village. Chagall, however, left the Soviet Union forever in July 1922. Habimah left in 1926. Shterenberg remained but had little further "Jewish" artistic activity.[84] Altman, whose many portraits of Lenin and whose Soviet Russian artistic activities gained him much renown, also provided, throughout the 1920s, Yiddish book covers and contributed stage designs to the Yiddish State Theatre.[85] These efforts, however, were not central to his career as a Soviet artist. Of all the Jewish artists, no doubt the most fascinating metamorphosis occurred with Tchaikov, who, from a Jewish national artist in Paris 1912, in Moscow 1917, and in Kiev 1919, passed into abstraction, then accepted Soviet Socialist Realism and became a professor of sculpture at Moscow University and even a dean. With his death at the age of 98 in 1986, one year after Chagall, the last significant representative of the tragic Jewish Modernist art renaissance brought to a close the Russian chapter in Jewish art history.[86]

## Afterword

The Russian Jewish artists did perform a miracle: within the space of a generation (1910-25), from being peripheral artistic provincials, they made their way to the forefront of the international avant-garde. Some, like the Pevsner brothers, went straight to abstraction. They were the exception. The majority moved through figurative art and most stopped at the borders of non-objective art.

The Russian Jewish artists who were drawn to the creation of a specific Jewish art came from a traditional Yiddish-speaking milieu – but not necessarily an ultra-religious one. They rejected the legacy of traditional Jewish shtetl life and were quite open to European acculturation. They believed a synthesis of European and Jewish perspectives was possible and highly desirable. In the short period of their activity they succeeded in fusing Eastern European Jewish folk motifs, themes and ornaments with European Modernist styles, particularly Futurism, Cubism, and Expressionism. Their works were well received in the international avant-garde for their freshness, exoticism, and technical accomplishment. Their graphic work for Yiddish books in particular can well be considered their most unique contribution. By treating the page simultaneously as canvas, verbal window and aesthetic object-in-itself, the artists raised textual illustration to a modern polysemous art form. The interplay of the figurative image with the Hebrew alphabet or the many abstract designs conflated from the Hebrew letters produced at once a verbal symbol and a visual icon. A new typographical "layout" came into being. The graphics of Lissitzky, Altman, Tchaikov and Chagall, and others, later brought these developments to Russian and Western modern art and typography.

Nevertheless, the thrust of Modernism towards increasing abstraction, the dominance of formal and painterly concerns over traditional themes or narrative content, finally affected Jewish artists like Lissitzky or Tchaikov, not to mention their Jewish disciples. No doubt external pressures and new ideological temptations or commitments hastened their abandonment of earlier artistic and Jewish national perspectives, but more overriding was their self-perception as professional artists. Their passage from Jewish figurative art to abstraction must be recognized as a personal development, a willful decision to explore elsewhere. The aesthetic successes of their "Jewish period" exhausted that vein in the same way that the Russians Malevich, Goncharova, Larionov, Popova, etc., passed through their "Russian" period of folk motifs and themes on *their* way to pure abstraction. Even Ryback, the diehard of the Jewish nationalist painters,

having worked through "Jewish Expressionism" in 1923, retreated to painting French landscapes. The inter-war Polish Jewish painters (with the exception of Henryk Berlewi and Karol Hiller), under no overt or covert political pressure to practice any particular form of art, never went beyond the victories of the Kiev Kultur Lige art productions of 1920 with their intended manifestations of a Jewish Modernist art.

Jewish art of this period with its use of national "icons" performed an essential mediating role by fortifying national pride and personal emotional legitimacy. It strengthened modern Jewish secular identity by its participation in the general European Modernist current, which privileged the folkloric, the "primitive" and the "childlike" in its explorations of new forms and new techniques of expression. By 1920, the Jewish national elements in art had served their function well for the most original Russian Jewish artists. The latter were now confident equals of their Russian contemporaries and eager to move into the brave new world.

Those Jewish artists who hesitated to join the international avant-garde in abstraction ultimately remained stifled in Jewish figurative art, the weakest of whom endlessly depicted nostalgic images of passing types, the Hasidic rabbi, the wagon-driver or the wooden synagogue. Eschewing personal artistic exploration, they passed, at best, into recording Jewish ethnology.

The real tragedy of the Russian Jewish artists was the imposition of Socialist Realism at the expense of both a Jewish national art and participation in the universal trend toward abstraction.

1   James H. Billington, *The Icon and the Axe*, New York: Vintage Books, 1970 (originally published 1966), p. 405.
2   John E. Bowlt, *The Silver Age: Russian Art of the Early Twentieth Century and the "World of Art" Group*, Newtonville, Massachusetts: Oriental Research Partners, 1979, pp. 217-19.
3   Franz Meyer, *Marc Chagall* (French version by Philippe Jaccottet), Paris: Flammarion, 1961 (original in German, Verlag M. Dumont Schauberg, Cologne, 1961), p. 50.
4   Mark Etkind, *Nathan Altman*, Dresden: VEB Verlag der Kunst, 1984 (based on the 1971 Russian edition), p. 14.
5   Yitzhak Lichtenstein, "Vitebsker Kinstler," *Vitebsk Amol*, ed. Gregor Aronson, New York, 1956, p. 447.
6   Matthew Frost, "Marc Chagall and the Jewish State Chamber Theatre," *Russian History*, 8, pt. 1-2 (1981), p. 93. This sensitive and important article with valuable dates and new information (gleaned from the Russian) must be read with some caution regarding the Yiddish contents of the productions. Shalom Aleichem's theatre was not in the "carnival" mode, but, on the contrary, was heavily sentimental. Granovsky, the great director, reworked all the plays of the classic Yiddish writers – and

usually against their intentions. One must also take with a grain of salt the Chagall quotations from *My Life* (the English seemingly based on the French version) or from his Russian texts. Chagall shaded his remarks for the supposedly linguistic audience of his writings.

7  Franz Meyer, op. cit., p. 272.

8  Sarah Bodine, "Unovis: Art as Process," *Ilya Grigorevich Chasnik*, New York: Leonard Hutton Galleries, 1979, pp. 26-7 (catalog).

9  Legally only Jewish merchants of the First Guild, certain rabbis and select Jewish prostitutes and servants were permitted to live outside the fifteen official residence zones (the Pale of Settlement). They all required permits, which were expensive. For Jews, obtaining a residence permit outside the Pale required skill, "friends," patience, and gifts.

10  Antokolski noted, "He [Stasov] loved passionately all of Russia, not differentiating people by class or religion. He wanted only that everyone keep his individuality and would perfect it for the common good and progress," in Yuri Olkhovsky, *Vladimir Stasov and Russian National Culture*, Ann Arbor, Michigan: UMI Research Press, 1983, preface IX.

11  Vladimir Stassof et David Gunzburg, *L'Ornement Hébreu*, Berlin: S. Calvary et Co., 1905, p. 7.

12  Ibid., p. 6.

13  Olkhovsky, op. cit., p. 29.

14  *The Golden Tradition*, ed. Lucy S. Dawidowicz, Boston: Beacon Press, 1967, p. 328.

15  Joachim Braun, *Jews and Jewish Elements in Soviet Music*, Tel Aviv: Israeli Music Publications, 1978, p. 37.

16  Y. L. Peretz in Warsaw must be given particular credit for encouraging the appreciation of Hasidism and Eastern European Jewish folk traditions. His own reworkings of Hasidic tales aroused interest from 1910 on. The westernizing Jewish intelligentsia and cultural activists recognized the authentic "Jewish" qualities of this material and saw it as a springboard for new works of art. See *Di Yidishe Velt*, St. Petersburg, no. 1, 1912, p. 96.

17  Braun, op. cit., p. 39; Saul Ginsburg, *Amolike Peterburg*, New York: Cyco Farlag, 1944, p. 239.

18  Marc Chagall, *My Life*, New York: Orion Press, 1960. The first extracts from Chagall's autobiography were in *Shtrom* (Moscow), 1922 (in Yiddish).

19  Isaiah Trunk, "Historians of Russian Jewry," *Russian Jewry*, eds. J. Frumkin, Gregor Aronson, and Alexis Goldenweiser, New York: Thomas Yoseloff, 1966, p. 465.

20  An-Sky's letter, *Fun Yakov Dineson's Arkhiv*, 1913, p. 26, in the Jewish National and University Library, Jerusalem.

21  Marc Chagall, "Eygns," in *Vitebsk Amol*, op. cit., p. 442.

22  Max Osborn, *Jüdische Graphik*, Petropolis: Reiner, 1923, p. 26.

23  M. Etkind, op. cit., p. 28.

24  *An-Sky's letter*, op. cit.

25  Robert C. Williams, *Artists in Revolution*, Bloomington: Indiana University Press, 1977, p. 54.

26  Kenneth Silver, *The Circle of Montparnasse: Jewish Artists in Paris 1905-1945*, New York: Universe Books, 1985, p. 25; Khil Aronson, *Bilder un geshtaltn fun Montparnasse*, Paris, 1963, pp. 11-12; Borvine Frenkel, *Mit Yidishe Kinstler*, Paris: Yidisher Kultur-Kongres in Frankraykh, 1963, pp. 7-9.

27  Chagall, "Eygns," op. cit., p. 433.

28  Saul Bellow takes the same position. He repeatedly denies being a Jewish writer – only a writer using Jewish material.

29  Both Jean-Claude Marcadé ("Le contexte russe de l'oeuvre de Chagall," *Marc Chagall*, Paris: Centre Georges Pompidou, 1984, pp. 18-26) and Susan Compton ("The Russian Background," *Chagall*, London: Royal Academy of Arts, 1985, pp. 30-45) correctly emphasize the importance of Chagall's Russian artistic training and the St. Petersburg cultural milieu. It is now time to question the generally sincere but simplistic handling of Chagall's Jewish background or that of the other Jewish artists from Russia. Thorough studies of their *heder* training and their socio-cultural context are now essential. The two articles by Z. Amishai-Maisels, "Chagall's Jewish In-Jokes," *Journal of Jewish Art*, vol. 5, 1978, pp. 76-93, and "The Jewish Jesus," *Journal of Jewish Art*, vol. 9, 1982, pp. 84-104, are particularly valuable beginnings in uncovering Chagall's manipulations of Jewish folk traditions and Western iconography. It is striking how little the Yiddish sources are used, be they Chagall's writings or others. Where translations do exist, they have been heavily edited.

30  Verbal communication to Avram Kampf from Yitzhak Lichtenstein. Kampf, op. cit., p. 206, note 44.

31  Leo Koenig, manuscript in the archives of the Jewish National and University Library, Jerusalem, no. 4○1269/173. He is one of the most astute Yiddish critics and deserves a full-scale study.

32  Marek Shvarts, "The National Element in Jewish Art," *Literarishe Bleter* (Warsaw), 3 April 1925, I, 48, p. 1.

33  Ibid., p. 1.

34  Koenig, op. cit., p. 6.

35  Ibid., p. 6.

36  Marc Chagall, "Eygns," op. cit., pp. 441-42.

37  Nathan Altman, *Jüdische Graphik*, Berlin: Razum-Verlag, 1923. In 1913 the Jewish Ethnographic Society had already published a series of photographs of old Jewish tombtones in Lublin by Sh. B. Nusenbaum, *Evreyski Nagrobnie goroda lyublina* (sixteenth to nineteenth centuries), St. Petersburg: Lire, 1913.

38  Rachel Wischnitzer, "Jüdische Kunst in Kiev und Petrograd," *Der Jude*, Berlin, 1920-21, pp. 351-56.

39  Shmuel Niger, "Lirishe Siluetn," *Tsukunft*, New York, 1920, vol. 25, no. 8, p. 485.

40  Moshe Broderzon, *Sikhes Kholin*, illustrated by Eliezer Lissitzky, Moscow: Shamir, 1917. (The publisher originally was Nashe iskusstvo, but the name is crossed out and replaced with Shamir in the Israel Museum copy.) *Sikhes Kholin* was one of the first Yiddish texts printed in Russia after the Tsar's fall. The revolution rescinded the *ukase* of 1915, forbidding publication in Hebrew letters.

41  Alan Curtis Birnholz, *El Lissitzky*, Yale University Ph.D. thesis in art, 1973, p. 20; Sophie Lissitzky-Küppers, *El Lissitzky*, London: Thames and Hudson, 1968, 1980 edition, p. 20. His widow, for whatever reasons, has excised from her study most of Lissitzky's Jewish works and any allusions to his writings in Yiddish.

42  Franz Meyer, op. cit., p. 246.

43  Professor Yakov Kagan-Shabshai had remarkably modern taste for a Jewish collector in those years in Moscow. The Chagalls he owned are reproduced in Boris Aronson, *Marc Chagall*, Berlin: Razum-Varlag, 1924, p. 31.

44  Mark Etkind, op. cit., p. 232, and the German original of Franz Meyer, op. cit., p. 733, where he explicitly states that it took place at Galerie Lemercier and that Chagall provided 43 works in ". . . Catalog No. 238-281."

45  *Oyf der Vakh*, Kiev, 12 July 1918, no. 9, p. 28.

46  Ibid., p. 28.

47  Ibid., p. 28.

48  *Oyf der Vakh*, Kiev, 24 May 1918, p. 27.

49  An-Sky's letter, op. cit., 1 October 1918, p. 36.

50  *Vystarki Sovetskogo Isobrazitel'nogo iskusstva spravocnik*, ed. Butorin, Moscow: Sovetskij Khudoznik, 1965, p. 16.

51  *Kultur un Bildung*, Moscow, 6 September 1918, no. 3-4, p. 21.

52  *Der Emes*, Moscow, 11 August 1918, p. 2.

53  See David Bergelson, "Dikhtung un Gezelshaftlikhkayt," *Bikher-Velt*, Kiev, 4-5, 1919, p. 8, and and Seth Wolitz, "The Kiev-Grupe, 1918-1920, Debates the Function of Literature," *Modern Jewish Studies Annual Two*, Queens, New York, 1978.
54  *Oyf der Vakh*, Kiev, 12 July 1918, p. 28.
55  *Oyf der Vakh*, Kiev, 7 June 1918, no. 6, p. 18.
56  *Der Emes*, Moscow, 20 October 1918, no. 49, p. 2.
57  Sophie Lissitzky-Küppers, op. cit., color illustration, nos. 20, 40.
58  The participants were Altman,* Burliuk, (D.D.), Beigun,** Brazer,* Veksler,** Volkhonsky, Gerasimov, Grishchenko, Gurvich,* Le-Dantyu, Zevin, Zeldin,** Ivanov, Kandinsky, Kliun, Konchalovsky, Kuznetsov, Kupin, Lentulov, Libakov, Lissitzky,* Malevich, Meerson,** Pain,* Pen,** Potekhina, Rodchenko, Rozhdestvensky, Romm,** Rozanova, Strazheminsky, Falk,** Fedorov, Fridlender,** Khidekel,** Chagall,** Shevchenko, Exter, and Yudovin.* (*Appeared in Moscow Jewish Artists Exhibit 1918. **Of Jewish origin but did not appear in Moscow exhibit.)
59  Howard Aster, *Jewish-Ukrainian Relations: Two Solitudes*, Oakville, Ontario: Mosaic Press, 1983, p. 26; Salomon Goldelman, *Jewish National Autonomy in Ukraine, 1917-1920*, Chicago: Ukrainian Research Information Institute, 1968, p. 67; Zvi Y. Gitelman, *Jewish Nationality and Soviet Politics*, Princeton: Princeton University Press, 1972, pp. 156-59.
60  *Der Fraytog*, Berlin, 1 August 1919, no. 2, p. 6.
61  *Di Grunt-Oyfgaben fun der Kultur-Lige, 1918-1919*, Kiev: Kultur Lige, 1919.
62  *Kultur Lige Zamlung*, Kiev, November 1919, p. 36.
63  I. Rabitchev would later become an important set designer for the Moscow Jewish State Chamber Theatre. In 1923, he did the sets for *200,000* and in 1924, for *Three Little Jewish Grapes*.
64  *Kultur-Lige Zamlung*, op. cit., p. 37.
65  Ibid, p. 38. All titles cited by artists published by the Kultur Lige.
66  It was in Kiev, not Vitebsk, as Camilla Gray asserts in her splendid and seminal work, that the "Jewish tradition" of "the first post-Revolutionary experiments in typology" took place. Camilla Gray, *The Russian Experiment in Art, 1863-1922*, New York: Harry Abrams, 1971, p. 253.
67  *Kultur-Lige Zamlung*, op. cit., p. 38.
68  I. Ryback and B. Aronson, "Di Vegn Fun der Yidisher Moleray," *Oyfgang- ershter zamlbukh*, Kiev: Farlag Kultur Lige, 1919, p. 99-124. A translation of the final part of this article appears in the Appendix.
69  Ibid., p. 110.
70  Ibid., p. 114.
71  Ibid., p. 124.
72  Ibid., p. 115.
73  Ibid., p. 114.
74  Ibid., p. 115.
75  Ibid., p. 115.
76  Yeheskiel Dobrushin, "Kunst-primitiv un kunst-bukh far kinder," *Bikher-Velt*, Kiev, no. 4-5, August 1919, p. 18.
77  *Kultur un Bildung*, Moscow, no. 1 (24), 1920, p. 39.
78  Joseph Tchaikov, *Sculpture*, Kiev: Melukhe Farlag, 1921, p. 12-13; Eliezer Lissitzky, "Memoirs Concerning the Mohilev Synagogue," *Milgroim*, Berlin, no. 3, 1923, pp. 9-13.
79  *Jewish Exhibition of Sculpture, Graphics and Drawing*, Kiev, 1920, p. 8. See I. Shmidt, *Iosif Chaikov*, Moscow: Izd. Sovetskii Khudoznik, 1977. For a translation of the catalog, see Appendix.
80  *Vystarki Sovetskogo Izobrazitel'nogo iskasstva spravocnik*, op. cit., p. 69.
81  *Kultur-Lige Bulletin* 2, Kiev, June-July 1920, p. 55.
82  Rabinovich became quite active in Goset. In 1921 he did the sets for *Before Dawn* (Voyter) and *God of Vengeance* (Asch); in 1922, *The Witch* (Goldfaden); in 1930, *The Deaf Man* (Bergelson); and in 1931 *No Worries* (Markish). Tyshler was to contribute sets to the highly successful *King Lear* (1935). See Béatrice Picon-Vallin, *Le Théâtre juif soviétique pendant les années vingt*, Lausanne: La Cité–L'Age d'Or, 1973, pp. 175-85.
83  Catalog of Kultur Lige: Nathan Altman, Marc Chagall, David Shterenberg, March-April 1922, Moscow (in Russian); Mark Etkind, op. cit., p. 232; also see Marc Chagall, *Oeuvre sur papier*, Paris: Centre Georges Pompidou, 1984, pp. 103-13, which contains rare drawings from his theatre period in Moscow 1920-22.
84  He did the sets of *Luftmensh* (1928) for Goset.
85  His stage sets were among the most original in the Soviet Union in the 1920s. In 1921, he completed for the Habimah theatre sets for their celebrated production of *The Dybbuk*. In 1922, he designed for Goset the sets for *Uriel Accosta*. In 1925, he collaborated with Goset on the set designs for the film *Jewish Happiness*. In 1926, he designed for Goset the sets for *The Tenth Commandment* and *137 Children's Homes*. In 1927, his last set designs for Goset were for *Trouhadec* (Jules Romains). See Picot-Vallin, op. cit., pp. 175-85; Mark Etkind, op. cit., pp. 218-23.
86  The Tchaikov illustrations cited appear in: Moshe Broderzon, *Temerl*, Moscow: Farlag Khaver, 1917; Reuveni, *Kinder*, Kiev: Kiever Farlag, 1918; *Far Kleyne Kinder*, Kiev: Kiever Farlag, 1918; Leib Kvitko, *Lemel Nasher*, Kiev: Kiever Farlag, 1919; *Finf Arbeslakh*, Kiev: Farlag Anhoyb (Yidisher Folks-Farlag), 1919; Mendele Mokher Seforim, *Dos Kelbel*, Kiev: Kultur Lige, 1921; and Joseph Tchaikov, *Skulptur*, Kiev: Melukhe Farlag, 1921.
The Lissitzky illustrations cited appear in: Moshe Broderzon, *Sikhes Kholin*, Moscow (Nashe iskusstvo): Shamir, 1917; Mani Leib, *Yingl Tsingl Khvat*, Kiev: Yidisher Folks-Farlag, 1918; *Had Gadya*, Kiev: Yidisher Folks-Farlag, 1919; Ben Zion Raskin, *Der Ber*, Kiev: Yidisher Folks-Farlag, 1919.
A close study of the names of the publishing houses reveals their original ideological commitments but as the Bolshevization continued – particularly from 1919 onwards – the names become hyphenated and finally, the older ones disappear. The changing names of the publishing houses, in short, reflect the continual decline of Jewish cultural autonomy. The later publications of illustrated children's books in Yiddish (published in Berlin in 1922-24, usually in Schwellen Verlag and Vostok) contain drawings that were composed earlier (in the case of Lissitzky) or were being transposed from another medium to the printed page (Ryback) or were fresh creations (Ryback, Tchaikov), but in an earlier Kiev Cubo-Futurist style with greater simplification, influenced, no doubt, by exposure to the Berlin Expressionists. By late 1924, even this late Berlin idyll was over.

This paper was made possible through a fellowship granted during 1984-85 by the American Council for Learned Societies, which permitted me to use the Jewish National and University Library and the Israel Museum Archives.

# From the Pale of Settlement to the Reconstruction of the World*

## John E. Bowlt

## Preamble

In 1905 Baron David Guenzburg and Vladimir Stasov published their elephantine folio *L'Ornement Hébreu* (cat. 159).[1] In 1939 the State Museum of Ethnography in Leningrad organized the exhibition "Jews in Tsarist Russia and the USSR," the last official panorama and propagation of Jewish culture in the Soviet Union.[2] Between those two dates, but especially during the 1910s and 1920s, the issue of Jewish artistic tradition and innovation received unprecedented attention in Russia, inspiring not only the search for, and rediscovery of, the Jewish literary, musical, and artistic heritage, but also the creation of a new Jewish visual art – perhaps of a new Jewish visual artist – which made a vital contribution to the development of the Russian avant-garde. It was, as Abram Markovich Efros wrote, "our aesthetic rebirth."[3]

What is especially remarkable about the pre-revolutionary period in this context is that, in spite of the pogroms and emigrations, and the institutional quotas and censorship of the Yiddish/Hebrew press, Jewish artists and critics, whether rightist or leftist, manifested a strong collective spirit, dedicated much energy to the refurbishing of Jewish culture and, to that end, projected and founded an impressive number of societies in St. Petersburg, Moscow, Kiev, Odessa, and Kharkov that championed and disseminated Jewish cultural concepts and values. The strategic role and ideological influence of organizations such as the Jewish Historical and Ethnographic Society, the Society for the Enlightenment of Jews, and of particular relevance to this exhibition, the Jewish Society for the Encouragement of the Arts (all in St. Petersburg/Petrograd) have received very little attention in scholarly examinations of Russian Jewish art: one aim of this essay, therefore, is to provide information on the activities of these organizations as they relate to the development of modern Russian art.

* "Reconstruction of the World" paraphrases the title of El Lissitzky's 1920 manifesto, "Suprematism in World Reconstruction." See S. Lissitzky-Küppers: *El Lissitzky*, London: Thames and Hudson, 1968, pp. 327-30.

## The Ethnographical Heritage

Before we explore this important component of Russian Jewish culture, we must confront several fundamental issues that intrigued many artists and critics of the 1910s-20s. The most widely discussed and most inadequately defined of these burning questions was the very notion of Jewish art: if there was such a commodity, what did it signify and how did it differ from French, Italian, or Russian art? Answers were as diverse and as contradictory as the artists and critics themselves. For ethnographic historians such as M. Balaban, Jewish art was the

> object created by the Jew, bearing all the features of distinctive Jewish creativity – articles of synagogue use, drawings and paintings, carvings, candlesticks and reflectors, illustrated manuscripts. . . the synagogues themselves and their constituent parts.[4]

Stasov, too, identified the Jewish style with "the ornamental talent of the Jewish race," with its decorative flourishes in the synagogue and the cemetery. Efros, one of the pioneering researchers of modern Jewish art, was much more guarded in his definition of the subject, preferring to stress the internationalism of the Jewish artist or, at best, to limit his characteristics to a "certain abstraction, a generalizing tendency, an elegiac contemplativeness."[5] Maxim Syrkin, a regular contributor to the Russian Jewish press, also formulated his response in broad terms, maintaining that "there has never been a *Jewish style.* . . . In any case, the main thing in art is created not by a tribe, but by the individuality of the particular artist."[6]

An-Sky (S. A. Rapoport), in his many discussions of Jewish culture, old and new, identified the strength of Jewish artistic creativity precisely with its ethnic and ethnographical traditions, with the basic religious rituals and customs of the Jewish way of life, which formed the common denominator of Jewish society whether in Kiev, Kishinev, Vilna, Vitebsk, Zhitomir, Vinnitsa, Odessa or, for the fortunate few, St. Petersburg and Moscow. Indeed, the late 1900s and 1910s witnessed a flurry of activity, inspired to a considerable extent by An-Sky, to preserve, analyze, and propagate this unifying principle – reflected in the wide-ranging articles of the "thick" journal *Evreiskaia starina* published in St. Petersburg/Petrograd/Leningrad from 1909 through 1930, and, of course, in the Baron Horace Guenzburg Jewish ethnographic expedition that An-Sky supervised in 1911-14 (for related material, see cat. 1-17).[7] True, the latter has only limited relevance to the question at hand, but it should certainly be mentioned in the general context of Jewish and Russian art of the early twentieth century: not simply because

young Russian Jews (Solomon Yudovin, El Lissitzky, and Issachar Ryback) were involved in the recording and collating of data but rather because the expedition and its results represented the same kind of rediscovery of indigenous culture that was being undertaken by the primary members of the Russian avant-garde at exactly the same time. Natalia Goncharova, Mikhail Larionov, Kasimir Malevich, and Vladimir Tatlin were deeply affected by their recognition and analysis of Russian primitive art (icons, *lubki*, painted trays, signboards, etc.). Although many young Jewish artists chose *not* to study their past, some were visibly influenced by it – for example, Nathan Altman, Marc Chagall, and Lissitzky.

According to a letter from An-Sky to the editor of *Evreiskaia starina* in 1915,[8] the research materials that he had collected in "more than 60 towns and villages" during his expedition through the Volynia and Podolia provinces were to be deposited with the Jewish National Museum in Petrograd.[9] An-Sky described this collection on several occasions and it is possible to reconstruct its composition from the moment when it entered the museum in 1916.[10] It contained over 2000 photographs of synagogues, Jewish historical buildings, monuments, domestic scenes and types; a collection of around 1800 folktales, legends and parables; more than 1500 folk songs; 500 cylinder recordings of songs and folk motifs; a substantial amount of purely anthropological material such as descriptions of rituals; more than 100 historical documents; 50 antique manuscripts and record books; a large number of antique silver, brass, and wood religious articles, etc. It is also known that An-Sky himself acquired many documents and illustrations relating to the predicament of the Jews during the First World War and these, presumably, were also passed on to the Jewish National Museum.[11]

This major assemblage of Jewish culture was operative as a museum by May 1915 and its materials were preserved in a "special fireproof facility."[12] During late 1915 and 1916 the museum and its archive continued to expand through donations from well-wishers such as Emanuel Lavin (a Petrograd collector of Jewish antiquities and books) and the sculptor Ilya Ginzburg, and its staff expected to publish a complete inventory in 1917.[13] According to one source, the materials from the Guenzburg expedition, transferred to the museum at the end of 1916, were located in cases in a spacious hall of the Jewish Almshouse in Petrograd, where the public could study them three times a week.[14] In the fall of 1917, the museum was closed because of robberies and pogroms and a report of 1918 indicates that many items were lost.[15] But the museum reopened on Vasilii Island on 17 June 1923 under the directorship of Ginzburg and with a council that included A. M. Bramson and Yudovin. Later that year Bramson took over the directorship and, until at least 1928, Yudovin was chief curator.[16]

It is tempting to assume that the visual arts section of the Jewish National Museum, with its "synagogue ornaments . . . rich albums with extremely interesting illustrations, ornamental title pages and initial letters,"[17] acted as an immediate source of inspiration for young artists. After all, An-Sky himself hoped that the collection would be used by:

> Jewish writers, poets and artists who henceforth would not reject their roots, who would not lose themselves in their search for motifs and whose works . . . would not wander among those of other nations like pale shadows, but would live their own forms.

In spite of An-Sky's sentiment, connections between the museum and modern artists were tenuous, and there is no written record of its collection being used by Altman, Isaac Brodsky, Lissitzky, or any of their circle. Conversely, the museum concentrated on antiquity and at no time manifested a commitment to modern Jewish art. Renderings of synagogue ornaments and tombstones by Lissitzky and Yudovin were an important part of the collection, and perhaps the designs inspired Altman, B. Kh. Kratko, Lissitzky, and others in their own decorative graphic work, but there does not seem to have been a particularly enthusiastic response on the part of young Russian Jewish artists to the museum – or vice versa. What was needed, therefore, was an institution that would support the cause of modern Jewish art, not within the context of local folklore, but in the arena of the latest Russian and European trends.

## Antokolskis of the Future[19]

It is important to remember that, in spite of pressures to the contrary, Jewish social and cultural traditions were still very strong in the Modernist period, and that for a young Jew like Altman or Chagall to renounce his "folklore" was an audacious, iconoclastic gesture. Even though the development of modern European art came about through the inauguration and assimilation of Cubism and Futurism, not all Jewish artists were able to embrace these systems wholeheartedly: An-Sky was never very involved with these new trends and his views found many sympathizers. Still, An-Sky, like Stasov, was an archivist and *littérateur* who tended to identify artistic development with narrative content rather than with formal quality. He appreciated painting and sculpture for their documentary and representorial or, at least, philosophical value, and his natural inclination was towards the thematic art of Mark Antokolski[20] rather than towards, say, the Cubist concepts of Robert Falk. In this sense, An-Sky represented a powerful faction of Jewish intellectuals in Russia who maintained that Jewish art had flourished, and would continue to flourish, only on the basis of its ethnographical tradition. Efros, for example, was not hostile to this viewpoint, although he was also willing to consider other resolutions of the problem.

Many members of the avant-garde contended that the future path of Jewish art lay in its anonymity and international commitment. In the 1920s, of course, this idea was shared by artists of many nations who strove to formulate the International Style in architecture and the plastic arts, sympathizing with the sincere attempts of their linguistic colleagues to accelerate the application of Esperanto. In the immediate context of Jewish art and the Russian avant-garde, this argument held a particular logic: few modern Jewish artists derived all their artistic inspiration from the patriarchal traditions of Jewish culture observed in the tortured environment of the shtetl, although, certainly, Chagall, Ryback, and Yudovin did. In many cases, they attempted to interweave these traditions with the aesthetic systems of Cubism, Futurism, Suprematism, etc.; i.e., "foreign" styles that, apparently, had little to do with the Jewish calendar, the synagogue or the rabbi. A case in point is the Kiev artist Abraham Manievich (1881-1942), who had a large one-man show at the Dobychina Bureau in Petrograd in 1916.[21] Born and raised in the ghetto, Manievich ignored all reference to this background in his art with a persistence that astonished his public.[22]

But the total rejection of the familiar and tribal past is impossible, and there are many interpretations of – or, at least, allusions to – tradition in the achievements of modern Russian Jewish artists. We think of Leonid Pasternak's covers for the three cycles of Joel Engel's Yiddish folk songs (cat. 163); Joseph Tchaikov's book on sculpture published in Kiev in 1921 (cat. 171) (translated in part in the Appendix); Lissitzky's designs for *Legend of Prague* (cat. 72, 74), for the covers of *U rek vavilonskikh* (By the Rivers of Babylon) (fig. 12) and for the exhibition catalog of Jewish art in Moscow (both 1917) (fig. 15) and the sheet music published by the Society of Jewish Music (1919) (fig. 67, cat. 82);[23] Altman's *Head of a Young Jew* – the self-portrait that Efros identified as the beginning of a national art[24] – and his impressive album *Evreiskaia grafika* (Jewish Graphics) (cat. 30);[25] and Boris Aronson's equally impressive work with a similar title (cat. 174) and his monograph on Chagall, etc.[26] Aronson, Isaac Rabinovich, and Alexander Tyshler also evoked their upbringing in their book illustrations and stage designs,[27] but, even

12

so, we should be careful not to overemphasize their reliance on "Jewish life" as the guiding principle of their artistic inquiry – and one reason for this lies simply in the rapid transformation and diversification of their life-styles as their contacts with the Russian and European avant-garde movements increased and intensified.

As at any moment when patriarchal values are challenged by the vicissitudes of demographic shifts, industrialization, and accessibility of alternative world views, Jewish society in Russia at the end of the nineteenth century was exposed to an entire range of external and internal pressures. The pattern that the Jewish family had followed for centuries (described in detail by Lazar Rokhlin in his study of the village of Krasnopolie)[28] began to crumble, and the more diligently ethnographers began to collect and categorize the relics of ancient Jewish culture, the more enthusiastically young Jews embraced other cultural systems.

Perhaps that is why famous Jewish artists at the turn of the century, such as Antokolski, Naum Aronson, Leon Bakst, Ginzburg, and Valentin Serov, were recognized and praised for their non-Jewish themes. As Efros observed in one of his articles, Antokolski, for example, was remembered largely for his themes drawn from *Russian* history.[29] Syrkin also noted that, in general, Jewish artists of the late nineteenth century, such as Michel Blokh, Mariia Dillon, Ginzburg, Arnold Lakhovsky, Isaac Levitan (and his brother Adolf), Pasternak and, of course, Antokolski, were remarkably close to the Russian *Peredvizhniki* (Wanderers) on account of their "ideological saturation . . . and absence of plastic culture."[30] Still, this is not to say that the Jewish Realists and academicians born in Russia ignored their natural identity; they were often proud of it, even if they did not emphasize it in their art. Antokolski's correspondence with Stasov makes this quite clear, and Naum Aronson wrote an entire tract on the subject.[31] Moreover, we should not forget that Antokolski and Aronson chose to live and work in Paris not only because it was an artistic center, but also because they felt that residence in Russia and the anti-Semitic bias of the Russian public would ruin their chances of artistic success.[32]

By 1909 -10, just at the time when the most important surveys of ancient Jewish art began to appear in the Russian press (e.g., *Evreiskaia starina*, *Perezhitoe* [Experience] [St. Petersburg, 1909-10], *Novyi voskhod* [New Sunrise], [St. Petersburg, 1910]), it was generally recognized that at least part of the Jewish community was moving away from strict religious observance toward a more secular or profane culture. An-Sky himself touched on this problem in his article "Jewish Popular Creativity" of 1909, where he identified a distinguishing feature of modern Jewish art as its highly developed civic sentiment and its orientation away from the rabbi towards the doctor, the professor and the writer.[33] An-Sky's sister, Sarah Rapoport, also broached the subject in her 1910 article "Religious and Secular Education," in which she implied that both systems of upbringing were legitimate.[34] In 1916 Maxim Vinaver (now remembered for his financial support of Chagall in St. Petersburg) even argued in his capacity as president of the first Jewish Social Club in Petrograd that the synagogue had already lost its status as the cultural center of Jewish life – and that new organizations were essential for the spiritual well-being of Jews. Such arguments coincided with the establishment of a whole complex of institutions and facilities – outside the jurisdiction of the synagogue – especially in St. Petersburg and Moscow, that promoted the cause of Jewish art. They arranged exhibitions, organized cash competitions for Jewish artists, invited artists and critics to talk about their work, and maintained close connections with sister organizations (e.g., Alexander Krein's Society of Jewish Music). Chief among these was the Jewish Society for the Encouragement of the Arts.

## The Jewish Society for the Encouragement of the Arts

This was one of several important cultural centers founded in Petrograd in 1916-17. Mention should be made of the Jewish Literary and Art Society (also called the Y. L. Peretz Society), established in 1916 by the writers L. M. Eisenberg and V. S. Mandel and by the State Duma member M. Kh. Bomash – which aimed to encourage the use of the Yiddish language, specifically in the theatre. The Jewish Theatre Society, chaired by S. A. Beliatsky, O. O. Grusenberg, L. I. Leonidov and M. S. Rivesman, also opened in Petrograd in 1916 and staged plays in Yiddish and Hebrew. The same year also saw the establishment of the Jewish Historical Museum in Odessa by the artist S. Ya. Kirshinevsky. All these institutions were short-lived, but the Jewish Society for the Encouragement of the Arts (JSEA) in particular achieved much of permanent value in the eighteen months of its active life (January 1916-summer 1917). True, the JSEA was not exactly an avant-garde group and owed much of its physical and spiritual health to the presence of the academician Ginzburg, but a number of young experimental artists were associated with it, including Altman and Brodsky. Although based in Petrograd, the JSEA opened a Moscow affiliation in March 1916 (supported by the archi-

tect A. N. Zelikson, the painter Adolf Milman and the engineer A. F. Kagan-Shabshai), and also announced the formation of branches in Kiev and Kharkov.[35]

The JSEA was modelled on the Society for the Encouragement of the Arts founded in St. Petersburg in 1821 by Prince Ivan Gagarin and others, and while its goals were far more modest, it clearly sympathized with the essential program of Gagarin's brainchild – to help underprivileged students receive a sound art education through subsidies, introduction to the Academy of Arts, and publications. The president of the JSEA was I. Ginzburg, who influenced, although did not necessarily dominate, its activities.[36] Inasmuch as the JSEA listed several august academicians among its ranks, including Isaac Askenazi and Moisei Maimon as well as the sculptor Ginzburg, it was in close contact with the Academy of Arts and reported dutifully on any event that happened to connect a Jewish artist to one of the Academy's spheres of activity. The JSEA rarely criticized the Academy, even though, with the institutional quota system, it had every right to do so. Rather, it tended to present the Academy as the highest arbiter of artistic taste, reporting proudly that, in 1914, Bakst and Osip Braz had been made academicians, that Blokh received a prize of R1000 at the Academy's Spring Exhibition in 1916, that Ginzburg lectured on Antokolski at a meeting of the Imperial Society of Architects and Artists at the Academy in 1916, and that the Academy Museum contained works by Askenazi, Brodsky, Levitan, Pasternak, and Savelii Sorin.

The JSEA was born at a time just when "searches for new values in Jewish artistic creativity were beginning to manifest themselves in the centers of intellectual Jewish society and in the capital cities."[37] At the first general assembly held in Petrograd on 11 January 1916, chaired by the architect S. K. Genshtein, Ginzburg emphasized that the goal was "to develop and encourage the plastic arts among Jews" and that an immediate concern was to organize exhibitions of Jewish art because "Jews don't know their own artists."[38] He then called for the establishment of a special Jewish art library and museum inasmuch as the collections of artifacts compiled by An-Sky had little to do with modern art. "He's interested only in ethnography," said Ginzburg. "It is essential to found an art museum where purely artistic works will be preserved."[39] Altman agreed, adding that it "is not a case of Jewish artists, but of whether they are working in the national spirit and whether they are creating national values."[40] Blokh, Lakhovsky, and Maimon also spoke on the organizational aims of the Society, mentioning the need to compile and publish a catalogue raisonné of Jewish art and to create a special subsection that would cater to the needs of painters, sculptors, and architects. The assembly continued with a series of lectures by Maxim Syrkin ("Art and the Jews"),[41] Lev Antokolski, nephew of Mark ("Jewish Artistic Creativity in Podolia and Volynia"), and Ginzburg ("Jews and Sculpture")[42] and concluded with the election of members of the Art Council (Anisfeld, Altman, Dillon, Peter Geller, Blokh, M. Katz, Genshtein, and the architects Moisei Sinianer and Moisei Zamechek). On 27 January, the JSEA reconvened to confirm its charter and to announce that a permanent exhibition of works by Jewish artists was to be opened at the Jewish Almshouse in Petrograd.[43] This proposal was restructured in December 1916 when the JSEA discussed the organization of a permanent commercial exhibition at the Jewish Club.[44]

In March 1916 the JSEA opened a competition for the design of its emblem with a special jury consisting of Anisfeld, N. Aronson, Brodsky, Ginzburg, and Mayzel. On 10 May the winning entries were nominated from the 24 submitted: the first prize of R100 went to Altman for his composition called "Drink the Water from its Source" (fig. 13), the second prize of R50 went to Kratko for his candlestick design (fig. 14), and G. A. Shakh was commended for his "Let Us Be Like the Sun." In spite of protests by Maimon, who did not like the designs and who from the very first had been against the idea of an emblem, Altman's black-and-white drawing was adopted as the insignia.[45]

During the spring of 1916 the JSEA embarked on a number of ventures that involved young Jewish painters and sculptors. Plans were developed to build a special art gallery with the proceeds of auctioned works, and Zamechek prepared the initial designs for the Society's library.[46] But perhaps the most important event was the organization of the "Exhibition of Members of the JSEA," which opened in Petrograd in April-May 1916. With over 150 paintings and sculptures by Altman, Blokh, Brodsky, Chagall, Geller, Lakhovsky, Maimon, Simkhovich, Slepin, et al., the exhibition was both an ideological and a financial success (works were sold for R3600) even though it was visited by only 500 people.[47] Elated, the JSEA immediately convoked a commission to arrange a second Petrograd exhibition (led by Altman, Blokh, Brodsky, Chagall, Ginzburg, Maimon, et al.) for the spring of 1917, but this does not seem to have materialized. On the other hand, the Moscow affiliate of the JSEA did organize an ambitious exhibition of around 400 paintings, sculptures, architectural designs and applied arts by 70 artists at the Galerie Lemercier in April 1917 – called the "Exhibition of Pictures and Sculpture by Jewish Artists." The Lemercier was Moscow's only professional private art outlet and while not especially supportive of the avant-garde, it was an eminently respectable, middle-class gallery – indicating a dramatic change in the

Moscow public's attitude towards "things Jewish." The "exhibition" had both a contemporary and a retrospective section, included an entire room devoted to Levitan, and showed several bronzes by Antokolski. Among the contemporary contributors were Anisfeld, Bakst, Brodsky, Chagall, Lissitzky, Nina Nis-Goldman, and Rabinovich; the catalog cover, designed by Lissitzky (fig. 15), carried motifs similar to those in his filigree drawings for his concurrent *Legend of Prague.*[48]

These two exhibitions in Petrograd and Moscow were the first exclusive panoramas of works by older and younger Jewish studio artists ever held in Russia. Of course, there had been several one-man shows of paintings and sculptures by Russian Jewish artists such as Levitan, his brother Adolf (Moscow, 1911)[49] and Manievich (Dobychina Bureau, Petrograd, 1916),[50] and many of them were contributing regularly to general exhibitions such as the "Jack of Diamonds" (Moscow, 1916) and the "Exhibition of Contemporary Russian Painting" (Dobychina Bureau, Petrograd, 1916). Even the Academy of Arts' "Spring Exhibition" in 1916 contained an inordinate number of Jewish contributions, by Brodsky, Dillon, Maimon, and others.

14

13

КАТАЛОГЪ
ВЫСТАВКИ
КАРТИНЪ
И
СКУЛЬПТУРЫ
ХУДОЖНИКОВЪ
ЕВРЕЕВЪ.

ЕВРЕЙСКОЕ
ОБЩЕСТВО
ПООЩРЕНІЯ
ХУДОЖНИКОВЪ
МОСКВА

1917

15

There was also a precedent to the JSEA exhibitions in the show of modern Jewish art organized in Warsaw in 1911. But this was the first time that the Russian public had been confronted with the notion of a school of modern Jewish art, a phenomenon that must have seemed as exotic as the shows of Persian miniatures, oriental *lubki*, and children's drawings that were a part of the eclectic art world in Moscow and St. Petersburg just before and after the Revolution.

The exhibition activities of the JSEA in Petrograd and Moscow were important for several reasons. They drew attention to the presence of a *new* Jewish art not totally reliant on ancient traditions and convinced observers that young artists like Altman, Chagall, Falk, and Lissitzky, while aware of their national past, were seeking original artistic resolutions that also owed much to their direct assimilation of Cubism and Futurism. In this respect, it was thanks to the JSEA exhibitions that professional critics, especially in Petrograd and Moscow, began to analyze their art in detail – for example, Syrkin wrote on Chagall in *Evreiskaia nedelia* (Jewish Week) (Moscow, 1916)[51] and Yakov Tugendkhold ran a major appreciation of Chagall in the prestigious review *Apollon* (Apollo) (Petrograd, 1916).[52]

Moreover, the exhibition activities of the JSEA acted as a valuable precedent to the several Jewish exhibitions organized just after the Revolution, such as the wide-ranging "Exhibition of Paintings and Sculptures by Jewish Artists" held in Moscow in 1918[53] and the several undertakings by the Kultur Lige in Kiev (see below). Perhaps one can also find a link between this early attempt to "institutionalize" Jewish culture and the subsequent state-controlled centers such as the Jewish Museum in Samarkand (1923), the Jewish Printing Industry School in Leningrad (1924), the Department of Jewish Culture at the Ukrainian Academy of Sciences in Kiev (1926), the St. Petersburg Institute of Higher Jewish Learning (existing in 1923), and the Jewish Popular University in Moscow (existing in 1918-21).

## An Age of Enlightenment

The JSEA achieved its aims, albeit modestly, through its exhibitions, lectures and regular press coverage, while maintaining its independence of traditional Jewish strictures. In this sense, its position typified the new secularism of the St. Petersburg and Moscow intelligentsia/plutocracy – part of the liberal bourgeoisie that contributed so much to the Silver Age of Russian culture. Of course, as Ginzburg made clear at the outset, the JSEA wished to "encourage the plastic arts among Jews" and he certainly did not wish to reject the ethnographical question out of hand. But, by its very nature, the JSEA extended the philanthropic activities of the Jewish lawyers, businessmen, politicians, writers and artists themselves who hoped for a rebirth of Jewish culture through its acquaintance with the latest aesthetic trends in Russia and Western Europe. While the propagational efforts of the Barons Guenzburg and of An-Sky on behalf of traditional Jewish art deserve the highest commendation, the flowering of modern Jewish art was not exclusively dependent upon them, and we must also look elsewhere for the material and spiritual forces that enabled Altman, B. Aronson, Tchaikov, Chagall, et al., to develop as members of the international avant-garde.

In general, the intelligent Jewish Maecenas were not particularly interested in art created by Russian Jewish artists – "as if they [were] ashamed of something that ought to be especially close to their hearts and tastes."[54] One exception to this rule was Chagall's supporter in St. Petersburg, Vinaver, a lawyer and member of the First State Duma. While an essential member of the Jewish Historical and Ethnographic Society (he gave the keynote speech at its opening in 1909), Vinaver was deeply interested in the new Jewish art and was an energetic champion of the JSEA.[55]

In fact, he was one of the few St. Petersburg Jews who tried to forge a link between the new generation of experimental artists and Jewish antiquity, in contrast to many of his colleagues, who either continued to concentrate on traditional art or disregarded the Jewish question completely.

As far as the artists and critics themselves were concerned, Ginzburg should be recognized for his impressive services to the cause of Jewish art as well as for his own sculptural work. Ginzburg used every opportunity to inform the Russian public about developments in this sphere – through his articles, lectures, supervision of the art section of the Jewish encyclopedia,[56] and extensive correspondence with many luminaries of his time. However, we should also remember the activities of Lev Antokolski, a painter and teacher who also did much to propagate the new Jewish art. Although based in Vilna where he taught painting at the Industrial Art Society (he and his students decorated a synagogue there),[57] Antokolski was also partly responsible for the organization of the JSEA exhibition in Moscow in 1917, lectured widely on Israels, Levitan, and other Jewish artists, and published a number of books on painting and decorating. As early as 1907, he proposed – together with Ginzburg – the establishment of a Jewish art museum and a regular art lottery.[58]

The surest channel for disseminating the new Jewish art in Russia was the Russian-language press.[59] Paradoxically, just at the moment when artists and critics like Altman, Chagall, Efros, and Tugendkhold were coming to the fore, virtually all Yiddish/Hebrew periodicals were closed down in Russia (1915), a measure that was expanded to include all other such publications in July-November 1916.[60] In other words, the Hebrew typography itself was banned, producing, for example, incongruous blank spaces in *Evreiskaia starina* where authors had been quoting from the original language. As a result, Russian-language magazines and newspapers became the prime vehicle for Jewish intellectual thought during these crucial years (although it would seem that, in any case, the leading Jewish art critics of the time – Efros, Syrkin, Tugendkhold, Nikolai Lavrsky – wrote in Russian, French, or German just as well, if not better than in Yiddish and Hebrew).

In this context, it is worth referring to a curious document published in Nikopol (Ukraine) in 1913-14 called *Otchet o deiatelnosti biblioteki (pri molitvennom dome) m. Shirokoe, Khersonsk gub* (An Account of the Activity of the Library, at the Prayer-House, at Shirokoe in Kherson Province).[61] The two volumes provide statistical information on the Jewish library in the village of Shirokoe in the years 1911-14, adducing analyses of

the tastes of its reading public based on the checkout ratio. Although, in 1911-12, only 128 titles of the library's 1298 volumes were in Yiddish, it transpires that, in any case, Gogol, Ostrovsky, Pushkin, and Tolstoy were more widely read than Shalom Aleichem and Mendele Mokher Seforim. A similar pattern continued for 1912-14. Certainly, before 1915 there were many books and magazines printed in Hebrew and Yiddish, especially at provincial centers (e.g., chromolithographic illustrations to the Biblical texts [fig. 16], tracts on calligraphy, etc.),[62] but those Jewish publications that were illustrated and/or supported by modern Jewish artists tended to appear in Russian. A case in point is the three-volume anthology of Biblical stories, fables, poems, and factual descriptions for Jewish children called *Nashim detiam* (For Our Children) (St. Petersburg, 1911-12), edited by M. G. Eisenstadt and M. I. Daiches and designed by Maimon (fig. 17). This contained many reproductions of works by modern Jewish (and non-Jewish) painters and sculptors, including M. Antokolski, Geller, Ginzburg, Levitan, Pasternak and Savelii Zeidenberg. Mention might also be made of *Evreiskii almanakh* (Jewish Almanac) (Kiev, 1908), illustrated by the Vilna Art Nouveau artist E. M. Lilien, and even the impressive first volume of the *Istoriia evreiskogo naroda* (History of the Jewish People) (Moscow, 1914), edited by M. Wischnitzer et al., and designed by R. Bernstein-Wischnitzer (fig. 18, cat. 166). The principal cultural reviews of the Jewish communities also appeared in Russian, e.g., *Evreiskaia starina, Voskhod* (Sunrise) – which with its particular connotations might also be translated as "Renascence" for the Jewish reader – *Novyi voskhod* (St. Petersburg, 1881-1906; 1910-15), and *Vestnik evreiskogo prosveshcheniia* (Herald of Jewish Enlightenment) (St. Petersburg, 1910-16), etc. The only full-length study of Jewish art published in Russia; i.e., Lavrsky's *Iskusstvo i evrei* (Art and the Jews) (Moscow, 1915), also appeared in Russian.[63]

It is important to remember that many Modernist Russian writers and critics also gave serious attention to the question of Jewish art and literature, and some of them knew Hebrew. The two numbers of the literary miscellany called *Shchit* (Shield) (Moscow, 1915), edited by Leonid Andreev, Maxim Gorky and Fedor Sologub, were dedicated to the Jewish theme. With Hebrew poetry translated into Russian by Ivan Bunin, Viacheslav Ivanov, Valerii Briusov, et al., with scholarly essays such as "Zion" by Sergey Bulgakov, "On the Ideology of the Jewish Question" by Ivanov, and "The Jewish Question as a Russian One" by Dmitrii Merezhkovsky, and with a cover that incorporated one of Pasternak's pictures, *Shchit* was, indeed, a welcome gesture to the cause of Jewish culture in Russia. There were also many Russian journals before and

16

17

18

after 1917 that combined the intellectual forces of both Jews and Russians such as the three collections called *Safrut* (Literature) published in Moscow in 1917-18. With front covers by Altman (fig. 19) and back covers by Lissitzky, *Safrut* introduced the Russian public to a wide variety of poems and articles by An-Sky, Bialik, Briusov, Bunin, et al. Mention should be made of *Evreiskaia antologiia. Sbornik molodoi poezii* (A Jewish Anthology. A Collection of Young Poetry) as well, also published by Safrut in Moscow in 1918 (cat. 76). Edited by Vladislav Khodasevich and L. B. Yaffe and introduced by Mikhail Gershenzon, this collection contained poems by Peretz, Bialik, and others, translated into Russian by Yurgis Baltrushaitis, Briusov, Marshack, et al.[64] Also noteworthy are the miscellany *Den iskusstva* (Day of Art), published in Polish, Ukrainian, Russian, and Yiddish in Vilna in 1914, and, more important, *Germes*, an "annual of art and humanitarian knowledge" published in Kiev in 1919 with contributions by Nikolai Aseev, Ilya Ehrenburg, Nikolai Evreinov, Alexandra Exter, Nikolai and Vladimir Makkaveisky, Osip Mandelstam, Viktor Shklovski, and Natan (Moisei) Vengrov.

These circumstances explain in part why the primary responses to the new Russian Jewish art (at least before 1917) were published in Russian, and why the journals *Evreiskaia nedelia* (Moscow, 1916, and Petrograd, 1917) and *Novyi put* (New Way) (Moscow, 1916-17) played such a crucial role in the propagation of Altman, Anisfeld, Brodsky, Chagall, Falk, Kratko, Manievich, Zuckerman, et al. Quite simply, the articles by Efros, Syrkin, Vermel, and their colleagues could be read by Russians, something that introduced Jewish art automatically into a more universal context – just as modern Russian art had entered the European mainstream thanks in part to the bilingual texts (Russian and French) of the leading Modernist journals, *Mir iskusstva* (World of Art) (St. Petersburg, 1898-1904, last issue, 1905) and *Zolotoe runo* (Golden Fleece) (Moscow, 1906-09, last issue, 1910). Furthermore, the new professional critics, while concerned with the general question of "Jewish art," tended to describe the intrinsic qualities of the work in question (paint, texture, rhythm, etc.) and referred to trends in Paris, Munich, and Milan rather than to the shtetl, the Pale of Settlement, and the synagogue.

19

Efros, in particular, tried to approach the young Jewish artists as members of a cosmopolitan community. He realized that Altman, Chagall, and their colleagues bore within them the "enormous, intact deposits of their 'national stratum',"[65] but that their pictorial styles derived largely from Cubism, Futurism, and (later) Suprematism. It was a fortunate coincidence, indeed, that a sophisticated critic such as Efros (who did not underestimate the significance of Jewish antiquity and of An-Sky's endeavors, and who studied and translated the ancient Hebrew texts) was able to avoid the prejudices of the past and recognize that the distinctive merit of the new artists lay in their commitment (conscious or unconscious) to the International Style. Such issues lay at the basis of his pioneering article "Aladdin's Lamp," which appeared in Moscow in 1918.[66]

## Cubism in Kiev and Suprematism in Vitebsk

Parallel to their assimilation of Cubism and Futurism, some Russian Jewish artists still alluded to their heritage. As noted above, Lissitzky embellished his designs of 1917 with "Assyrian script,"[67] no doubt recalling his ethnographic sketches for the An-Sky expedition. Tchaikov also participated in many Yiddish editions, illustrating stories, poems, and articles, as, for example, in the collection *Baginen* (Beginning) (fig. 11, cat. 50), published in Kiev in 1919 by the Jewish Section of the All-Ukrainian Literary Committee.[68] Yudovin was also active in this area after the Revolution, although his slightly angular style could hardly be regarded as avant-garde.[69] But in general, Russian Jewish artists were not well represented in the new Yiddish press, and important cultural reviews such as *Kultur un Bildung* (Culture and Education) (Moscow, 1918) published by the Cultural Enlightenment Section of the Jewish Commissariat, *Der Yidisher Artist* (The Jewish Artist) (Kharkov, 1918), and even the album *Velikoe desiatiletie v zhivopisi i skulpture* (A Great Decade in Painting and Sculpture) (Moscow, 1927 – Russian and Yiddish) were published without the involvement of Altman, Chagall, Tchaikov, Lissitzky, et al.[70]

The new generation of Russian Jewish artists who grew up with the Revolution (e.g., B. Aronson, Rabinovich, Shifrin, Tyshler, Chashnik, Khidekel, and Kogan) had every reason to maintain the international tradition. Born in remote parts of the Ukraine, White Russia, and the Baltic area, such artists aspired – from the very beginning – to leave their environment and enter a more cosmopolitan artistic community. All the major Jewish contributors to modern Russian art moved from their native towns and villages to Moscow or Petrograd/Leningrad or Paris and New York (often via Kiev and Odessa) and they achieved eminence precisely as Soviet or European or American artists later.

No doubt, this state of affairs explains in part the success of Exter's school in Kiev in 1917-19 and of Malevich's pedagogical experiments in Vitebsk in 1919-22. The majority of Exter's and Malevich's students were local Jews who esteemed their mentors not only because – from all reports – they were charismatic individuals, but also because they upheld aesthetic systems that transcended ethnic folklore. Writing to Shifrin from Kiev in April 1919, Rabinovich referred to Exter as a "champion of the French," adding "only now, after studying painterly disciplines, does one understand one's helplessness and dilettantism."[71] Tyshler later recalled of Exter that "in her hands a simple paper lampshade turned into a work of art."[72] Indeed, Exter's Kiev studio became a point of pilgrimage for many displaced intellectuals just after the Revolution and, as the Soviet historian Flora Syrkina has observed,[73] it was the permanent or temporary presence in Kiev of writers such as Ehrenburg, Benedikt Livshits, Mandelstam, Shklovski, and Vengrov, as much as Exter herself, that influenced Aronson, Rabinovich, Tyshler, and their colleagues.

During those turbulent years, Kiev was a cultural hub: cabaret life thrived to the strains of Ri-ba-bo and Junk; art magazines and literary reviews mushroomed, reflecting the most diverse tendencies – from the weekly *Teatralnaia zhizn* (Theatrical Life) (1918) to *Germes*, from *Literaturno-kritichni almanakh* (Literary Critical Almanac) (1918) to *Baginen*; Exter presided over the Art Section of the Ministry for Great Russian Affairs, while her friend Elsa Krüger performed evenings of dance at the Arts Theatre; an exhibition of Chinese and Japanese engravings opened at the Society of Art Workers just as Alexander Deich announced the end of proletarian art.[74] Here was an atmosphere that could only inspire young artists to forget the misery of the *mestechko*, where "the streets are cleaned only sporadically,"[75] and to experiment at all costs. Quite logically, therefore, B. Aronson, Rabinovich, Shifrin, and Tyshler proceeded to follow Exter's Cubist teaching, to which their artistic achievements in studio painting, street decoration, and stage design (e.g., Rabinovich's decorations for *Salome* and Shifrin's for *The Green Island* in 1919) owe a large debt, completely rejecting the Jewish milieu. Only when these artists reached Moscow, around 1918, did they recall their Jewish past, involving themselves in productions at the Jewish Chamber Theatre – a development now well documented and researched.[76]

Of course, the presence of so many Jewish artists in Kiev c. 1917-20, whether connected with Exter or not (as in the case of Tchaikov), still focused attention on the issue of modern Jewish art within the Russian (and Ukrainian) development. Rabinovich, Shifrin, Tyshler and, on a different level, B. Aronson seized the opportunity to display their works under the aegis of the Kultur Lige in Kiev; e.g., at the "Jewish Exhibition of Sculpture, Graphics and Drawings" organized by Aronson in February-March 1920. This was a major showing of works by second-generation artists of the Russian Jewish avant-garde; i.e., Aronson, Tchaikov, Lissitzky, Isaac Pailes, Shifrin, Tyshler (represented under his real name and his pseudonym, Dzhin-Dzhikh-Shvil), et al. Although a number of the works treated Jewish themes and illustrated Yiddish tales, the catalog (with a cover designed by Tchaikov) (fig. 20, cat. 169) was printed in Ukrainian, Russian, and Yiddish. Even in this specific context, we become aware once again of the fundamental dichotomy in Russian Jewish Modernism

20

– the parallel aspiration to preserve an ethnic loyalty and to participate in the international community.

Actually, the Kultur Lige played an important role in Jewish cultural life at that point both in Kiev and in Moscow. In 1921, for example, it opened its own theatre studio in Moscow and the following year organized a three-man show of works by Altman, Chagall, and Shterenberg, also in Moscow (cat. 172);[77] it continued to be active as a propaganda center through the mid-1920s, at least. In 1922, for example, it organized another exhibition of sculptures, reliefs, and paintings in Kiev.[78] In 1924 it sent a special section to the "Exhibition of All-Union Art Workers" there, and in 1926 published I. Yakhinson's important architectural tract, i.e., *Istoriia zhilishchnogo i stroitelnogo iskusstva* (The History of Residential and Building Art).

Like Kiev, Vitebsk enjoyed a remarkably rich cultural life just after the Revolution, serving as the meeting place for many important writers and artists – from Mikhail Bakhtin to Chagall, from Pavel Medvedev to Malevich. It also became a focus of experiment in art, music, literature, and pedagogy, which stimulated the

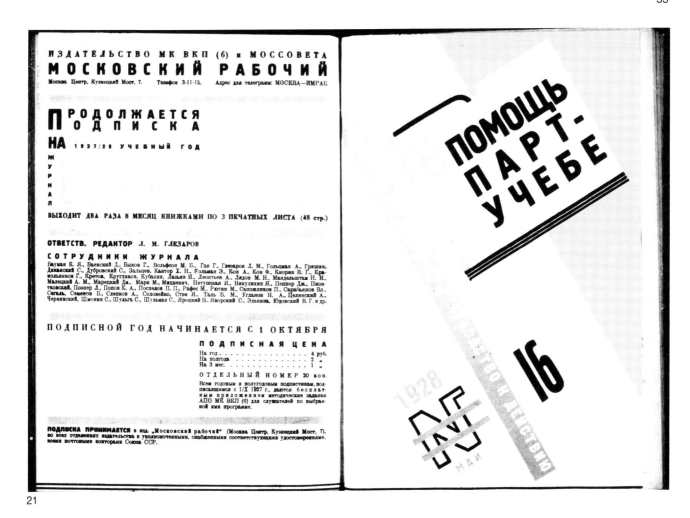

21

publication of several innovative journals, such as *Shkola i revoliutsiia* (School and Revolution, 1919), *Vestnik kooperatsii i kultury* (Herald of Cooperation and Culture, 1921), and *Zhurnal Vitebskogo otdeleniia Rosta* (Journal of the Vitebsk Section of ROSTA, 1921) as well as the leaflets published by Malevich's group.[79] Some of these publications did pay attention to the Jewish community in Vitebsk, but most ignored it – and it was precisely in the "neutral" journals that the avant-garde Jewish artists ran their articles on the new art, such as Chagall's description of the Vitebsk Popular Art Institute and Lissitzky's "New Culture."[80]

Chagall and Lissitzky published together in the June 1919 issue of *Shkola i revoliutsiia*, but by September of that year, when Malevich ousted Chagall from his position as director of the Popular Art Institute, there remained little sympathy between the two Jewish artists. Given the size and strength of the Jewish contingent in Vitebsk at this time, and of its cultural organizations (e.g., the Jewish Literary Society), it seems reasonable to assume that for a Jew to avoid this association was a gesture of blatant defiance. However tolerant Chagall may have been, he was surely shocked

when some of his students transferred to Malevich, not simply because this was a blow to his self-esteem, but also because, in so doing, they were converting from their natural allegiance, to the universal philosophy of Suprematism.

From 1919 through 1922 Malevich taught at Vitebsk, preaching his faith of total abstraction to a group of devoted and brilliant disciples. With Vera Ermolaeva as rector of the Institute, with Kogan in charge of the preparatory studios and with Lissitzky heading the graphic and architectural studios, the members of Malevich's circle – Unovis (Affirmation of the New in Art) – implemented many exciting projects: they produced a version of the opera *Victory over the Sun* and a Suprematist ballet, published theories and manifestos, and undertook an entire series of futurological schemes. But in spite of the marked Jewish composition of the group, not to mention the close proximity of Yehuda Pen ("one of the most important prerevolutionary Jewish artists")[81] and Yudovin, Unovis avoided all reference to the Jewish heritage.[82] Examination of the Vitebsk works by Chasnik, Khidekel, Kogan, Roiak, Yudin, et al., reveals a complete dedication to, and mastery of, the principles of Cubism and Suprematism. It was as if they were quite unaware of the great national traditions that An-Sky and his colleagues regarded as the true wellspring for the renaissance of Jewish art.

## Conclusion

Even Lissitzky, who for several years had tried to "modernize" Jewish art through his highly schematic renderings of traditional motifs (e.g., his sheet music cover [cat. 82] and his designs for *Had Gadya* [One Kid] [cat. 90]), submitted to the full force of Suprematism after his encounter with Malevich. Throughout the 1920s-30s he seems never to have "relapsed," and whether in architecture, interior design, posters, or polygraphical design (e.g., his cover for the journal *V pomoshch partuchebe* [An Aid to Studying the Party] of 1928 [fig. 21]), he eschewed folklore in favor of abstract reduction.

Many young, experimental artists of Jewish background earned recognition in the 1920s, but, more often than not, their work was so "anonymous" and so international as to be almost indistinguishable from the concurrent work of their Russian, German, and American colleagues; Naum Gabo and Anton Pevsner, Saul Rabinovich, Beatrisa Sandomirskaia, and Dmitrii Tsaplin, to mention but a few, were clearly more at home with Cubism and Constructivism than with Jewish arts and crafts and were sometimes highly indignant at being categorized as "Jewish" artists. The absorption of the Jewish artist into the Russian milieu, especially after the October Revolution, is of course not surprising. The Jewish artist used Russian, not Yiddish, as the first language of communication; for him freedom and democracy were promised by the Soviets, not by the shtetl, and there seemed little point in maintaining a grand isolation when the avant-garde, made up of so many nationalities, manifested a remarkable racial tolerance.

It would be misleading to assume that the associations with the Jewish tradition, evident, for example, in Tyshler's work for the Jewish theatre in the 1920s onwards, or B. Aronson's designs for the leftist Yiddish press and theatre in New York in the 1920s, or Altman's illustrations of the Bible of c. 1930, were of central importance to their artistic development. In some cases, these concerns did reflect a genuine appreciation of the Jewish cultural heritage, but more often than not they derived from a momentary nostalgia or a material incentive. As Aronson implied in his large photomontage (c. 1925) (fig. 22), with the Gabo torso in the center, or as Louis Lozowick implied in his eulogies of

22, detail

the big, industrial city, the Jewish artist was now free to operate within all systems, with all media, and in all countries. Many young Jewish artists who stayed in the Soviet Union, such as Samuel Adlivankin (fig. 23) and Viktor Midler, also quickly passed from depictions of Jewish ceremonies to young pioneers and collective farm scenes.

At the same time – as the Israel Museum exhibition proves – there was a Jewish movement within the Russian avant-garde, and many artists used Jewish themes in their work. Consequently, there is no legitimate reason for the consistent omission of the Jewish connection in the standard monographs on Russian Jewish artists such as Pasternak, Rabinovich, and Tyshler. True, their interest in the ethnic environment did not play a crucial role in the development of their sophisticated artistic styles and aesthetic values, but, on the other hand, there is no need to conceal or underestimate it. This exhibition may raise more questions than it answers, but, at least, for the first time since the heyday of the avant-garde, it focuses public attention on the issue of the Jewish presence in the "great experiment"[83] that for too long has been regarded as an exclusively Russian accomplishment.

22

23

1   D. Gunzburg and V. Stassof, *L'Ornement Hébreu*, Berlin: Calvary, 1905. This was the French version of the original edition of 1886, i.e., W. Stasov and D. Gunzburg: *Drevne-evreiskii ornament po rukopisiam* (Ornementation des anciens manuscrits hébreux de la Bibliothèque Impériale Publique de Saint Pétersbourg), St. Petersburg: Gunzbourg. Stasov was an ardent supporter of Jewish culture and did much to enlighten the Russian public in this respect. See, for example, his articles: "Evreiskoe plemia v sozdaniiakh evropeiskogo iskusstva," *Evreiskaia biblioteka*, St. Petersburg, 1873, vol. 3, pp. 286-322; 1875, al. 5, pp. 34-73; 1878, vol. 6, pp. 49-64; and "Posle vsemirnoi vystavki," ibid., 1879, vol. 7, pp. 257-81.

2   The exhibition opened on 10 March 1939, coinciding with the Eighteenth Party Congress, and was dedicated to the history of the Jews in Tsarist Russia and the Soviet Union. Although it was basically an ethnographical and historical exhibition, it contained an art section (book illustrations, broadsides, etc.) and a number of important Russian Jewish artists, including Isaac Askenazi and Solomon Yudovin, were involved in the exhibition design. A catalog was published.

3   A. Efros, "Lampa Aladina," *Evreiskii mir. Literaturnye sborniki*, Moscow, 1918, book I, p. 301.

4   M. Balaban, "Evreiskie istoricheskie pamiatniki v Polshe," *Evreiskaia starina*, St. Petersburg, 1909, vol. 1, p. 55.

5   A. Efros (Rosstsii), "Zametki ob iskusstve," *Novyi put*, M., 1916, nos. 48-49, p. 64.

6   M. Syrkin, "Vystavki," *Novyi voskhod*, St. Petersburg, 1911, no. 10, p. 36.

7   An-Sky himself refers to the expedition that he directed within the period "1911-14" in his note called "O rabotakh Etnograficheskoi ekspeditsii" in *Evreiskaia starina*, 1915, vol. 8, p. 239. However, an untitled, anonymous note in the following volume (1916, p. 479) gives 1912-14 as the duration of the expedition. For further commentary by An-Sky on the expedition see *Novyi voskhod*, St. Petersburg, no. 16, 25 April 1914, p. 31.

8   An-Sky, op. cit.

9   Ibid.

10   According to An-Sky (ibid., p. 240), his colleague Lev Shternberg was compiling a list of "2000" questions and answers that was to be published under the title *Programma dlia sobiraniia svedenii po etnografii* (A Program for Collecting Materials on Ethnography), which was closely related to the museum collection.

11   An-Sky, op. cit., p. 240.

12   Supplement to *Evreiskaia starina*, 1915, vol. 8, p. 14.

13   *Evreiskaia starina*, 1916, vol. 9, p. 479.

14   *Evreiskaia starina*, 1918, vol. 10, p. 319.

15   Ibid.

16   See *Evreiskii vestnik*, ed. S. Ginzburg, Leningrad: Society for the Dissemination of Enlightenment Among Jews, 1928, p. 225. Part of the collection of the Jewish National Museum is now housed in the Museum of the History of Leningrad, Leningrad. According to unconfirmed reports, another part of the collection is in the Museum of Religion and Atheism in Leningrad.

17   *Evreiskaia starina*, 1924, vol. 11, p. 397.

18   According to a letter written by An-Sky and quoted by F. Shargorodskaia in the article "O nasledii An-skogo" in *Evreiskaia starina*, 1924, vol. 11, p. 307.

19   In his article "Zametki ob iskusstve" in *Novyi put* (1917, no. 8, p. 36), Efros mentioned that Jewish children who showed talent for drawing and painting were often nicknamed "future Antokolskis."

20   It is known, for example, that An-Sky met with Antokolski in Paris in 1894. See Shargorodskaia, op. cit., p. 307.

21   Manievich was given his one-man show at the Dobychina Bureau, Petrograd, in March 1916 where it was visited by about 2000 people, and pictures were sold for R6000. For a review see Emgal, "Syn 'cherty'," *Novyi put*, 1916, no. 15, pp. 25-28. Nadezhda Dobychina, a Jewess, was sympathetic to the cause of Jewish art. She regularly bought and sold works by Altman and Chagall and in March 1915 offered her gallery (the so-called Bureau) for an auction of works by Jewish artists, the proceeds from which were to have gone to war relief. See *Novyi voskhod*, 1915, no. 10/11, p. 49.

22   See Emgal, op. cit., pp. 26-27.

23   It is of interest to note that Joel Engel, whose sheet music Leonid Pasternak designed c. 1912, had also taken part in the Jewish Ethnographic Expedition of 1911-14. He described his findings in his lecture "At the Source of the Jewish Song," which he gave in Odessa in November 1915. See *Teatr i kino* (Theatre and Cinema), Odessa, 1915, no. 2, p. 14.

24   Altman's *Head of a Young Jew* (1915) is in the State Russian Museum, Leningrad. Efros, who at one time regarded Altman as the primary Russian Jewish artist, described Head of a Young Jew in these terms in his "Zametki ob iskusstve," *Novyi put*, 1916, nos. 48-49, p. 64.

25   N. Altman, *Evreiskaia grafika*, Berlin: Petropolis, 1923.

26   B. Aronson, *Shagal*, Berlin, 1923. Mention should also be made of Aronson's splendid collection, reproduced in the checklist of this catalog.

27   See, for example, Tyshler's illustrations for Natan Vengrov's Petukh, Kiev, 1918, or Altman's illustrations for Vengrov's *Zverushki. Stikhi malenkim*, Moscow-Petrograd, 1923.

28   L. Rokhlin, *Mestechko Krasnopolie Mogilevskoi gub.*, St. Petersburg: Scvcr, 1909.

29   Efros, "Zametki ob iskusstve," *Novyi put*, 1917, no. 8, p. 37.

30   Syrkin, "Vystavki," op. cit. In fact, Lakhovsky, who tried to become a "Jewish" artist by emigrating to Palestine and working for the Bezalel School in 1908 as a professor of drawing, found the conditions there to be totally alien to his artistic temperament and returned to Russia. See N. Lavrsky, *Iskusstvo i evrei*, Moscow: Zhizn, 1915, p. 26. It is not by chance, incidentally, that Stasov was an enthusiast of both the *Peredvizhniki* and Jewish artists.

31   Aronson's discussion of the Jewish artist (written in Russian) covers many pages. The manuscript of this document is in the possession of his widow, Mrs. Naum Aronson, New York City.

32   For example, according to a note in *Novyi voskhod*, 1911, no. 27, p. 18, Naum Aronson refused to take part in a competition for the design of a monument to Suvorov in St. Petersburg precisely because he was afraid of the anti-Semitic prejudice of the Russian jury. Like Bakst, Aronson had experienced the ignominy of being denied a residence permit in St. Petersburg. See M. S., untitled note in *Novyi voskhod*, 1910, no. 28, 7 October, pp. 25-26.

33   An-Sky, "Evreiskoe narodnoe tvorchestvo," *Perezhitoe*, St. Petersburg, 1909, vol. 1, p. 297.

34   S. Rapoport [An-Sky], "Religioznoe i svetskoe vospitanie," *Novyi voskhod*, 1910, no. 19, pp. 6-9.

35   *Novyi put*, 1916, nos. 36-37, p. 19.

36   Ginzburg did try to persuade the Moscow affiliation of the JSEA to give him a one-man show and to publish a monograph on him in 1917 (see *Novyi put*, 1911, no. 28, p. 26), but this does not detract from the sincerity of his endeavor to propagate the cause of Jewish art in Russia. Unfortunately, the single published collection of Ginzburg material avoids this aspect of his career, i.e., *Skulptor Ilia Gintsburg. Vospominaniia. Stati. Pisma*, ed. A. Lebedev, Leningrad: Khudozhnik RSFSR, 1964. Among Ginzburg's own publications relevant to this exhibition are his books *Iz moei zhizni* (From My Life), St. Petersburg: Trud, 1908; *Iz proshlogo* (From the Past), Leningrad: Gosizdat, 1924; and his articles, e.g., "Tolstoi i evrei," *Novyi voskhod*, St. Petersburg,

1910, no. 34, pp. 29-31; untitled note on Savelii Zeidenberg, ibid., 1910, no. 9, pp. 29-30; ditto on the synagogue in St. Petersburg, ibid., no. 10, pp. 25-26.

37 F. Edvabnyi, "Zametki dilletanta. Evreiskii teatr i Klara Yung," *Teatr i kino*, Odessa, 1917, no. 6, p. 8.

38 As reported in *Evreiskaia nedelia*, M., 1916, no. 4, in the article "V. 'Evr. OPKh' " signed M. L-n, p. 29.

39 Ibid., p. 30.

40 Ibid.

41 Syrkin's lecture was published as "Iskusstvo i evrei" in *Evreiskaia nedelia*, 1916, no. 25, pp. 37-40; no. 26, pp. 37-40.

42 Ginzburg gave the same lecture at the opening of the Moscow section of the JSEA on 19 March 1916. See *Novyi put*, 1916, no. 9, p. 40.

43 See *Evreiskaia nedelia*, 1916, no. 6, p. 33.

44 See *Novyi put*, 1916, no. 50, pp. 30-31.

45 For information on the competition see *Novyi put*, 1916, no. 18, p. 13; and *Evreiskaia nedelia*, 1916, no. 21, p. 26.

46 Ibid., no. 13, p. 34.

47 Ibid., no. 21, p. 26. For a review see A. Benois, "Po povodu 'Evreiskoi vystavki' " in *Rech*, Petrograd, 22 April 1916, no. 109.

48 *Evreiskaia nedelia*, 1916, no. 51, p. 37. Also see *Novyi put*, nos. 13-14, 23 April 1916, p. 73, which mentions that the JSEA would be publishing an illustrated catalog. A catalog was, indeed, published but without reproductions; moreover, it does *not* refer to the retrospective sections (Antokolski and Levitan) mentioned in *Novyi put*.

49 The Adolf Levitan exhibition opened in Moscow in April 1911. For a review see *Novyi voskhod*, 1911, no. 16, p. 26.

50 See note 21.

51 M. Syrkin, "Mark Shagal" *Evreiskaia nedelia*, 1916, no. 20. pp. 43-48.

52 Ya. Tugendkhold, "Mark Shagal," *Apollon*, Petrograd, 1916, no. 2, pp. 11-23.

53 This exhibition, held in Moscow in July-August 1918, included 233 works by 41 artists. It represented all trends of the right and left – from Baranoff-Rossiné to Lakhovsky, from Lev Antokolski to Altman, from Lissitzky to Shkolnik, from Zeidenberg to Shterenberg.

54 Untitled note signed I. G. (Ginzburg) in *Novyi voskhod*, 1910, no. 9, p. 30.

55 Vinaver's memoirs are of some interest for the cultural historian, although they concentrate on his legal activities, not on his art sponsorship. See *Medavnee. Vospominaniia i kharakteristiki*, Petrograd: Yakor, 1917.

56 The Lev and Mark Antokolski archive at the Central State Archive of Literature and Art, Moscow (F. 698, op. I, ed. khr. 7), contains references to Ginzburg's activities as supervisor of the art section for the Jewish encyclopedia. The same archive contains an interesting set of letters between Lev Antokolski and Ginzburg, in which the question of Jewish art is often discussed.

57 For details see *Novyi voskhod*, 1911, no. 33, p. 12; no. 51, p. 22. Subsequently, Lev Antokolski published a number of practical guidebooks on painting and decorating, e.g., *Programma kruzhkov po izucheniiu maliarnykh rabot*, Moscow: Central Committee of the Union of Construction Works, 1928; *Spravochnik po maliarnym rabotam*, Moscow-Leningrad: Gosstroiizdat, 1933; *Maliarnoe delo*, Moscow: VZITO, 1933.

58 See letter from I. Ginzburg to M. Antokolski at the Central State Archive of Literature and Art, Moscow (F. 698, op. I, ed. khr. 7, 11. 1-9).

59 For details on the position of the Jewish press in Russia see U. Ivask, *Evreiskaia periodicheskaia pechat v Rossii*, Tallinn: Society of Friends of the Yiddish Scientific Institute, 1935.

60 See I. Yashunskii, *Evreiskaia periodicheskaia pechat v 1917 i 1918*, Petrograd: Vestnik, 1918, p. 3.

61 Published by Vainshtein and Moldavskii, Nikopol, 1913; the second volume by Trud, Nikopol, 1914.

62 See, for example, Girtovich's manual on Hebrew calligraphy published by Iegudiia in Vilna in 1914, and also the reproductions in this catalog.

63 Mention should also be made of the following books concerned with Jewish culture in Russia that appeared in Russian at this time: P. Marek, *Ocherki poistorii prosveshcheniia evreev v Rossii* (Sketches in the History of Enlightenment Among the Jews in Russia), Moscow: Society for the Dissemination of Correct Information on Jews, 1909; L. Saminsky, *Ob evreiskoi muzyke* (On Jewish Music), St. Petersburg, 1914; I. Cherikov, *Istoriia obshchestva dlia rasprostraneniia mezhdu evreiami v Rossii 1863-1913* (The History of the Society for Propagation Among Jews in Russia 1863-1913), St. Petersburg: Fleishman, 1913, vol. 1 (no longer published); Yu. Gessen, *Istoriia evreev v Rossii* (History of the Jews in Russia), St. Petersburg: Pravo, 1906, and subsequent editions. Gessen was also coeditor of the multivolume Jewish encyclopedia published in St. Petersburg by Brokgauz and Efron, i.e., *Evreiskaia entsiklopediia*, 1908-13.

64 The inside back cover of *Evreiskaia antologiia* advertises a third volume of the miscellany Safrut (see main text), which was to include a contribution by Efros. There is also a reference to Efros' Russian translation of Plach Ieremii (Wail of Jeremiah) – which was not, however, published.

65 Efros, "Zametki ob iskusstve," *Novyi put*, 1916, nos. 48-49, p. 32.

66 See note 3. The entire text is on pp. 297-310.

67 Lissitzky, in his note at the end of Broderzon's *Legend of Prague* (Moscow, *Nashe iskusstvo*, 1917), mentioned that he was attempting to fuse the "marvellous Assyrian script" with his graphic designs for the mythological tale.

68 For a review of the miscellany see *Rabochii zhurnal*, Kiev, 1919, no. 1, p. 30 (the back cover of which also, incidentally, carries a vignette by Tchaikov). This journal (p. 25) refers to forthcoming collections in Yiddish, including an anthology of Yiddish social lyrics and illustrated children's stories. The dissemination and illustration of this kind of literature were recurrent interests among the avant-garde Russian Jewish artists, especially c. 1917-23, and the activities of Lissitzky, Rabinovich, Tyshler and Chagall, in particular, in this area constitute a separate and rich avenue of enquiry. A special conference was even held by the Society for the Protection of the Health of the Jewish Population in Petrograd in December 1917 to discuss this problem – at which Chagall, *inter alia*, welcomed the idea of increasing the publication of creative literature for Jewish children. See *Evreiskaia nedelia*, nos. 47-48, 31 December 1917, p. 28.

69 Yudovin was a prolific illustrator throughout the 1920s-30s although nothing quite equalled his 28 linoleum cuts in M. Malkin's *Evreiskii narodnyi ornament*, Vitebsk: Peretz Society, 1920 (cat. 170). For comparative work see his cover for P. Guber, *Khozhdenie na vostok venitseiskogo gostia Marko Polo prozvannogo millionshchikom*, Leningrad: Brokgauz-Efron, 1929; or his woodcuts for S. Rozenfeld, *Starinnaia povest*, Leningrad: Izdatelstvo pisatelei, 1934; E. Kish, *Rasskazy o semi getto*, Leningrad: Khudozhestvennaia literatura, 1937. For commentary on Yudovin see I. Ioffe and E. Gollerbakh, *S. Yudovin. Graviury na dereve*, Leningrad: Academy of Arts, 1928; V. Brodsky and A. Zemtsova, *Solomon Borisovich Yudovin*, Leningrad: Khudozhnik RSFSR, 1962.

70 An important exception seems to have been the Yiddish journal *Di Roite Velt*, Moscow, 1926, which did, indeed, pay attention to the new artists, e.g., A. Romm wrote on Falk and Tchaikov in nos. 5-6 and 10, respectively.

71 Letter from Rabinovich to Shifrin dated 19 April (year not indicated) in Central State Archive of Literature and Art, Mos-

cow: Fund 2422, opus 1, ed. khr. 311, 1. 5.

72   Quoted in O. Voronova, *V. I. Mukhina*, Moscow: Iskusstvo, 1976, p. 43.

73   F. Syrkina, *Alexander Grigorievich Tyshler*, Moscow: Sovetskii khudozhnik, 1966, p. 11.

74   A. Deich, "Krakh proletarskogo iskusstva," *Teatralnaia zhizn*, Kiev, 1918, no. 18, pp. 8-10.

75   Rokhlin, op. cit., p. 11.

76   See, for example, A. Deich, *Maski evreiskogo teatra*, Moscow: Russkoe teatralnoe obshchestvo, 1927; A. Efros, "Khudozhniki teatra Granovskogo," *Iskusstvo*, Moscow, 1928, Books 1-2, pp. 53-74; B. Picon-Vallin, *Le Théâtre juif soviétique pendant les années vingt*, Lausanne: L'Age d'Homme, 1973.

77   For reviews see N. Tarabukin, "Altman, Shagal, Shterenberg," *Vestnik iskusstva*, Moscow, 1922, no. 5, pp. 27-28; E. Beskin, "Altman, Shagal, Shterenberg," *Izvestiia VTsIK i Mossoveta*, Moscow, no. 115, 25 May 1922, p. 4.

78   For a review of this 1922 show see E. Kuzmin, "Laborantskoe iskusstvo," *Iskusstvo*, Kiev, 1922, no. 5, pp. 14-16.

79   For details on the Unovis leaflets see L. Zhadova, *Malevich, Suprematism and Revolution in Russian Art 1910-1930*, London: Thames and Hudson, 1982.

80   M. Shagal (Chagall), "O Vitebskom narodnom khudozhestvennom uchilishche," *Shkola i revoliutsiia*, Vitebsk, 1919, nos. 24-25, pp. 7-8; L. Lisitzky (Lissitzky), "Novaia kultura," ibid., p. 11.

81   *Evrei v tsarskoi Rossii i v SSSR*, Leningrad: State Museum of Ethnography, 1939, p. 21. This is the catalog of the exhibition mentioned in note 2. Chagall, no doubt, agreed with this statement. See his article on Pen (in Yiddish), "My First Teacher. For the Jubilee of the Artist Y. Pen," in Shtern, Minsk, 1927, no. 3, pp. 41-42. Also see G. Brazer, "Yehuda Pen," ibid., 1937, no. 4, pp. 103-07.

82   Representative of this polarization in Vitebsk just after the October Revolution is the simultaneous publication of the profoundly "national" album of Jewish ornaments compiled by Yudovin and Malkin (see note 69) and Malevich's "international" album, *Suprematizm. 34 risunka* (Suprematism. 34 Drawings). Both works were published in Vitebsk in 1920.

83   The reference is to Camilla Gray's pioneering monograph on the Russian avant-garde, i.e., *The Great Experiment. Russian Art 1863-1922*, London: Thames and Hudson, 1962 (and subsequent editions).

# Yiddish Book Illustrations in Russia: 1916-1923

## Chimen Abramsky

The renaissance of modern Yiddish poetry commenced a few years before World War I, about 1912, in Russia, Poland and the United States, in each case bearing the stamp of its country. Particularly marked were the strident, almost aggressive tones of the new wave of Russian poetry. Its earliest Yiddish exponent was the brilliant lyric poet David Hofstein, who made major innovations in language and form. Next to him were the volcanic poet Peretz Markish and the magical poet who endeared himself to children, Leib Kvitko. There were many others too, but here we will mention only those who wrote in Russia. Their early literary activities were interrupted by the war in 1915, when the Russian government banned all publications in Yiddish and Hebrew. This changed dramatically with the outbreak of the February Revolution in 1917. All bans on publications in Yiddish and Hebrew were rescinded and all other restrictions on Jews were abolished. A veritable explosion of books, pamphlets and periodicals began to be published, reflecting many different political outlooks and affiliations. This lasted for about a year in Russia and for over two years in the Ukraine. Young Jewish artists had come into their own.

At the time Marc Chagall was the central figure among Jewish artists. In March 1914, Anatoly Lunacharsky, who would later become the first Commissar of Culture and Education in Lenin's government, hailed him as a great artist. This opinion was also echoed by the two famous Russian art critics Ya. Tugendkhold and Abram Efros (both Jewish), who wrote extensively about him for many more years. They were enthralled by his art. It is not surprising, therefore, that by the beginning of 1917 Chagall was asked and he readily agreed to illustrate the first Yiddish children's book, containing two stories by Der Nister: *A Mayse Mit a Hon, Dos Tsigele* (A Story about a Rooster, The Little Kid) (Vilna: B. A. Kletzkin, 1917) (cat. 144).[1] The illustrations have all the mannerisms of Chagall – the little house (cat. $144_1$), the old woman hugging the rooster (cat. $144_2$), the woman sick in bed (cat. $144_3$), the rooster at the top of the steps facing the sick, old woman (fig. 24, cat. $144_4$), and the death of the old woman as viewed by the rooster (cat. $144_5$). Some of these illustrations have their beginnings in Chagall's drawings and paintings of 1910-11.[2] The woman symbolizes the death of the old order, and the rooster heralds in a new age. Both motifs appear frequently in Chagall's paintings. The little goat (fig. 25, cat. $144_6$) is a continuous motif in Chagall's art and reappears in Lissitzky's drawings, under Chagall's influence.

Chagall then illustrated *The Magician* (Vilna: B. A. Kletzkin, 1917) by the great Yiddish classic writer Y. L. Peretz.[3] Some of these illustrations, like the Sabbath eve meal and the magician himself, recur in his

24

25

turned upside down. Yiddish literature itself expressed the liberation felt by many young Jews and non-Jews at the events spurred all over Russia by the Revolution. Although the war was still on, the first phase of the Revolution evoked hopes of a Utopian age; catastrophe mixed with the hope that after the enormous bloodshed a new world would be ushered in, a world of harmony without discord or hate, as seen in the prophecies of Isaiah and Micah. Poets and artists would have to learn the hard way, however, that the teachings of Lenin on bitter class war would prevail, rather than the dreams of the prophets.

studies of the circus and of the Jewish home. Chagall's drawings and paintings strongly oppose the ossified, classical sculptures of Mark Antokolski and the academic paintings of Leonid Pasternak, who represented the established art style of the time. Chagall's works vibrate with new ideas flowing from Paris, and represent a dream world of poetry and magic. The most impressive Yiddish book illustrations by Chagall during 1917-22 are the drawings he made for *Troyer* (Mourning), a collection of poems by David Hofstein (Kiev: Kultur Lige, 1922) (fig. 26, cat. 150), which movingly portrays the feelings of the poet after the pogroms against the Jews in the Ukraine during the civil war. Chagall first ornamented the words of the title (fig. 26); e.g., where the last Hebrew letter, a "ר," contains an illustration of a funeral for a Jew (part of it can already be seen in his drawing of 1908).[4] Another illustration shows a man with "weeping hands" (cat. 150$_3$); the next refers to "blood dripping amid sunshine" (cat. 150$_4$); and the last is a moving drawing of a series of houses over a headless body symbolizing the pogroms (cat. 150$_6$). Chagall also illustrated the title page of the short-lived monthly *Shtrom* (Stream) (Kiev, 1922) (fig. 27, cat. 151), in which each letter of the title is a miniature in black and white of waves and a world

Two major cultural events followed the outbreak of the Revolution: the establishment of the Hebrew theatre Habimah (Moscow, March 1917), under the direction of Nahum Zemach and with the artistic guidance of Yevgeny Vachtangov, and the establishment of the forerunner of the Yiddish State Theatre (Petrograd, Moscow, 1918), under the direction of Alexander Granovsky (1890-1937) with Solomon Mikhoels (1890-1948) (Chagall's childhood friend), as the principal actor. Both theatres commissioned stage sets from Chagall and Nathan Altman, which they carried out in a masterly fashion, thus extricating the Jewish theatre from the doldrums and planting it firmly on the European stage. Two radically different theatres proclaimed, in opposing ways, Jewish national culture in ultra-revolutionary forms.

In April 1917, the Russian Jewish merchant and art lover Yakov Kagan-Shabshai commissioned El Lissitzky to illustrate Moshe Broderzon's folktale *Sikhes Kholin* (Small Talk) (cat. 74), based on old Jewish folklore of Prague. The booklet was published in an edition of 110 numbered copies. The text was written by a professional scribe (a *sofer*, or one who writes Torah scrolls, tefillin, and mezuzot). Each page of the

26

27

text was surrounded by illustrations, partly inspired by both Chagall and medieval Hebrew illuminated manuscripts, but with many geometric designs hinting at Lissitzky's attempt to distance himself from Chagall, although his style is still far from Constructivist. The drawings closely follow the story, with its miracles and messianic hopes of the Jews, a clear reference to the Revolution in apocalyptic terms. Lissitzky himself clarified the aim of his illustrations:"to fuse the style and content of ornament-drawing with the wonderful Hebrew square script." A few copies were issued in the form of a scroll.

Poetic childish fantasy reached its peak with two booklets illustrated by Lissitzky – the first, a children's poem by Mani Leib (Brahinsky), *Yingl Tsingl Khvat* (The Mischievous Boy) (Moscow, 1918) and the second, *Had Gadya* (One Kid), the last poem of the Passover *seder*, in Yiddish translation. Both booklets represent a remarkable synthesis of illustrations, text and script, containing strong Cubist elements. Chagall's influence is still felt, but still there is considerable artistic independence, pointing the way to Lissitzky's Constructivism and his Prouns. The drawings are also full of poetic fantasy and playfulness. In *Yingl Tsingl Khvat* (cat. 79), there is a panoramic picture of life in the Jewish town,

the shtetl: children playing, the busy housewife, the activities of man, beast and bird, the religious teacher with children. Beautiful typographic vignettes are based on an arch reminiscent of the synagogue ark, the hands with the priestly blessings, again within an arch, and the cock crowing. Lissitzky was to later use these typographic vignettes in a number of Yiddish books. *Had Gadya* (fig. 28, cat. 90) seems to have captivated Lissitzky's imagination, for it is one of the few Yiddish booklets that he illustrated in color. In it, Lissitzky vividly portrays the Jewish world of man and beast, and the symbolism of man's tragic destiny. Cubist and Fauvist influences are totally merged with the Hebrew letters to create a remarkable effect of harmony within the architectural arches. No other illustrated Yiddish book reached such a poetic blend of fantasy and artistic perfection. Lissitzky's restless, innovative art reached its peak in this poem, which ends – surprisingly for an artist who fully identified himself with the Revolution – with the final authority of God over man.

דער בער האָט אָפּגעדאַנקט דעם שעפּס,
און די מעשה/לע איז אויס.

10

29

30

The later Yiddish booklets illustrated by Lissitzky are extremely effective, and combine some of Chagall's influence with the new ideas of Constructivism. This is noticeable in the stories of Ben Zion Raskin (cat. 92, 94), where the illustrations are within circles and cubes and the animals often evince an anthropomorphic element, together with architectural designs that also appear in some of Léger's paintings; as seen in [Uncle] Ben Zion Raskin's *Der Ber* (The Bear) (fig. 29, cat. 94) (Kiev: Yidisher Folks Farlag, 1919); *Kinder Gortn* (Kindergarten) (cat. 92) (Kiev: Yidisher Folks Farlag, 1919-20); *Hatochen, Hatochenet, Veavnei Hareihaim* (The Miller, His Wife, and Their Millstones) (Warsaw: Tarbut, 1922) (cat. 93), incidentally the only Hebrew booklet illustrated by Lissitzky; Yakov Fichman's *Shabes in Vald* (Sabbath in the Forest) (Kiev, 1919) (cat. 84); and particularly the second title page of Hans Christian Andersen's fairy tales *Mayselekh* (fig. 30, cat. 85), which was translated into Yiddish by Der Nister (Kiev, 1919) and is pure Constructivism, with the initials E. L. joined in a manner taken directly from medieval Ashkenazic Hebrew manuscripts.

The last two Yiddish booklets that Lissitzky illustrated were *Ukraynishe Folkmayses* (Ukranian Folktales)

(cat. 103) and *Vaysrusishe Folkmayses* (White Russian Folktales) (cat. 108), both translated into Yiddish by Kvitko and published in Moscow in 1922 and 1923, respectively. The illustrations have a sculptural element, remote from Chagall, but influenced by the Russian *lubok* and late Cubism. The artist shows close familiarity with the life of the Ukrainian and White Russian peasantry, but, naturally, the pictures have no specific Jewish content. Such illustrations are not uncommon in Russian illustrated books by Favorsky or Popova. Probably the last Yiddish work whose title page was illustrated by Lissitzky, is Kipnis's book of poems *Oksn* (Oxen) (fig. 31), in the best Proun style, with the letter "L" within the Hebrew letters ק"א (Kiev: Widervuks, 1923) which has, by the way, been overlooked in all studies of Lissitzky.

In any discussion of Lissitzky's illustrations of Yiddish books, one must touch on his drawing (fig. 32, cat. 105) which is, perhaps, his most original work on a Jewish subject. This is an illustration, not in a Yiddish book, but in the Russian work by Ilya Ehrenburg, *Six Stories with Easy Endings* (Moscow-Berlin, 1922). The illustration represents a Hamburg-New York steamer superimposed on two triangles forming the Star of

31

32

David, over a collage of a portion of the Mishnah (order Kodoshim, tractate Midot, chapter 4.6, dealing with the measurements of the Temple), and over it a hand drawn in heavy black ink, and on the hand the Hebrew letters פ״נ, acronym for the Hebrew tombstone inscription "here lies." The irony of the drawing is biting. It could mean, the Jews are saying goodbye to the old world; it could also mean, goodbye to the Revolution, and that Russia and the whole of Europe lie buried, and the future is in the new world.[5] It is not surprising that he did this drawing on his arrival in Berlin, not having decided whether to stay in Germany or return to the Soviet Union.

After 1923, Lissitzky ceased illustrating Yiddish books and concentrated his great talents on Constructivism, photomontage and architectural design, making significant contributions in all of them.

Undoubtedly, Chagall was a greater painter than Lissitzky, but one can argue that Lissitzky's innovative genius exerted far more influence on the development of abstract art, photomontage and revolutionary ideas in typography. His illustrated Yiddish books remain unsurpassed to this day.

Issachar Ber Ryback was another artist who illustrated Yiddish books, and who was, of all his peers, primarily a Jewish artist. All his paintings, drawings and illustrations are on Jewish subjects: the shtetl (cat. 136), pogroms and Jewish Symbolist motifs. Younger than Chagall, Lissitzky and Altman, he was chiefly influenced by Chagall, but his illustrations are reminiscent of early nineteenth century Russian woodcuts interspersed with strong Cubist sculptural elements. This can be seen clearly in his illustrations for Kvitko's poems, *Foyglen* (Birds) (Berlin: Shveln, [1922]) (fig. 33, cat. 137). The book ends with a vase of flowers, a motif copied from Jewish cemeteries, when he and Lissitzky were sent by An-Sky on their expedition. The same can be seen in his illustrations for Kvitko's book of poems, *Gringroz* (Green Grass) (Berlin: Vostok, 1922) (cat. 138) in which he reproduces many symbols from Jewish tombstone and synagogue carvings. The only exception in his artistic work is the booklet by Kvitko, *Pionern Bichl* (Pioneer Book) (Kharkov: Knihaspilka, [1927]) (fig. 34, cat. 140), where his illustrations are plagiarisms of George Grosz's satirical drawings, especially those on pages 7 (cat. 140₃) and 9 (cat. 140₄). The first word of the title is made up of letters symbolizing the red flag, the five-pointed star, the hammer and sickle, the factory chimneys, and a floral wreath, all symbols of the rising Socialist Realism tendency. Ryback lacks the innovativeness of Lissitzky and the fantasy of Chagall's dream world; he is a very straightforward artist, free from any sentimentality. His artistic work is much more moving in his albums on Ukrainian Jewish types, the pogroms there, and the profound portrayal of the vanishing shtetl (cat. 136). His sense of tragedy is evident in his portraits of old Jews, or of the synagogue in Dubrovna (his albums were issued in Berlin in 1923, 1925 and 1926).

Another artist, Nathan Altman, painter, sculptor, stage designer, and master of many styles, began to work long before the Revolution. Among his early works are the funeral of 1911 and the powerful Cubist portrait of the old Jew of 1913, the first purely Cubist paintings on Jewish subjects. Although he already showed a great interest in Jewish art as far back as 1911, he became more deeply involved during 1917-23 in studying Jewish ornamental art as found on embroidered Torah ark curtains (*parochot*) and engraved tombstones. As a result he produced a masterly album, *Jüdische Graphik* (Berlin, 1923) (cat. 30). But as an illustrator of Yiddish books he was less impressive. Thus, the design for the book of poems by David Hofstein and Aaron Kushnirov, *Shtam/Azkore* (Branch /Memorial) (Kiev, 1922) (cat. 29), is simply Constructivist in style, influenced by Lissitzky's Prouns, leaving the Hebrew letters enlarged but not decorating them. His later illustrated Yiddish books belong to the school of Socialist Realism. He also revolutionized stage design at Habimah and the Yiddish State Theatre (Goset) by replacing the old patriarchal, sentimental motifs with Cubist-Constructivist designs, not unlike Tatlin's. In addition, he became an outstanding portraitist, known for his many portraits of Lenin. In the late 1930s and during World War II he returned to make stage designs for the Moscow State Yiddish Theatre, for plays by Shmuel Halkin and Y. L. Peretz. After the war he illustrated the Russian translations of Shalom Aleichem stories, in a rather conservative, classical style.[6]

The last major artist in our discussion is Joseph Tchaikov, who studied sculpture in Paris in 1910-14. He was deeply involved in producing *Makhmadim* (The Precious Ones), the artistic periodical produced in Paris by Jewish artists in 1912, consisting of illustra-

tions without texts in a style fusing Art Nouveau and Cubism (cat. 160-162). On his return to Russia, Tchaikov launched an effort to create a group of artists who would form a Jewish national style both in sculpture and in book illustration. He wrote the first book in Yiddish on sculpture, *Skulptur* (Kiev, 1921) (cat. 171). Between 1919 and 1924 he illustrated a large number of Yiddish booklets, many of them for children, in a style modelled on Cubist sculpture. He signed the drawings with the Hebrew letter "ט," but unlike Lissitzky and Chagall, he never decorated the Hebrew letters of Yiddish texts. The illustrations closely follow the texts, but lack the poetic imagination so abundant in the works of Chagall, Lissitzky and Ryback.[7] His finest illustrated Yiddish book is Peretz Markish's *Der Galaganer Hon* (The Arrogant Rooster) (Berlin, 1922) (fig. 35, cat. 63). The illustrations are bold and expressionistic, adhering almost literally to the text.

In 1925, a group of young Hebrew writers in the Soviet Union decided to establish a Hebrew literary miscellany, for which they received official support from the Soviet government. Edited by Abraham Krivoruchko (later known in Israel as A. Kariv), the writers called their publication *Bereishit* (In the Beginning – the first word in the Hebrew Bible). (Rumors are current that the Soviet Commissar for Education, Anatoly Lunacharsky was in favor of its publication.) It was set up in Leningrad, but for unknown reasons it was printed in Berlin. The cover (fig. 36, cat. 66) by Tchaikov, is a striking design of revolutionary ideas. On the right are factories and a railway with red flags fluttering, while the lower right corner contains a pastoral scene with trees, a bridge and railways. In the center a nude man stands holding aloft a red flag with two people, one in a theatrical gesture of defiance. On the left are two dancing girls dressed in green, and below them a girl in a very dramatic gesture, calling on the world to

33

35

34

rebel. The combination of colors and theatrical effects is striking. In many ways it seems to be the most brilliant cover designed by Tchaikov, who after 1925 became a conformist to the demands of Socialist Realism. Even the letters of the title are striking, beginning and ending with red. Though lacking the brilliance of Lissitzky, it has the challenging element of a dramatic opening. Tchaikov never reached this brilliance in his Yiddish book designs.

Other minor artists in Russia at the time who illustrated Yiddish books were N. Shifrin, who illustrated two Yiddish books by Itzik Kipnis: *Dos Tsigayner* (The Little Gypsy) (Kiev: Kultur Lige, 1923) (cat. 157) and *Dos Pantofele* (The Little Slipper) (Kiev: Kultur Lige, 1923) (cat. 156); and Chasia Shor, who illustrated three children's books by Kipnis: *A Ber is Geloyfn* (A Bear Has Run Away) (Kiev: Kulture Lige, 1924), *Rusishe Mayselekh* (Russian Tales) (Kiev: Soravkop, 1924); and *Mayselekh* (Little Tales) (Kiev: Soravkop, 1924). They are interesting but lack originality. The works of the remarkable painters Robert Falk, I. Sternberg and Alexander Tyshler are outside the scope of this essay.

Great original Yiddish illustrations by avant-garde artists ceased when art was forced to serve the demands of official Soviet policy. However, Yiddish poetry and prose continued to flourish – albeit with growing restrictions – until it perished in Stalin's fatal attack on Yiddish culture, launched in October 1948, and culminating in the murder of the foremost Yiddish writers and actors in August 1952. This is a tragic story that still awaits its historian.

In conclusion, Yiddish children's literature essentially began with the Russian Revolution, which provided an exceptional stimulus for the creation of children's stories and poems between 1917 and 1927. With the onset of the Revolution, writers felt they were seeing a new age dawning. Hope for a harmonious world of sunshine and bliss was visualized, bringing an end to war and misery, as also reflected in Russian and Ukrainian literature.

The artistic freedom during the first five years of Lenin's government indicates that the Bolsheviks slowly were gaining power and could be considered emancipators in the eyes of poets and artists. Artistic and poetic experimentation took place and then was consolidated in all spheres of life before Bolshevik rule asserted its unlimited authority on all creativity.

Then, in 1927 Stalin defeated the opposition led by L. Trotsky, S. Zinoviev and L. Kamenev. Stifling repres-

sion set in and conformity to the party line became the order of the day.

In November-December 1918, Rosa Luxemburg wrote the following profound prophecy, which is a fitting epitaph for this brilliant, short-lived, and unique period in modern art: "But with the repression of political life in the land as a whole, life in the Soviets must also become more and more crippled. Without general elections, without unrestricted freedom of press and assembly, without a free struggle of opinion, life dies out in every public institution, becomes a mere semblance of life, in which only the bureaucracy remains as the active element. Public life gradually falls asleep."[8]

1   As Vilna was under German occupation, the book was printed in Petrograd.
2   Franz Meyer, *Marc Chagall, Life and Work*, New York, 1964, p. 18 and the paintings of 1908 on p. 65.
3   Again, printed in Petrograd as Vilna was still under German occupation.
4   Meyer, op. cit., p. 66.
5   The American art historian, Alan Birnholz completely misunderstood this, thinking that it was a Kabbalistic text: obviously not knowing Hebrew, he invented an unfounded theory of the influence of Kabbalah on Lissitzky.
6   For a chronology of Altman's work see M. Etkind, *Nathan Altman*, Moscow, 1971 (in Russian).
7   For the many books he illustrated, see *Jewish Publications in the Soviet Union, 1917-1960*, ed. Chone Shmeruk – see under Tchaikov in the index.
8   *The Russian Revolution*, introduction by Bertram D. Wolfe, Ann Arbor, 1961, p. 71.

# Chagall and the Jewish Revival: Center or Periphery?*

## Ziva Amishai-Maisels

In 1922, on the verge of leaving Russia, Marc Chagall published an article, in Moscow, in the new Yiddish journal *Shtrom*, where he reviewed his position vis-à-vis the renaissance of Jewish art in which he had participated, and stated his own ideas on the subject. Since this article is seminal to an understanding of his works in this context, it is translated here in full:

A few words, comrades, on the subject on which you asked me to write at length – my opinion of Jewish art.

How long ago did I first hear in Jewish artists' circles a controversy over so-called Jewish art?

In the midst of this tumult and uproar, a group of Jewish artists stood forth and amongst them also Marc Chagall. I was still in Vitebsk when this misfortune occurred – I had just returned from Paris, [and] I smiled to myself. At that time I was preoccupied with something entirely different.

On the one hand – 'New World Jews' – with that world which Litvakov so detested[1] – my small village lanes, hunchbacked, herring-like inhabitants, green Jews, uncles and aunts with their questions: – God be praised, you've grown, you've become an adult! And I captured them in painting. . .

On the other hand – I was then younger by a hundred years and I loved them, I simply loved them. . .

It was with them that I busied myself; they attracted me more than the idea that someone had labeled me a Jewish artist.

Already in Paris in my room in La Ruche, while I worked, I heard through the partition the voices of Jewish immigrants arguing:

What you mean, in the long run, is that Antokolski is not a Jewish artist, – and neither is Israels nor Liebermann!

The lamp had already burnt low and illuminated my painting, which was standing upside down (that's how I work – enjoy yourselves!), and in the end, when at daybreak the skies of Paris began to glow, I gaily laughed at the futile ideas of my neighbors on the fate of Jewish art – Okay, you talk – and I will work.

Representatives of all lands and peoples! – to you I turn (I cannot help but think of Spengler).

Admit it: now, when Lenin sits in the Kremlin, when there is no splinter of fire wood, the fire smokes, the wife is angry – are you now making 'national art'?

You, wise German Walden and all you others who preach an international art, noble Frenchmen Metzinger and Gleizes (if you are still alive), you will answer me – Chagall, you were right.[2]

Jews, if you take this to heart (I certainly do), you will weep that the painters of the wooden shtetl synagogues (why was I not buried along with you in one grave) and the carvers of wooden 'synagogue-clappers' – 'Sh!'[3] (I saw some in An-Sky's collection and was frightened) – have all passed away. But what can we deduce is really the difference between my hunchbacked great-grandfather Segal from Mohilev, who painted the [walls of the] Mohilev synagogue, and I, who painted the [walls of the] Jewish Theatre (a good theatre) in Moscow?

Believe me, neither of us had less lice when I followed him on the floor of the workshop, in the synagogue and in the theatre.

Moreover, I'm sure that if I were unshaven, I would be his very portrait. . .

Incidentally, my [fore]father. Believe me, no less did I work hard, no less love (and how!) did we both exude. The difference is only in that he received commissions for shop signs and I studied in Paris, which he also knew about.

But yet, neither I, nor he, nor others (many others) are all there is of Jewish art.

And why not actually tell the truth? From where should one take it?

Heaven forbid that it should come into being because of some command or other! Because of Efros writing an article, or Levitan giving me an 'academic dose'!. . .[4]

There was Japanese, Egyptian, Persian, Greek art. Only from the Renaissance on has national art been on the wane. The boundaries have dissolved. Artists arrive – individuals, citizens of some country, born somewhere (blessed are you, my Vitebsk), and one must have a good registration or even a passport expert (from the Jewish section) in order to be able to 'firmly establish the nationality' of all the artists.

And then I think to myself:

If I weren't a Jew (with the content that I give this word), I would never have become an artist, or I would have become a different one.

This is also news to me!

I myself know very well what this little people can produce.

Unfortunately, I am too bashful and cannot express what it can produce.

Just a word on what this little people has produced! It felt like it – it created Christ and Christianity.

It wanted to – it gave forth Marx and Socialism.

Can it be that it will not show the world some kind of art?

It will do so!

Kill me, if it doesn't.[5]

This article is Chagall's declaration of faith on his complex attitude towards Jewish art. On the one hand, he was fully aware of the international nature of modern art and, on the eve of his return to Western Europe, even partially concurred with it. On the other, he was

proud of his Judaism, defending its pronounced influence on his art against past and future critics. However, he did not see himself as consciously reviving Jewish art, but – on the contrary – as naturally continuing it, even stressing a family relationship with Chaim ben Isaac Halevi Segal of Slutsk, the artist of the Mohilev synagogue, whose paintings had been studied and "documented" by El Lissitzky and Issachar Ryback (cat. 67-70; 119; 173$_{1-6}$). Unlike them, Chagall suggests that he had no need to "document" the synagogue; rather, its folk art was in his blood.[6] This identification is echoed in his "differentiation" of himself from his "forefather," who, he states, had also been a sign-painter, since in his autobiography, Chagall claimed that he had himself painted signs, again suggesting that his roots lay in folk art.[7]

Furthermore, Chagall states that a conscious revival of Jewish art, attended by oral and written polemics, is utterly beside the point. The only polemics possible are the works of art themselves, and he sees himself not only as having produced such works, but stakes his life on his ability to create a world-shaking Jewish art in the future. Moreover, he did it; the name Chagall is almost synonymous with the term "modern Jewish art," and his fame today lies less in his being a pre-Surrealist than in his having brought Jewish themes into the international art arena, portraying them in a way equally fascinating to Jews, Christians and even Japanese, to the point that *Fiddler on the Roof* was named after one of them. It is also in his work rather than in his theories that his importance to the Jewish revival movement lies, for he was producing the art on which it would model itself long before it had worked out its theories. Yet his relationship with the movement was much more complex than such a statement infers, for he was simultaneously a guiding inspiration to it and the earliest exponent and beneficiary of its still embryonic ideas. To study this symbiotic relationship, we must return to the beginnings of Chagall's career in Vitebsk, St. Petersburg and Paris, for it was there that the seeds of his contribution to the Jewish renaissance were sown.[8]

Chagall began his studies in Vitebsk under the tutelage of Yehuda Pen, an academic artist whose work at this time – as can be seen from An-Sky's article on him in *Ost und West* – partook not only of the style of the Russian Wanderers, as Meyer claims, but of the style and sad ghetto iconography of the Jewish artists of Eastern Europe, led by Mauriczy Gottlieb, Samuel Hirszenberg, Leopold Pilichowsky, and Leopold Horowitz.[9] In fact, one of the reasons Pen set up his studio in Vitebsk may have been to be close to his ghetto subjects. It was thus from Pen that Chagall first learned both academic drawing, which he never fully assimilated,[10] and the idea that Jewish shtetl themes were legitimate subjects in art.

Pen also seems to have been the one to introduce Chagall to modern Jewish art, using the pages of *Ost und West* to demonstrate his ideas.[11] There Chagall could see reproductions of Hirszenberg's new painting, *Exile* of 1904, which inspired him to sketch his own version, *Exodus*, adding a guardian angel to the wandering Jews.[12] On the other hand, these early volumes of *Ost und West* would also have brought to his attention the fact that folk art – synagogue and tombstone decorations, Haggadah illustrations, etc. – were beginning to be highly appreciated as precursors of modern Jewish art.[13] That Chagall became interested in this type of art is suggested by his small painting of a cemetery, in which he – like the photographers of *Ost und West* – concentrated on the cemetery itself rather than on mourners, even sketching in the paintings and letters decorating the tombstones.[14]

It may also have been due to Pen that Chagall first met some of the Jewish artists who would participate with him in an attempt to create modern Jewish art: Lissitzky, who seemingly began studying with Pen in 1903-4, and speaks of being in 1905, "one of a group of comrades who worked together"; Solomon Yudovin, who studied with Pen for a time before 1910, and may have met Chagall during the latter's summer vacations in Vitebsk; and Ossip Zadkine, whom Pen introduced to Chagall on Zadkine's return from London in the summer of 1908, at the same time that Zadkine met with Lissitzky.[15]

To further his art studies, Chagall travelled to St. Petersburg and, following in the tradition of a yeshiva student, immediately made contact with other Jews whom he hoped would help him. He turned first to the sculptor Ilya Ginzburg and through him met Baron David Guenzburg, who paid Chagall a monthly stipend, accompanied by little lectures on art. These contacts were particularly important for Chagall's development: Ginzburg introduced him to the world of his recently deceased teacher Mark Antokolski, and to a different, officially recognized and more assimilated form of modern Jewish art. Baron Guenzburg, who had collaborated with Antokolski's friend Vladimir Stasov in searching for the roots of Jewish art, had not only published *L'Ornement Hébreu* in 1905 (cat. 159), but was – at the time Chagall was in contact with him – actively involved in organizing the Jewish Historical and Ethnographic Society in St. Petersburg with another native of Vitebsk, An-Sky.[16] Chagall thus had a front-row seat to observe the preparations for the investigation of Jewish folk art, which would get under way only in 1912 after he had moved to Paris, and

would be documented by another of Pen's pupils, Yudovin, with whom Chagall may well have been acquainted.[17]

His connections with this movement are further clarified by his friendship with Maxim Vinaver, who would eventually give him money to study in Paris. Vinaver was not only a member of the Duma, but another of the organizers of the Jewish Historical and Ethnographic Society, and he took a deep interest in modern and folk art.[18] Even the story of Vinaver's permitting Chagall to sleep in the office of a Jewish Russian-language newspaper ties him to the beginnings of this movement. This must have been in 1910, when *Novyi voskhod* (New Sunrise) began to be published, and the first volume of this magazine shows a concern both for modern Jewish academic art and for Jewish folk art, illustrating wooden synagogue architecture on its pages. Furthermore, Chagall mentions being encouraged by Syrkin at this time, who just happens to have written the articles on wooden synagogues in Poland and Lithuania in the first volume![19]

At the same time that Chagall was open to these influences, he came under the tutelage of Leon Bakst and Mstislav Dobujinsky at the Zvantseva art school.[20] On the one hand, Bakst – a supposedly fully assimilated Jew who was, however, still subject to anti-Semitic attacks – was a role model even more advanced than Antokolski, and completely different from Pen and other Eastern European artists. Bakst would have strongly reinforced Chagall's growing ambivalence to his Judaism, showing him that the way to liberation as an artist lay through full emancipation from his Jewish bonds.[21] On the other hand, Dobujinsky, who occasionally painted shtetl scenes and synagogues, introduced him to a world of mystery and symbols, in which humor and irony were basic components.[22] Both artists would also have pointed out to him the artistic merit of children's art: Dobujinsky exhibited a "child's drawing" of *Paradise* at the St. Petersburg Salon in winter 1908-9, and Bakst's article in *Apollon* of early 1909 suggested that both children's and folk art have a lot to teach the modern artist.[23] It was in this environment that Chagall began to develop a "primitivist" style of his own, one which in many ways paralleled that developing on a purely Russian level in the art of Natalia Goncharova, Mikhail Larionov and the Burliuk brothers.[24]

This multi-faceted environment had a profound effect on Chagall. He was surrounded by Jews intent on exploring their Jewish roots as well as by those trying to assimilate into their Russian Christian surroundings. In neither one of these groups did he feel entirely at home: alienated from his own Jewish roots, he was unable to assimilate into the culture of the Russian city,

37

and felt almost equally rejected by both. Witness, on the one hand, his comments on his rejection by the Academy and other modern art groups, and on his arrest for being in St. Petersburg without a permit, and, on the other, his family's reaction to his becoming an artist.[25] In retaliation, he withdrew into a world of his own, a childlike world with a strong touch of ironic humor that could pass for "naive" poetry or mystery, getting his message across to his fellow Jews by turning Yiddish idioms into visual metaphors in paintings such as *The Dead Man, Circumcision, and The Holy Family*, some of which play games with Christian iconography.[26] However, his irony could as easily be turned against traditional Jewry, as is obvious in his drawing of *The Mikveh* (fig. 37, cat. 141). A mikveh is a ritual bath, where men and women are strictly segregated. Women usually come for "purification" after having menstruated and before having sexual relations with their husbands, and men usually bathe there in preparation for the Sabbath. Chagall presents his view of this ritual in a thoroughly sarcastic way, showing men and women bathing nude together. On each side, a couple reclines on a bed, spied on in their lovemaking by a witness of the "primal scene" hiding under the bed, while men and women – segregated by sex – gossip about what is going on around them. He turns this ritual connected with sexual purity into the kind of orgy a child might imagine if he had never been to the mikveh, having only partially understood the connection between it and sexual intercourse. This mockery of religious Jewry may well have been his reaction to his mother's horror at his portrayal of his beloved Bella in the nude, and to the gossip going on about Bella's presence in his studio at all hours of the day and night.[27]

In other works of this period, he tried to unite the Jewish and Christian worlds in which he moved. Thus in *Kermesse*, he combined Russian sources, such as the circus atmosphere from Alexander Bloch's play *Balaganchik*,[28] with that of a *Purimspiel*, from which he took the detail of the woman (Zeresh) emptying the slop pail from a second-story window on the head of her husband (Haman), who is taking part in the procession. Here again the iconography would only be fully open to those who could partake of both of Chagall's worlds, Russian and Jewish.

In this period, Chagall stood between different worlds, searching for his identity. He achieved a stylistic *blend* of children's and folk art – Jewish and non-Jewish – while his iconography – Jewish and Christian – is composed of *contrasts* and hidden meanings. Fully sensitized to both internationalist and nationalist folk conceptions of Jewish art, he had begun to create a modern Jewish "folkic" art.

On arrival in Paris, Chagall again made contact with Russian Jews who could help him get established, from a painter named Ehrenberg, who lent him a studio, to Sonya Terk Delaunay, who helped introduce him to avant-garde art circles.[29] From the start, primed by the exhibitions he had seen in St. Petersburg and having studied the latest paintings at the Salon d'Automne, he "instinctively" chose the most avant-garde groups to join, absorbing Fauve color and Cubist faceting, and blending them convincingly with his own "folkic" style.[30] For the French, the results were strikingly modern and had the fresh *naiveté* of their beloved Douanier Rousseau, who died a few weeks after Chagall's arrival, and they welcomed him readily into the avant-garde fold, exhibiting his new Paris works at the Salon des Indépendants in March 1912.[31] Yet despite this welcome and the many friends he made, Chagall remained alienated from his surroundings.[32] Rather than painting Paris, he preferred to redo his major Russian Jewish works – *Birth, The Wedding, Death* and *The Funeral* – in his new "French" style, starting the series off with the eery *Sabbath* of 1910.[33] However, his main themes during his Paris period usually concerned non-Jewish Russian peasants painted in an overtly childlike, "folkic" style, to which Cubist elements were sometimes added.[34] His fluctuations between these styles, his ability to add or leave out Cubist or Fauve elements at will, are due neither to his being merely an eclectic artist, nor to his simply "learning" these styles, nor to his use of different styles in different mediums. It seems rather to have been a matter of conscious choice. This can be seen in his playful juxtaposition of different styles in a single painting, as in *I and the Village* and *The Soldier Drinks*. Thus on the one hand, he emphasized his cosmopolitan sophistication, while on the other, he constantly insisted on his childlike "folk" nature.[35]

Chagall's divided personality is consciously asserted on many levels in his *Self-Portrait with Seven Fingers* of c. 1912, in which he portrays himself in Cubist style standing before a "naive" folk-style painting, *To Russia, Asses and Others*, which was actually executed in a much more Cubist fashion. Behind him he displays the three components of his style and personality. On the right, he sets the Eiffel Tower to represent Paris; on the left, he places his memories of Russia, symbolized by a Russian church; and he labels both of them in Yiddish. Furthermore, the Yiddish inscriptions point up the fact that both his seven fingers and the figures in the painting on the easel are visual translations of Yiddish idioms.[36]

It is at this time of divided inner loyalties and outer stylistic assimilation that he came into contact with the Jewish artists who inhabited the room next to his in La

38

Ruche – e.g., Joseph Tchaikov, Leo Koenig, Henry Epstein, Yitzhak Lichtenstein – and heard their interminable arguments on the need to create a modern Jewish art.[37] His reasons for mocking them should now be clear: he had not only heard all this before in Vitebsk and St. Petersburg, but he saw himself as actually being involved in accomplishing what they were still discussing. Furthermore, a comparison of his works of this period with the weak academic designs they produced in 1912 in their journal, *Makhmadim* (The Precious Ones) (cat. 160-162), will highlight the reasons this avant-garde artist could have nothing to do with them.

Yet those all-night sessions overheard through the paper-thin walls of La Ruche were not without their influence on Chagall. Since *Makhmadim* was published in 1912, these talks must date from late 1911 through 1912, and they parallel – or may even have inspired – Chagall's earliest Biblical themes. In fact, a comparison between these drawings and Chagall's Biblical works suggests that he saw himself to be competing with them, choosing the same themes they had chosen in their Shavuot (late spring) 1912 issue in order

to show them how to produce the art of their dreams. Thus his *Cain and Abel* (fig. 38)[38] can best be explained by referring to the *Makhmadim* version (cat. 162₅): the figure holding his head has been turned from Cain into Abel, and the moment shown is one of aggression between the brothers rather than remorse. The most obvious change is, however, in the style, which Chagall makes clearly primitivist rather than academic. He purposely turns the weak zig-zag pattern of the frame, antlers and loincloth of the *Makhmadim* drawing into a strong, staccato pattern that is echoed in the brothers' bodies and augments the expressive tension in the work in a manner utterly beyond the grasp of the Makhmadim artists. Whereas their interpretation remains highly traditional, Chagall shows them the way to break new ground stylistically, keeping his colors uncharacteristically limited to brown, black and white, so as not to take unfair advantage in competing with a drawing.

In a similar manner, his two versions of *Adam and Eve* of 1912 contain stylistic plays and details which suggest that they answer Marek Schwarz's and Tchaikov's versions of the theme in the same journal's

Shavuot and Sabbath issues (fig. 5, cat. 162$_4$, 160$_5$). In the version Chagall exhibited in 1913 (fig. 39),[39] he depicted a Cubistic Adam and Eve flirting with each other while Eve plucks the fruit from the serpentine tree, whose forms may owe something to the twisted columns that frame Schwarz's drawing. Chagall has, however, turned this form into one which makes the erotic connotations of the story fully apparent: the tree not only offers the couple realistic apples and a pair of fig leaves, but it has a somewhat phallic protrusion, reminiscent of Adam's genitals, pointed directly towards Eve's genital area.[40] These Cubist figures inhabit a "folk" Paradise: they are surrounded by innocent animals rendered in the pure folk-art style of Russian and Polish synagogues, papercuts and tombstone decorations.[41] By inserting these animals, Chagall was apparently again working on several levels. First of all, he was restating the meaning of each style: the folk style is that of the innocent animals, while Cubism is the style of "knowledgeable" man in the act of plucking the apple from the Tree of Knowledge. Secondly, this folk-art element is Chagall's answer to *Makhmadim*: it is in Jewish folk art that the roots of Jewish art lie, but the way to use this style is not that in which Schwarz drew his "naive" birds above the columns of his frame, but in the full folk tradition to which Chagall is heir. His renewed interest in making a statement on this style may have been spurred by contact with Vinaver, who would have kept him abreast of the expedition to study Jewish folk art undertaken that very year.[42] Finally, the goat on the left is one of Chagall's favorite animals, depicted in the manner he had already developed in *Rain* and *Full Moon*.[43] The stag and bird, on the other hand, seem to have been elicited by *Makhmadim*: the stag was sacrificed in Cain and Abel and the bird appears in both versions of Adam and Eve.[44]

Chagall added still another level of Jewish meaning to his other version of Adam and Eve in *Homage to Apollinaire*. Here he moved away from the folk-art style of his first sketches to a more modern and sophisticated, semi-Cubist conception, adding by means of the clock, which chimes the hours around the Fall, a Midrashic level utterly lacking in the work of the Makhmadim artists.[45]

At the same time, this contact with the Makhmadim group had another effect on Chagall, inspiring a series on Jewish religious life, which has no known parallel in his early works before 1912. He portrays the eve of the Day of Atonement, the blowing of the shofar, the prayer for the new moon, the sick old Jew being forced to break his fast, and devout Jews praying, studying and holding the Torah.[46] This phase of his art may also have been influenced by the article on Pen

40

published in *Ost und West* in August 1912, in which Chagall is mentioned as his student. In these works, Chagall answered both the Makhmadim artists and his former teacher, declaring that *this* is the way a modern Jewish artist should deal with traditional themes.

This interplay – especially with Pen – can be seen when one of the works reproduced in *Ost und West, The Morning's Lesson in Talmud* (fig. 40), is compared to Chagall's *The Pinch of Snuff* and *Jew in Prayer. The Pinch of Snuff* (fig. 41), shows an almost identical situation: a devout Jew with a long, gray beard, his sidelocks curled and emphasized, and a large skullcap on his head, sits in the Beth Midrash (House of Study) before a Torah ark whose curtain is decorated with a Star of David, with a book open on the table before him. Chagall has added part of a menorah on the left and the inscription ס״ת, the initials for *Sefer Torah* (Torah Scroll) on the curtain at the right.[47] But instead of studying, the Jew here refreshes himself with a pinch of snuff, a traditional form of taking a break,[48] and displays his book for all to see. This book clearly sets forth Chagall's Hebrew name, "Segal Moshe," and this, combined with the way the Jew stares out of the picture, seems to call on the artist to reaffirm his Jewish identity and to return to his roots. But whereas his Hebrew signature is turned towards us, Chagall sets his usual international signature upside down in the lower right-hand corner, so that it can be read in turn by the Orthodox Jew, to whom Chagall declares his non-Orthodox identity.[49] Chagall has thus taken this traditional subject and changed not only its style, but its content: no longer a depiction of simple faith, it is a statement of the conflict between the artist and his religious background.

The same kind of ambivalent message is found in *Jew in Prayer* (fig. 42), in which he seems at first to have merely done a stylistic variation on Pen's devout Jew, bending him still further over his book, and emphasizing his devotion by setting a phylacteries box on his head and showing him in prayer. Yet this Jew does not sit *before* a Torah ark, but – portrayed in profile – he literally and somewhat sacrilegiously turns his back to the Torah scroll held up *behind* him and bisected by the frame. He is anchored to the chair by the fringes of his *tzitzit*, and the way he bends over his book – whose text has been crossed out – is accented by the sharp point of the Star of David above his head: it pushes his head down to the breaking point and threatens to prick him should he stop praying. The positioning of this star may have been suggested by its location in Pen's painting, but the formal expression here – and the understanding that the positioning of the star can have a formal meaning – is far beyond Pen's academic training. Moreover, as opposed to the relatively light room in Pen's work and in *The Pinch of Snuff*, this world of prayer is dark, lit only by the tiny window behind the Jew at the upper right, with its cruciform grill. Whereas in *The Pinch of Snuff*, the Jew is flanked by symbols of Judaism, here a Christian element intrudes, albeit a very small one. The confined feeling of this painting demonstrates that although Chagall had begun to tackle themes from his Jewish background, he was far from having made peace with his Judaism or even with the kind of painting of Jews he had learned from Pen.

Thus in Paris, Chagall launched his first concrete exposition of his views on Jewish art. While highlighting his ambivalence to his own position vis-à-vis Judaism, it also shows him to have succeeded in creating new forms of modern Jewish art, complete with a new style and new personal, Midrashic and idiomatic meanings.

In the spring of 1914, Chagall travelled to Berlin for his major one-man show at Der Sturm Gallery, a show which was a clear indication that he had "arrived" on the international avant-garde art scene. From there, he went on to Russia to claim his fiancée of many years, Bella. He undoubtedly saw himself as the "new Antokolski," the established modern artist, returning home, as Antokolski had done, to claim the reward for his success – the hand of the daughter of the *gvir*, the wealthy and important community leader.[50] Yet this was far from a *joyeuse entrée*. Halfway through what was meant to be a three-month visit, World War I broke out and trapped him in Vitebsk with no visible means of support since all his new works were still in Berlin. Although he was known in avant-garde Russian circles, he had never shown his major new works in Russia.[51] Moreover, he now had a competitor for the title of leader of modern Jewish art, in an artist whom he himself had influenced: Nathan Altman.

41

Altman had met Chagall, Zadkine and Archipenko in Paris in 1911, and, on his return to Russia, had done his own Cubist version of *The Dead Man* lying on the floor, undoubtedly inspired by Chagall's 1910-11 Cubist rendition of the theme. However, Altman displayed none of Chagall's humor or irony; his is a deep expression of mourning, which reflects his feelings on the death of his grandfather.[52] Since then, Altman had been developing his own attitude to Jewish art. His *Old Jew* of 1913 used suggestions of Cubist faceting to modernize his academic style. It presented the Jew according to the tradition of Eastern European Jewish art, but with a good deal of inner pride and strength. His modernism is not as far-reaching as Chagall's, and his attitude to Judaism far less ambiguous.[53]

In 1913, Altman also "discovered" Jewish folk art around his native Vinnitsa and in Volynia, probably inspired by the expedition of the Jewish Historical and Ethnographic Society, which was investigating this area. He produced a series of graphics based on tombstones and other artifacts, which he stylized in a lightly Cubist fashion (cat. 30) rather than presenting them as documents as Yudovin had done (cat. 170). He thus "digested" folk art into his own Cubist idiom,

42

producing – at least externally – the same kind of combination of Cubism and folk art that Chagall had developed in Paris by the time of Altman's visit. Altman exhibited these works at the "World of Art" show in Moscow in December 1913.[54] Possibly in reaction to word of Chagall's *Adam and Eve*, exhibited in the Salon des Indépendants of that year on which Apollinaire had commented, or as a result of seeing the Shavuot copy of *Makhmadim*, Altman did his own highly erotic version of the *Temptation of Eve* (cat. 30₁), in which the serpent crawling up the tree has legs and his tail winds down suggestively between the legs of the reclining Eve.[55]

Yet, initially, despite his highly competitive personality, Chagall showed no consciousness of this rivalry. As he wrote in *Bletlakh*, he was too busy on his arrival in Vitebsk with personal concerns. He drew and painted his family over and over again.[56] This intense preoccupation with his family led to a change in his style: they are painted in his closest approach to Realism since leaving Pen's studio, although his angles of vision – from above, below and the side – derive rather from Degas and the Post-Impressionists he had seen in Paris. In these portraits, Cubist elements are almost entirely missing and primitivist ones are minimized: only his Fauve color remains intact.[57] Irony and humor

are also almost absent, and what emerges from these works – as Chagall wrote – is his intense love for the family he had missed for so many years, a love he would continue to develop in his paintings of Bella, their married life, and his first child.[58]

At the same time, he was directly influenced by the outbreak of the war and did an entire series of works on the soldiers and nurses who flooded the town on their way westward towards the front or returning wounded from it. Most of these works are done in his folkic style and treat the subject from a purely Russian point of view, but a number of them, such as *The Departure*, specifically relate to Jewish soldiers going off to fight for their country, whereas in *War* and *Smolensk News*, he shows the effect of the war on the Jewish population, many of whom became refugees at this time.[59]

Finally, Chagall did a small series of very important works on distinctly Jewish themes, in which he took a serious and deeply felt look at his roots. Careful scrutiny of these works reveals both several levels of personal meaning and a confrontation with the work of his former teacher Pen, with whom he was again in close contact, and the entire tradition of Eastern European Jewish painting. This emerges from his translation of Pen's *Shamash* (fig. 43) into his own style in *Jew in Red* (fig. 44), substituting a sack for the basket on his arm, and thus turning him into a Wandering Jew.[60] The main changes in the figure are stylistic: the treatment is slightly more naive, the hands foreshortened "incorrectly" and their color unreal – one is white, the other red like the flames in the background which have caused the Jew to set out on his wanderings.

Chagall also added a personal element here, which gives this representation a new perspective. On a pale background on the left, from which the Jew is almost entirely isolated, Chagall inscribed the names of Cimabue, El Greco, Fouquet, Van Gogh, and other European masters whose works he had seen in the Louvre, writing them in a strange combination of Latin and Cyrillic script, which is especially apparent in the central name: Brueghel-Mouzjik (peasant Brueghel). To this, he adds in Yiddish the name of Rembrandt, as though adopting the Christian artist who painted Jews into Judaism. The message of these names and their location can be interpreted in two ways. On the one hand, the sad wandering Jew lives in a totally different world than these august artists, a world which pushes Western art aside. He thus parallels Chagall, who feels that he has been exiled by the war from these artists. On the other hand, an attempt is being made to mold these artists – and Chagall's various personalities – into one whole by combining Cyrillic and Latin letters in their names,

43

44

calling Brueghel *a mouzjik*, and making Rembrandt a Jew.[61] Thus, while bringing Pen's work up to date, Chagall also expressed his own alienation from and re-identification with his roots.

This same message is found in his *Jew in Bright Red* and his *Jew in Green*, both of which also combine up-dated traditional Jewish types with texts, this time in Hebrew. In *Jew in Bright Red*, the depiction of the Jew himself is quite traditional, and is similar in kind to the type Altman had used in his own *Old Jew*, albeit in a more depressed condition.[62] His face, however, with the closed left eye and the right eye looking over to the side, may have been inspired by Hirszenberg's *Jeru-salem Jew*, reproduced in *Ost und West* in 1912.[63]

The more interesting comparison is, however, with *Jew in Green* (fig. 45), whose pose and dejected mood seem to have been inspired by two works repro-duced in *Ost und West*: Israels' *Son of an Ancient Peo-ple* (fig. 46), which depicts a second-hand dealer sit-ting almost on the ground, and shows the depths of despair to which this ancient people have sunk; and its source, Rembrandt's *Old Jew* (fig. 47), where the age of the figure and his position are very similar to those used by Chagall, while the position of the hands is an almost exact quotation.[64] This return to tradition

and to *Ost und West* was due to the renewed influence of Pen, both on a personal level, and because he would have insisted that his former student see the *Ost und West* article on him, in which Chagall himself was mentioned.

Next to these modernized traditional representations of Jews, Chagall inserted texts which had a national as well as a personal meaning. On the national level, they stated that the Jews were the Chosen People, an idea which – set against the sorrowful, almost pitiable Jews represented in these pictures – recalls Israels' ambiguous use of the title *Son of an Ancient People* for his Jewish second-hand dealer. On the personal level, the texts show Chagall's re-identification with his people: he even included his Hebrew name again – Moshe Sega[l] – in the middle of the inscriptions in *Jew in Bright Red*.[65] He was now more at peace with this identification than he had been in *The Pinch of Snuff*, even though he sees this process through depressed eyes. Because of this depression, both texts refer to Chagall's need to leave Vitebsk for Paris as well as to his return home to marry Bella. In these works, Chagall's symbolism had become more open: he wrote messages which fellow Jews could easily read rather than relying on them to understand his visual translation of Yiddish idioms. Indeed, after painting

45

46

47

48

*Over Vitebsk* at the beginning of his stay, with its visualization of the expression "going over the town," which means passing through town, he seems to have continued to use such idioms mainly in his drawings, often accompanying his figures with an inscription in Yiddish.[66] His strong sense of alienation had waned, and his works seem more relaxed and peaceful.

This lessening of tension is particularly evident in *Jew in Black and White* of 1914 (fig. 48), the first of the series that he exhibited in March 1915 in Moscow in a show meant to introduce his latest work to Russia.[67] Its mood is entirely opposed to the *Jew in Prayer* he had done in Paris. The 1914 Jew is rather a straightforward modernization of another traditional type, the revered, wise, Orthodox Jew in his prayer shawl and phylacteries, set in a pose similar to that of Altman's *Old Jew* but on an abstract background. The head is treated realistically, as is the left arm with the phylactery bands, and the stylization of the figure is kept to a minimum. He has even completely renounced his Fauve coloring here, creating instead an aesthetic play on the black and white of the prayer shawl, its stripes and serrated edge echoing the black phylactery bands to the right.[68]

It is no wonder that this painting had a strong effect on the young Jewish artists who saw it at the "Year 1915" exhibition in Moscow, which opened on April 1st: they hailed it as a masterpiece of modern Jewish art and proceeded to base their own style on it and on Chagall's Jewish themes in general.[69] The reasons for this evaluation become clear when one studies the Jewish "competition" in this show: Altman re-exhibited his Paris works, including *Jewish Funeral*, while Robert Falk showed only non-Jewish subjects. Chagall's painting appeared, on the other hand, both completely avant-garde, easily able to stand comparison with the works of the Burliuk brothers, Larionov and Goncharova, and it displayed a Jewish subject.[70]

As in his friendly "competition" with the Makhmadim group, Chagall perceived himself as having emerged victorious from this confrontation. He had proved himself both the leader of the Russian Jewish artists and a member in good standing of major avant-garde circles of Russian art.[71] As a result, he was not only finally able to marry Bella,[72] but, re-establishing himself in St. Petersburg, he also renewed his contact with Syrkin, from the Novyi voskhod group, and with Altman, who was shortly to be come extremely active in the organization of the revival of Jewish art, helping to found the Society for the Encouragement of Jewish Art with Chagall's old mentor, Ginzburg, in January 1916.[73] This contact, and the friendly competition between Chagall and Altman, may even have spurred the latter

to make a further statement as a Jewish artist in his sculpture *Portrait of a Young Jew (Self-Portrait)*, which he exhibited at the end of the following year.[74]

It was in this environment of growing interest in Jewish art that Chagall, while working at an army desk job, began to illustrate Yiddish books. Since there was a ban on publication, he exhibited them in St. Petersburg in December 1916 through January 1917.[75] His choice of texts is completely in keeping with his previous choice of styles. Two poems by Der Nister (the Hidden One), *The Rooster* (cat. $144_{1-5}$) and *The Little Kid* (cat. $144_{6-8}$), are deceptively childlike in style, hiding a more sophisticated, metaphysical message beneath the surface: the first poem involves the death of an old woman, while the second deals with a fantastic wandering goat who lulls a wakeful child to sleep, leaving his horns in her hands.[76] On the other hand, Y. L. Peretz's humorous, sarcastic approach to shtetl life represents an acute sharpening of Chagall's subtle irony. But the choice of *The Magician* is even more personal, as Chagall may well have identified with the magician who goes around in rags and a top hat, helping others but unable to provide for himself. On Passover eve, the magician comes to a house and conjures up a *seder* feast for a poor man and his wife (cat. 143), whereupon they recognize him as the prophet Elijah. The ambiguity of this figure undoubtedly appealed to Chagall: he looks Jewish down to his nose, but has no beard; he comes from Paris and, on the way to London, detours through an East European shtetl. He doesn't pray with the community, and when they try to pin down this strange being with questions, he disappears, turning up somewhere else. Both books are decorated with simple, literal drawings. However, these illustrations – along with Altman's illustrations for a children's book – opened the way for one of the most fruitful fields that artists interested in reviving Jewish culture pursued in the coming years.[77]

It may have been through the Society for the Encouragement of Jewish Art that Chagall got his commission to paint decorations for a Jewish secondary school housed in the building of the main synagogue of St. Petersburg in 1916-17. For this commission – his first for a Jewish organization – Chagall eschewed both Cubism and Realism, choosing his more easily comprehensible folk style, which he undoubtedly felt was not only the most suitable for a school, but would be most easily recognized as "Jewish," and would be in strong opposition to the "Moorish" architecture of the synagogue housing the school.[78]

That this is a "Jewish" style is evinced by the fact that Chagall based *The Feast of the Tabernacles* (fig. 49) on a representation of the Passover *seder* in the

*Mantua Haggadah* (fig. 50), a reproduction of which he found in *Ost und West*.[79] The composition is divided in a similar tripartite fashion, with the table in the center, in a separate room drawn in incorrect perspective. Instead of a servant presenting a dish to a whole family, Chagall merged the servant with the mother, setting her in the same position outside the *sukkah*, passing a dish through the window. The woman cooking on the right of the *Haggadah* illustration, has been turned into a small boy with a chicken, set in the same area in exactly the same pose. On the left, the beggar at the door – a traditional representation for a *seder* – has been transformed into a Jew holding a *lulav*, who is headed away from the *sukkah* to pray in the synagogue, although the only building visible behind him is a church. This kind of quotation of Jewish art became a basic ingredient of all the works Chagall did for Jewish institutions throughout his life.

Meanwhile, Chagall had been busy exhibiting. In November 1916 he showed 45 of his Vitebsk paintings at the "Jack of Diamonds" show in Moscow, including *Jew in Green, Holiday* and *Jew in Red*.[80] This show brought both him and Altman, who exhibited his *Portrait of a Young Jew*, into close contact with the Moscow Jewish artists, and led to their founding – along with Lissitzky, who was based in Moscow – the Union of Moscow Jewish Artists, which apparently merged shortly afterwards with the Moscow branch of the Society for the Encouragement of Jewish Art.[81]

This contact with other Jewish artists and the Society's interest in researching Jewish folk art, as well as Altman's slightly Cubistic versions of Jewish tombstones, may have inspired Chagall – once more in Vitebsk, with the Revolution raging around him – to return to a theme he had originally treated c. 1907-9: the Vitebsk cemetery. In 1917-18, he executed two paintings on this theme, one of which was simply a new version of his old painting, translated into a more Cubistic idiom but with somewhat more care being taken to depict both the tombstone decorations and the cemetery's thoroughly dilapidated condition. The facets in the sky add to the upheaval caused by those of the ground, and the way the tombstones fall over makes one feel that he has caught the scene just before its total destruction.[82]

On the other hand, the contemporary *Cemetery Gates*, although open to reveal the tombstones, has a more comforting message set forth on the pediment in phrases taken out of sequence and with spelling and quotation mistakes – from Ezekiel's "Vision of the Dry Bones" (Ezekiel 37:12,14), a text occasionally found on such gates: "Behold, I will open up your graves . . .[and raise] you up from your graves, my

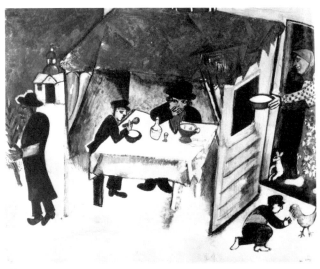

49

50

people, and I will bring you to the land [confused lettering] [and I will] put my spirit in you, and you will live." This message of hope is echoed in the facets of the sky, which, rather than disrupting the cemetery, repeat and harmonize with the shapes of the gateway, stressing its spiritual quality. This message would be equally appropriate to the Revolution in general, to the hopes it engendered among Russian Jews, and to the revival of Jewish art, all of which Chagall was involved with at the time.[83]

After the Revolution, Chagall's importance as a leader of Russian Jewish art was immensely enhanced by the publication of the book on him by Efros and Tugendkhold, hailing him as a great Jewish artist, and by his appointment as Art Commissar of Vitebsk in August 1918.[84] This appointment filled Chagall with enthusiasm and he immediately began rounding up teachers for his ideal art school, his selection indicating the ideals he had in mind. The staff he organized consisted for the most part of Jewish artists. He could not bring in Altman, who was a member of Narkompros in Petrograd and was fully occupied with the creation of a "proletarian art" in an increasingly abstract style.[85] However, he did import two fellow avant-garde Jewish artists, Falk and Ivan Puni, with his wife, and – after they left – two others who had taken part in the ethnographic expeditions, Yudovin and Lissitzky. He also brought in his own teachers, first Dobujinsky and, following him, Pen.[86] The predominance of Jews among the staff and the presence of his own teachers suggest that Chagall not only saw himself as founding an avant-garde school, but saw the school as a golden opportunity to carry on the work of the Society for the Encouragement of Jewish Art under his own leadership. At first, he concentrated on those artists whom he saw as being universally avant-garde, including a teacher who had helped form *this* part of his own personality. When this failed, he turned to those artists involved in the Jewish renaissance, and to the teacher who had formed *that* side of his personality. At this point, he undoubtedly saw Yudovin and Lissitzky as talented disciples working under his influence. He encouraged Yudovin to publish a brochure on Jewish folk art (cat. 170), recalling this book during his last visit to Israel, as a very important contribution to the field.

Chagall's relationship with Lissitzky at this time deserves special attention. Lissitzky, who had studied architecture after leaving Pen's studio, had recently become an extremely prolific book illustrator. Like Altman, he apparently began this work as part of the Russian avant-garde movement, and his 1916 cover for K. Bolshakov's *The Spent Sun* (fig. 56) is in the approved Cubo-Futurist style.[87] In his illustrations for Yiddish and Hebrew books, Lissitzky turned his back on this style, seeking one of his own, and eventually opting for a naive folk style with Cubist elements strongly influenced by Chagall. This is most clearly seen when his *Violinist* from the *White Russian Folktales* (cat. 108$_3$) is compared to Chagall's drawing and painting of a violinist from his Paris period. The pose and conception of the figure in the two drawings are very similar, down to the position of the feet, the awkward fingers holding the violin, the incorrect perspective of the bench, and the mixture of straight and curved geometric elements of which the violinist is composed. Furthermore, the checkered pattern of the background and the curled lines at the feet of the chair suggest that Lissitzky had seen either the original painting or a photograph of it.[88] Further influence is evident in a drawing for his *Ukrainian Folktales* (cat. 103$_4$), in which the pose of the woman and the overall composition are very similar to those in Chagall's unused sketch for Peretz's *The Magician* of 1915 (cat. 143), while the incorrect perspective of the house recalls the kind of perspective Chagall had developed in Paris and continued to use after returning to Russia.[89]

It is, however, with the *Had Gadya* illustrations of late 1918 that Chagall would have been most pleased, seeing in them the full development of a style of illustration based on his paintings. The goat was one of his favorite animals, and it had been featured in his 1915 illustrations for Der Nister (cat. 144$_{6-8}$) in the same pose and naturalistic style favored by Lissitzky (cat. 90, 90$_{10}$). The way this animal prances in from the side, half cut off by the frame, in the frontispiece and last illustration of *Had Gadya* can be seen almost as echoing several of the farm animals in Chagall's works.[90] Even the strong geometric elements in these illustrations would have pleased Chagall: had he not used them at least equally forcibly in his Paris works, from *The Wedding,* through *I and the Village, Russian Village from the Moon* and *Golgotha,* to *Homage to Apollinaire*?[91] Thus he would doubtless have cheerfully welcomed Lissitzky to Vitebsk, seeing in him his most successful "beloved disciple."

Chagall's exaltation during this period is expressed in his contribution to the decoration of Vitebsk in November 1918. He not only filled the town with his distinctive figures and animals, but made a clear, personal statement in *The Traveller* (fig. 51, cat. 145), inscribing it originally, "Onward, onward without a Pause." This image is, in fact, a "portrait" of the artist, as it perfectly interprets his name: "Chagall" means "march forward." He hints at this meaning in quoting Mayakovski's pun on his name: "God grant that everyone may *chagalle* like Chagall."[92] This "chagalling" traveler thus expresses both his identification with the Revolution and his feelings on his own progress as an artist.

Kasimir Malevich's arrival – whether precipitated by Vera Ermolaeva, Lissitzky or Chagall himself – and his takeover of the school at the end of 1919 thus proved to be a stunning double blow to Chagall's ego.[93] Malevich's Suprematist style not only appealed to the students as being more comprehensible and revolutionary than Chagall's teachings, but it could be shown to be more "Jewish" in its adherence to the Second Commandment. Here Chagall found himself once more confronted with the theoretical arguments of which he complained in his 1922 article, and the results – as he suggested – were catastrophic, at least for himself. Lissitzky's "betrayal" of him in wholeheartedly supporting Malevich was a crime he never forgave, and he comments on it in his autobiography without "soiling his pen" with either his name or that of Malevich: "My most zealous disciple swore friendship and devotion to me. To hear him, I was his Messiah. But the moment he was appointed professor, he went over to my opponents' camp and heaped insults and ridicule upon me."[94]

Despite this, Malevich's art and personality were so persuasive that Chagall himself succumbed, trying to

51

understand the style that had defeated him. His attempts in this direction are fascinating for what they reveal about his reaction to events. The most Suprematist works of this series – *Profile at the Window, Joy of Living, Man with Whip, The Circus, Composition with Circles and a Goat* and *Composition with Goat* – show Chagall making a serious effort to work out a Suprematist composition, but categorically unable to refrain from including figurative elements from his own folk style.[95] He tries here to find a way to adapt the new style to his own ends just as he had previously adapted Cubism and Fauvism. However, Suprematism had too many painful connections for it to become part of Chagall's own style. In fact, his pain at the blow to his self-esteem is set forth all too clearly in these works. In all but two of the paintings mentioned above, Chagall "repossesses" his goat from Lissitzky. This is particularly evident in the way the half-figure of the goat enters the painting in *Composition with Circles and a Goat*, cheerfully watching the Suprematist circles knock his opponent over, and in the way he trots in from behind the large rectangle which has blotted out all but the feet of the man on the left in *Composition with Goat*. In *Man with Whip*, he reclaims his juxtaposition of animal and human heads, which Lissitzky had used in his frontispiece, reminding us through the man with a whip who had appeared beside the goat in *Rain* that this whole symbolism was invented by him during his Paris period.[96]

These esoteric meanings become still plainer in *Cubist Landscape*, done in Vitebsk either during the fight or during his abortive return there in 1920.[97] Here Chagall turned to the composition he had used to stress his sense of alienation and identification in *Jew in Red*. The main area on the right is composed of Cubist elements of the kind Chagall had used in Paris, even including a panel of *trompe-l'oeil* wood graining and a piece of wallpaper at the upper left. He thus stressed his own use of this style before Malevich had adopted it. Although the main areas are abstract, he sets them around figurative elements: an eye, a naive depiction of the Vitebsk Academy, and suggestions of a Cubist face in the pink area. This combination may at first recall Malevich's juxtaposition of a cow and violin in a Cubist composition, and some of the details may even be based on that work. However, this is not being done in emulation of Malevich, but as part of the battle with him over priority and leadership.[98] This is evinced both by the representation of the Academy building in the center of the composition, and by the area on the left, where instead of writing the names of the artists he loves as he did in *Jew in Red*, Chagall endlessly repeats his own name in Latin and Cyrillic letters and once even in Hebrew, setting them between the Russian words for "Art School."[99] Another work, *Collage*

52

(fig. 52), done after June 1921, is even more explicit, but its message is now addressed directly to the Russian *Jewish* public. Here Chagall has pasted two inscriptions onto a purely abstract composition. The first, in Hebrew, enclosed in a triangle, proclaims Justice (צדק). The second, in Russian, separated from the first by a mottled black band which serves as a level on a fulcrum, is cut out of the invitation to the exhibition of Chagall's murals for the Jewish Theatre in Moscow.[100] The clipping stresses the word "Chagall" and lists four of his works. Here, Chagall is not only demonstrating his ability to do abstract compositions at will, he is also demanding justice, setting in the balance the proof of his importance: his new wall paintings for the Jewish Theatre, a commission which had come as balm to his wounded ego.

The 1920-21 murals for the Jewish Theatre were, in fact, Chagall's clearest claim to a major role in the Jewish art revival, and they perfectly blend his various styles – folkic art, Cubism, Fauvism and Realism – and bear inscriptions in Hebrew or little folk-art animals to stress the Jewish context.[101] This is even true of the almost abstract design for *Love on the Stage*, in which the man's shoes are decorated with Hebrew letters, those on his left foot indicating that the stage is in the "Yiddish theat[re]." In the other scenes, he used a particularly Jewish group of characters to symbolize the arts: the *klezmer* fiddler as *Music*; a woman dancing

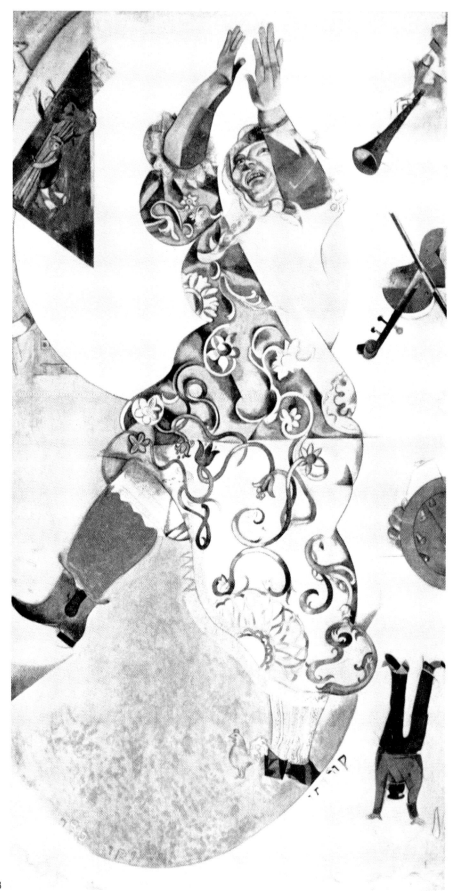

at a wedding to the popular Jewish wedding tune "The Voice of the Groom, the Voice of the Bride" for *Dance* (fig. 53); the *badkhan* who makes people laugh and cry at weddings for *Theatre*; and the Torah scribe for *Literature*.[102] It is with the latter that Chagall identifies by setting a cow above his head, from whose mouth the name "Chagall" emerges in Hebrew with the "l" reversed.

Chagall appears in person in the largest mural (fig. 82), along with Efros, who had helped him get the commission, and Granovsky, the director – each one carefully labeled in Hebrew. However in the names of Chagall and Granovsky, the Hebrew letters are composed as in Russian, from right to left. Much has been written about this mural, its *klezmer* band and Jewish acrobats,[103] but it is in some of the small details that Chagall reveals his ideas on Jewish art and his place within it. Thus at the very top of the composition, he set his version of the St. Petersburg synagogue, with its distinctive double-arched window above a row of columns, the building which was to have housed his murals for the Jewish high school.[104] In like manner, he added a Torah ark curtain decorated with the Tablets of the Law directly behind his head (fig. 54) as *his* background, and in part Efros's, but definitely not Granovsky's. Directly below his portrait, at the bottom of the wall, he did a variation on the hand emerging from a cloud holding a shofar, probably from the Mohilev synagogue, with which Yudovin and Malkin had decorated the back cover of their folder *Jewish Folk Ornament* (cat. 170$_{29}$).[105] He then did his own variations on these disembodied hands holding an instrument: in the central area near the goat, hands hold a drum (as they hold a tambourine to the right of *Dance*), and below – in typical Chagallian fashion – he reversed the imagery, setting disembodied *feet* beside a fiddle. To balance the hands on the right of the mural, he set a fiddler in front of a variation of the cemetery entrance from his 1917-18 painting. Thus the repeated stress on his "forefather," the painter of the Mohilev synagogue, in connection with these murals was not just a written device, but a translation of his pictorial declaration there and even a clue to his message: he is both heir to the Jewish traditions of his "forefather," an innovator in modern Jewish art, and the natural leader of that art because of his background and works.

A further statement is made in his curtain decoration of a "two-headed" goat against an abstract background, which is related to a drawing of a bearded man standing behind a goat.[106] The latter follows the traditional design of *Had Gadya*, and here as well as in his curtain design and his insertion of a goat into the scene in the center of his mural, Chagall "reclaims" his goat, setting it forth clearly as his own in the theatre

designs with which he hoped to overcome Lissitzky's "betrayal."

This "in-fighting" is also apparent on another level in the choice of the Jewish wedding as a leitmotif for the arts. Although Chagall does not explain this choice, he gives us several clues in his writings on his work for the theatre in Moscow. Chagall says he saw these murals as an expression of his ideas on modernizing and regenerating the Yiddish theatre. He stressed that the actor Solomon Mikhoels found in them a new way of acting. He also tells us that he was invited to design the costumes and sets for *The Dybbuk* at Habimah, something he had wished to do at least since An-Sky had broached the idea to him during the war. He prepared sketches with which he went to see the director, J. B. Vachtangov, and Nahum Zemach, but his ideas on the design and staging of the play were rejected. In one version, he says that Vachtangov spent a year studying his sketches, in another that he spent hours studying the murals at the Kamerny. This discrepancy is not a mistake, but a slip that indicates that the *klezmer*, the dancer and the *badkhan* set under a frieze that Chagall has designated "The Table for the Wedding Feast" may actually be based on his designs for the big wedding scene in the second act of *The Dybbuk*.[107]

Meanwhile, Chagall was busy designing the opening three playlets by Shalom Aleichem for the Kamerny, which premiered in January 1921. His designs here resume his battle with Suprematism. The decor of the train for *The Agents* is basically abstract, and Chagall heightened the Constructivist effect in the final staging of the scene (fig. 84) by removing the locomotive and most of the Hebrew writing he had drawn in his original sketch (fig. 83).[108] The design for *The Lie* is primarily a backdrop utilizing a rectangle inscribed with a few words in Yiddish, around which figures and objects behave in an unnatural way, as Chagallian motifs overshadow abstract ones. The sketch for *Mazeltov* (fig. 85), on the other hand, shows a fully Chagallian interior, with a tilted table and chairs, an upside-down painting of a goat on the wall, and an inscription in which parts of the letters are missing. It seems to read "Aleichem Shalom," not only a reversal of the author's name, but the traditional answer to the greeting which makes up his name: "Peace be with you" – "With you be peace."[109] In this set, only the large, black quadrant on the left, the beam across the ceiling and the material rectangle at the right recall Suprematist or Constructivist compositions. After the setback in Vitebsk, Chagall now felt fulfilled: not in the provinces, but in Moscow itself, he had proved himself not only a second Antokolski, but a second Bakst, a worthy heir to his teacher.[110]

54, detail

54

This euphoria did not last long. Altman arrived in Moscow and, after designing Mayakovski's *Mystery-Bouffe* in June 1921 – just at the time of the exhibition of Chagall's wall paintings – he was given the coveted commission for *The Dybbuk*, under conditions that filled Chagall with envy. Whereas Chagall had to make costumes out of second-hand clothes, painting them – and the actors – almost as they went on stage, Altman could order any cut and material he liked.[111] Furthermore, Altman's set for act 1 must have seemed to Chagall a variation on his own *Mazeltov* set. Whereas Altman's original sketch shows a fairly naturalistic representation of a synagogue, his final version – as seen in his sketch (fig. 86, cat. 19) – has a lot in common with Chagall's sketch. The entrance is from the left, from a geometric area (a quadrant in Chagall's version and a set of rectangles in Altman's), in front of which stands a table and two chairs at exactly the same angle. Altman's Ark of the Covenant with its folk motifs and animals at the top is set in the background, where Chagall had placed small pieces of furniture dominated by his upside-down goat, while the right side of the stage contains a main object – the stove or the *bimah* (Torah reader's podium) – dominated by a large, flat sign with Hebrew writing.[112] However, a comparison of both sets shows that out of this conglomeration, Altman created a unified set, using the rectangular "flag" forms he had developed in his decorations for *Storming of the Winter Palace* in Petrograd in October 1918 as a frame.[113] Furthermore, instead of Chagall's light fantasy, as seen in the goat and the unintelligible inscription, Altman's set makes sense,

and the inscription "Hear O Israel" sets the correct atmosphere for the first act.[114] Moreover, while Chagall's design is primarily a background set, Altman uses space more theatrically: he has steps which provide various levels for the action, the possibility of appearing behind the *bimah*, etc. In other words, Altman has not only been influenced by Chagall, but has had the nerve to go him one better!

The same is true of the costume sketches (figs. 88–89, cat. 21–26). Whether Altman created their sharp and awkward poses or the movements of the actors inspired him, the fact remains that these poses and many of the details have no precedents in Altman's art or theatre designs – while they do have precedents in Chagall's paintings, especially in his murals, as well as in his costume designs. On the other hand, Altman's designs, and particularly his faces, are much more expressionistically grotesque than are Chagall's light-hearted figures.[115] In fact, if Altman's sketches of the beggars in the wedding scene are compared with Chagall's approach to this scene in his murals (fig. 82), one will become convinced that Chagall's style was much too joyful for the drama involved in An-Sky's tragedy. Yet anyone who has seen the second act of *The Dybbuk* will be struck by its transformation of Chagall's view of the shtetl, which is present at the beginning of the act, and seems to have dominated not only its conception by his fellow artists but that of the actors and even of Vachtangov himself, into an increasingly grotesque and frightening Expressionist experience far beyond Chagall's ken.[116]

Chagall was present at the dress rehearsal of *The Dyb-buk*, which premiered on January 31, 1922, and pro-claimed it an "act of genius,"[117] but it marked the end of his friendship with Altman, and heightened his bitter-ness over his treatment in Russia. To add insult to in-jury, Granovsky invited Altman to design the sets and costumes for *Uriel Accosta* at what Chagall consid-ered to be *his* theatre. Altman not only accepted, but he again did a more successful variation on a Chagall set: the truncated arch and rectangular forms he used in one of his sets for this play recall and improve upon Chagall's Constructivist set for *The Agents* (fig. 84).[118]

Chagall's feeling of betrayal by his comrades found expression in the tone he gave to the ending of *My Life*, and it colored his view of the Jewish revival move-ment, which he called a "misfortune." His revolt against this situation led him to write his declaration that *he* would create modern Jewish art. He tried to rectify matters by exhibiting his theatre designs together with works by Altman and Shterenberg, and expressed his own sorrow by publishing his drawings for David Hofstein's *Troyer* (Mourning) (cat. 150).[119] When this failed to improve things, he decided to leave Russia, which he now felt had refused to award him the place he deserved, and went to Berlin, where another Jewish revival was in progress. There he studied with the "Pen" of that group, Hermann Struck.[120]

Chagall's phrasing of his determination to create a Jewish art illuminates the path he now set for himself – a different one from that trodden by the Revivalists. He does not say "They wanted to – they created a Moses," or a "David," or a "Maimonides," but rather "a Christ" and "a Marx," specifically choosing two Jews who had abandoned Judaism, and created in its place the two international movements that dominated Rus-sia. Instead of perpetuating the more Jewish part of his personality, now that he had soured on the revival movement, he embraced a more universalist position, and he continued to do so until he came up against Fascism. This threat drove him back to a concern for his people, and even inspired him to visit Poland, where he – like the Russian ethnographers – did paint-ings of synagogue interiors "to preserve them."[121] Fi-nally, the internationalist artist returned to his roots – and even to the use of Yudovin and Malkin's *Jewish Folk Ornament* – for the only synagogue commission he received, at the Hadassah-Hebrew University Medi-cal Center in Jerusalem.[122] At long last, he – like his "forefather" – had a synagogue to decorate, and pro-duced his own sophisticated version of the Jewish folk-art animals that were "in his blood."

\* I would like to thank Mirjam Rajner, Helena Tolstoy-Segal, Yerahmiel Cohen, Moshe Barasch and Rachel Sukman for their help with the Russian and Yiddish texts utilized here.

1 A reference to Jews in the post-revolutionary period who were rejecting their past and assimilating. Moshe Litvakov was a Jewish writer who tried to put Yiddish culture to the service of the Communist party, which he joined in 1919. In 1921, he became a leading member of the Yevsektsiya in Moscow (*Ency-clopedia Judaica*, Jerusalem: Keter, 1971-72, vol. 11, pp. 404-5).

2 Herwarth Walden, originally Georg Lewin, was the Jewish editor of *Der Sturm* magazine in Berlin and organizer of exhibi-tions of modern art to which Chagall had contributed. Jean Metzinger and Albert Gleizes were Cubist painters in Paris with whom Chagall was friendly. They all apparently warned him about the "Jewish" elements in his art, which were unfashiona-ble before World War I.

3 Shul– or synagogue-clappers, often elaborately carved, were sounded to wake people for early morning prayers.

4 Abram Efros was a Jewish art critic who wrote both on Cha-gall and on Jewish art. Isaac Levitan was a famous Russian Jewish landscape painter usually classified with the Wander-ers, and Chagall had copied some of his works in his youth (John E. Bowlt, *The Silver Age: Russian Art of the Early Twenti-eth Century and the "World of Art" Group*, Newtonville: Oriental Research Partners, 1979, pp. 24-27 and opp. p. 91; Marc Cha-gall, *My Life*, New York: Orion, 1960, p. 97; and Franz Meyer, *Marc Chagall*, New York: Harry N. Abrams, 1963, p. 57, and cat. no. 6).

5 Marc Chagall, "Bletlakh" (in Yiddish), *Shtrom*, no. 1, 1922, pp. 44-46, repeated with minor changes in Marc Chagall, "Eygens" (in Yiddish), *Die Zukunft*, June 1925, pp. 409-10.

6 Chagall repeated his claim to this relationship in 1928 in con-nection with his work in the Jewish theatre (Marc Chagall, "Meyn Arbet in Moskver Yidishen Kamer-Theater" [in Yiddish], *Di Yidishe Velt*, no. 2, May 1928, pp. 276-82, reprinted in *Di Goldene Keyt*, no. 43, 1962, pp. 170-74), where he suggests that Segal also painted in Lyozno, and in Chagall, *My Life*, p. 159. Although his claim is not usually accepted, it is at least pos-sible. Chagall's Hebrew name, as he signed it on *The Pinch of Snuff* of c. 1912-14, was "Moshe Segal" (Meyer, p. 195), and both Vitebsk and Lyozno, his maternal grandfather's town, are closer to Mohilev than is Slutsk, Chaim ben Isaac Halevi Segal's hometown. In fact, Lyozno was in Tsarist times part of the Mohilev district, and it was in that district that Chagall's birth was registered (ibid., p. 21). On the other hand, we know practi-cally nothing about Segal other than the fact that he painted in the Mohilev synagogue in 1740, and possibly also in those of nearby Kopys, which is north of Mohilev in the direction of Vitebsk, and in Dolginovo, which is equidistant from Slutsk, Vi-tebsk, Mohilev and Vilna (David Davidovitch, *Tziyurai Kir B'vatai Knesset B'Polyn* [in Hebrew], Jerusalem: Bialik Institute, 1968, pp. 46-48 and pl. 21; and Rachel Wischnitzer, *The Architecture of the European Synagogue*, Philadelphia: Jewish Publication Society of America, 1964, pp. 141-44). Whether or not the rela-tionship did in fact exist, Chagall is clearly using it here for ideo-logical purposes. One must also take into account that he may have been acquainted from childhood with other synagogue paintings in Vitebsk and Lyozno that have been neither docu-mented nor preserved.

7 Chagall, *My Life*, p. 85. *My Life* was written, apparently in Russian (Meyer, p. 313, and note at the end of "Meyn Arbet,"

*Di Yidishe Velt*, p. 282), as Chagall left Russia and constantly revised before its publication. It was conceived – like Gauguin's *Noa Noa*, which had just been published in Russian in 1918 with a frontispiece by Lissitzky, and was thus known to Chagall – to reintroduce his "exotic" subject matter to the European public. This point is underlined by Chagall himself when he ironically states: "It's all one to me if people are pleased and relieved to discover in those innocent adventures of my relatives the enigma of my pictures. How little that interests me! My dear fellow-citizens, help yourselves!" (*My Life*, p. 13). The facts related in this book must therefore be taken with an even larger grain of salt than is usually required when reading a memoir. In it, Chagall plays with the reader as he does with the spectator of his paintings. He drops hints of important Jewish contacts in Russia, using names which mean little or nothing to the Western reader, without explaining their true value to him. In the Yiddish versions of his autobiography, many of these names are either missing or played down, as the Yiddish reader might be more aware of who they were.

8   The period to be studied is still shrouded in uncertainty, compounded by Chagall's habit of affixing dates to his early works at a later time and lumping the dates together in a highly impressionistic fashion, so that "1908" does not mean that the date is 1908, but that the painting was done before Chagall went to Paris (see also Meyer, pp. 10-11 and 143). Although it is impossible to redate these works at the moment, we may re-evaluate them in connection to the problem under discussion.

9   S. An-Sky, "Jurij Paen," *Ost und West*, vol. 12, August 1912, pp. 733-40ff. Also see the same article, with an additional picture, in *Novyi voskhod*, no. 38, 1912, pp. 31-36; and Fr. Dr. Patai, "Der Maler der jüdischen Mutter," *Aus alter und neuer Zeit*, January 2, 1931, p. 194. Information on Eastern European artists was disseminated through *Ost und West*, and they all await more up-to-date studies. The date Chagall began studying with Pen is problematic. Meyer (p. 616) sets it in 1906, when Chagall would have been 18-19 years old, which seems rather late considering Chagall claims he was in the "fifth form" at the time (Chagall, *My Life*, pp. 52-58). Chagall claimed to have studied there for barely two months (ibid., p. 58), which is doubtful, considering the debt he owed to Pen. The problem of dating is compounded by his tales of courting girls and painting at the same time, which he seems to have begun when he was 14-15 years old (ibid., pp. 68 and 70; and Chagall, "Eygens," *Die Zukunft*, May 1925, p. 291). Chagall may have minimized Pen's influence on him after becoming exasperated with him during 1920, a feeling reflected in the version of his autobiography quoted in Walter Erben, *Marc Chagall*, New York: Frederick A. Praeger, 1957, p. 70. At the time he wrote the final versions of his autobiography, he felt neglected by Pen, who had not answered his letters (Marc Chagall, "Moi pervie uchitelya" [in Russian], *Rassviet*, Paris, no. 4, 1927, pp. 6-7). On the other hand, he had previously respected him enough to show one hundred of his works in an exhibition of Vitebsk artists that he organized in 1918 (Meyer, p. 265), and in his 1927 article, he begged people not to forget Pen.

10   The problem of the degree to which Chagall was amenable to academic training is difficult. Although some of the works of this period – e.g., *Old Man* (Meyer, cat. no. 2), which is very close to Pen's recordings of old Jews (An-Sky, "Paen," pp. 739-40, 743-46), and the drawings illustrated in *Marc Chagall*,

*Oeuvres sur papier*, Paris: Centre Georges Pompidou, June 30-October 8, 1984, nos. 1 verso, 2-3 – show considerable ability for a beginner, others, such as *Woman with Basket* and *The Musicians* (Meyer, pp. 54-55), combine well-drawn elements – parts of the woman's face and the head and upper body of the musician on the left – with a clumsy rendering of hands and legs. The question is whether these are willful distortions, as Chagall later claimed (ibid., p. 47), or show an inability on the part of the young artist. This problem, which is especially important in determining Chagall's connection with folk art, will unfortunately remain impossible to evaluate until more of his early works have been discovered and set in chronological order. The problem is further complicated by the other ideas he may have absorbed in Pen's studio, by his early realistic portrait of one of his sisters on the reverse side of the "naïve" *The Ball* (*Chagall*, Paris, 1984, no. 1), and by his return to academic portraiture in 1914, which will be discussed below.

11   *Ost und West* was a Zionist monthly issued in Berlin which sponsored a revival of Jewish art, and included articles on Jewish art and artists, along with coverage of other cultural fields. It was profusely illustrated, and thanks to its need to advertise itself, we can be sure that copies were available throughout Russia, for instance in Vitebsk, Vinnitsa (Altman's hometown), Mohilev and St. Petersburg (distributor's list, *Ost und West*, vol. 4, July 1904, p. i).

12   Meyer, cat. no. 33; "Sie Wandern . . .," *Ost und West*, vol. 4, August-September 1904, pp. 553-62ff; and B. Samuel, "Samuel Hirszenberg," ibid., October 1904, pp. 665-74 and passim. Chagall seems to have added to his sketch the two figures from Max Fabian's *Emigrants* of 1902, also published ibid., June 1904, pp. 369-70. Further and rather more startling proof that Chagall was familiar with these early volumes, and may even have had copies of his own, is given by the extremely strong resemblance between several of his self-portraits and the reproductions illustrating "Maurice Heyman's 'Symphonie d'expressions'," (*Ost und West*, vol. 5, January 1905, pp. 35-44). Thus the expression of the model in *Pain III* (p. 37) and *Scorn III* (p. 44) should be compared to two of Chagall's highly expressive self-portraits, the second of which he dated to 1911 (Eberhard W. Kornfeld, *Verzeichnis der Kupferstiche, Radierungen und Holzschnitte von Marc Chagall*, Berne: Kornfeld und Klipstein, 1970, vol. 1, nos. 42-43; and Meyer, p. 19). He apparently combined the types of expression he found in this source with reminiscences of Rembrandt's self-portraits (A. Bredius and H. Gerson, *Rembrandt Paintings*, London: Phaidon, 1971, pls. 25 and 5, respectively).

13   See, for instance, S. B., "Die 'Hagada'," and Binjamin Segal, "Synagogale Kunst," *Ost und West*, vol. 1, April 1901, pp. 259-68, 275-90. These articles featured details of Eastern European synagogue decoration (pp. 281-82) as well as *Haggadah* illustrations close in style to those of the Russian *lubki* and Jewish folk-art prints with which Chagall would have been familiar (e.g., pp. 289-90 and 311-12). Also see S. Weissenberg, "Juedische Kunst und Juedisches Kult– und Hausgeraet," ibid., vol. 3, March 1903, pp. 201-6; Ben Samuel, "Synagogale Kunst," ibid., June 1903, pp. 417-22; illustrations from the *Sarajevo Haggadah* (ibid., vol. 4, March 1904, pp. 197-98); and Theodor Zlocisti, "Die Haggadah von Mantua (1560)," ibid., April 1904, pp. 265-82. The latter included *lubok*-like prints as well as Hebrew letters illuminated with animals and heads in the way Chagall was later to use during his second Russian period (e.g., fig.

27, cat. 151). This art was also given a prestigious place in the major exhibition of modern Jewish art (Berlin, Galerie für alte und neue Kunst, "Ausstellung Jüdischer Künstler," November-December 1907, pp. 10-13), which was reviewed by Alfred Nossig ("Ausstellung Jüdischer Künstler," *Ost und West*, vol. 7, December 1907, pp. 743-52ff) in an article which raised many of the basic questions on the essence of modern Jewish art.

14 Meyer, cat. no. 7. For comparison to cemetery photographs, see Max Grunwald, "Portugiesengraeber auf Deutscher Erde," *Ost und West*, vol. 2, August 1902, pp. 527-34; and Josef Winternitz, "Der alte Prager Jüdische Friedhof," ibid., vol. 4, February 1904, pp. 119-28. For the more popular manner of depicting cemeteries as a background for mourners, see Hirszenberg's painting (ibid., vol. 2, October 1902, pp. 685-86). It should be noted in this context that Boris Aronson and Issachar Ryback stated in 1919 that Chagall had admired Jewish folk art in tombstone and synagogue decorations in his childhood (see Appendix).

15 Sophie Lissitzky-Küppers, *El Lissitzky*, London: Thames and Hudson, 1968, pp. 15-16; Ossip Zadkine, *Le Maillet et le Ciseau*, Paris: Albin Michel, 1968, pp. 47-48. See also the misdated encounter between Zadkine and Lissitzky in Eindhoven, Stedelijk van Abbemuseum, *El Lissitzky*, December 3, 1965-January 16, 1966, p. 60. Information on Yudovin is courtesy of Mirjam Rajner.

16 Chagall, *My Life*, pp. 79-81; and Meyer, p. 50. For information on Ilya Ginzburg, see Lothar Brieger-Wasservogel, "Elias Jacowlewitsch Guenzburg," *Ost und West*, vol. 4, March 1904, pp. 162-68, 192, 195-96, 201-2, 205 and 210. The illustrations emphasize his interest in children. Ginzburg also wrote an article on Jewish national art in *Ost und West*, vol. 5, October-December 1905, pp. 703-8, 775-80, in which he stated – as Chagall would later – that although artists were individuals, their backgrounds and nationality influenced them. He added that nationalism in art was the best kind of cosmopolitanism, as in it each people was free to express itself, and this, in the long run, would bring different peoples closer together. He also lectured on Jewish art at the Jewish Academy run by David Guenzburg. For information on this background, see Avram Kampf, "In Quest of the Jewish Style in the Era of the Russian Revolution," *Journal of Jewish Art*, vol. 5, 1978, pp. 49-51.

17 By 1912, An-Sky knew about Chagall, as he mentions him as one of Pen's students who was exhibiting in Paris (An-Sky, "Paen," p. 740).

18 *Encyclopedia Judaica*, vol. 16, pp. 152-53. Chagall was undoubtedly aware of Vinaver's activities at this time, as he was apparently acquainted with his whole family: it was Vinaver's brother-in-law, Leopold Sev, who gave him an introduction to Bakst c. 1908 (Chagall, *My Life*, p. 87; and Meyer, pp. 57-59). See also Marc Chagall, "Pamyati M. M. Vinavera" (in Russian), *Rassviet*, Paris, no. 43, 1926, p. 11.

19 Chagall (ibid., loc. cit.) and Meyer (p. 57) mistakenly called him N. G. Syrkin. The original paper, *Voskhod*, which is the name Chagall used, ceased publication in 1906, and so cannot be the paper in question. It and its successor, *Novyi voskhod*, were the Russian-language organs of assimilated Jews who had not yet cut their ties with Judaism. In 1899, *Voskhod* was acquired by Vinaver and a group of his colleagues, with the intention to serve Jews through developing their national consciousness (*Encyclopedia Judaica*, vol. 16, pp. 225-27). This continued to be the goal when they resumed publication as

*Novyi voskhod* in 1910. Chagall's story here is close to that which he told of his Paris days. He describes himself as painting while listening to the newspaper staff at work in the same room: "My thoughts on art mingled with the voices of the editors who came to discuss and work" (Chagall, *My Life*, pp. 97-98). For an example of Syrkin's articles, published while Chagall lived in the office, see *Novyi voskhod*, no. 11, March 18, 1910, pp. 27-30. He continued writing on the subject throughout the year. It is interesting in this context that Chagall dated his earliest consciously primitivizing works to 1908, the year the Society was founded, although the paintings may well have been done in 1909 and were only exhibited in 1909-10 (Meyer, pp. 28, 92-93). This date may also have been inspired by a wish to achieve chronological parity with the Burliuks, Larionov and Goncharova, who exhibited their first Neo-Primitivist works that year (J. C. Marcadé, "Chronologie du Futurisme Russe," *Europe*, vol. 53, April 1975, p. 209).

20 For information on the Zvantseva school, see Bowlt, *The Silver Age*, pp. 230-31. Although Chagall only mentions Bakst in his autobiography and his relationship with this teacher was undoubtedly helped by the fact that they both came from a similar Jewish background, he was also close to Dobujinsky. This can be seen by the fact that he later invited Dobujinsky to teach in the Vitebsk art academy (ibid., p. 255).

21 Ibid., pp. 217-18. It is interesting in the light of what has been said above about his other Jewish contacts in St. Petersburg that, writing of their first meeting, Chagall stressed Bakst's Jewish appearance, his background, and the "strange" juxtaposition on his walls of "paintings of Greek gods" and a "black velvet altar-curtain, from a synagogue, embroidered in silver" (Chagall, *My Life*, pp. 87-88).

22 Rachel Bernstein-Wischnitzer, "Umschau: Jüdische Kunst in Kiev und Petrograd (1918-1920)," *Der Jude*, vol. 5, 1920-21, p. 354; Donald E. Gordon, *Modern Art Exhibitions 1900-1916*, Munich: Prestel, 1974, vol. 2, p. 112, nos. 125 and 136, and p. 267, nos. 64 and 80; Bowlt, *The Silver Age*, pp. 264-65 and opp. p. 118; Berlin: Akademie der Künste, *Sieg über die Sonne*, September 1-October 9, 1983, pp. 15, 187 and 189. Wischnitzer stresses that since Dobujinsky was not Jewish, he painted these scenes like Romantic landscapes, unlike Chagall's more intimate approach. Tugendkhold was the first critic to mention Dobujinsky's influence on Chagall (A. Efross and J. Tugendhold, *Die Kunst Marc Chagalls*, Potsdam: Gustav Kiepenheuer, 1921, p. 34, translated from the Russian edition of 1918). Also see Susan Compton, *Chagall*, London: Royal Academy of Arts, 1985, pp. 32-33. For an example of this influence, compare Dobujinsky's placement of a funeral cortege between an organ-grinder's monkey and a poster with a laughing woman and a portion of a word, *kaka* (excrement), on it in *Autumn* of 1905, with Chagall's use of acrobats, clowns and a woman pouring water on the head of a mourner in a like situation in *Kermesse* (Bowlt, *The Silver Age*, opp. p. 252 and p. 265; and Meyer, p. 79).

23 Gordon, p. 298, no. 79; and Leo Bakst, "Puti klassitzizma v iskusstv," *Apollon*, no. 3, 1909, pp. 54-61. See also Bowlt, *The Silver Age*, p. 260. Marcadé ("Chronologie," p. 210) states that children's art had become so popular by the end of 1909 that it was exhibited at the first Salon of Vl. Izdebski in Odessa in December 1909-February 1910, an exhibition in which Altman participated, although neither Altman nor children's drawings are mentioned in connection with this exhibition by Gordon (pp.

356-62). This interest in children's art could not but find an echo in an artist who constantly reiterates in his autobiography his refusal to grow up (Chagall, *My Life*, pp. 46-47, 49, 51, 65, 67-68, 71 and 107).

24 Chagall had previously studied under Nicholas Roerich, an associate of Bakst, at the art school of the Society for the Encouragement of Jewish Art, where Chagall was exposed not only to Roerich's academic style, but to his interest in Russian folk art, especially in his work for the theatre (Camilla Gray, *The Great Experiment: Russian Art 1863-1922*, London: Thames and Hudson, 1962, pp. 40-41; Bowlt, *The Silver Age*, pp. 29, 42, opp. p. 42 and opp. p. 118; and Compton, *Chagall*, p. 32). The interrelationship between Larionov, Goncharova and Chagall, all of whom were apparently influenced by Roerich's ideas, is highly problematic as none of their dates from this period has been adequately fixed. It is clear, however, that Chagall reacted to some of Larionov's works. For instance, his *Barber* of 1912 is later than Larionov's version of this theme, which was exhibited in St. Petersburg in March 1910, while Chagall was still there (Meyer, *Chagall*, cat. no. 116; Berlin, *Sieg über die Sonne*, 1983, p. 153; and Gordon, p. 380, no. 76). Chagall's sketch *The Ball*, usually dated c. 1907, which is unlikely, seems also to be based on Larionov's *Cafe* of c. 1907 rather than on Van Gogh, who had influenced Larionov (*Chagall*, Paris, 1984, no. 1; and Waldemar George, *Larionov*, Paris: Bibliothèque des Arts, 1966, p. 71). On the other hand, Larionov's and Goncharova's Jewish subject matter may well have been influenced by Chagall, whose work they exhibited in 1912 at the "Donkey's Tail" and in the "Target" show, in which their own paintings of Jews were exhibited (Mary Chamot, *Goncharova, Stage Designs and Paintings*, London: Oresko, 1979, p. 40; and Gordon, p. 565, no. 286, and pp. 708-9, nos. 125-27, 34, 36, 39 and 80). See also Jean-Claude Marcadé, "Le contexte russe de l'oeuvre de Chagall," *Chagall*, Paris, 1984, pp. 19-21.

25 Chagall, *My Life*, pp. 78, 83-84, 105-6.

26 See Ziva Amishai-Maisels, "Chagall's In-Jokes," *Journal of Jewish Art*, vol. 5, 1978, pp. 76-80. The first hint that he was using Yiddish idioms is Tugendhold's comparison of his imagery with that in Yiddish (Efross and Tugendhold, p. 30). Tugendhold also repeatedly stresses the comic, ironic and cynical qualities of Chagall's messages (ibid., pp. 30, 32 and 34). On the other hand, throughout this period, the influence of *Ost und West* was still in force for his Jewish scenes. *The Dead Man* (Meyer, p. 65), set strangely outside the house, should be compared to the drowned Jewish martyr photographed on his bier outside his house in "Rumaenische Greuel" (*Ost und West*, vol. 2, August 1902, pp. 543-44), while *The Wedding* (Meyer, p. 78) should be compared to A. Trankowski's *Jewish Wedding in Lithuania* (ibid., September 1902, pp. 581-82).

27 Chagall, *My Life*, pp. 75-77. Also see his comments on his grandfather pretending not to have seen a drawing of a nude (ibid., p. 13). The figures under the bed witnessing the "primal scene" are also suggested in Chagall's story of hiding under his mother's bed (ibid., p. 68). The kind of negative comment made here is echoed in Chagall's remarks on the Sabbath, whose candles "cut my throat the way that a cow's throat was cut in my grandfather's barn. Sanctity of blood. It was warm and offensive" (ibid., pp. 22-23), which describe the atmosphere of his eery *Sabbath* of 1910, painted on his arrival in Paris (Meyer, pp. 98 and 101).

28 Compton, Chagall, pp. 32-33 and 155.

29 Ibid., pp. 36 and 162; and Meyer, p. 95.

30 Before leaving St. Petersburg, Chagall undoubtedly saw the "Salon Izdebsky," which ran from May 2 to June 7, 1910, and thus overlapped the exhibition of the Zvantseva school in which he took part, as that lasted from April 20 to May 9 (Gordon, pp. 401-7; and Meyer, p. 92). This salon included such leading foreign modern artists as Balla, Braque, Gleizes, Kandinsky, Matisse, Metzinger, Van Dongen, and Rousseau, who exhibited his enigmatic *Gay Jesters* (no. 462) – monkeys overturning a bottle of milk with a back-scratcher – a painting which had been widely exhibited in Russia since the end of 1909. Chagall claims that he went to the Salon des Indépendants on arrival in Paris (Chagall, *My Life*, p. 101). As Meyer points out (pp. 93 and 96), this can hardly be so as he arrived in August. The Salon d'Automne opened on October 1 (Gordon, pp. 426-29), and it would simply have reinforced the impression he had already received of French art at the "Salon Izdebsky."

31 Ibid., p. 559, nos. 652-54. The coupling of Chagall's name with that of Rousseau was echoed in Russia, and is stated in Boris Aronson, *Marc Chagall*, Berlin: Razum, 1924, pp. 11 and 19.

32 For an account of these friendships, see Chagall, *My Life*, pp. 109-16. At the start of his stay, Chagall felt he had left the ghetto and become "a man" rather than "a Jew" (ibid., p. 106), but the fact that he was turned down by the Salon d'Automne of 1911 (Meyer, p. 147) would have renewed his feelings of rejection by his environment.

33 Ibid., pp. 105, 112, cat. no. 66, pp. 157 and 101, respectively. For the rare Paris scenes, see ibid., pp. 106 and 207, and cat. nos. 41-42.

34 Ibid., pp. 117-18, 121-22, 158-59, 163, 184-86, 200, 210-11, and cat. nos. 57-65, 76-79, 100-9, 112-16.

35 Ibid., pp. 162 and 184. Given Chagall's interest in children's art, it would be very interesting to know more about the drawing of his sister, Sima (Zina?), which he displayed at the Malpel Gallery in mid-1914, which reminded Apollinaire of "the earlier paintings of her brother" (*Apollinaire on Art: Essays and Reviews 1902-1918*, ed. Leroy C. Breunig, London: Thames and Hudson, 1972, p. 403).

36 Meyer, pp. 169 and 159. The Yiddish expression for doing something "with all seven things" – e.g., seven eyes, seven fingers – means to do something wholeheartedly. For the Yiddish idioms he used in the painting on the easel and his other Paris paintings, see Amishai-Maisels, "In-Jokes," pp. 83-87. Compton recently pointed out that the title *To Russia, Asses and Others* refers to the "Donkey's Tail" exhibition of 1912, in which Chagall participated (*Chagall*, p. 36). Since the name of this exhibition was itself a "Dadaistic" slap in the face of the public, this in no way lessens the sarcasm of Chagall's title, but rather stresses the connection between his ironic attitude in many of his Paris works and those of his comrades in the Cubo-Futurist and Zaum groups in Russia. On the other hand, Chagall's split identity here is far from unique among Jewish artists who had left the ghetto. The closest parallel would be in the works of Gottlieb, who in the 1870s portrayed himself in turn as a Polish patriot, the Wandering Jew, a sophisticated cosmopolitan, a religious Jew and a witness to Christ's teachings and trial (Mojzesc Waldmann, *Maurycy Gottlieb* [in Polish], Cracow: Narodowa, 1932, pp. 16, 39, 41, 50-51 and opp. p. 70).

37 For information on Makhmadim, see Kampf, "In Quest," pp. 64-65. Koenig and Lichtenstein had previously studied at

Bezalel in Jerusalem, where the argument over a national style was in full swing, *Bezalel 1906-1929*, ed. Nurit Shilo-Cohen, Jerusalem: Israel Museum, 1983, pp. 40, 371-72.

38 Color reproduction in Paris, *Chagall*, 1984, p. 53. This work was mistakenly dated 1911 by Chagall.

39 Compton, *Chagall*, pp. 72 and 173; Gordon, p. 690, no. 556, dated in the catalog to 1912.

40 This may have been suggested by the rather phallic branch Eve is holding in Tchaikov's *Adam and Eve* (cat. 160₅).

41 For comparisons, see M. Malkin and S. Yudovin, *Yidisher Folks-Ornament* (in Yiddish), Vitebsk: Y. L. Peretz Society, 1920 (cat. 170), inside front cover and pls. 6-7 and 17; Giza Frankl, *Migzerot Niyar* (in Hebrew), Givataim: Massada, 1983, pp. 35, 122-23; and Davidovitch, p. 66 and pls. 4 and 22. This combination of animals at the foot of the Tree of Knowledge is quite traditional. See, for instance, Yeshayahu Shachar, *Jewish Tradition in Art: The Feuchtwanger Collection of Judaica*. Jerusalem: Israel Museum, 1981, no. 1.

42 Meyer (pp. 146-47) states that Vinaver visited Chagall in Paris several times to see how he was progressing. Chagall ("Vinavera," p. 11) mentions meeting him only once, but since Vinaver seemingly provided the funds on which Chagall lived, there must have been contact between them throughout the Paris period.

43 Meyer, cat. nos. 78, 101-3, and p. 158. The goat is cut here by the frame in the same way that the lamb was cut by the tree in the parallel area of Tchaikov's *Adam and Eve*.

44 In like manner, he may have taken the blessing hands of the priest and the Stars of David that appear between and above them in a drawing by Arieh (Leo Koenig) in the Shavuot issue (cat. 162₇), and turned them into a tombstone motif on a mausoleum in *Raising of Lazarus* (Meyer, p. 199), thus returning the motif to its folk origins. The choice of Lazarus in this context is a slap in the face to the Jewish nationalism of the Makhmadim group, as it stresses the Judeo-Christian tradition. On the other hand, as opposed to the sketch (ibid., cat. no. 131), he specifically excludes Christ from this representation: Lazarus apparently resurrects himself – a statement which would be equally unacceptable to Christians. One must bear in mind here that although this article deals with Chagall's ambivalence toward Judaism, he was equally ambivalent at this time toward Christianity, as I have shown in an earlier paper (Amishai-Maisels, "In-Jokes," pp. 84-88). Norbert Lynton recently pointed out a mistake in that article, indicating that Félah, the name he originally gave his *Maternity* of 1913 refers to Fela Cendrars (Compton, *Chagall*, pp. 24 and 29, n. 31). This in no way alters either the idiomatic meaning of that picture or the fact that it pokes fun at the Virgin Birth. Understanding Chagall's irony and his habit of making fun of all sacred cows at this time – Christian as well as Jewish – is a prerequisite for understanding both his first Paris period and the changes that later took place in his art and philosophy. His attitude is very much in line with the iconoclastic approach of the Cubo-Futurists, and what he does there to the *Blachernitissa* is in many ways similar to what Larionov did to that icon when he turned it into a fertility goddess in *Autumn* (*Chagall*, Paris, 1984, p. 19).

45 Meyer, p. 155. The date of this work is usually given as 1911-12, but it was exhibited only in 1914, and Compton suggests that it is later than the version discussed above (Compton, *Chagall*, p. 170). For a fuller interpretation, see Amishai-Maisels, "In-Jokes," pp. 88-89.

46 Meyer, p. 187 and cat. nos. 126 and 111; Compton, *Chagall*, pp. 78 and 177; and Meyer, pp. 194-95 and cat. no. 127, respectively. The only one of these motifs which may have a direct precedent is the *Man Eating* figure eating out of a bowl marked "kosher" in Hebrew (ibid., cat. no. 124). This may be a reprise of the lost painting with a similar name (ibid., pp. 28, 92-93) which Chagall had exhibited in St. Petersburg in 1910 along with *The Dead Man* (*Chagall*, Paris, pp. 66-67).

47 Not מ"ת as Compton believes (*Chagall*, p. 177): there is no break in the letter at the top or bottom as there would be in a מ, and as there is when Chagall writes that letter in his signature in this painting. The inscription is Chagall's variant on the traditional כ"ת (Keter Torah – Torah crown), which he seems in fact to have written at first, and then altered. For an example of the original inscription, see the Torah ark curtain in the background of Isidor Kaufmann's painting *From the Tribe of the High Priest* (*Ost und West*, vol. 3, September 1903, p. 597). The sketch with חי (Life) inside the star (Meyer, cat. no. 128) refers to a verse from Psalms that says the Torah is a "Tree of Life for those who believe in it." The comparison to Pen's painting is reinforced by the fact that Chagall used this work to illustrate his own later article on his teacher ("Moi pervie uchitelya," p. 7).

48 For additional meanings, see Compton, *Chagall*, pp. 177-78.

49 The identity problem and ambivalence to Judaism discussed here are not unique to Chagall, but are almost symptomatic of the trauma felt by Jewish artists throughout the nineteenth century on leaving the ghetto. It can be found in the works of Hirszenberg, who constantly stressed the dark side of shtetl life, and in those of Leopold Horowitz, Kaufmann and Alphonse Levy, who often mock the ghetto life they continue to depict, occasionally pushing their works in the direction of caricature. See, for instance, *Ost und West*, vol. 2, pp. 85-86, 661-62, 677-79, 710; vol. 3, pp. 509-10, 581-82, 589-90, 593-94 and 614; vol. 4, pp. 689-90; and vol. 5, pp. 293-94, 301-2, 306, 318, 321-22, 327-28, all of which would have been known to Chagall.

50 After the success of his *Ivan the Terrible* in 1871, Antokolski married the daughter of a wealthy Jew of his hometown, Vilna. Bella Rosenfeld's father was equally wealthy and had undoubtedly until then looked down on the son of a poor herring-porter, who had no visible means of support, and – even worse – wanted to be an artist. For the reaction of Bella's family to Chagall, see the second half of her memoirs, *First Encounters* (Bella Chagall, *Nerot Dolkim* [in Hebrew], Tel Aviv: Dvir, 1970, pp. 216-19), and Chagall, *My Life*, pp. 121-22. Chagall's fame as both a Russian and a Jewish artist emerges from Apollinaire's comments on the Sturm exhibition: "The Jewish race has not yet distinguished itself in the plastic arts. . . . The Sturm Gallery, in Berlin . . . is currently exhibiting the works of a young Russian Jewish painter, Marc Chagall . . . a colorist imbued with an imagination that occasionally finds its source in the fantasies of Slavic folk illustration but always goes beyond them. He is an extremely varied artist, capable of painting monumental pictures, and he is not inhibited by any system" (*Apollinaire on Art*, p. 400).

51 Meyer (p. 147) claims that he sent *Birth*, *Interior II* and *The Dead Man* to Russia for exhibition at the "World of Art" show in January-February 1912, but the catalog for that show (Gordon, p. 546, no. 338a) lists only *Corpse on the Street*, seemingly the same painting exhibited as *Death* at the "Donkey's Tail" in

March-April 1912 (ibid., p. 565, no. 286). Since Meyer identifies *A Street in My Town*, exhibited at the Salon d'Automne in October-November 1912, as the Cubist version of this painting (Meyer, p. 177; and Gordon, p. 620, no. 318), and since Chagall exhibited the Cubist version of *Birth* at the Salon des Indépendants the following year (ibid., p. 690, no. 555), unless the paintings were being shipped back and forth, it would seem that the works in question were his early versions of these themes rather than those done in Paris. Meyer (p. 206) also states that the Paris paintings *The Drunkard* and *The Herdsman* were exhibited at the "Contemporary French Art" show in Moscow at the end of 1912, but I have been unable to trace the catalog. This again seems problematic, as *The Herdsman* was on exhibit in Paris in October-November 1912 at the Salon d'Automne (Gordon, p. 620, no. 319). Trapped by the war, Chagall made an abortive attempt to exhibit at the "World of Art" show in the autumn of 1914 (Meyer, p. 243). His perception of his problem at this time is expressed in *The Clock* of 1914, which he exhibited in April 1915 (ibid., p. 228; and Gordon, p. 870, no. 191). This "simple" still life tells the tale through a combination of images and words. On the clock face, he wrote "Le Roi à Paris" – referring not only to the maker of the clock, but to the important position Chagall felt he had held in the Paris art world. As opposed to this French inscription, Chagall signed the work at the lower right in *Russian*, while on the left, he portrayed himself wistfully looking out the window at the black sky as time runs out.

52   Mark Gregorievich Etkind, *Nathan Altman* (in Russian), Moscow: Sovetskii Khudoznik, 1971, pp. 16 and 23; and Meyer, cat. no. 66. Altman exhibited this painting along with those he had done in Paris (e.g., Gordon, p. 767, no. 1-3). He used the same broad facets as had Chagall to create a mesh of planes around his figures, thus separating them from their simple but realistic background, and not intruding overly into the figures themselves. This decorative faceting is quite unlike the more moderate but correct use of Cubism Altman displayed in his Paris works and in the Cubist portraits he executed in Russia upon his return (e.g., Etkind, *Altman*, pp. 18, 21-22, 27, 29-31 and 33). Neither Chagall nor Altman was at all forthcoming about his contacts with the other: Chagall doesn't even mention Altman in his autobiography – even when discussing his work. The reasons for this will become clear later in this article.

53   Ibid., pl. 29. For comparisons, see *Ost und West*, vol. 1, pp. 578 and 625; vol. 3, pp. 197-98 and 598; and vol. 4, p. 402. Altman exhibited *Old Jew* in November 1913 (Gordon, p. 754, no. 2).

54   Ibid., p. 770, nos. 5-6. They were only published in 1923, but this early exhibition dates them firmly to 1913. For a discussion of these works, see Kampf, "In Quest," pp. 56-57.

55   Gordon, p. 690, no. 556; and Compton, *Chagall*, p. 173. The erotic idea here, as well as the serpent's legs and the giant flowers, owes a good deal to Gauguin's conception of the subject in "Te Nave Nave Fenua" (Ziva Amishai-Maisels, *Gauguin's Religious Themes*, New York: Garland, 1985, pp. 181-85 and pls. 69-70).

56   Meyer, pp. 226-27, 229 and cat. nos. 165-91. He also did "portraits" of Vitebsk and Lyozno at this time (ibid., p. 273 and cat. nos. 219-28, 271-73 and 275).

57   For another explanation of this stylistic change, see Compton, *Chagall*, p. 37. Chagall's return to his version of an academic style has many parallels at this time. Kandinsky returned to figuration from abstraction on his return to Russia (*Kandinsky: Russian and Bauhaus Years, 1915-1933*, New York: Solomon R. Guggenheim Museum, 1983, nos. 3, 6-8), and Picasso startled the art world by returning to Classicism at the very beginning of 1915, after Braque had been drafted, and developed both Classicism and Cubism as two distinct styles for many years thereafter (*Pablo Picasso, A Retrospective*, New York: Museum of Modern Art, 1980, pp. 179, 192-245). Chagall's return to academic painting furthers the impression generated by his dual style of Cubism and "naive" art in Paris that he was not as natural a folk artist as he would have us believe, but that he adopted his "naive" style for his own purposes.

58   Meyer, pp. 258-63, 267, 275-76, and cat. nos. 235-50, 263, 265, 267-70, 285-89.

59   Ibid., pp. 188 (misdated), 242, 249, 251, 255, and cat. nos. 192, 210-16; *Chagall*, Paris, 1984, pp. 80 and 89; and Efros and Tugendkhold, p. 61.

60   An-Sky, "Paen," p. 743; Meyer, p. 232; and color reproduction in *Chagall by Chagall*, ed. Charles Sorlier, Tel Aviv: Steimatzky, 1979, p. 65. This comparison indicates even more sharply than that between *The Pinch of Snuff* and *Jew in Prayer* the importance of Pen for Chagall's development, and the need for much deeper research into his career than anyone has so far attempted.

61   Also see Haftmann's explanation of these names, some of which Chagall repeats in discussing Vitebsk in his autobiography (Werner Haftmann, *Marc Chagall*, New York: Harry N. Abrams, 1972, pp. 20-21). An early photograph of this painting (Karl With, *Marc Chagall*, Leipzig: Klinkhardt and Biermann, 1923, unnumbered) shows that Chagall had removed or altered some of the names he originally used, probably in keeping with the names he mentioned in *My Life*.

62   Meyer, p. 223. It could be based on any of a number of works from Eastern Europe, an unknown Pen painting, or Israels's *Alone in the World*, reproduced in *Ost und West* (vol. 11, August-September 1911, pp. 741-42), in obituaries which generated controversy among the Makhmadim artists, as – in Chagall's story – they denied that Israels was a Jewish artist. See G. Kutna, "Jozef Israels," ibid., pp. 689-98; and L. Pilichowsky, "Jozef Israels," ibid., pp. 713-16. Chagall here may still be reacting to this controversy, and making Israels Jewish by changing the subject from a Dutch to a Jewish one.

63   *Ost und West*, vol. 12, February 1912, p. 136. This article on Hirszenberg illustrates several heads which may have inspired Chagall. For instance, the study of an Oriental Jew (p. 134) may have given him the idea for the staring eyes and lined forehead of the Jew in *The Pinch of Snuff*, while the heads on pp. 137-38 will bear comparison with that of *Jew In Green*.

64   Ibid., vol. 11, August-September 1911, pp. 729-30, and vol. 2, September 1902, pp. 629-30; and Bredius and Gerson, pl. 207. The Rembrandt is usually designated as *Old Man*, but it was called *Old Jew* in *Ost und West*. Note that vol. 2 had also reproduced Israels's painting, translating its title into Hebrew as "Ben-Ami" – "Son of *My* People" (pp. 293-94). The same volume also featured a similarly depressed and bent *Old Jew* by Leonid Pasternak in the Russian garb used by Chagall (pp. 413-14). *Jew in Green* also bears comparison with Pasternak's *After the Pogrom* of 1904 (Chaim Nachman Bialik and Max Osborn, *L. Pasternak*, Berlin: Stybel, 1924, p. 3). This wealth of comparisons shows to what extent this figure relies on nineteenth century Jewish imagery, as well as on Rembrandt, who

strongly influenced Chagall at this time, especially in his paintings of old men (e.g., compare the heads of his old Jews with Bredius and Gerson, pl. 154). He not only converted Rembrandt to Judaism, as described above, but his *Double Portrait with Wine Glass* (Meyer, p. 275) is a variant on Rembrandt's *Self-Portrait with Saskia* (Bredius and Gerson, pls. 25-26).

65    For a full explanation of the quotations and their meaning, see Amishai-Maisels, "In-Jokes," pp. 89-93. The use of what is apparently part of his Bar Mitzvah Torah portion in *Jew in Green* adds to this personal identification, as may the opening phrase of the inscription, "The Preacher of Slutsk," given his identification with his "ancestor," Chaim ben Isaac Halevi Segal of Slutsk, the painter of the Mohilev synagogue.

66    Ibid., p. 89; Meyer, pp. 233, 269, 279, 293 and 320; and his illustrations to *Troyer* (cat. 150).

67    Color reproduction in Compton, *Chagall*, p. 84; and Gordon, p. 870, no. 189. The other works he exhibited were landscapes, still lifes, portraits of his family and genre scenes. They showed his three styles: folkic art, Cubism and Realism, and combinations thereof. The selection of the paintings, chosen on the advice of Tugendkhold (Meyer, p. 243), is a fair representation of the work he was doing at the time.

68    The similiarity in pose among *Jew in Black and White*, *Jew in Bright Red* and Altman's *Old Jew* (which had been exhibited the previous year) raises the question as to whether Chagall had kept in touch with Altman and, aware of this work, saw himself as competing with it and correcting it, as he had the works of Pen and Israels. The writing behind *Jew in Bright Red* would thus take the place of the closed books in Altman's painting. It should also be stressed that despite his deeply felt rendering of Orthodox Jews, which is also seen clearly in the drawing *Old Rabbi Reading the Torah* (cat. 142), Chagall could still manifest his ambivalence to Orthodoxy. Thus in *Feast Day* of 1914 (color reproduction in Compton, *Chagall*, p. 85), he portrays a Jew in a prayer shawl, carrying a *lulav* and *etrog* to synagogue. Yet his treatment of the purple synagogue, whose almost black interior is as inviting as was Lazarus' tomb (Meyer, p. 199), causes the Jew to turn gray and his "other self" to scurry away from it on his head.

69    See the translation of the 1919 article by Aronson and Ryback in this catalog, and the discussion on it in Kampf, "In Quest," pp. 62-64. Aronson and Ryback saw either the exhibition or the illustration of this work, along with *Jew in Bright Red* and *Over Vitebsk*, in *Apollon* (Ya. Tugendkhold, "Marc Chagall" [in Russian], *Apollon*, no. 2, 1916, between pp. 10-11 and 14-15). For Chagall's general influence on Ryback, compare the head in *Jew in Bright Red* to the latter's *Portrait of a Jew* of c. 1917 (Kampf, "In Quest," p. 56), and note the unstable arrangement of shtetl houses in Ryback, *Shtetl*, pp. 3-4, 18 and 20 (cat. 136$_{2-3,17,19}$), the use of folk art and comedy on p. 9 (cat. 136$_8$), the attempts to combine Cubist and folkic elements in most of these designs, and the inclusion of a Yiddish inscription around the rabbi on p. 31 (cat. 136$_{30}$), which paraphrases that around *Jew In Green*: "Thus the rabbi said to me." Also see Aronson's graphic (cat. 38) in which the figure in Chagall's *Jew in Black and White*, retaining all his accoutrements, and even the zigzags of his prayer shawl, is turned into a martyr.

70    Gordon, pp. 869-71, nos. 1-4, 8-20, 59-65, 147-60.

71    He had moreover been mentioned in two major reviews by Efros and Tugendkhold, the latter hailing him as "a new talent" (Meyer, pp. 243 and 717).

72    See the comments of the wedding guests: "He's already famous . . . he even gets money for his pictures" (Chagall, *My Life*, p. 124).

73    Meyer, p. 243; and Nathan Altman, *Jüdische Graphik*, Berlin: Razum, 1923, introduction by Max Osborn, pp. 22-23.

74    Etkind, *Altman*, p. 37; and Gordon, p. 894, no. 6.

75    Gordon, p. 898, nos. 204-54. For the reasons for the restrictions on Yiddish publishing, see Simon Dubnov, *History of the Jews*, New York: Thomas Yosseloff, 1973, vol. 5, pp. 833-37. The books were eventually published after the Revolution, in Vilna in 1917. In the same show, Altman exhibited drawings for a children's book, dated to 1913 (Gordon, p. 898, nos. 2-12), so that the collaboration/competition between the two was clearly continuing.

76    *Der Nister* was the pseudonym of Pinhas Cohenovich, whose father – like Chagall's – made a living selling herring. He went into hiding to avoid army service. He was a member of the generation – as was Chagall – that seriously questioned its Jewish background and its values and sought to find a personal modern style without abandoning its roots. His earliest book, published in 1907, deals with the difference between dream and reality, naiveté and birth, and mixes Christian and Jewish imagery, paralleling the elements present in Chagall's early works. In 1910, he came under the influence of Y. L. Peretz, and turned to fables and fantasy, apparently writing these poems during the war (Der Nister, *HaNazir V'Hagaddya* [in Hebrew], Jerusalem: Bialik Institute, 1963, introduction by Chone Shmeruk, pp. 9-12, 17-28). Chagall and Der Nister, both doing bureaucratic work instead of serving as combat soldiers, may have met at this time, perhaps through Dr. I. Eliashev (cat. 146), who had written a review on Der Nister in 1908 (ibid., p. 23) and with whom Chagall was friendly (Meyer, p. 243). Eliashev had also been influenced by Peretz and had published *Ironic Tales* after 1910. He believed that one's ethnic background determined one's creativity, and wrote an essay on the impact of South Russian Jewish life on Yiddish literature (*Encyclopedia Judaica*, vol. 4, pp. 4-5). Here, too, Chagall's choice of friends was not accidental.

77    This interest in book illustration should be seen against the background of modern Russian book design as outlined by Susan P. Compton (*The World Backwards*, London: British Library, 1978), especially as in 1914, Altman had done a drawing for Alexei Kruchenykh's *Explodity* (ibid., p. 104). That Chagall was seen as a pioneer in this field by other Jewish artists emerges from Aronson's statements (*Chagall*, p. 28).

78    Meyer, pp. 246 and 248, and cat. nos. 255, 257-61. For a photograph of this building, see Wischnitzer, *Architecture*, p. 208.

79    Compton, *Chagall*, p. 90; and Zlocisti, p. 279.

80    Gordon, pp. 894-95, nos. 336-80, especially nos. 338, 340-41. *Old Man with Letters* (no. 342) is probably *Jew in Bright Red*, as it, along with *Jew in Green* and *Jew in Red*, were bought by Kagan-Shabshai, one of the founders of the Moscow branch of the Society for the Encouragement of Jewish Art, for a Jewish museum (Meyer, p. 246).

81    Compton, *Chagall*, pp. 38-39. Chagall had apparently known Lissitzky for many years, although neither of them discusses their early relationship. Both had studied with Pen at about the same time, and Lissitzky had gone to Paris in 1911 or 1912, visiting his good friend Zadkine (Lissitzky-Küppers, pp. 18-19), who was equally friendly with Chagall. It is quite proba-

ble that Lissitzky saw Chagall during this visit. Lissitzky must have come into contact with Chagall on his return to Vitebsk in the summer or early fall of 1914, as it is hard to imagine that an aspiring artist, who had been studying in Germany, would have failed to notice that a hometown boy and fellow student of Pen's had "made it" with a show at Der Sturm, or that he would have failed to get in contact with this artist on returning home, particularly given the fact that Chagall had renewed his ties with Pen. It may even have been through Chagall's and Pen's contacts with the Jewish Historical and Ethnographic Society that Lissitzky eventually undertook with Ryback the expeditions to document Jewish folk art in general and the Mohilev synagogue in particular in the summers of 1915-16. Here again, the reasons for the reticence of both artists on this subject will be discussed below.

82   Color reproduction in Lionello Venturi, *Chagall*, Geneva: Albert Skira, 1956, p. 52. The inscriptions, although containing some traditional features such as the פ״נ (Here Lies) and some names, are for the most part undecipherable.

83   Meyer, p. 247. Erben (p. 69) suggests that these paintings were inspired by Chagall's visit to his parents' graves, which he seems to discuss in *My Life* (pp. 7-10). However, his parents died only several years after the paintings were done (Meyer, p. 304; and Sidney Alexander, *Marc Chagall*, London: Cassell, 1978, pp. 210-11, 237-38 and 313).

84   The cover of this book (*Chagall*, Paris, 1984, p. 92) was designed by Chagall, and stressed the fantastic world he had developed in Paris. The main figure is shown with his head upside-down ("fardreiter kop" in Yiddish, signifying confusion), parallel to the upside-down title of the book: *The Art of Marc Chagall*. He holds a memory of Vitebsk in his hand, but now, instead of it consisting primarily of a church, as in *Self-Portrait with Seven Fingers*, Chagall sets the church farther back, blending it with the other buildings, and places a village scene with animals in the foreground, stressing Vitebsk's shtetl character.

85   See, for instance, his 1918 article in John Bowlt, *Russian Art of the Avant Garde: Theory and Criticism 1902-1934*, New York: Viking, 1976, pp. 161-64; and Etkind, *Altman*, pp. 43, 46-47 and 51.

86   Compton, *Chagall*, p. 40; and Meyer, pp. 268-72. According to Meyer, Pen was offended by his exclusion from the original teaching staff, and thus he was probably one of the instigators of the Y. L. Peretz Society's complaint against Chagall in the spring of 1919 (ibid., loc. cit.). Information on Yudovin courtesy of Mirjam Rajner.

87   Compton, *The World Backwards*, color pl. 18.

88   Meyer, pp. 203 and 198. The checkered pattern in the original painting resulted from the material on which it was done (Compton, *Chagall*, p. 180), and the curling lines may have been suggested by the smoke issuing from the chimney to the left of Chagall's violinist's foot. Lissitzky could easily have been shown a photograph of this work by Chagall, who must have brought either photographs or sketches of the work to Russia, as he was to develop this theme in his *Music* for the Kamerny (Meyer, pp. 282 and 295). It is noteworthy that in both that painting and the variant of it, Chagall himself transformed the smoke rings into spirals connected to the bench. It is also possible that Lissitzky had traveled from Düsseldorf to Berlin in June 1914 to see the exhibition of Chagall's works at the Sturm Gallery, or that he saw the drawing, which was published in *Der Sturm* in May 1917 (p. 25), a magazine that could have been available

to him once Russia had withdrawn from the war.

89   E.g., see Meyer, pp. 105, 122, 163, 210, 214, 267, 276 and cat. nos. 61-63, 66, 78-78, 93, 100-4, 145, 147, 257-60, all of which predate Lissitzky's works. The sources of this perspective in Chagall's work date back to his early, naive drawings (ibid., cat. nos. 13, 23 and 33), but it was only fully developed in Paris. As was pointed out above (n. 69), Ryback had also been strongly influenced by this type of perspective.

90   Ibid., pp. 120 and 138 and cat. nos. 78 and 101; and fig. 2 above. See also the eye-to-eye confrontation between the calf and the man in *I and the Village* (ibid., p. 163), which Lissitzky intensified in the contact between the child and the kid on the frontispiece.

91   Ibid., pp. 113, 163, 158, 175 and 155, respectively. For Chagall's iconographic influence on Lissitzky in this series, see Haia Friedberg's "Lissitzky's *Had Gadiá*," *Jewish Art* (formerly, *Journal of Jewish Art*), vol. 12/13, 1986-87, pp. 292-303.

92   Meyer, pp. 265-66; and Chagall, *My Life*, p. 154.

93   Chagall could have seen Malevich's *Zaum* and Cubist works exhibited in St. Petersburg in 1915, and certainly saw the 50 Suprematist compositions Malevich exhibited at the "Jack of Diamonds" show in 1916, where Chagall had also shown (Gordon, p. 868, nos. 9-26, and pp. 894-96, nos. 140-99, 336-80). He might also have learned of him from Puni, who was one of the organizers of the "0.10" exhibition, which was dominated by Malevich's Suprematist works (Marcadé, "Chronologie," p. 214; and Gordon, p. 884, nos. 39-77), and Compton (*Chagall*, p. 37) suggests that he may even have seen this exhibition, which was held during his stay in St. Petersburg at the end of 1915 and the beginning of 1916. This seems probable as Altman and Puni had also exhibited in this show (Gordon, pp. 883-85, nos. 1, 98-120). The usual supposition is that Chagall invited Malevich at the instigation of Lissitzky, who had met Malevich and seen his works in early 1919 (V. Rakitin,"El Lissitzky 1890-1941," in O.A. Shvidkovsky, *Building in the U.S.S.R. 1917-1932*, New York: Praeger, 1971, p. 35; and Meyer, p. 272). It is not clear on what basis Rakitin claims that Lissitzky knew of the invitation to Malevich before he went to Vitebsk. Compton (*Chagall*, p. 40) states that Ermolaeva invited Malevich, which would have been natural no matter who had initiated the invitation, as she was director of the school and, according to Chagall, a close friend of Lissitzky (Meyer, p. 272).

94   Chagall, *My Life*, p. 142. Chagall's comments on Malevich, just above these lines, are much more insulting. Also see the heartbreak behind his anger at being pushed out of the school, his bitterness against his former "friends," and his comment: "Don't worry, I shan't remember you" (ibid., pp. 144-46).

95   Meyer, p. 305 and cat. nos. 298, 301, 323-24. Also see Compton's analysis of this problem (*Chagall*, pp. 197 and 201). His positive attitude to this style is seen both in *Painter at the Easel* (Meyer, cat. no. 282 and p. 277), where he shows himself painting a circle and pyramid, and in the story of his discussion with Stepanova after leaving Vitebsk for Moscow (Compton, *Chagall*, p. 42).

96   For Chagall's *Rain*, see Meyer, cat. nos. 101-3.

97   Color reproduction in *Marc Chagall*, July 7-October 15, Saint Paul: Foundation Maeght, 1984, p. 58. For his return, see Chagall, *My Life*, pp. 151-52; and Meyer, pp. 272 and 277.

98   Ibid., p. 278; and Donald Karshan, *Malevich, The Graphic Work: 1913-1930*, Jerusalem: Israel Museum, 1975, p. 127. The details that are related to this work are the wood graining, the

spiral at the lower left which may derive from the concentric circles in the corners of Malevich's work, the sloping planes, and the empty background at the left, which Chagall promptly utilized.

99  Also see the drawing in which – emerging from a Suprematist background to which he has added a folkic house almost entirely composed of geometric elements – he sets forth the first four letters of his name in Russian (color reproduction in *Chagall*, Paris, 1984, cover).

100  Color reproduction in *Chagall*, Paris, 1984, p. 126. The text can be compared to the photograph of the invitation (Meyer, p. 33), dated June. There is apparently a Realist portrait on the verso (*Chagall*, Paris, 1984, p. 103).

101  Meyer, pp. 281-85. The murals and sketches are often misdated 1919-20 because of Chagall's signature on some of the sketches. They could not have been started before 1920, when Chagall moved to Moscow, and probably not before November, when the Kamerny theatre arrived from Petrograd. The works were finished at least by June 1921, when they were exhibited, and more probably for the opening of the theatre in January 1921 (Meyer, p. 292; and Matthew Frost, "Marc Chagall and the Jewish State Chamber Theatre," *Russian History*, vol. 8, nos. 1-2, 1981, p. 93).

102  Meyer, pp. 282-83. The song "The Voice of the Groom" is based on Jeremiah 33:10-11. Chagall's use of the fiddler here may again represent a reclaiming of his motif from Lissitzky.

103  For new views, see Compton, *Chagall*, p. 42; and Frost, p. 95.

104  For a photograph of the St. Petersburg synagogue with the dome cut off and the"gable" and double-arched window emphasized, see *Novyi voskhod*, no. 10, March 11, 1910, pp. 25-26, an issue produced during the time Chagall was living in the office, so that he may have preserved a copy.

105  The Torah ark curtain behind Chagall is seen most clearly in the detail of the colored sketch in *Chagall*, Paris, 1984, p. 125. Yudovin and Malkin do not label the end-paper drawing, but they mention the zodiac designs at Mohilev in their introduction, and the design is similar to those Ryback and Lissitzky did at Mohilev (cat. 67 and 69), one of which Ryback included in his own depiction of a synagogue in his *Shtetl* series, p. 14 (cat. 136₁₃), and this would have been enough for Chagall. For Chagall's attitude to Granovsky's "Jewishness," see his comments: "He spoke Russian in the Yiddish theatre. . . Granovsky was trying to find something new – not with the warmth of a Jewish soul, but ponderously, as though from books" (Erben, p. 70). Also see the comments on him of Beatrice Picon-Vallin, *Le Théâtre juif soviétique pendant les Années vingt*, Lausanne: La Cité, 1973, p. 55. This mural must be examined in much greater depth than can be done here, as the small details give us a wealth of information about Chagall. For instance, in the detail of the upper right-hand corner published in Aronson (*Chagall*, opp. p. 23), around the upside-down cow, he drew a nude woman with hands reaching towards her rather bulging stomach from below, and two chickens facing in opposite directions, on one of which a figure is riding – one of the first such groups in Chagall's work. The source here is apparently the paintings of *Hell* by Bosch and Pieter Huys, which were reproduced with details of the birds from Huys' version in *Apollon*, no. 3, 1911, between pp. 8-9 and 14-15.

106  *Chagall*, Paris, 1984, p. 105, doc. 50, and p. 107, no. 78.

107  Chagall, *My Life*, pp. 165-67; Chagall,"Mein Arbet," pp.

281-82 (pp. 173-74); Erben, p. 71; and Gray, *The Great Experiment*, pl. 163, where the wedding feast is reproduced overlapping the mural. This suggests that Chagall was invited to design *The Dybbuk* either while still working on the murals, or even before he began them, at the time he was designing Constructivist and Chagallian sets for the Moscow Theatre of Revolutionary Satire (Meyer, pp. 286, 289, 291-92, and cat. no. 307). This would explain Chagall's arrival in Moscow well in advance of the Kamerny (ibid., p. 277; and Compton, *Chagall*, p. 42). This idea is borne out by Binyamin Zemach's statement that Nahum Zemach had turned to Chagall in *1920* for *The Dybbuk* designs (Debora Gilula,"Nathan Altman – Tzayar 'HaDybbuk'" [in Hebrew], *Bamah*, nos. 101-2, 1985, p. 19). Chagall's ideas for the wedding scene probably also influenced his designs for an evening devoted to Jewish and Hasidic dance in December 1921, staged two months before *The Dybbuk* opened (Meyer, p. 298). For the influence of the murals on Jewish stage design and acting, see also Picon-Vallin, pp. 66-67 and 72.

108  *Chagall*, Paris, 1984, p. 127; and Meyer, p. 33.

109  *Chagall*, Paris, 1984, pp. 128 and 130; Picon-Vallin, opp. p. 65; and Frost, pls. 9-10.

110  This was especially important for Chagall because he had originally failed the test Bakst had set for him in set painting in 1910 (Chagall, *My Life*, pp. 92 and 105).

111  Ibid., p. 164; and Gilula, pp. 26, 31-32, n. 51.

112  Etkind, *Altman*, p. 67; Avram Kampf, *Jewish Experience in the Art of the Twentieth Century*, South Hadley: Bergin and Garvey, 1984, p. 38; and *Chagall*, Paris, 1984, p. 130. It is highly instructive to compare the folk motifs Altman used here with those he translated into slightly Cubist terms in his *Jewish Graphics* (cat. 30). The animals – at least in the sketches – have the freer, rounder treatment usual in Chagall's work. To see to what extent Altman adopted Chagall's view of the shtetl, one has only to compare his set for act 1 to the more traditional Eastern European view of the shtetl seen in Jakob Steinhardt's sketch for act 1 of *The Dybbuk*, seemingly also executed c. 1921 (Hans Tietze, *Jakob Steinhardt*, Berlin: J. J. Ostens [c. 1930]).

113  Gray, *The Great Experiment*, nos. 164-67; and Etkind, *Altman*, pp. 44-45.

114  Altman used such inscriptions for the second and third acts as well: "The Voice of the Groom, the Voice of the Bride," as in Chagall's painting *Dance*, for the wedding scene in act 2; and "This is the Gate of God" for act 3 (fig. 87).

115  Kampf, "In Quest," pp. 70-71; Meyer, pp. 268 and 288, especially the figure on the bottom left; *Chagall*, Paris, 1984, p. 103; and Gilula, pp. 20 and 25. This similarity is much more pronounced in photographs of the actors, with their awkward, almost primitivist angular movements (e.g., Bernhard Diebold, *Habima Hebraïsches Theater*, Berlin: Heinrich Keller, 1928, pls. 8-9, 14-16), to the point that Asriel's makeup (ibid., pl. 12) is practically a translation of Chagall's *The Pinch of Snuff* and *Jew in Green*, and is markedly different from Altman's *Old Jew*. The break-up of forms in the costumes (e.g., ibid., p. 15) also recalls Chagall's attempts in this direction in his Shalom Aleichem sketches (especially *Chagall*, Paris, 1984, p. 103), and in his paintings and drawings, while the group scene from the beggars' wedding, with the stiff, doll-like figures in the background and the awkward figures in the foreground (Diebold, pl. 16), recalls Chagall's paintings (e.g.,compare the figures at the table with those in his *Sabbath* of 1910, Meyer, p. 101). On the other

hand, both Chagall and Altman were influenced by Mayakovski's costume designs for his *Mystery-Bouffe* of 1919 (Larissa A. Zhadova, *Malevich*, London: Thames and Hudson, 1982, pls. 180-84), and at least one of Chagall's designs for Gogol's *Inspector General* (Meyer, cat. no. 320) shows the influence of Malevich's 1913 designs for *Victory over the Sun* (Zhadova, pls. 31-35). Furthermore, Chagall got his idea of painting little figures on Mikhoels's face (Erben, p. 75) from Burliuk, Larionov and Goncharova (e.g., *Sieg über die Sonne*, Berlin, 1983, p. 272). This does not decrease Chagall's influence on Altman, but it does show that neither of them worked in a vacuum.

116   Gilula (p. 24) stresses that Chagall's genre was comedy, and that it is impossible to translate his comic gestures into a tragedy. That, however, is just what occurs in act 2 of *The Dybbuk*, and what is so impressive about it: it builds up slowly from a gay – almost comic – scene into a nightmare. She further notes that Vachtangov simply decided that Realism would be wrong for this play, and he changed his style because the actors gave him details on Jewish life and culture. On the other hand, Chagall claimed that it was his art which was responsible for this decision. In fact, whether or not Chagall was involved in the mises-en-scène of the Kamerny (ibid., p. 28, n. 3), his paintings had already had a massive psychological effect on all concerned, and it is not really important whether they influenced Vachtangov directly or whether their impact was subconsciously transmitted to him by the actors. Considering that Vachtangov had previously used Stanislavsky's Realist style, it would otherwise be hard to explain why both he and Granovsky, who had strong Symbolist propensities, suddenly turned – while depicting shtetl scenes in their plays – to an Expressionistic, awkward, stylized approach, and why Granovsky, once free of Chagall, immediately reverted to the Symbolist mode (Picon-Vallin, pp. 55-57, 68, 81-83, 120-24). To see to what extent Chagall's conceptions continued to dominate, see Picon-Vallin's comments (pp. 101-2, 113, 146, n. 16); and the sets (which often use Chagall's unstable perspective), the costumes and especially the poses illustrated ibid., opp. p. 81, between pp. 96-97 (*200,000*) and between pp. 144-45 (*Voyage of Benjamin III*); and in *Shtrom*, nos. 5-6, 1924, pp. 88-89. Also see Aronson's costume designs in Meira Perry-Lehmann, *One Hundred Works on Paper from the Collection of The Israel Museum Jerusalem*, Jerusalem: The Israel Museum, 1986, p. 209, and in *Rimon*, no. 4, 1923, pp. 29-30. Although they bear a resemblance in their geometric forms to Altman's designs as well as to Chagall's paintings and drawings, their details give away their source. *The Hasid* retains the zig-zag from Chagall's *Jew in Black and White*, while Baruch Agadati's costume bears a Biblical inscription on his thigh, recalling both the inscriptions in the background of Chagall's paintings and the letters decorating the man's shoes in *Love on the Stage*. See also Meyer, pp. 292-96, who stresses the contemporary critics' view that Chagall had set his seal on the Kamerny's future productions, although this does not emerge from Efros's article as translated by Frost (p. 97) and Picon-Vallin (p. 66).

117   Gilula, p. 20 and p. 29, n. 14.

118   Chagall's influence on Constructivist sets has been noted by Linton, in discussing the Constructivist and kinetic elements of Chagall's set for *Playboy of the Western World* (Compton, *Chagall*, pp. 26-27); the Constructivist nature of his set for *The Agents* is mentioned by Frost, p. 96. Although Altman had previously used geometric forms both in his paintings and in his work for the stage, most prominently in *Mystery-Bouffe*, on which he had worked with Granovsky (Picon-Vallin, pp. 68-69, 81-83), the similarity of his set to that of Chagall is striking.

119   For Chagall's use of this exhibition, to "settle accounts," see Frost, p. 98. *Mourning* was published in Kiev in 1922, and was most probably done either after the debacle at Vitebsk or after that in Moscow. It deals primarily with the Ukrainian pogroms of World War I, and is dedicated to "all those who died before their time." Chagall here does variations on certain lines, mixing them up in a way that has meaning for him, but is completely out of context and out of step with the expressive quality of the poems. Thus he illustrates a sad poem, "The Sunset" (cat. $150_3$) with "broken" hands and "slipping" feet which emerge in a very lively fashion from rectangles bearing these words, below a row of tombstones, an image which does not convey the poet's idea that his return to the ruins of the ghetto seems to break his hands and make his feet slip out from under him. In like manner, Hofstein's mixture of disgusting images of slaughter with visions of beauty turns into a seemingly comical scene of animals and an upside-down woman with her pants pulled down beside an outhouse, and only the quotation "a string of drops of blood, bright and clean" connects the illustration with the text (cat. $150_4$).

120   The exact date Chagall left Russia is unclear, but it could not have been before his exhibition with Altman and Shterenberg in April, several months after *The Dybbuk* had opened (Compton, *Chagall*, p. 43). See Chagall, *My Life*, pp. 100-1, 173-74, for his feelings on Russia. Chagall went to Berlin to recover his Paris paintings from Walden, and because he had received a letter telling him of his success there (ibid., p. 173). His experience in Russia at this time was not unique; it is paralleled by that of Kandinsky, who had strongly influenced the development of abstract art in Russia, but found himself outflanked on his return there by Malevich and the Constructivists. Kandinsky and Chagall both revolted against their treatment and left for Germany within weeks of each other. Their problems in Russia turned out in the long run to be blessings in disguise, as both of them escaped before the Communist government clamped down on avant-garde art, trapping their former colleagues and recent "enemies," and seriously damaging their style.

121   Meyer, p. 409, and cat. nos. 622, 624-25.

122   Ziva Amishai, "Chagall's Jerusalem Windows: Iconography and Sources," *Scripta Hierosolymitana*, vol. 24, *Studies in Art*, Jerusalem: Magnes, 1972, pp. 146-82 and pls. 27-32.

# El Lissitzky's Jewish Works

## Ruth Apter-Gabriel

El Lissitzky was an extremely dynamic and intense artist with tremendous intellectual powers. The first aim he set himself as a young aspiring artist in pre-revolutionary Russia was to participate in the creation of a new avant-garde Jewish art.

Until now, this effort has been largely eclipsed by his later Suprematist works, designs, and typography. Added to this, his Jewish works are very rare and, apart from a few exceptions, have never been reissued since they appeared. In an attempt to restore the balance, we shall present Lissitzky's Jewish works, as completely as possible, with illustrations and in chronological sequence.

Born Lazar Markovich Lissitzky on 10 November (23 November New Style) 1890, in Pochinok in the province of Smolensk, the artist grew up in Vitebsk in traditional Jewish surroundings. Already as a child he loved popular art.[1] At age thirteen he met Yehuda Pen, later Chagall's teacher, and at fifteen he created his first artistic work, a revolutionary almanac. He also tried his hand at woodcuts, and under the influence of Mikhail Vrubel, did portraits on canvas, none of which has been preserved. He went to high school in Smolensk, staying with his grandfather. Upon matriculation, he was denied admission to the St. Petersburg Academy of Arts because of the Jewish quota, entering instead the Darmstadt Technische Hochschule in 1909.[2] He graduated as an architect in 1914, and left soon afterwards for Russia, with the outbreak of the war.

Lissitzky's growing interest in a Jewish art form evolved as a direct reflection of the spreading renaissance of Jewish culture and nationalism (as outlined in Seth Wolitz's article in this catalog). As Lissitzky recalled some five years later, a whole generation of Jewish school children and yeshiva students had found that the study of sacred texts did not satisfy them; their Jewishness demanded more. Questions as to the place of the Jews as a nation, Jewish culture, even Jewish art were evoked, demanding solutions.[3] "Seeking to find ourselves and the shape of our time, we tried to peer into the old mirrors in order to penetrate deeply into the so-called 'folk creations.' At the beginning of our era, this path was trodden by almost all the various nations. My own case in point followed this same logic when, suddenly one summer, I let myself return to 'the folk'."[4]

Lissitzky's and the other Jewish artists' search for past sources was not an isolated phenomenon; Russian artists also turned to the provinces in quest of their cultural roots, as well as showing interest in Russian folk art. For Lissitzky this meant going on an exploratory tour, together with Issachar Ryback, along the Dnieper

River in White Russia.[5] Financed by the Jewish Histori-cal and Ethnographic Society in St. Petersburg, they set out to copy old wall paintings in synagogues and do architectural drawings of them, for which Lissitzky, with his background in architecture and engineering, was eminently suited.[6]

The dating of this expedition is open to different inter-pretations due to Lissitzky's recording: "It took place between 19.. and 1916."[7] Rachel Wischnitzer[8] inter-prets this to mean that the first exhibition of Jewish art-ists of 1916 was the event which triggered Lissitzky's wish to explore his nation's artistic heritage and spurred him to set off on the tour. Avram Kampf, in his groundbreaking article on the topic of Russian Jewish avant-garde art,[9] also writes that the tour took place in 1916, but Lissitzky's text seems to indicate that he set off in the summer of 1915, continuing into 1916. The tour may well have been broken up into different stages, as Lissitzky also visited the Druya synagogue in Lithuania, quite far from White Russia, as well as studying for a new diploma in engineering and archi-tecture in Moscow c. 1915-17,[10] and starting to work at an architectural atelier in Moscow in 1916.[11]

It is difficult to trace Lissitzky's activities on behalf of an avant-garde Jewish art, or even his general interest in the Jewish cause, before his synagogue tour. Al-though he explored ancient Jewish synagogues, man-uscripts and graveyards while studying in Germany, he showed no less interest in Christian medieval mon-uments. As mentioned he returned to Russia from Darmstadt in 1914, but what he did or how he earned his living is unclear. Claims that Lissitzky spent some time drawing with Ossip Zadkine in Vitebsk are erro-neous,[12] although he may have stayed with relatives in Vitebsk at the outset, perhaps meeting with Pen, and with Chagall, who also returned to Vitebsk with the outbreak of the war. Presumably, he socialized with in-tellectual Jews, and if not before, then certainly now, he was exposed to the ideas of Jewish cultural auton-omy. J. Leering[13] claims that Lissitzky now took an ac-tive part in the Jewish Society for the Encouragement of the Arts; however, no details are available concern-ing specific activities.

## The Beginning

The first visual example of Lissitzky's awakened inter-est in the Jewish cause which we are certain of are the surviving sketches from his exploratory tour, mainly from the Mohilev synagogue. The most interesting is the lion's head with a human face, one of the zodiac signs (cat. 67), which the artist copied with careful at-tention to detail. "Isn't that a rabbinic face on the lion's head in the zodiac painting in the Mohilev syna-gogue?" Lissitzky asks in his 1923 article (cat. 173).[14]

Lissitzky was clearly overwhelmed by the synagogue; " . . . this is the fruit of a great culture," he writes. The surprise in store was tremendous when the doors were opened; " . . . the entire shape was organized by the painter [Chaim ben Yitzhak Halevi Segal from Slutsk] with just a few basic colors, but so saturated that an entire, vast world lives here and blossoms forth and fills up this none-too-large cube." He illustrated his article with a photograph of lions holding the descrip-tions above the western entrance (fig. 55, cat. $173_2$), and drawings of a ship (fig. 78, cat. $173_3$), Jerusalem (cat. $173_6$), Worms (cat. $173_1$) and the zodiac sign of a lion (cat. 68). In addition, he includes a sea horse and bird (cat. 71) from the synagogue of Druya.

An additional zodiac sign of an archer (cat. 69) from the Mohilev synagogue exists, " . . . depicted with one hand holding the bow, the other drawing on the string. The latter is the 'strong hand,' the 'punishing hand' of the Bible . . ."[15] and a peacock (cat. 70) – " . . . on the western side above the entrance are gigantic lions with peacocks below them . . . " – can easily be identi-fied as standing behind the lion at the left side in fig. 55.

When studying these early drawings one should bear in mind that they are copies rather than Lissitzky's own creations. Thus those from Mohilev (cat. 67-70, $173_{1-6}$) have a special, sturdy quality to them: "some of his [the original artist's] drawings are remarkably laconic and vigorous,"[16] compared to the lighter, more curvilinear sea horse from Druya (cat. 71, $173_7$), no doubt reflect-ing the hand of its original creator.

Regrettably, we have no information on Lissitzky's other possible Jewish artistic enterprises of 1915 and 1916. He exhibited two paintings, *The Leader* and *Jeri-cho*, at the "World of Art" exhibition in 1917 in Petro-grad, although no illustrations exist to help us deter-mine either their content or his artistic style.

cat. 70

55, detail

ופו ישמור שלא כאש שמן ריח

55

שלא לאבד נפשו והוחז יפשפש כמעשיו ביד שהוא בכורה לוחמ כי הוצר הרים מער לא בפה יחן לשומו ופו ישמור שלא כאש שמן ריח

## Lissitzky's Jewish Works in 1917

By 1917, Lissitzky had developed his early version of a Jewish modernist style, which he pursued most fully in *Legend of Prague* (Moscow: Shamir, 1917. Text by Moshe Broderzon), which appeared in April 1917. Also called *Sikhes Kholin* (Small Talk), the book (fig. 8, cat. 74), which is based on an entry in the chronicles of the Jewish community in Prague, contains a title page, fifteen illustrated pages folded together and a colophon. It was printed in 110 copies, some of which[17] were hand-painted by the artist and backed with thin cloth, and presented in scroll form in an oak casket (fig. 9) like a Scroll of Esther. And to lay to rest a frequently disputed point: although the text is such an integral part of each illustration, it was not written by Lissitzky but by an anonymous scribe.[18]

In spite of the fact that *Legend of Prague* is Lissitzky's first Jewish work to have come down to us, it is important to note that it is not necessarily an example of his early style, but constitutes a conscious attempt by the artist to create a particularly Jewish style. Any attempts to connect the flowing lines of *Legend of Prague* to the lingering of Jugendstil influences from Darmstadt are misplaced. A comparison to Lissitzky's cover illustration for Bolshakov's *The Spent Sun* (fig. 56), which appeared in 1916, makes it clear that Lissitzky had already absorbed the latest avant-garde trends before his first purely Jewish creation appears. Using the swirling curvilinear line like decorative calligraphic writing, Lissitzky makes a statement of intention: he wants to create an ornamental drawing, fusing the style and content of the story and "the wonderful Assyrian script."[19] Lissitzky cites "Assyrian script," the term for Hebrew square letters,[20] probably in order to evoke the spirit of ancient Jewish tradition. Expressed differently, he is creating an old-new book, fusing sources from the Jewish past with modern form.

At the same time, we already sense Lissitzky's inventiveness as a designer. Although the text is not written by him, his illustrations create a very dynamic interplay with it, constantly varying the relationship between image and text with each turn of the page. Strong, fluid color is used as an expressive vehicle in a totally imaginative way. The choice of color varies from scroll to scroll, sometimes extending to the title page of the black-and-white book edition.

Among the themes are old Jews, scenes from the shtetl, and architectural elements of synagogues used in various scenes. The most remarkable are probably the title page (fig. 8, cat. 72$_1$) and colophon (cat. 72$_2$), both with a similar outline. The colophon is clearly based on the shape of a Torah ark; the title page is

56

57

comparable to ancient Hebrew printed prototypes. Lissitzky obviously draws on his impressions of his ethnographic tour with Ryback[21] and on similar finds from An-Sky's first ethnographic expedition in 1912, which probably influenced Lissitzky's decision to do his own.

Compared to the rich design of the title page, the additional, extremely rare copy of the original cover[22] (fig. 57, cat. 73) of *Legend of Prague* has a surprisingly simple composition, based on typography rather than narration. Two-dimensional and austere, it is basically built on the dramatic effect achieved by switching the black-and-white of letters vis-à-vis background, and juxtaposing round against square. (See the Appendix: Aronson, *Contemporary Jewish Graphics*, Chapter Four.) It offers further proof that Lissitzky's determined choice of an ancient style and form inside the book comes close to being the content.

Lissitzky was among the organizers of the exhibition of "Pictures and Sculpture by Jewish Artists" at Galerie Lemercier in Moscow in April 1917. The front cover of the catalog (fig. 15) surprisingly carries a copy of his colophon design, lifted straight from *Legend of Prague*. We do not know why Lissitzky failed to create an original design; however, during those years, existing designs were sometimes integrated into new works.

*Legend of Prague* is unique in its exuberant style. However, with its reference to the Scroll of Esther and ancient Hebrew prayer books, its symbolism could be seen as pretentious. Lissitzky may have had an inkling of this too, as his next important undertaking for the advancement of a new Jewish art, a set of watercolors for the *Had Gadya* (figs. 58-61), is much less "hectic," and he abandons the ancient for more recent folk-art sources, presenting the story of the kid in a purely narrative way. Curvilinear though no longer calligraphic, the line carries the traditional task of folk art; it is descriptive and separates different color areas. As in *Legend of Prague*, the colors are non-realistic, and are used for expressive purposes. Each illustration is framed by an arch, around which the text is placed, with the number in Hebrew letters on top offset by the two last words of each verse below. Lissitzky's preference for asymmetrical compositions and diagonal axes is apparent especially in figs. 58 and 59.[23]

Quite different in concept and style is Lissitzky's hand-colored linoleum cut of the Vitebsk synagogue (fig. 62, cat. 75). Placed off-center and silhouetted against a darkened sky, the building rises massively, dominating the cityscape with its sheer size. It is a suitable visualization of Lissitzky's later writings: "Synagogues were

usually placed in such a way that they would dominate the surrounding valleys. This was true of Druya, Dubrovne, and other small towns: the synagogue with its imposing mass, and especially its high roof, gives the entire town its characteristic contours, just as the character of old European cities is recognizable by its towers and cathedrals."[24]

Lissitzky's closeness to Chagall during these years has often been stressed. True, both artists frequented Pen's studio in Vitebsk, Lissitzky preceding Chagall by a couple of years, and they may well have met there. According to several sources, Lissitzky visited Zadkine, whom he knew from home, in Paris during a summer vacation sometime between 1911 and 1913.[25] Roaming the art galleries together they may have met Chagall and seen his Parisian work, although again, we do not know for sure. Upon returning to Russia, there is circumstantial evidence to suggest that he may have met Chagall in Vitebsk as the latter spent the first year there upon his return from Paris, and Lissitzky had family there. According to Sophie Lissitzky-Küppers, he soon arrived in Moscow. He may have seen the large show "Year 1915" which opened there on 5 April 1915, and in which Chagall exhibited 24 works, including five items titled *Vitebsk Landscapes*.[26] He probably saw the "Jack of Diamonds" show in November 1916 in Moscow,[27] where items 336-380 were Chagall's, including works painted in Vitebsk in 1914-15, and incidentally, items 140-199, Malevich's *Suprematism of Painting* series.[28] Efros was later to stress Chagall's "Vitebsk period" as having been important as a model for the younger generation of Jewish artists.[29]

The world of the shtetl too, as portrayed by Lissitzky in his earliest works, is thematically close to Chagall's. But then, both artists grew up in a similar milieu, and basically focused on the surroundings of Vitebsk. A certain thematic and compositional affinity can be detected occasionally, for instance by comparing Lissitzky's *Vitebsk Synagogue* (fig. 62, cat. 75) to Chagall's *Blue House* of the same year,[30] or Lissitzky's illustration for *White Russian Folktales* (cat. 108₆) to Chagall's illustration for Der Nister (cat. 144₇). Nevertheless, there is no way of knowing whether Lissitzky had seen these works or whether the similarities are coincidental.

Stylistically, the differences between the artists are greater than the affinities. Lissitzky from the very beginning attaches great importance to the typographical element, and his architectural background is reflected in his feeling for space, volume and precise line. While Chagall presents a somewhat dreamlike world with floating figures, Lissitzky solidifies his fig-

די קעצעלאך, אי׳ מֻלֻן׳טעס, גערשחט, גערשחט
אויף אײ׳ך!

58

דעסאַר האַט אים אַ שטעקעלע געמײ׳ט
אויפֿן אָרט!

59

און איבּעגשויפט האַס יאַמערל דאַס גאַנצע
פֿעלד טײ׳ך!

60

דער טוואַרבק טלאַר בליתֿל, אז ער זאַל
עלעכֿן טױט...

61

ures, and creates dynamic movements through asymmetrical compositions. The portrayal of the Vitebsk synagogue demonstrates how avant-garde Lissitzky's Jewish style can be when he chooses, and how undreamlike even his nocturnal view is.

The sign of the publishing house "Yidish" on the title page of *Kunst-Ring Almanakh* (vols. I and II, Kharkov) (fig. 63, cat. 78) appeared for the first time in 1917. Small in size, but loaded with Jewish symbolism, two miniature shtetl views are separated by Hebrew letters placed vertically to form the name of the publishing house, enclosed in the shape of a tombstone. The company name, "Yidish," is blessed by two giant, priestly hands appearing above in the dark sky, as if blessing the whole modernistically rendered Jewish world.

As of now, Lissitzky's only known illustration for a Hebrew text[31] is for C. N. Bialik's "Shlomo Hamelekh" (King Solomon) appearing in the journal *Shtilim* (Saplings) (23 October 1917, nos. 6-7) (fig. 64, cat. 77). In addition to a final major illustration, it includes eleven narrative vignettes. Each small illustration also carries a Hebrew letter instead of a number, prominently displayed in the center, though not integrated into the overall composition. Contrasting with the lively vignettes, the major illustration is static and, like the *Kunst-Ring Almanakh* logo, loaded with Jewish symbolism; the references to God, the Tablets of the Law, the seven-branched candelabrum, Solomon's Temple, and the attire of King Solomon – from the black-and-white borderlines resembling the pattern of a prayer shawl, to the Star of David topping his oriental head covering – must have touched a core of hope for a better Jewish future, shared by Lissitzky and the Jewish reader alike at this particular time.

The final known work Lissitzky did in 1917 in the pursuit of a Jewish art are designs for the front and back covers of *U rek vavilonskikh* (By the Rivers of Babylon) (fig. 12), published by Safrut in Moscow. We recognize the figure on the back cover as identical to that in one of the vignettes in "Shlomo Hamelekh" (cat. 77₄). On the front cover, a floral folk design is combined with a deer, a popular motif on Jewish gravestones. New, or rather different, is Lissitzky's treatment of it, indicating that he has studied the formal and stylistic foundations of Jewish folk art, reaching conclusions similar to Altman's in his *Jewish Graphics* (cat. 30). The treatment of the deer, together with the crystallized space surrounding the title, which is a foreign element in Jewish folk art, shows that Lissitzky has definitely given up conjuring an ancient aura as well as pure decoration, for the portrayal of Jewish folk art, fused with a more avant-garde style. This is the path Lissitzky would follow and explore for the next year and a half.

62

64

63

## The 1918-19 Works

The year 1918 saw few works by Lissitzky; the only Jewish one was *Di Vayse Tsig* (Kiev: Kiever Farlag), a Yiddish translation of Alphonse Daudet's *La chèvre de M. Seguin*, in addition to two non-Jewish commissions.[32] However, in that year Lissitzky was probably busy preparing several of the many works which appeared in 1919.

The major book illustration of 1919 to be prepared in 1918 was undoubtedly *Yingl Tsingl Khvat* (The Mischievous Boy) (cat. 79), containing children's poems written by Mani Leib (Brahinsky). In comparison to the rather small books to follow, this is an impressive edition with a three-color cover in blue, red, and yellow on white, and large black-and-white illustrations interacting with the text. Consequently each page, as in *Legend of Prague*, is composed in a different way. Lissitzky's interest in the Hebrew letter is clearly felt in the play with several of the starting letters, quite like the letter in an illuminated manuscript, though produced in a modernist shape. The page numbers too are integrated in a decorative way to form small illustrations. This is done more successfully than in "Shlomo Hamelekh" (cat. 77).

This is a children's world, portrayed against the backdrop of the shtetl, much like Lissitzky's own childhood must have looked, and capturing an atmosphere similar to Ryback's in his *Shtetl* (cat. 136). Especially impressive is page one (fig. 65), with the old, devout Jew in his prayer shawl bridging the two worlds, represented by the synagogue and the church and augmented by the small figures of a pig and a goat below. The line is either fluid or somewhat jerky, and shading and volume are treated much like the cover of *By the Rivers of Babylon* (fig. 12). The trademark of the Yidisher Folks Farlag publishing house appearing on the title page (cat. 79) is clearly inspired by Jewish folk art. The custom of borrowing illustrations for use in different publications has already been noted. Thus the upper left side of the last page in *Yingl Tsingl Khvat* (cat. $79_{10}$) has been lifted, number and all, to mark the end of *Hob Ikh Mir a Liedele* (I Have a Little Song) (fig. 66), a collection of Yiddish folksongs and poems, published in 1922 by the Kultur Lige in Warsaw. This certainly testifies to the decorativeness of Lissitzky's number! In addition to illustrations borrowed from Chagall, Ryback, Tchaikov, Yudovin and Szyk, Lissitzky is also represented in this book with a smaller version of the chicken taken from *Yingl Tsingl Khvat*, walking alone without additions below, and by the interior view from the center of page four (cat. $79_5$).

Appearing in 1919, but probably planned earlier and echoing the illustrations of "Shlomo Hamelekh" (see especially fig. 64), is Lissitzky's cover for notes to Joel Engel's music (fig. 67, cat. 82), published by the Society for Yiddish Music in Moscow.[33] Rather surprisingly for Lissitzky, whose compositions are usually dynamic and asymmetrical, even when portraying a single person (see cat. $79_9$), this cover is static and symmetrical almost to a fault. Even the typography is unimaginative. The main attention is drawn to the two crowing cocks, and the strangely dressed men at the top. In the only thematic connection to the context they lift up their heads, which recall those of Assyrian warriors, and blow their rams' horns. We do not know whether the reserve stems from demands made by the commissioning society on our artist, or from the fact that Lissitzky is addressing the adult Jewish public.

In D. Dolgopolski's *Dem Zeydns Kloles* (Grandfather's Curses) (Moscow: Tsentraln Yidishn Komisariat, 1919), a children's comedy in one act, the cover illustration of a boy with a mask in hand (cat. 83) already sets the context, with the typography assuming an important part of the composition. The two illustrations inside are also meant for the theatre; one shows three figures in a theatrical scene (cat. $83_1$), the other looks like a stage design for a typically Jewish interior (cat. $83_2$). Regrettably the printing is of rather bad quality, and the illustrations very small, thus diminishing their power.

This is true also for Jacob Fichman's *Shabes in Vald* (Sabbath in the Forest) (Kiev: Kiever Farlag, 1919). Its three small illustrations (cat. 84) are stylistically and thematically close to *Yingl Tsingl Khvat* although they lack the latter's visual and typographical interaction.

By now Lissitzky must have been one of the most sought-after artists among the Jewish publishing houses, as is attested by the designs he made for them. The sign for "Yidish" in *Kunst-Ring Almanakh* (fig. 63, cat. 78) has already been mentioned. So too has the logo of the Yidisher Folks Farlag (fig. 68), which, starting from *Yingl Tsingl Khvat*, appears on a large number of books published by this house. On this as well as on an additional logo for this publishing house (fig. 69), lettering is integrated into the composition, which is architectural, prefiguring *Had Gadya* in its structure. Also frequently appearing is the design for Kiever Farlag (fig. 70, cat. 81), bearing the influence of Jewish folk art.

A children's illustration showing the first inklings of Suprematist influence is the cover for *Mayselekh*, Der Nister's translation into Yiddish of Hans Christian Andersen's *Fairy Tales* (Kiev: Kiever Farlag, 1919)

האָב אַ מעשהלע אַ שיינע,
פאַר די קינדער מײַנע קליינע,
זײַט זשע, קינדער, שטיל און שאַ
ס׳איז מײַן מעשהלע אַזאַ:

ערגעץ ווײַט, ווײַט, ווײַט פון דאַנען,
צוצוקומען ניט מיט באַנען,
ניט מיט שיפן, ניט מיט פערד —
ערגעץ אויף אַ ווײַטער ערד

האָט אַ טאָל זיך דאָרט געפונען,
און אין טאָל איז דורכגערונען,
ווי אַ שנירל ווײַט און גלײַך,
ווײַט און גלײַך, אַ קליינער טײַך.

און בײַם טײַך פון ביידע ברעגן,
זײַנען שטיבער פיל געלעגן.
שטיבער, גאַסן און אַ מאַרק,
און בײַם זײַט פון מאַרק אַ באַרג.

און די גוים און די ייִדן
האָבן דאָרט געלעבט צופרידן.
ווער אין פרייד און ווער אין נויט,
יעדער האָט געהאַט זײַן ברויט.

(fig. 30, cat. 85). The typography is again an important part of the dynamics of the design, in which mass and voids interact with the stylized contour of the flying bird carrying a child. While the typography still has a folksy appearance, the bird and the child are stripped of their natural look and infused instead with an "industrial" touch. The picture is signed very discreetly with initials in the lower right corner.

The *Had Gadya* of 1919 (Kiev: Kultur Lige, edition of 75) (cat. 90) and its watercolor illustrations are acknowledged to be Lissitzky's most splendid Jewish work. This sumptuous edition of ten color lithographs with a title page comes as a change after the small and low-keyed illustrations preceding it. Lissitzky was one of the founders of the newly established Kultur Lige in Kiev and it was thus natural that he should undertake a large-scale, color lithographic printing endeavor.

Compared to the 1917 *Had Gadya* watercolors (figs. 58-61), the change in Lissitzky's style as well as outlook vis-à-vis his Jewish works is striking. The Hebrew letters have been given a geometric character, creating an architectural order on each page; the folk-art line has given way to a crisp edge, the colors have become more somber, the elongated figures in diagonal "slow" movement are now locked in circular, even turbulent states, and naturalistic volume has yielded to large, flat masses. Still narrative, the illustrations show a clear tendency towards greater abstraction, and a new spatial experimentation is especially evident in pages five and six of the set. If ever there was a closeness to Chagall in Lissitzky's illustrations, it has now given way to other influences of a more radical nature. The most obvious inspiration comes from the charismatic Malevich and his circle. In 1916, while Lissitzky was probably working in Moscow, Malevich showed Suprematist works twice there and published Suprematist manifestos that Lissitzky presumably read, although his art as yet remained unaffected by them. By 1918, however, Malevich's powerful influence was felt by a large group of artists, its first effects seemingly also touching Lissitzky.

More remarkable than the change in Lissitzky's style over the two preceding years is his change in outlook. In order to encompass this we have to divert our discussion from Lissitzky's Jewish works to his view of the new social order, well summed up by his statement:
> In Moscow in 1918 there flashed before my eyes the short circuit which split the world in two. This single blow pushed the time we call the present like a wedge between yesterday and tomorrow. My efforts are now directed to driving the wedge deeper. One must belong on this side or on that – there is no mid-way.[34]

The Jewish masses generally welcomed the Bolshevik Revolution as a harbinger of freedom, ending Tsarist repression. Lissitzky too, like most of his Russian colleagues, not only hailed it, but very enthusiastically employed his art in its service. He designed the first flag for the Central Committee of the Communist Party for the 1918 May Day celebrations,[35] and possibly took part in producing the propaganda works in Moscow in autumn 1918, although information on this is scarce.[36]

While intellectually moving over to the left at an early stage, Lissitzky gives no visual indication of this in his Jewish artistic output up to *Had Gadya*. Likewise, while putting his art into the service of the revolutionary cause, his few non-Jewish graphics also remain unaffected by his new ideas until 1919.

The set of watercolors (fig. 71, cat. 87-89) was lithographed with minor changes; the colored backgrounds in some of the arches of the watercolors have been replaced with white (except for the illustration of "Then Came Death and Took the Butcher"), the colors are more subdued, and the diminutive figures which are inside the page number are usually omitted. Leaving out this decorative addition which was common in ancient Haggadot indicates Lissitzky's diminishing concern for old Jewish sources.

66

68

69

A single watercolor page (fig. 72, cat. 86), which surprisingly shows a different version of the first verse of *Had Gadya*, is presently known of, although it has been overlooked in all previous discussions of *Had Gadya*.[37] This page, with its animal-filled letter א standing for page number one, and its curious jerkiness of movement, was clearly conceived before the watercolors. Although the general composition is similar to the watercolors, there are striking changes, primarily in the treatment of the central group.

Whereas in the earlier version the old Jew fed the goat while the boy carried it, forming a rather tightly knit group encircled by the rainbow, in the later watercolor the relationships are reversed. The old man and the goat stand together, separated by the upper part of the rainbow from the boy, who is now offering nourishment to the goat. The rainbow ends in a point directly above the head of the boy, as if forming a covenant with him exclusively.[38] For Lissitzky the perfectionist, the switching of tasks and positions within the group must have been meaningful,[39] and artistically confirms his move away from Jewish tradition to a belief in the new.

While the traditional *Had Gadya* story demonstrates the ultimate power of God over evil and death, Lissitzky illustrates the story in such a way as to also include his new messianic view of redemption through the Communist Revolution. *Had Gadya* traditionally carries an allegorical meaning in which the goat symbolizes the oppressed Jewish people.[40] Lissitzky's change in composition, with the goat being fed by the young boy and not the old Jew, signifies his own switch of allegiance.

This assumption is reinforced when we consider that Alan Birnholz has already concluded that "Lissitzky presented a parable of the final, complete victory of the Revolution"[41] in *Had Gadya*, basing himself in particular on the final episode, "And God Slays the Angel of Death," the angel in the 1917 version being drawn dying (fig. 61) and in 1919 being drawn dead (fig. 73).

In a convincing article, Haia Friedberg goes one step further. Scrutinizing all the illustrations, she found numerous examples that "Lissitzky tries to persuade the Jewish public of the justice of the Communist way by using traditional language symbols and characteristic Jewish values."[42] Thus, the Angel of Death enters through the door wearing a crown closely resembling Russian folklore depictions of the Tsarist crown, and symbolically also lies dead wearing the same crown in the last illustration. Here too, the divine hand is similar to that "on one of the first series of stamps printed after the Revolution in 1918, the hand of the Soviet people of the Revolution uprooting slavery and oppression."[43]

70

דוֹבְּן אַבָּא

73

The arguments of both Birnholz and Friedberg are significantly strengthened by the comparison of the hitherto overlooked "extra" version of *Had Gadya*.

In this period of political turmoil, the world of art saw innovations and rapid changes, as also reflected in Lissitzky's art. While *Had Gadya*, which is Lissitzky's most "advanced" creation thus far, carries the revolutionary message in Jewish folk terms, a real transition appears in its exceedingly rare dustjacket[44] (figs. 74, 75), published for the first time in 1982.[45]

The dustjacket shows a new artistic language: here Lissitzky has essentially abandoned figuration and the Jewish world and entered into the world of abstraction. It carries the date 6.2.1919, predating Lissitzky's arrival in Vitebsk, which, according to most sources, occurred sometime during the late spring or summer of 1919. The *Had Gadya* lithographs must, stylistically, have been executed towards the end of 1918, with the watercolors preceding them. The remarkable change in concept and style in the dustjacket proves that Lissitzky was exposed to powerful influences, at the latest around January 1919.

Until more material in the Soviet Union is made available to art historians, we have little information on

Lissitzky's activities in 1917 and 1918. All we know is that "at this time of great unrest Lissitzky was restlessly travelling from place to place."[46] During 1918-19 he was a member of IZO Narkompros (People's Commissariat for Enlightenment),[47] and he probably arrived in Vitebsk from Kiev, where he had been influential in setting up the Kultur Lige.

In addition to Malevich's at least indirect influence on Lissitzky's *Had Gadya* lithographs, his new language on the dustjacket may also bear the mark of Suprematist works by Alexandra Exter, who had her own studio in Kiev at this time. Finally, Malevich's works at the "Tenth State Exhibition," which opened in January 1919 in Moscow, may well have been seen by Lissitzky and influenced him strongly, as demonstrated by the dustjacket.

It is tempting to decipher in the abstract play the lower part of a powerful striding figure, perhaps standing for the newly liberated Russian masses, marching for the Revolution.[48] Putting a dark shoe forward, the figure pushes up the Yiddish text for *Had Gadya*, the other foot prodding a sun-like disk, which brings to mind Lissitzky's opening text from his album *Victory Over the Sun* (Hanover, 1923): "The sun as the expression of the world's age-old energy is torn down from the sky

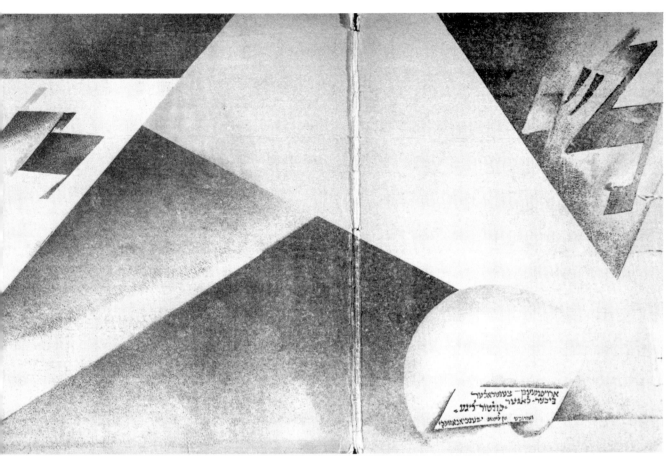

74

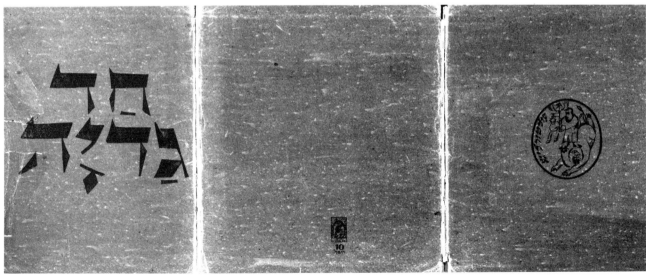

75

76

by modern man; the power of his technical supremacy creates for itself a new source of energy."

Lissitzky was hopeful that the younger generation would accept the Revolution: "The educated were expecting the 'new era' to arrive in the shape of a Messiah . . . mounted on a white horse. But . . . it came in the shape of Russian Ivan . . . in tattered and dirty clothes, barefoot . . . only the youngest generation recognized this. . . ."[49]

Did the Jewish public understand and appreciate Lissitzky's new message, intertwined in *Had Gadya*? In a review a year later the illustrations for it were criticized as "too schematic and generally 'overworked,' and having no value for children except as a gift from a child to an adult."[50] Nevertheless *Had Gadya* must have been popular, as is testified by a second, smaller black-and-white edition of 1,000 copies, published in 1923 in Warsaw (cat. 91).[51]

It was probably necessity that forced Lissitzky and the writer Ben Zion Raskin, on 22 April 1919, to sign a contract with the Yidisher Folks Farlag Kooperativ in Kiev, selling their rights to the publishing house for a series of eleven children's stories in Yiddish under the general title "Kindergarten." Lissitzky and Raskin undertook to do all the necessary work (writing, illustrating, matching text to pictures, supervising the lithographic process, etc.). Both would receive 1.600 rubles together for each story, and 15 percent of the price of all copies sold after the first 5000. Five stories were to be delivered by July 1st, the rest by the end of September 1919.[52]

The Herculean task of finishing eleven books within five months indicates Lissitzky's need for money during this tempestuous time. As he wrote in a letter to his beloved, Sophie Küppers, when faced with a simi-

lar situation six years later: "In order to make some money, I have to devote myself once again to book covers and posters; then maybe I can bring my earnings up to 500 rubles a month, but that means ruining myself physically and artistically. . . ."[53] The "mass production" also may explain the rather sketchy quality of *Der Milner, di Milnerin un di Milshtayner* (The Miller, His Wife and Their Millstones) (cat. 92), and *Der Ber* (The Bear) (cat. 94). In a possible attempt to make *Der Milner* more appealing, the illustrations in the later edition published by the Kultur Lige in Warsaw in 1922 were enlarged and printed in green, with the text in red (cat. 93).[54] The above-mentioned two books and *Di Hun vos hot Gevolt hoben a Kam* (The Rooster that Wanted a Comb) seem to have been the only ones to appear in this series. All three have the same cover design, although in *Di Hun* this design has been pushed to the left side and Lissitzky introduces the first purely Suprematist elements in a children's book (fig. 76, cat. 95), also splurging on a two-color printing.

Why didn't Lissitzky fulfill his contract? We can only speculate that by now he was moving to Vitebsk to start teaching in Chagall's art school, thus securing a more regular income.

77

## The Last Jewish Works

All major studies on Lissitzky so far were written before the discovery of the dustjacket. It proves, however, that Lissitzky arrived in Vitebsk not only supporting the Bolshevik Revolution, but also with an artistic vocabulary, fully ready to assimilate Malevich's Suprematism and create his own Proun (acronym of "Project for the Affirmation of the New") works.

Birnholz has attempted to see Lissitzky's Prouns as "transcending" the old Jewish tradition and as a continuation of his Jewish themes on a higher level,[55] even suggesting that restrictions on Jewish art and the desire to create a new art made Lissitzky turn to a literal acceptance of the Second Commandment.[56] Chimen Abramsky has voiced the opposing view that Lissitzky devoted the years 1917-22 to Yiddish illustrations and that they constitute a period somewhat isolated from his works to come.[57] The Polish-Jewish artist Henryk Berlewi has written dramatically about the high price Lissitzky had to pay when sacrificing Jewish art on the altar of Constructivism.[58]

Lissitzky himself acknowledges only 1917-20 as a time of Yiddish illustrations.[59] In the light of all his subse-

78

quent statements, there is no reason to doubt the fact that Lissitzky's shift of interest from a Jewish renaissance to involvement in the Revolution resulted in an artistic language directed not only towards Jews, but, stripped of any national connotations, towards everyone. Or to put it more bluntly "we . . . blasted aside the old work of art . . ." and ". . . the subject with its plague-ridden aura of individualism."[60]

Lissitzky saw the Revolution as the start of a new era, in which he wanted to be an active participant as an artist and architect. In fact, given the outlook of the "leftist" artists, any other choice at that time would have been inconceivable, and artists not willing to serve the new era through their art generally left Russia rather than compromise themselves.

En route to Berlin in 1921, Lissitzky stopped in Warsaw, where he met Berlewi, at this time intensively engaged in Jewish emancipation and art. However, he failed to involve Lissitzky, who by then was only interested in Suprematism.[61]

In spite of Lissitzky's newly adapted "radical" outlook on art – and his own statement that he dealt with Jewish themes only up to 1920 – we have to consider his impressive collage, often called *A Journey to America*, which illustrates the story "Shifs Karta" (fig. 32, cat. 105) in Ilya Ehrenburg's *Six Stories with Easy Endings* (Moscow, Berlin: Helikon, 1922). This collage is one of six illustrations for the book; as one of the other illustrations includes a collage cut out from a newspaper dated 20 April 1922, our work may be dated to the same period.

That this work – the only one in the book – includes Jewish symbolism should not be seen as a continuation of Lissitzky's former plans to create a Jewish avant-garde art. In spite of the profound layers of meaning given to the work,[62] the illustration was, after all, created to complement Ehrenburg's story, in which the reader, through the Jewish watchmaker Hirsch, is introduced to the horror of pogroms. Hirsch has a son in the United States, who writes him letters in poor Russian. Writing that something happy will soon occur, he promises Hirsch a *shifs karta* (boat ticket), but although Hirsch repeatedly asks everyone what this means, nobody knows and he is finally considered mad. One Yom Kippur (the Day of Atonement), Communists break into the synagogue, burning the Torah scroll. Hirsch is unable to understand why God allows this. After a discussion including much Kabbalistic talk, Hirsch comes to believe that new pogroms are a sign of the coming of the Messiah. He hears shooting one morning and runs outside. Seeing a tall man riding by on a white horse he cries, "He's here, he's here, the *shifs-karta* is here," whereupon the man shoots him.

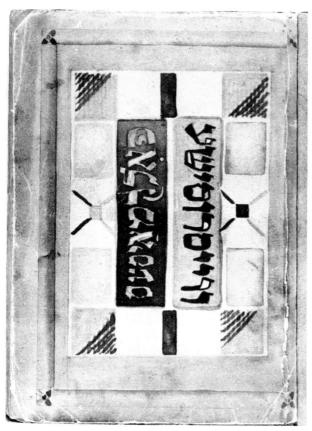 

79

The collage is enigmatic, as is the story itself. Whether the "new world" implied by the boat ticket to New York glued to the work should be considered as the future hope, or whether belief in it equals death, as implied by the black, forbidding hand with the Hebrew letters פ"נ ("here lies"), still remains unsolved.

Two richly illustrated books then appeared in 1922 and 1923, respectively, although judging from both style and content, we would have expected them to be executed in 1919 at the latest. *Ukraynishe Folkmayses* (Ukrainian Folktales) (Der Yidisher Sektsie bam Komisariat far Folkbildung, 1922, translated from Ukrainian into Yiddish by L. Kvitko) contains ten illustrations (cat. 103, see also cat. 96 - 102). Solidly drawn, with strongly shaded contours, the figures, which are basically two-dimensional, if sometimes slightly Cubistically rendered, appear surrounded by added details in fine lines. Here and there are elements we recognize from his earlier works. For instance, the elongated bird (cat. 100) and the cat (cat. $103_7$) in their curvilinearity hark back to the 1917 works, while the ship (fig. 77) is practically identical to the one Lissitzky copied at Mohilev (fig. 78), and the bear (cat. 101) looks like a visualization of a description from Lissi-

tzky's memories of Mohilev: "A bear climbs a tree looking for honey." Simultaneously, stylistic elements such as the cylindrical movement of the chicken (cat. $103_7$) approach the more fully developed similar turbulence in *Had Gadya* (cat. $90_{5,6}$).

The fourteen illustrations in *Vaysrusishe Folkmayses* (White Russian Folktales) (Der Yidisher Sektsie bam Komisariat far Folkbildung, 1923, translated from White Russian into Yiddish by L. Kvitko) (cat. 108) are similar in style albeit more restrained, with less details, the focus being solely on the figures. Several of the figures lack any reference to a background setting. The delicate treatment and Chagallian airiness in cat. $108_6$ is exceptional for these two books. Nevertheless, unlike Chagall, Lissitzky has a need to solidify even his floating figures and give them a reference. The comparison of the two covers offers an interesting juxtaposition. The *White Russian Folktales* cover (fig. 79) is astonishingly naively designed, as if by a real folk artist, in yellow, brown, and pink. The *Ukrainian Folktales* cover (fig. 80), on the other hand, is done by a sophisticated designer. Reference to the folktales is given in the geometrical ornamentation around the edges while the Hebrew lettering, apart from the first letter – larger

80

in scale than the rest, and freestanding as the opening letter in an ancient, illuminated prayer book – is kept within an avant-garde design, repeated on the back cover.

Probably stemming from the time of printing (1922), or perhaps from 1921, when Lissitzky visited Warsaw, is the new title page for the second edition of *Yingl Tsingl Khvat* (Warsaw: Kultur Lige, 1922) (fig. 81), added after the original cover design drawn in 1918. Here, Lissitzky bases his purely typographical design on the expressivity of the Hebrew lettering combined with the dynamics of diagonal thrusts, creating an ultra-modern page. The change in style and concept within the timespan of the first and second edition is striking.

In Berlin, Lissitzky also designed the cover for *Rabbi* (cat. 107) by Olga Forsch (A. Terek) (Berlin: Verlag Skythen, 1922), and published his "Memoirs of the Mohilev Synagogue" (1923) (cat. 173).[63] Still, Lissitzky's major works at this time had no connection to anything Jewish. As Ehrenburg recalls from this period: "Lissitzky firmly believed in Constructivism. In ordinary life he was mild, exceedingly kind, at times naive. . . . He fell in love in the way that people used

to fall in love in the past century – blindly, self-sacrificingly. But in art he was like a fanatical mathematician, finding his inspiration in precision and working himself up over austerity. . . ."[64]

cat. 108₁, detail

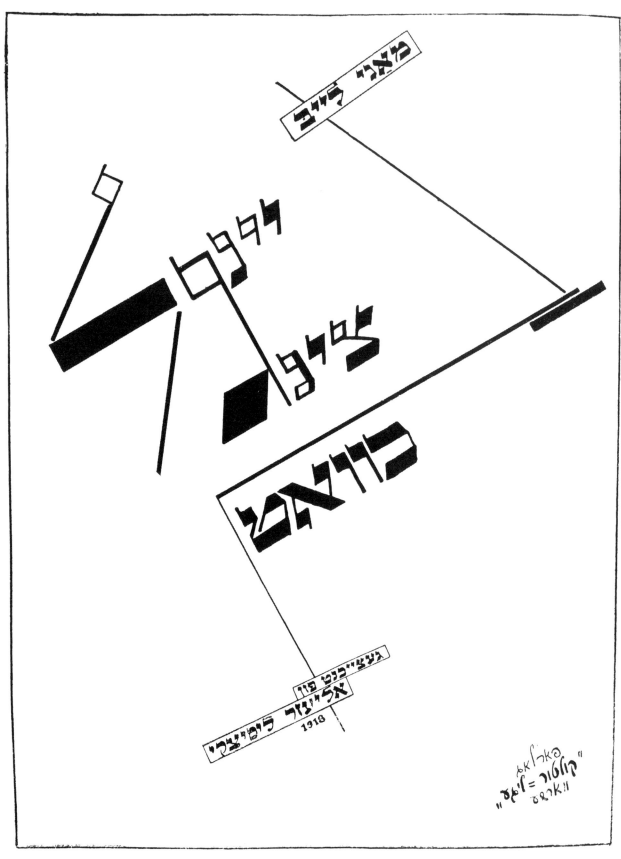

## Epilogue

Lissitzky's Jewish works, which stem from a very short period in his creative life, also mark the beginning of his development as a maturing artist, his student years now a closed chapter. In the quest for new solutions to new challenges, a certain eclecticism is unavoidable. On the other hand, certain forms can be discerned in Lissitzky's work from the very beginning. We see the first hints of crystallized space already in 1917, in the space surrounding the title of *By the Rivers of Babylon* (fig. 12) and in the rays of the sun in the 1917 *Had Gadya* (fig. 60). It reappears in a more advanced form in the cover to Hans Christian Andersen's *Fairy Tales* (fig. 30, cat. 85), becoming even more avant-garde in nos. 7 and 9 of the 1919 *Had Gadya* (cat. 90$_{7,9}$), finding its final form in the dustjacket (fig. 74).

Another, even earlier shape is that of a flying or ascending figure combined with a round shape. This composition appears for the first time at the top of the drawing *Reminiscence of Ravenna*, c. 1914.[65] A variation on the theme appears in *The Spent Sun* (1916) (fig. 56), another one on the title page of *Legend of Prague* (fig. 8), and still a third one in the portrayal of God in the 1917 *Had Gadya* (fig. 61). Stripped of figuration, the round shape in the 1919 *Had Gadya* (fig. 73) has gained in importance. Pulled down in the dustjacket (fig. 74) it becomes a prominent compositional element to appear fully developed in Lissitzky's Prouns.

Although Lissitzky's attempt to create a modernist Jewish art was brief, his output is impressive. Within the period of three to four years one can follow a fascinating development from his 1916 copies of Jewish folk art and his exuberance in the 1917 decorative work of *Legend of Prague*, with swirling lines, to the crystallization and maturity of his concept and growing political awareness in *Had Gadya* and its dustjacket, up to his breakthrough from a national, cultural background to an international, abstract framework, free of any local connotations.

This study is only concerned with Lissitzky's graphic works that appear in the West. It is hoped that a systematic search for additional graphic works and early oils by him will eventually be undertaken in the Soviet Union itself. Uncovering more examples from Lissitzky's early career would greatly add to our understanding of this artist, who is so important for the study of Jewish avant-garde and international art alike.

1   Sophie Lissitzky-Küppers, *El Lissitzky. Life. Letters. Texts.* London: Thames and Hudson, 1968, p. 15.
2   For more biographical data, see especially ibid., pp. 15-19; J. Leering, "Einführung," in *El Lissitzky* [Eindhoven exhibition catalog], Stedelijk van Abbemuseum, Eindhoven, and Kestner-Gesellschaft, Hanover, 1965, pp. 8-9; and Alan C. Birnholz, *El Lissitzky* (book-length study of the art of El Lissitzky, 1890-1941) Ph.D. thesis, Ann Arbor: University Microfilms, 1974, pp. 1-15.
3   El Lissitzky, "The Synagogue of Mohilev," *Milgroim/Rimon*, no. 3, Berlin, 1923. A translation of the entire article appears in the documentary section.
4   Ibid.
5   Prof. Chimen Abramsky remembers being told by Boris Aronson that he also took part in this ethnographic tour, and that his collection (see cat. 1-17, 67-71) consists of materials copied then, mostly by Lissitzky.
6   This type of travelling exploration was not new to Lissitzky. He writes, "I received my basic education in my wanderings through Europe – for example I traversed Italy on foot in 1912, making sketches of it and studying it." In "Information on the Work of the Book Artist," *El Lissitzky*, Cologne: Galerie Gmurzynska, 1976, p. 81.
He also took other trips during his holidays, for instance when he drew the interior of the ancient synagogue at Worms, and especially its lion reliefs, later to appear in his Jewish works (Küppers. op. cit., p. 16).
7   *Milgroim/Rimon*, op. cit.
8   Rachel Wischnitzer, "The Wise Men of Worms," *Reconstructionist*, vol. XXV, no. 9, 15 June 1959, p. 10.
9   Avram Kampf, "In Quest of the Jewish Style in the Era of the Russian Revolution," *Journal of Jewish Art*, vol. 5, 1978, p. 51.
10   Different scholars date his studies at various dates between 1915 and 1917.
11   Küppers, op. cit., p. 19.
12   This conclusion probably stems from Zadkine's short article on Lissitzky, first published in the Eindhoven catalog, op. cit., p. 60, and reprinted in Küppers, op. cit., p. 393. Zadkine's dates, however, are wrong. At the outbreak of World War I Zadkine remained in Paris, eventually volunteering for the French army. Prior to all this, he returned from a sojourn in England to Smolensk in 1908, and spent that summer in Vitebsk. In his memoirs he mentions meeting Pen and Chagall on this occasion. See: Ossip Zadkine, *Le Maillet et le Ciseau: souvenirs de ma vie*, Paris: Editions Albin Michel, 1968, p. 82.
13   J. Leering, op. cit., p. 8.
14   *Milgroim/Rimon*, op. cit.
15   Ibid.
16   Ibid.
17   The most commonly accepted number is 20, as stated, for instance, by Küppers, op. cit., p. 20, and by Angelica Rudenstine in *The George Costakis Collection/Russian Avant-Garde*, New York: Harry N. Abrams, 1981, p. 243. However, there seems to be no way of verifying this number.
18   The three stars in the Russian text of the colophon make this clear. For the opposing view, see Birnholz, op. cit., pp. 18, 56-57, footnote 19.
19   As stated in the colophon.
20   The term "Assyrian script" was given to the Hebrew square letters in which the Talmud was written, to distinguish it from the ancient Hebrew "daats" script. See *The Hebrew Encyclopedia*, vol. 26, pp. 625-626 (in Hebrew).
21   For more details on the Mohilev synagogue and Ryback's contribution, see: Ruth Apter-Gabriel, "A Drawing Comes to Light: The Ceiling of the Mohilev Synagogue by Ryback," *Israel Museum News*, vol. VI, 1987, pp. 69-74.
22   See *Christie's London, Important Modern and Contempo-*

*rary Prints*, Wednesday, 25 June 1986, lot 649. This writer is aware of only two copies.

23  Unfortunately, only the illustrations for numbers 3, 4, 7 and 10 have been published (in Küppers, op. cit., illus. 16-19). The entire set is kept in the Tretyakov Gallery in Moscow.

24  *Milgroim/Rimon*, op. cit.

25  According to Küppers, op. cit., p. 19, it was the summer of 1911, but a photograph of both in 1912 is printed; Birnholz, op. cit., p. 7, claims it was in the summer of 1912; Christina Lodder in *Russian Constructivism*, New Haven and London: Yale University Press, 1983, p. 248, says it occurred during 1912 and 1913.

26  According to Donald E. Gordon, *Modern Art Exhibitions 1900-1916*, Munich: Prestel-Verlag, 1974, p. 870.

27  Camilla Gray relates that Lissitzky also participated in it. *The Great Experiment: Russian Art 1863-1922*, London: Thames and Hudson, 1962, p. 291.

28  According to Gordon, op. cit., p. 896. At the show "Modern Russian Painting," Petrograd, Dec. 10, 1916 – Jan. 14, 1917, Chagall included two drawings (nos. 204, 205) for the book by Der Nister, Gordon, op. cit. At present there is no way of knowing whether Lissitzky was in Petrograd on this date.

29  Franz Meyer, *Marc Chagall*, New York: Harry N. Abrams, 1963, p. 256.

30  For illustration see ibid., p. 273.

31  Although Raskin's *Hatohen, Hatohenet Ve'avnei Harehayim* appeared in Warsaw in 1922, this is only a Hebrew translation of the Yiddish text *Der Milner, di Milnerin un di Milshtayner*, Kiev, 1919, and Lissitzky's illustrations for both are identical.

32  Unfortunately, I have not seen a copy of *Di Vayse Tsig*. The two non-Jewish works are the design for Paul Gauguin's *Noa Noa*, Moscow, 1918 (illus. p. 20 in Küppers, op. cit.) and the design for the Helikon Press, appearing in Abram Efros and Yakov Tugendkhold, *Iskusstvo Marka Shagala* (The Art of Marc Chagall), Moscow: Helikon, 1918, illus. p. 97 in Troels Andersen, *Moderne russisk kunst 1910-1930*, Copenhagen: Borgen, 1967.

33  The same composition appears on several of Engel's music notes.

34  From a typescript in the Lissitzky archive. Central State Archives for Literature and Art (TsGALI), Moscow, no. 58. Quoted in Küppers, op. cit., p. 325.

35  Ibid., p. 20.

36  Birnholz, op. cit., p. 43.

37  It was published in Camilla Gray, op. cit., illus. 162.

38  The rainbow is an ancient Jewish symbol for universal peace and tranquility, based on Genesis 9:13: "My bow I do set in the cloud, and it shall be for a token of the covenant between Me and the earth."

39  Other minor differences: the letters are on an orange background, as opposed to white. A large goat's head is sketched in very thinly behind the young boy and the tiny house, whereas we see the red contour of a small cat in the later watercolor and lithograph.

40  For a concise explanation of *Had Gadya*, see *Encyclopedia Judaica*, Jerusalem: Keter, 1971, vol. 7, pp. 1048-49.

41  Alan C. Birnholz, "El Lissitzky and the Jewish Tradition," *Studio International*, London, vol. 186, no. 959, October 1973, p. 131.

42  Haia Friedberg, "Lissitzky's *Had Gadîá*," *Jewish Art* (formerly, *Journal of Jewish Art*), vol. 12/13, 1986-87, pp. 292-303.

43  Ibid.

44  Each *Had Gadya* set originally was enclosed in a dustjacket, as listed in Ratner-Kvitni, *Dos Yidishe Buch in F.S. S.R. far di Yohren 1917-1921*, Kiev, 1930. This writer knows of only three copies.

45  For the first note on the appearance of the dustjacket, see:

John Bowlt, "A Child's Topography of Typography," *Art News*, vol. 81, no. 7, September 1982, pp. 13, 14, 17.

46  Küppers, op. cit., p. 20.

47  *Russian Art of the Avant-Garde*, John E. Bowlt, ed., New York: The Viking Press, 1976, p. 151.

48  The figure is formalistically close to Malevich's *The Woodcutter* of 1912 in the Stedelijk Museum, Amsterdam, although it is doubtful whether Lissitzky saw this work, as it was shown at the "Union of Youth," in St. Petersburg, 4 Dec. 1912 - 10 Jan. 1913, while Lissitzky was abroad studying, and again at the Sixteenth State Exhibition in Moscow, 1919-20 (i.e., long after the dustjacket had appeared). These dates are according to Troels Andersen, *Malevich*, Amsterdam: Stedelijk Museum, 1970, p. 87.

49  Lissitzky in "New Russian Art: A Lecture," Küppers, op. cit., p. 331.

50  *Kultur un Bildung* (Culture and Education), Moscow: Der Kultur un Bildungs Abtaylung dem Komisariat Far Yidishe Inyonim, no. 1 (24), 1920, p. 39.

51  Only the title page is in blue with red letters. Otherwise it is similar except that on the cover, the place "Kiev" and the word "lithographed" have been removed, and the last letter of *Had Gadya* was changed from the Hebrew letter ה to א.

52  Communicated by Peter Nisbet, curator at the Busch-Reisinger Museum, Harvard University, U.S.A.

53  Lissitzky in a letter to Küppers, 5 November 1925. Küppers, op. cit., p. 70.

54  The name of the series, *Kindergarten*, was exchanged for *Far Klayne Kinder* (For Small Children). Similarily the Hebrew edition (Warsaw: Tarbut, 1922) kept the larger format, with dark green illustrations combined with brown text.

55  Birnholz, "El Lissitzky and the Jewish Tradition," op. cit., p. 32.

56  Ibid.

57  Chimen Abramsky, "El Lissitzky as Jewish Illuminator and Typographer," *Studio International*, London, vol. 172, no. 882, October 1966, p. 182.

58  Henryk Berlewi, "El Lissitzky in Warschau," *El Lissitzky*, [Eindhoven exhibition catalog], op. cit., pp. 61-63 (German).

59  "Autobiography by El Lissitzky," Galerie Gmurzynska, op. cit., p. 88.

60  From Lissitzky's essay, "Suprematism in World Reconstruction" (1920), Küppers, op. cit., pp. 327-329.

61  Berlewi, op. cit.

62  See Birnholz, "El Lissitzky and the Jewish Tradition," op. cit., pp. 132-34, and also Abramsky's article in this catalog.

63  Küppers also mentions that as a 1923 Christmas present from Lissitzky, her sons received a picture book illustrated with watercolors called *Das Neugierige Elefantlein*. These, according to her, "were sketches for the Jewish children's book which was eventually published in Berlin in 1923 by the Helikon Verlag" p. 37. These illustrations, devoid of Jewish content, depict animals.

It should be noted that Küppers, op. cit., illus. 15, also includes *The Four Billygoats*, Warsaw, 1924, as illustrated by Lissitzky. Although similar in style to Lissitzky these illustrations are, according to the information in the book, by an artist named Uriel Kahana.

64  Ilya Ehrenburg, *Memoirs. 1921-1941*, transl. Tatania Shebunina, Cleveland and New York: The World Publishing Company, 1963, p. 23.

65  Illustrated in Küppers, op. cit., illus. 5.

# Art And Stage Design: The Jewish Theatres of Moscow In The Early Twenties

## Avram Kampf

During the 1920s two Jewish theatres from Moscow, the Jewish State Chamber Theatre and the Hebrew-speaking Habimah, stunned Jewish, Russian, and European audiences with their performances. Both groups were born within the Russian Revolution, when hopes for the blooming of a national art ran high, and both achieved extraordinary artistic standards within a span of a few years. Both theatrical groups were heirs to the Jewish historical tradition, although they made different use of this tradition and ultimately had different goals. Their acting style, their blending of reality and fantasy, their lively national temperament, and the intensity and vigor of their exaggerated gestures and their painted, masklike faces earned them a reputation far beyond the borders of Russia. The rapidity of their movement, their sharp humor and deep sorrow, the unity of word, gesture, music, light and dance were born from the rhythm of Jewish crowds in the marketplace, and from the wondrous, naive Hasidic folktales. Their plays, which were acted before imaginatively designed stage sets, granted them a rare distinction.[1]

The particular style of the actors and the specific energies of the individual and the ensemble derived largely from Marc Chagall's work for the Yiddish theatre. This assumption is shared by Meyer,[2] Erben, and Lubomirsky. The latter stated:

> His influence was visible not only in the stage sets, costumes and make-up techniques, but even in the gestures of the actors. . . . The actors found in the grotesque stylization of European gestures and the exaggeration of the Jewish, as well as in folklore, what they needed to express their idea of the Jewish character. In many cases they came close to the conception expressed in Chagall's forms. Their efforts, together with the trend started by Chagall, gave rise to what was later considered the national form of that theatre.

Biographies of Chagall have largely overlooked the impact of his student years in St. Petersburg, in the winter of 1906-7 and where he stayed, with some interruptions, until the summer of 1910. Thus, significant influences he may have absorbed in the Russian capital have not been given enough weight in assessing his total work and the evolution of his style and philosophy, at least not until recently.[3] The St. Petersburg of Chagall's student years was ablaze with artistic, musical, and theatrical activity comparable to any of the West European capitals.

All of Chagall's teachers were leading members of the Mir iskusstva (World of Art), the early modern art movement in Russia, and all of them exhibited a strong bent for stage design, book illustration, and graphic art. They were men of exceptionally wide horizons and accomplishments, who gave their students access to living modern art. Like the Art Nouveau movement in general, Mir iskusstva celebrated the concept of total art, and stage design was seen as the creation of a microcosm of the total art concept (*Gesammstkunstwerk*), which Richard Wagner had pioneered and which Gordon Craig, Appia, Max Reinhardt, and Stanislavsky further developed.

Among Chagall's teachers was Nicholas Roerich, director of the school of the Society for the Protection of the Arts. Roerich was, among other things, a painter, poet, and anthropologist with a keen knowledge of primitive art, who participated in several expeditions to Siberia. He worked with Igor Stravinsky and Sergei Diaghilev as stage designer for their ballet, *The Rite of Spring*. Mstislav Dobujinsky and Leon Bakst, with whom the young Chagall studied at the Zvantseva school of art, then the most modern art school in Russia, were also leading stage designers. Dobujinsky worked for Diaghilev, Stanislavsky, Vesevold Meyerhold, and Evreinov designing the stages of theatres, cabarets, and nightclubs. Bakst was one of the founders of Mir iskusstva, and his sensuous and colorful stage designs and wide knowledge of esoteric and oriental art doubtless contributed greatly to Diaghilev's success. For Bakst the lively, imaginative interplay of colors, their texture and the harmonizing of their tensions were the essence of composition and far more important than fidelity to nature or reproduction of reality.[4] Here his views about the nature of art paralleled those of the stage director Nikolai Evreinov, for whom Chagall did stage designs after his return from Paris,[5] but who already had extensively elaborated his theories about the nature of the theatre in 1908, theories in which many of the seeds of Chagall's artistic orientation can be found.

For Evreinov faithfulness to reality, simplicity, and naturalness were an anti-theatrical crime; sincerity and honesty on the stage utterly boring, the product of ignorance and lack of imagination, the realism of the nineteenth century theatre an appalling mistake. In 1908, Evreinov founded the Ancient Theatre in St. Petersburg with the aim of reviving historical plays. He restored Greek, Roman, medieval, and oriental theatre as well as the Italian theatre of the sixteenth and seventeenth centuries, the commedia dell'arte, which was based on improvisation. The commedia dell'arte actor was a prolific artist who sang, danced, declaimed, and performed acrobatics. Evreinov concluded that the aim of the scenic art was the theatricalization of life. Theatricality was the essence of the theatre and theatre meant art, not life or its faithful representation. Not the object but the image counted. Not the literary play, not faithfulness to text, not dialogue or self-expression,

not ideas or philosophical, social or political issues were the essence of the theatre but theatricality, the transformation of the self, the disguise, the masque, the marionette, the deep-seated desire to be someone else, the desire to play a different role than the one assigned to a person by life or circumstance. This urge for self-transformation Evreinov traced from the caveman through to the desire for the costumes and processions of the royal courts. The main function of the actor is not to create a true-to-life figure, but to masquerade as lover, servant, master, doctor, underlining the comic element in sharply exaggerated form. Acting was a bold magnification. Actor and audience alike were not to forget for a moment that they were in the theatre.[6]

Implied in Evreinov's views was the theatre of style, a challenge to the psychological realism and Stanislavsky's theatre of truth, then at its height. This challenge had already been voiced by Meyerhold, a former pupil of Stanislavsky, who subsequently broke with his teacher and came to St. Petersburg in 1906 to work with Vera Komisarzhevskaya. Meyerhold became director of Komisarzhevskaya's theatre, which had become the home of Symbolist writers, modern painters, and avant-garde composers. This theatre was enthusiastically supported by university, conservatory and art students, whom it attracted through special Saturday-evening performances, poetry recitals, and modern music concerts. There Meyerhold (Meyergold) put into practice his ideas about an unrealistic theatre, experimenting with stage design and movement influenced by ancient bas-reliefs. He abolished the stage in depth and brought the backstage closer to the front.

With the rise of a new avant-garde, advocates of folk art, icons, Suprematism, Cubo-Futurists, and Constructivists, new forms of stage design flooded the theatre. Alexander Tairov (Kornfeld), in 1914, introduced into his new chamber theatre abstract geometric forms, by the painters Alexandra Exter and Giorgi Yakulov, and the architect Alexander Vesnin. In the chamber theatre the stage floor rather than the set was the focus of attention since it was the most important element, the platform of the actors' work. In general, the floor offered a panorama of mighty spheric, cylindrical, cubic, and pyramidal shapes connected with stairs and platforms of various heights.[7]

With the coming of the Revolution in 1917 all latent tendencies reinforced each other and were accelerated. Meyerhold, who had fervently embraced the political goals of the Revolution, found fertile ground for experimentation and innovation. He abolished front curtains, backdrops, and stage sets altogether, playing against the bare brick walls of his theatre. Seeing in Constructivism the most meaningful contemporary expression of the Revolution's impulses and goals, he summoned the artists Popova and Stepanova to fill the empty stage with abstract structures. In the course of his experimentation, he introduced on the stage stairs, arches, escalators, lifts, monorails, cables, ropes, cranes, lifting devices, and rotating walls. He filled the stage with moving lights, projections, and musical instruments. The stage became a "factory," a motorized universe moving in perpetual rhythm. These innovations were complemented by the biomechanical system, in which actors expressed a state of mind or emotional experience through precise control of their movements. They turned individual emotions into a social and normative emotion suitable for theatre aimed at a mass audience. This new audience was not versed in Chekhov or Shakespeare; it consisted of soldiers and peasants who wanted to be entertained. Theatre therefore moved toward the circus, which could be enjoyed by everyone.

The Revolution gave rise to street theatres, pageants, processions, and carnivals in which thousands participated. These evolved their own techniques and devices, which influenced the avant-garde theatres in the major cities. The street theatre blurred the separation between stage and audience as well as between the various arts. In addition to acting there was dance, pantomime, music, painting, acrobatics, and clowning.

In the street theatre the stage director usually worked from an elevated podium, and assumed even greater authority. So did the stage designer. While the stage director knew the dramatic art and even literature and music, his knowledge of modern painting was usually minimal. A prime aspect of street theatre was assigned to the general composition and to improvisation of an idea rather than a precisely predetermined text. Psychological determination of individual characters gave way to forms of expression that could be absorbed from a distance.

From the vortex of these turbulent political, social, and artistic developments, the two major Jewish theatres emerged. The Hebrew-speaking theatre Habimah was committed to the renewal of Jewish national life and moved in the orbit of the cultural aspirations of Zionism. The Jewish Chamber Theatre (the Kamerny) was supported for different reasons by the Yevsektsia and by intellectuals of the Jewish Theatre Society, and was encouraged to develop a Yiddish national theatre, as were other national theatres. From the beginning, the Jewish Chamber Theatre aspired to be a world theatre performing in Yiddish.[8]

Alexander Granovsky, Nahum Zemach, Yevgeny Vachtangov, Chagall, Nathan Altman, Isaac Rabinovich, Robert Falk and many other painters, musicians, and actors participated in the creation of significant innovations of modern Russian art and theatre, and adapted their innovations and practices to the goals of the Jewish theatres and their audiences.

Granovsky, the founder of the Kamerny, was an experienced professional director, an assimilated Jew ignorant of Yiddish literature and culture, and unspoiled by any knowledge of the pre-revolutionary Yiddish theatre. He had studied at the University of Munich, was a pupil and assistant of Reinhardt, and had wide experience as a lighting designer, technician, and theatrical and cinematic director, in addition to possessing extraordinary organizational skills.

At the beginning of 1919 he assembled in Petrograd a group of thirty young students who had no experience in the theatre and trained them for the stage by exposing them to the most distinguished instructors in acting, voice, music, diction, movement, dance, and acrobatics, as well as intensive courses in Jewish literature, culture, and folklore, thus molding them into an artistically unified ensemble. Granovsky aimed to remove himself completely from the old Jewish ghetto theatre and establish a theatre in the Yiddish language fully equal in its standards to other Soviet avant-garde theatres. For the first performances of his group in Petrograd he used stage designers like Alexander Benois and Chagall's former teacher, Dobujinsky.

When Granovsky's group moved to Moscow, at the end of 1920, the theatre critic Abram Efros recommended Chagall as stage designer, and as decorator for the long drawing room of the half-destroyed luxury villa on Chernyshevsky Street, which was to be turned into the auditorium of a small theatre seating ninety. As Chagall recalls in his autobiography:

> Ah, I saw it, here is an opportunity to do away with the old Jewish theatre, its psychological naturalism, its false beards. There, on these walls I shall at least be able to do as I please and be free to show everything I consider indispensable to the rebirth of the national theatre.[9]

Here was Chagall's chance to make a significant statement about the theatre in general and the new Jewish theatre in particular. The very idea of a national Jewish art was appealing and brought him close to other Jewish painters who lionized him and saw in his work the realization of their goal. For several years they had been theorizing about the possibility of creating a modern Jewish art that would be utterly avant-garde. They had explored the various manifestations of Jew-

82

ish folk art, and investigated the art and architecture of wooden synagogues, Hebrew illuminated manuscripts, gravestones, the structure of the Hebrew letter, and the various ritual objects used for home or synagogue. On the basis of folk art they hoped to create the structure of a modern Jewish art. Issachar Ryback, El Lissitzky, Boris Aronson, Joseph Tchaikov, and Isaac Rabinovich had done significant work in this area, and in 1920 the political atmosphere still seemed promising for such endeavor.[10] Had not the Revolution promised the liberation of all nationalities of Russia and the development of their specific cultures?

Chagall himself had deep roots in the Jewish tradition and was firmly planted in the ideas and practices of contemporary art. His preoccupation with Jewish portraits, holidays, and folkways and his illustrations of Jewish books after his return to Russia in 1914 made him the logical choice. Defying the cold and famine of the Moscow winter of 1920, he worked on the mural and the sets for the theatre, while Granovsky and his group rehearsed for the forthcoming Shalom Aleichem evening.

Guided by a common purpose and believing in the redeeming power of their work, an intense and enthusiastic collaboration developed between the painters, composers, musicians, and actors and the director Granovsky. In Chagall's words:

I flung myself at the walls. . . .
The canvasses were stretched out on the floor. . . .
Workers, actors walked over them. Rooms and corridors were in the process of being renovated, piles of shavings mingled with my tubes of paint, with my sketches. . . I too was stretched out on the floor. . .
I remember a distant ancestor of mine who did the paintings in the Mohilev synagogue. . . . I set to work. I painted a mural for the main wall . . . introduction to the new national theatre. . . . to myself I silently implored the stage manager, the actors who passed me. . . 'Let us agree. Let us join forces and get rid of this old rubbish. Let's perform a miracle.'[11]

The murals, painted on canvas, filled the small auditorium and stunned the spectators. The introduction to the new national theatre, a 12×36-foot oil painting, was like a "Manifesto," as Meyer observed.[12]

The compositions of the murals (fig. 82) were firmly constructed, as Chagall then also employed Constructivist geometrical elements in his paintings.[13] Yet into this formal design of planes were integrated shafts of

bright color and wide bands and circles, lively, moving performers – musicians, actors, acrobats, clowns. The long-legged critic Efros carries the painter with his palette like a gift toward the director (fig. 54). In addition the painter introduced giants and dwarfs, goats and cows, umbrellas, heads and limbs. The informal air of the commedia dell'arte and its closest Jewish manifestation, the Purim jesters, dominate the canvas with their perpetual, frenzied movement, their exaggerated gestures, their mocking, farcical postures, and their jazz rhythm and abandoned dancing. The theatre became a circus. The actors wore pointed hats and round caps, crazy-quilt, diamond-shaped patches on their ill-fitting trousers decorated with Hebrew script, and dotted, wide, rectangular signs. These patterns also appear in the sketches for the costumes he designed for the forthcoming play. The scene of the mural evokes the quintessential spirit of the new Yiddish theatre. The movement must never stop.[14] One could apply to the mural the words of the review that a critic gave the Yiddish theatre when it performed in Berlin:

> In every theatre there are moments when one may relax. Not here. Cubistic liveliness . . . they talk not only with their hands but almost with their hair, calves, soles, and toes.

You think someone is walking and already he is lying down. You think someone is waiting and already he is fleeing.[15]

Not only does the mural mirror the rhythm, the farce, and clowning, but also the integration of acting, music, dance, literature, and painting into a unique Jewish theatricality. As pointed out above, the mural had a decisive impact on the actors' very acting style and their shaping of characters and gestures in their presentation of the Jewish type.

On the opposite wall, in the spaces between the windows of the Kamerny theater, Chagall painted personifications of music, dance, drama, and literature. The street musician on top of the wall playing the fiddle, the dancer (fig. 53), the wedding jester, and the Torah scribe were all part of the Jewish folk tradition and also symbols of the new Jewish theatre and modern Jewish secular culture.

On the back wall of the theatre Chagall placed a large Cubo-Futuristic composition of a pair of lovers dancing, hiding, and reappearing. At the bottom tiny figures of actors converse.[16]

83

At the opposite end of the hall, Chagall designed for the stage curtain a sketch of circular and angular motifs combined with two goat heads turning away from each other when the curtain opens.[17] Apparently this sketch was not used. Moshe Litvakov mentions a black curtain with the design of a white goat turned upside down.[18]

The murals and the sketch for the curtain are two-dimensional abstract forms that combine playful, figurative elements in a firmly unified composition. They form a stylistic unity that dissolved the walls of the small auditorium into a mass of color and movement. Erben writes:

> The effect of Chagall's pictures was extraordinary. The people who poured into the theatre were dismayed, bewildered, amused. They stood in front of them and discussed them, and more and more people came. The theatre itself had become a side issue. When anyone appeared on the stage to talk about the aims of the Jewish theatre he was forced by the audience to explain the pictures on the walls.[19]

84

85

We also find Constructivist and folkloristic elements in the sets Chagall painted for *Mazeltov*, *The Agents*, and *The Lie*, the three one-act plays that composed the Shalom Aleichem evening of the opening night of the theatre. Reacting against the crude, farce-like presentation of the traditional Yiddish stage, in his sets and costumes Chagall expressed the lyrical humor of Shalom Aleichem, the strain between dream and reality that the artist felt were in accord with the author's conception. Clearly, the artist was on home ground.

Central to Chagall's interpretation of Shalom Aleichem is the ephemeral existence of the *Luftmensch* who walks over roofs, in the air, and everywhere except on firm ground, and who proves to be an acrobat by the very fact that he survives in a world in which he is a stranger. By inventing new schemes and dreams about riches and greatness while discounting the misery and hopelessness of his situation, he carries on.

Undoubtedly, in the set design for *The Agents* (fig. 83), the artist intended the white arch that springs from the floor and stretches over the railroad carriage to represent the railroad tracks on which the carriage runs. The

arch ends in a white sign with a Yiddish inscription in Hebrew characters indicating that the carriage is for smokers. Frost has already pointed out that "Chagall's employment of formalist design concepts to convey his fantastic train of thought demonstrates his ability to transcend formal and associative problems by the power of his imagination."[20]

But the final stage set (fig. 84) points to the fact that formal analysis does not suffice. The small, cramped railway carriage, isolated in the center of the stage, is stationary, and we have no inkling where it is going; this may be the very essence of Shalom Aleichem's point as interpreted by the artist. The railroad carriage going nowhere is a microcosm of the Jewish ghetto as he saw it. One travels yet remains on the spot. Indeed, if continued, the white, wooden arch, the imaginary railroad track, would make a full circle enclosing the ghetto suspended between dream and disbelief: "Men fort. . . . men vayst vuhin men fort?" (One travels . . . . does one know whereto one travels?)[21]

In the set for *Mazeltov* (fig. 85), Hebrew letters are integrated like magic symbols on the fire screen and, together with the upside-down goat, break away from the conventional rendering of a kitchen of a wealthy Jew's house, occupied by servants and common people.

The design for *The Lie*, too, exhibits unreal features. Meyer describes a painted set "on which a street lamp reclines and behind which an actor dives head first."[22]

Although Chagall's murals helped the actors realize their unique style, his stage design evoked adverse critical comment. Abram Efros, who had urged Granovsky to invite Chagall, reacted:

> Chagall shows that he did not have a theatrical streak . . . he did not want to know the third dimension or the depth of the stage, and arranged all his sets parallel with the footlights, in the same way as he arranged his paintings on the wall or on an easel . . . he does not adapt to stage perspective . . . the objects that were drawn contrasted with the real objects; Chagall hated them because they legitimately violated his cosmos.[23]

Henning Rischbieter sees in Chagall's theatre work a classic case of the great artist as stage designer, whose decor are personal visions of the plays experienced through his own iconography. He was commissioned to do an original backdrop and costumes and instead he created magnified pictures of his own mythology.

> The scenic character of his own painting prevented him from giving to the theatre everything that he had perhaps to give . . . his mythology was already theatrical . . . and the outcome was a theatre within a theatre . . . instead of realizing itself through Chagall the theatre seemed to be celebrating Chagall, to be presenting his art with an apotheosis.[24]

Vachtangov arrived at Habimah in 1918, recommended by his teacher Stanislavsky to train the group of young amateurs who had gathered around Zemach. Vachtangov was the director of the first studio of the Moscow Art Theatre and was considered by Stanislavsky as his natural successor. At their first performance of three one-act plays, called *Neshef Bereshit* (Evening of the Beginning), Vachtangov still staged the performance on a realistic stage and the actors themselves arranged for the sets by placing on the stage a real bookcase, real books, and "real lamps, real candlesticks, a real wash basin, and other objects."[25] But between 1919 and 1922, when Vachtangov worked with the group on An-Sky's *The Dybbuk*, Habimah's most famous play, he was slowly moving away from the realism of his teacher, toward a fantastic realism and pure theatricality, which brought him closer to the ideas of Evreinov and put

him artistically somewhere between Stanislavsky, Tairov, and Meyerhold.[26]

There was apparently an attempt to consider Chagall as the stage designer for *The Dybbuk*, which opened in Moscow in 1922. A meeting between the painter Zemach and Vachtangov did not result in any agreement. Apparently Chagall was too surreal for Vachtangov. In any case, Altman was asked to do the sets and costumes.

Altman, like Chagall, had a distinguished record and a strong Jewish background. He had been in Paris, Munich and Vienna before World War I, had studied Jewish folk art motifs and Hebrew calligraphy at the cemetery of Shepetovke, a small town in southern Russia, and pioneered the creation of a modern Jewish art. Like many other artists, he was swept by the Revolution toward Cubo-Futurism, abandoned his plan to emigrate to America, and was appointed by Anatoly Lunacharsky, the Russian Minister of Culture, as Commissar of Art for Leningrad and the surrounding region. He designed the Uritzky Square spectacle of 1918, the mass festivity marking the first year of the Russian Revolution and the storming of the Winter Palace. He covered the Alexander column and other statues with a huge Cubo-Futuristic design of bright colors; he placed symbolic shapes around the columns in the center of the square and decorated the streets converging on the square as well as the façades forming it. He designed the first stamp of the Soviet Union and also became the portraitist of Lenin, "the Louis David of the Russian Revolution," as Ilya Ehrenburg put it.[28]

Altman's background and his personal and artistic loyalties are apparent in the design for *The Dybbuk*. *The Dybbuk* is about many things: It is a love story, it is a Hasidic mystery play, it is pure folklore. It is about the struggle of rich and poor, about restless souls floating in mid-air, rising and falling and attaching themselves to other souls. It is about the authority of wonder-working rabbis. For Vachtangov, an Armenian who did not know Hebrew, it was pure theatre, and he turned it into the most significant play the Hebrew stage has produced and into one of the most famous productions in the history of the modern theatre. The first act, which takes place in a synagogue (fig. 86, cat. 19), incorporates traditional Jewish folk-art motifs and Cubo-Futurist elements: the carved and painted Torah ark, the deep red, velvet curtain mounted under the Tablets of the Law, above them the hands of priestly benediction touching the crown, and high above on the gable, two guardian lions. Three steps flanked by railings lead to the ark, the architrave of which is supported by a column, and baroque scrolls widen it and

86

87

lend it dignity. On the left side of the railing stands the small lectern of the cantor. The centrality of the ark is accentuated by the white background wall, which resembles the ark's outline, making it the most overpowering and dominant object on the stage. The pronounced white background is formed by Cubo-Futuristic, overlapping planes suspended from the rear wall and the ceiling, masking and framing the ark. To the right of the ark in the foreground stand a small table and bench, and to the left four steps lead up to the *bimah* (platform), which is surrounded by a railing with a reading desk attached to it. Before the *bimah* stands a bench and on the left side, a reader's podium.

In the space above the *bimah* Hebrew cut-out letters are suspended from the ceiling in midair: *Shema Israel* (Hear, O Israel), suggesting mystical significance.

In the third act, Altman heightens the drama of his stage design (fig. 87) by moving toward a more abstract conception, introducing solid forms that add an awesome monumentality to the Hasidic play and which in turn are animated by the tension between high and low groups, by song, movement, and gesture, by the contrasting of white and black, and by the spirit of folk legend and mystery.

89

88

The set, predominantly white, was constructed rather than painted, and the sharp geometric volumes that cut through space intensify the action on stage. By raising the rabbi's table in the rear so that it slopes toward the front, Altman abolishes its customary function and appearance and turns it into a sharply angular structure, into a dramatic incline, driving it like a wedge into space. The sloping table also accentuates the position of the white figure of the rabbi, who presides from the far and high end of the table over the black-frocked assembled Hasidim. The artist realizes by plastic means the idea of *farbrengen* (communion) and also creates a visual and plastic metaphor for ascent and descent, which is the theme of the music and songs of the Hasidim. "Why does the soul fall from the high to the deep abyss? So it may rise again." The tilted table becomes a metaphor for impending doom for the here and beyond, for fate and betrayal, for a promise given and a promise broken. To realize the effectiveness of this design we must imagine the table in the ordinary horizontal setting. Could the effect of this particular scene be the same without the artist's inven-

tion? It can be safely assumed that Altman was strongly influenced by his former teacher Exter, who in Tairov's Chamber Theatre had produced *Salome* in 1917 and *Romeo and Juliet* in 1920.[29]

The nature of the play did not lend itself to a more radical abstract conception, and Altman aimed at a compromise between realistic and abstract forms, toward a social reintegration of new, non-objective art with the functional design demands of his specific cultural and religious ambience. This compromise is surely also due to the nature of the folk theme of *The Dybbuk*, the commitment to realism – albeit fantastic and theatrical – at which Vachtangov had arrived during his work on *The Dybbuk*, and perhaps even the conservative bent of the audience to whom *The Dybbuk* was directed.

The actors' costumes (fig. 88, cat. 26; fig. 89, cat. 25) in the second scene are remarkable. They are designed in angular, circular, and Cubo-Futuristic forms. Relying on disharmony, asymmetry, and arrhythmicality, Altman destroyed the central axis of the cos-

90

tumes and thereby intensified the deformity of the beg-gars. Their painted, masklike faces underlined the grimness of their fate. He dramatized the wretched-ness, the halting yet threatening steps of the crippled beggars on the stage. Their miserable lives glow for a moment as they dance one by one with the bride Leah, the beautiful daughter of the wealthy merchant. Vachtangov wanted to emphasize the monstrous and bitter and make the dance a tragicomic orgy:

> Our purpose will be unique, exceptional and signifi-cant. It may be one would not ordinarily encounter such cripples on the street but confess that it is true that if you happen to see an ordinary pauper you will not even pause, whereas if you see an unusual one, you will stop, and so will your friends and hundreds of others, to see the strange sight. But such people are not figments of our imagination, they exist; we have simply gathered them together and put them here on the stage.[30]

Vachtangov's dramatic choreography of the beggars' dance symbolized the Revolution. The beggars, repre-senting the downtrodden masses of the world, side with Hanokh against the bride's wealthy father. In their dance revenge is expressed. An element of actuality is introduced into An-Sky's mystery play.

Altman's design for *Uriel Accosta* (fig. 90), at the Kamerny, was far bolder and clearly measures up to those of Popova, A. Stepanova, Exter, and Vesnin. The year 1922 was the height of Constructivist stage design activity,[31] and the Yiddish theatre was fully committed to avant-garde design. Constructivist de-sign was seen by the left as expressing the spirit of the Revolution. It rejected illusionism and easel painting as speculative, parasitical, bourgeois aestheticism. It was austere, utilitarian, economical, and symbolic of a hard, matter-of-fact, positive attitude toward building the Soviet state. In the theatre, constructions replaced painted decorations. They were supposed to aid the actor in all his movements, just as a work-bench and tools were aiding the factory worker. Some saw Constructivist stage design as a machine for acting.

Carl Gutzkov's play was reinterpreted. Uriel was not the romantic lover victimized by the religious establishment for his love of Judith. He personified free thought, the victim of bigotry.[32] Altman here made dynamic use of immobile forms. Furniture was totally absent from the stage, the set reduced to different levels of platforms and stairs that made the stage an instrument of the actor rather than a specific location, making the actor the pivotal element. The extension of an arch across the set unites the disparate geometric forms. Altman rejects all illusionistic elements. All forms are real and occupy space like the actor himself. They are clearly defined, precise, and carefully proportioned. Measure, clarity, and pure rationality are strongly imbedded in the design. It becomes symbolic of the mind of Uriel Accosta as Altman and Granovsky interpret it. The set consists of three-dimensional volumes in real space. In the theatre Altman does not paint, but constructs, and builds. Color is only used as material, and not for imitation of other materials.

The stage as a box, defined by walls, did not satisfy Altman; yet he had to compromise because of the physical conditions of the theatre. He covered the walls with black felt in order to move them into the infinite. "We want to leave the box-like stage, we want to abandon the ramp and the curtain since these objects by themselves already create objects, the illusion, the picture."[33] The formal construction is subordinated to the definite tasks the play demands. But Altman attempted to affect not only the eye but also the feeling and consciousness of the audience. Yet there is some evidence that the Jewish theatre audience was not happy with this advanced design.[34] But in those heady days Altman, committed to the goals of the Revolution and convinced of the force of his art to shape the affairs of men, dreamt about the theatre of the future, the theatre of streets, piazzas, and masses, when life would be so well organized that every human gesture, every object would be beautiful and life and art would blend.[35]

At the beginning of 1922, Rabinovich designed the sets for Abraham Goldfaden's play *The Sorceress* (fig. 91), for the Jewish Chamber Theatre, and Granovsky, without much consideration for the original text, had changed the tearful melodrama about a young girl sold by her stepmother into a Turkish harem, into a hilarious comedy, a carnival in the spirit of Jewish commedia dell'arte. Word, song, movement, lighting, dance, and setting were fully orchestrated, and while a fantastic masquerade of endlessly changing characters and situations moved on the stage, the depths of Jewish folklore were plumbed. While the play ridiculed the old Jewish way of life, it also hurled barbs at known local party bureaucrats and Red commissars. Indeed, it has

been observed that the Jewish Chamber Theatre, in Moscow was the only place where stark and healthy humor "triumphed over the censored word and dictated 'revolutionary' pathos."[36]

Rabinovich was a product of Kiev and of the artistic circle nurtured by Exter. He had worked for Nemirovich Dantchenko, the co-director with Stanislavsky of the Moscow Art Theatre. He had designed the setting for *Lysistrata*, representing the Acropolis and the Parthenon by placing a few columns, curved pediments, staircases, and platforms against a deep blue sky. Indeed, he fused Constructivist stage design with classical tradition.

For *The Sorceress* (fig. 92), the Rabinovich design utilizes fully the height of the stage by erecting a two-tiered scaffolding with plain horizontal wooden beams and vertical poles. Platforms protrude at various levels; gangways, stairs, ladders, and ropes provide the setting for the acrobatic virtuosity of the actors. On this set the actors climbed up and down with leaps and somersaults, scaling the ladder, sliding down chutes, enlivening the scene with their acrobatic skills and keeping their audience in constant tension. The coordination between action and setting was complete. The setting molded the action just as the action molded the setting. A full aesthetic equilibrium was achieved among the various arts.

A similar but more simplified stage design, which was not a set in which the play is enacted but was integral to the play and intertwined with its action, was created by I. Rabitchev and Stepanova for the musical comedy *200,000* (fig. 93), an adaptation of Shalom Aleichem's story *Dos Groyse Gevins* (The Big Win). The set was built of wooden beams, unevenly shaped boxes, and brilliantly colored pieces of canvas. It was built for the carefully stylized and timed mass scenes for which Granovsky was famous. The Kamerny was also known for its ideologically slanted interpretations and adaptations. The stage design aided this purpose. The poor tailor Shimele Soroker, who became rich for one day by drawing the lucky number in the lottery and winning 200,000 rubles, loses his money to his rich partner's trick. The rich and the poor meet and clash in the tailor's open-air workshop, designed to accommodate mass scenes. The theatre critic who viewed the play when the Kamerny performed it in Berlin, in 1928, describes the interaction of set and play:

> The tailor's workshop is situated under the open sky. Into this sky the actor gingerly climbs. In the foreground there is a place for the family and all its members. But on the fence there stands suddenly the *shnorrer* (beggar). A chimney sweep has climbed on the roof – and who comes there from

91

high up? A violinist with tattered caftan wrapped in his romantic dreams.

The balcony gave me particular joy. It is nothing but a wooden plank and seems to protrude from the side of the right wall high up without any support. Suddenly a man sits on the plank and plays the flute. Then a servant appears with a giant broom and sweeps the dust onto the people below, or a marriage broker appears on the high plank and slowly descends to the ground with a red parachute.[37]

Another Berlin theatre critic called the scenery most eccentric:

The high scaffold, with its swinging platform on the upper right, hovers in the air with numerous voids and deletions which only interrupt and hint at the real structure. A Jewish Punch and Judy farce with top hats, and short, sloppy tuxedos.[38]

And Alfred Kerr, the most renowned of the Berlin drama critics of the twenties, the nemesis of producers, writers, and actors, admired the makeup and the interaction between stage and play:

They are 11 almost repelling types. With all the filth and ghetto-raggedness of their East. This ghetto-figure and ghetto-manner appears in concentrated form – until it almost frightens the Western Jewish burgher.

Oh, these maimed with the heavy protruding faces and large bellies . . . then the same mask-bearers from the rich Jewry of a little eastern town: with black beards and high hats all alike. The marriage broker in sparkling vivacity. The fiddler at the Purim festival; long and dark; something of the drooping willow in him. Peculiar. All these creatures stand below, above, on the level, on sloping planks, on dizzy distant boards, high up. They walk and they hover and shoot and climb and slide and hang and tower and seat themselves and twist like eels, beat each other, chase each other, make up again – and at the end arrange a solemn – wedding around humble people.[39]

In 1925, when the vogue of Constructivist stage design had abated, Granovsky staged the tragic poem by Y. L. Peretz called *Night in the Old Market* (fig. 94), and the painter Robert Falk designed the stage set and costumes. Falk had been praised by Ryback and Aronson as the ideal modern Jewish painter, yet his

92

93

94

work was strongly influenced by Rembrandt and Cézanne. Falk had been working for two years on the sketches in close collaboration with the director, changing his designs as Granovsky kept experimenting and changing the direction of the play, turning it into a tragic carnival and one of the most notable productions of the Yiddish theatre.

Before starting to work on the play, Granovsky wrote:

The atmosphere of the stage, the structure of its decoration and design must render the horror of the end, that horror which permeates the scene. Not one part of the stage should speak of life. Everything is condemned, everything is rotten, past generations must be felt in every bit of the play. One has to sense that the market and the cemetery are one and everything is but a shadow, and the living resemble the dead and the dead resemble the living.[40]

In the program for *Night in the Old Market*, Granovsky describes the mood:

Old square . . . old with centuries and with pain.
Decaying, almost rotten away.
Market square that becomes a cemetery.
A cemetery becoming a market, ghostly place.
Dead who return to life, and living who are like the dead.
The last dance of the dead before the coming of day.
Ghosts of yesterday.
Carnival of the shadows of our past.[41]

Since the text of the poem was short, it played a secondary role in the staging of the performance, and the burden of the play fell on the stage decoration, the costumes, the masks and composition of the figures, the frequently changing images, and the music. The tragedy was to be conveyed mainly by plastic and painterly symbols.

To convert the mood of the poem into visual and plastic expression, Falk sought morgues, cemeteries, and ruins. "I had to inhale by myself the dust of decomposition."[42] He created a nearly abstract version of the old marketplace around a low well. Crooked, slanting buildings barely upright, with steps and balconies, were framed by symbols of the church and synagogue on opposite sides of the stage. Sharp-edged, crumbling stone walls, holes, and pits filled the market. A catwalk connected the buildings. From above a huge, bony hand, without flesh, hung over the scene – fate, which had overcome everyone.

The same set presented the market of the living and the cemetery of the dead, a ghostly acting area for

95

ghostlike figures. By blending reality and fantasy, by distortion, through masklike, expressionistic makeup and by costumes of violent patterns, shape and color, Falk evoked a feeling of horror (fig. 95). The funeral atmosphere of the play was heightened "by ghastly masks and costumes," wrote Louis Lozowick, who viewed the performance in Moscow.

> This was the dying world of priests and rabbis, traders, and prostitutes, writhing in its last agonies and clinging desperately to its old superstitions. The dead regulate the customs of the living and the living are putrid with the germs of decay. The Last Judgement is upon them and when the dead rise, the difference between the dead and the living disappears.[43]

The performance, for which the constantly changing visual imagery on the stage was decisive, evoked extraordinary responses:

> The masks, comic and ghastly, masks of mummies, when worn by the living or the dead, were of ineffable expressiveness. Every bandage, every shroud, every ram's horn, every old rag, by light or graveside, was part of the play, was part of these bodies.[44]

So comments Alfons Goldschmidt, who, like Lozowick, was deeply impressed by the play. He also felt it to be a play about a worn-out tradition and a dying culture.

The periods of war, revolution, and their aftermath were also the periods of national awakening. Habimah and the Jewish Chamber Theatre were an expression of this awakening, of the will to live and develop a Jewish social, historical, and cultural identity.

Both theatres worked in the stream of Russian avant-garde art under the most advanced leadership in the art of the theatre, the visual arts, and stage design. The influences they absorbed and radiated were many and we cannot account for their achievement without seeing them as part of the flowering of the Russian theatre. Speaking about Granovsky, Zemach, and Vachtangov, we also must think about Evreinov, Meyerhold, and Tairov. When we consider the works of Altman, Falk, Rabinovich, and Chagall, we must also think of the works of Exter, Vesnin, Yakulov, and Popova. The new forms of artistic expression were created by all of them.

While the Jewish theatres were nourished by their own needs, temperament and literature, their art and stage design also became part of both the Russian theatre and the world theatre.

1   Habimah won glowing praise for its performances, even from people who had no knowledge of Hebrew. Gorky, Reinhardt, and Evreinov speak about being spellbound by the dramatic force, the rhythm, and the musical unity of its performance. Gorky, Meyerhold, Stanislavsky, Chaliapin, Tairov, and other members of the Russian cultural elite asserted that "Russian art is a debtor to Habimah's art."

Even Habimah's Communist detractors, who saw in the Hebrew theatre nothing but "a caprice of the Jewish bourgeoisie" not deserving the support of a regime of peasants and workers, had to acknowledge its high artistic merit. About Habimah's first years and its struggle to survive, see: "The Life Work of Nahum Zemach Against the Background of the Revival of Jewish Culture in the Soviet Union" (Ph.D. diss., Hebrew University, Jerusalem, 1974, pp. 163-68) (Hebrew); *The Birth of Habimah, Nahum Zemach, Founder*, ed. Itzhak Norman, Jerusalem, pp. 393-99 (Hebrew); Yehoshua Gilboa, *Fight for Survival, Hebrew Culture in the Soviet Union*, Tel Aviv, 1977, chapter 6 (Hebrew); and Emanuel Levy, *The Habimah, Israel's National Theatre 1917-1977*, New York, 1979, part I.

The Yiddish Chamber Theatre was received with great enthusiasm by drama critics and people close to the theatre. Thus Kerr of the *Berliner Tageblatt*: "This is great art. Great art. . . this is immortal. Something scarcely known to the stage before. . . here is an excellent example of complete knowledge of all the possibilities of theatrical art. Three, four, five fields intermingled: word, song, dance, picture, behavior. Stepped up to the end. Coordinated. Not a dead point the whole evening" (12 April 1928).

Alfons Goldschmidt wrote: "Every conception one brings to this theatre about the proverbial vivaciousness of the Jewish people was surpassed by the hasty and passionate gesticulation of the actors. These were Jews of a higher temperature, Jews who were more Jewish. Their passion was by several degrees more passionate, their melancholy even became fierce and savage, their sadness fanatical and their joy rapture. They were Dionysian Jews" (*Das Moskauer Jüdische Akademische Theater*, Berlin, 1928).

The two theatres had differences and similarities. Both took their work extremely seriously. Both reacted against the old Yiddish ghetto theatre. Both aimed to be an art theatre, and both wanted to be a modern theatre. They cultivated the ensemble, and devoted many months to intense training, rehearsal and preparation. Both took the best people available and measured themselves against the best theatrical groups.

2   Franz Meyer, *Marc Chagall, Life and Work*, New York, p. 294. Walter Erben, *Marc Chagall*, New York, 1957, p. 75.

Chagall's influence extended beyond the Yiddish stage into Habimah. An-Sky wanted Chagall to design the sets and costumes for his *Dybbuk*. Zemach confided to Chagall that Vachtangov, who directed the play for Habimah from 1919 to 1922, studied Chagall's murals at the Yiddish theatre long and hard (Marc Chagall, *My Life*, New York, 1966, p. 166.).

3   Susan Compton, *The Russian Background in Chagall*, exhibition catalog, London: Royal Academy of Art, 1985.

4   Close study of the artist's years in St. Petersburg shows that in his autobiography, Chagall minimized the impact of that city on his artistic development and especially minimized the impact of his teachers. It is hard to imagine that as Commissar of Art for Vitebsk and as head of the People's Art School of Vitebsk, Chagall, in his search to recruit the best teachers, would

have expended the great effort to persuade Dobujinsky to join his staff if he had not thought so highly of him. As for Bakst, Chagall, who in 1910 wanted to accompany him to Paris with the Diaghilev Ballet, failed the qualifying test of designing the scenery for *Narcissus*, a rejection that probably chagrined the artist deeply.

5   In 1916, Chagall did the backdrop for *To Die Happy* for Evreinov at the Comedians Halt Cabaret, for which he enlarged *The Drunkard* (Meyer, p. 123), a composition he had done in Paris, in 1911. For the performance he painted the hands of the actors green and their faces red.

The flat, airy drunkard is firmly constructed with hidden linear continuities and strong traces of Chagall's encounter with Orphic Cubism. The figure's severed head, suspended in mid-air, turns its profile and meets the corked bottle of absinthe at the apex of the triangular composition. The bottle seems to have jumped from the table towards the thirsty lips of the drunkard.

In 1919 Chagall prepared for Evreinov sketches for *Gogol's Marriage* and *The Gambler*, but the designs were not realized. For Chagall's stage designs in Vitebsk when he was Commissar of Art, see Matthew Frost, "Marc Chagall and the Jewish Chamber Theatre," *Russian History*, vol. 8, parts 1-2, pp. 90-107.

6   For an account of twentieth century Russian theatre see Nikolai Gorchakov, *The Theatre in Soviet Russia*, New York, 1957; Marc Slonim, *Russian Theatre*, New York, 1961; P. A. Markov, *The Soviet Theatre*, London, 1934; Jürgen Rühle, *Theater und Revolution*, Munich, 1963. For an account of the stage designs of Roerich, Dobujinsky, and Bakst, see John E. Bowlt, *Russian Stage Design*, exhibition catalog, Mississippi Museum of Art, 1982.

7   Tairov was most likely strongly influenced by Gordon Craig, who in 1911 had been invited by Stanislavsky and Nemirovich Dantchenko to the Moscow Art Theatre, where he put abstract, three-dimensional shapes on the stage. "The basic elements of Craig's Moscow *Hamlet* consisted of screens of coarse, undecorated canvas, sometimes covered with gold. The various combinations of the huge but narrow screens hinted at corners, towers, palace halls, narrow streets, and other places. These square neutral shapes used to augment Craig's various lighting effects. Craig asserted the need for blending the music, the lighting, and the movement of the architectural forms into a single musical quality." Gorchakov, op. cit., pp. 46-47.

8   "The Yiddish Theatre is first of all a theatre, a temple of shining art, of joyous creation, where the prayer is sung in the Yiddish language. The functions of this theatre are those of a world theatre and only in its language it differs from other theatres." Alexander Granovsky, *Dos Yidishe Kamer Teater*, Yidishe Teatrale Gesellshaft, Petrograd, July 1919.

9   Chagall, op. cit., p. 162.

10   See Avram Kampf, "The Quest for a Jewish Style in the Era of the Russian Revolution," in *Jewish Experience in the Art of the Twentieth Century*, South Hadley, Mass., 1984.

11   Chagall, op. cit., p. 159.

12   Meyer, op. cit., p. 296.

13   See, for instance, *Cemetery Gate of 1917*, Meyer, p. 247; *Profile at the Window*, 1919, Meyer, p. 305; *Cubist Landscape*, 1919, Meyer, p. 307; and Meyer, classified catalog, pp. 323-24.

14   Chagall, who made man and animal fly in his pictures, always felt drawn to the circus. But the theatre, which approaches the circus, was a general trend in the avant-garde. The circus was to compensate for the difficulties of daily exis-

tence. After the hard days of the Revolution the common man had a right to relax, claimed Lunacharsky. Elements of the circus were to appear in Meyerhold's productions of *The Magnanimous Cuckold* and *The Death of Tarelkin*, both done in 1922, and in Yakulov's productions for the Moscow Chamber Theatre of *Brambilla* (1920) and *Girofle-Girofla* (1922). The artist Yurii Annenkov recommended in 1919 the circus as a sanitorium for city dwellers whose soul is crippled and body unhealthy by living in the city. "Usually doctors send city dwellers to the country for recuperation but if you need medical treatment but are not able to go out of town – go to the circus – this merry sanitorium" (Compton, op. cit.). Chagall himself felt more sympathetic to Meyerhold than to all other artists, poets and directors. "I like him alone among them all. I am even sorry I have never worked with him" (Chagall, op. cit., p. 154).

15   Alfred Kerr, "The Jewish Academic Theatre of Moscow," *Berliner Tageblatt*, 12 April 1928.

16   Illustrated in Meyer, p. 281.

17   See Meyer, cat. 315.

18   Moshe Litvakov, *Finf yor Melukhisher Yidisher Kamer Teater, 1919-1925*, Moscow, 1924, p. 44.

19   Erben, op. cit., p. 75.

20   Frost, op. cit.

21   Litvakov, op. cit., p. 44.

22   Meyer, op. cit., p. 294. The artist's misgivings about his work for the Yiddish theatre can be felt from his frequent disagreements with Granovsky (op. cit., p. 163). In April-March 1922, when the Kultur Lige arranged an exhibition of theatre designs by Altman, Chagall, and Shterenberg, in Moscow, Chagall speaks in the catalog about his "painful love affair with the theatre and about my ideas about the theatre which were either realized with difficulty (the Yiddish stage) or not realized at all" (quoted from Frost, op. cit.).

As to the difficulties with the theatre, Chagall must also have referred to the Red commissars' reaction to his "street theatre," when, under his direction, Vitebsk was decorated for the 1918 anniversary of the Revolution with 450 posters, 7 arches, and hundreds of flags, banners, and garlands. He painted many of the horses and cows, which were copied by house painters. But the commissars wanted to know, "Why is the cow green and why is the horse flying in the sky? Why? What has that to do with Marx and Lenin?" No record is left of Chagall's work for Terevsat (revolutionary theatre), where he designed sets for nine performances of satirical sketches about White generals. The theatre played to the soldiers in the Vitebsk region.

Perhaps most unfortunate was when a director of Stanislavsky's theatre rejected his 1920 sketch for *Playboy of the Western World*, by Synge. In this sketch, among other things, a mutilated Christ puppet is impaled head down, spinning on a cable, and sliding to the ground while a red spiral rises diagonally, juxtaposed by a vertical ladder. Norbert Lynton has pointed out that this spiral refers directly to Tatlin's monument for the Third International, shown in model form in St. Petersburg and Moscow during the winter of 1920-21, which prompted much discussion. Lynton believes that the sketch can be read as representing a kinetic construction rather than a painted set and therefore could be seen as a forerunner of Popova's construction for *The Magnanimous Cuckold*, which Meyerhold performed in 1922 (Norbert Lynton, "Chagall Over the Roofs of the World," in Compton, op. cit.).

23   Quoted from Frost, op. cit.

24   Henning Rischbieter, *Art and Stage Design in the 20th Century*, New York, 1969, p. 60.

25   Raikin Ben-Ari, *Habimah*, New York, 1957, p. 28.

26   "Vachtangov proclaimed theatrical truth instead of truth to life. He opposed self-sufficient realism but he favored a realism that would be subordinated to the unreal laws of the theatre" (Gorchakov, op. cit., p. 251).

Ben-Ari, who participated in the original performance of *The Dybbuk*, remembers the rehearsals: "Vachtangov constantly searched in his work to reach higher levels, find new truths. He would begin rehearsals according to the Stanislavsky methods and techniques and would suddenly switch over to new theories. . . . One day Vachtangov gave voice to a new manifesto; 'No more superficial and unnecessary realism. The theatre has a realism of its own, its own theatrical truth. The emotion and the feelings of the actor must be true and that truth must be projected to the audience with the help of theatrical means.' The difference between natural and theatrical, Vachtangov explained to his actors by a simple illustration: 'It is as though you are served duck at home, and at a restaurant. The roast duck is the same in both places but in the restaurant it is served in a manner that you might call theatrical'" (Ben-Ari, op. cit., p. 47).

27   Chagall, op. cit., p. 165.

28   Kampf, op. cit.

29   Vesnin, who in 1922 designed Racine's *Phèdre* for Tairov's Chamber Theatre, may have also influenced Altman. He had the stage resemble a sloping deck, which signified for him "an impending inner catastrophe. It represented not only the list of a ship's deck at the point of disaster but also feeling over spirit." See Edward Brown, "Constructivism in the Theatre," in *Art in Revolution. Soviet Art and Design Since 1917*, exhibition catalog, London: Hayward Gallery, 1971, p. 72.

30   Ben-Ari, op. cit., p. 49.

31   The year 1922 saw significant Constructivist stage designs such as Popova's for *The Magnanimous Cuckold* and Stepanova's *The Death of Tarelkin*, both directed by Meyerhold, and Vesnin's design for *Phèdre* and Yakulov's design for *Girofle-Girofla*, both directed by Tairov.

Soon the original motives became blurred. Early in 1923, Ivan Aksenov wrote: "So-called Constructivism started with a most impressive programme for the total abolition of aesthetic methods, but once it appeared on the stage it began to show signs of being only too ready to adapt itself to its surroundings and now it has degenerated almost to a decorative device, albeit in a new style." (From Brown, op. cit., p. 72.)

32   Faina Burko, "The Soviet Yiddish Theatre in the Twenties" (Ph.D. diss., Southern Illinois University at Carbondale, 1978).

33   Nathan Altman, "Das Plastische Element in der Theater Decoration, Des Staatlichen Jüdischen Kammerspiel Theater, Moskau," *Kunstchronik und Kunstmarkt*, Leipzig, 1 December 1922, vol. 58.

34   Litvakov, op. cit., p. 46.

35   Altman, op. cit.

36   Joseph Roth, *Das Moskauer Jüdische Akademische Theater*, Berlin, 1928.

37   Monty Jacobs, "*200,000* Im Theater Des Westens," in *Vossische Zeitung*, Berlin, 4-12, 1928.

38   *Welt Am Abend*, Berlin, 4-12, 1928.

39   Alfred Kerr, "The Jewish Academic Theatre of Moscow," *Berliner Tageblatt*, 12 April 1928.

*The Sorceress* and *200,000* demonstrate how much Granovsky approached Meyerhold. Indeed, Louis Lozowick reports that the Kamerny was sometimes jokingly referred to in Moscow as Meyerhold's branch on Malaia Bronnaia Street. But he hastens to add that this was an exaggeration, since the Kamerny was among the most original theatres in Moscow.

40   Benjamin Zuskin, "Wi Mir Hoben Gearbet Oyf Perez's Bei Nacht Oyfn Altn Mark," *Literarische Blatter*, Warsaw, 1928, p. 879.

41   Beatrice Picon-Vallin, *Le théâtre juif soviétique pendant les années vingt*, Lausanne, 1973, p. 108.

42   Dimitri Sarabjanow, *Robert Falk*, Dresden, 1974, p. 291.

43   Louis Lozowick, "Moscow Theatre, 1920," in *Russian History 8*, parts 1-2, 1981.

Lozowick, who was in Berlin and Moscow in 1921-22, knew the Russian Constructivists. His own painting and printmaking link them and the American Precisionists. Being immersed in Russian, American, and Yiddish culture, he published broad and informative views in the journals *Broom* and *Menorah*. Speaking about the two plays, *The Sorceress* and *Night in the Old Market*, he writes: "The effect of the two plays on me was profound. Although I subsequently saw both in the Soviet Union and in Western Europe practically the entire repertoire of the Jewish State Theatre, no other play affected me as powerfully." Lozowick himself in 1926, a few years after his return from Europe, did a Constructivist stage set for George Kaiser's play *Gas*, which was produced at the Goodman Theatre in Chicago.

44   Alfons Goldschmidt, "Das Jüdische Theater in Moscau," op. cit.

# The Future in Search of Its Past: Nation, Ethnos, Tradition and the Avant-Garde in Russian Jewish Art Criticism

## Nicoletta Misler

The question of a specific Jewish tendency within the general panorama of Russian avant-garde art criticism does not invite a single, comprehensive solution. Indeed, the issue can be considered only in the ideological framework of the Jewish cultural renaissance at the beginning of the twentieth century – something closely identifiable, of course, with the Zionist movement. Furthermore, a Jewish art criticism within the Russian tradition (if such an art criticism existed) cannot be categorized as a simple aggregation of Jewish art critics. In this case, nationality does not have particular significance, since Jewish critics such as David Arkin[1] or Ieremii Ioffe[2] never paid much attention to the topic of "Jewishness" in their writings, even when they happened to deal with Jewish artists. Typical examples of such occasional references are Arkin's and Yakov Tugendkhold's reviews of Robert Falk,[3] and mention could be made of Nikolai Lavrsky's book on Jewish art.[4]

Since Russian avant-garde art was represented by leftist artists and critics, it can be easily argued that, especially after the October Revolution, those who wished to adopt Marxism rejected all traditions from their religious past. Those favoring a less radical position tried to adjust tradition to the new formal prerequisites, at once cosmopolitan and international. Simultaneously, there was the problem of satisfying the demands of both the Russian and non-Russian minorities: some artists wanted to reaffirm their national identity *and* to support an international, interracial solidarity. This contradiction had to be faced by all the intelligentsia then.

In art criticism, this state of affairs was reflected in the concurrent advocacy of two opposing approaches – the ethnographical argument versus the International Style, which, formulated differently, might read as arts and crafts versus streamlined, utilitarian design, the *mestechko (mestechko*, a diminutive of the Russian word *mesto*, denotes the specific locality or community inhabited by Jews in Russia. Cf. settlement or shtetl) or periphery versus the center. Of course, the Jewish people, particularly until the Revolution, had always been exposed to this contradiction, and in the 1910s and 1920s avant-garde artists such as Nathan Altman, Marc Chagall and El Lissitzky transferred from their peripheral birthplaces (Vinnitsa, Vitebsk, Pochinok, etc.) to St. Petersburg or Moscow or Paris and began immediately to experiment most audaciously. But as far as art criticism was concerned, perhaps only one Russian Jew made a sincere, though short-lived, effort to provide a theoretical basis for this dialectic: Abram Markovich Efros (1888-1954).[5]

A brilliant essayist, Efros (fig. 96) approached the work of art very sensitively, endeavoring to describe and re-

96

gnettes, end pieces and borders decorated according to the antique specimens reproduced in the Guenzburg/Stasov portfolio of Jewish ornament (fig. 98, cat. 159).[8] Even if Efros was responsible for the translation, footnotes, and literary apparatus, he had presumably been attracted to translating the Song of Songs because it represented an opportunity to provide the Russian reader with an authentic distillation of Jewish culture. Beyond that and perhaps of equal, if not greater, importance to Efros, this volume of the Song of Songs was an artistic totality in miniature – a synthesis of the printed word and the visual accompaniment. The idea of the book as an aesthetic whole, as an independent work of art, was supported strongly (both in theory and in practice) by Vladimir Favorsky,[9] a graphic artist Efros admired.[10] It was logical, therefore, that Efros's first sally into Jewish art was through a book – which anticipated one of his most prestigious accomplishments, i.e., his translation from Hebrew into Russian of the Book of Ruth, illustrated by Favorsky (Moscow, 1925) (fig. 99).[11]

Favorsky's concept of the book as an organic unit carefully integrating content, decoration, and design coincided with Efros' constant and concurrent interest in the relationship between literary text and visual expression, between the narrative or philosophical communication and the illustration – all of which seems to relate to a characteristic of Russian Jewish art criticism of the 1910s, i.e., the identification of intimate artistic forms with Jewish art. This is true of the critic Maxim Syrkin,[12] who was, however, very distant from Efros; it is also true of Tugendkhold,[13] the most "European" of the Russian Jewish critics. Suffice it to quote three passages to clarify this claim: 1) a short appraisal of Altman by Efros; 2) a comment on ancient Hebrew art by Syrkin; 3) a paragraph on Jewish ornament by Tugendkhold.

1) Altman's physiognomy is that of a creature that amasses rather than of an individual personality. His essential, inner temperament is penetrating and acute, although it hides its sting, as a cat does its claws, in the softness of its external behavior.[14]
2) Facts indicate that Jews . . . also sensed an unconscious need of beautiful forms. So if we are to seek individual features, here, we soon realize that they lay precisely in this unconscious intimacy, in this simple attitude towards this unseen aspect of their soul.[15]
3) Since Stasov, the collecting and study of Jewish antiquities have made great strides. There is no doubt now that, if the creative abilities of the ancient artists did not dwell within the sphere of *grand art* (or simply have not come down to us), they did find their application in the minor arts – synagogue and domestic utensils, embroidered curtains and Torah

cord the artifact's *Zeitgeist* while speaking of its formal qualities. Efros was at once ultra-archaic and ultra-modern. Inasmuch as he dealt specifically with the Jewish problem and was concerned with the debate outlined above, Efros is a key force in our discussion here and, indeed, in the general context of Russian Jewish art of the 1910s-20s. True, his relevance must be qualified since the Jewish question occupied only a small part of his critical activity. But Efros attempted to make Jewish artists conscious of their Jewishness and to articulate the problem in all its aspects. Unfortunately, the intricacies of his broad cultural activities and his Jewish concerns cannot be analyzed exhaustively until his personal archive, now in the Manuscript Section of the Lenin Library in Moscow, becomes freely accessible to those researching his critical *oeuvre*.[6]

It is not by chance that Efros' first "formal" publication (in 1909, two years before his graduation from Moscow University) was his translation from Hebrew into Russian of the Song of Songs (fig. 97) – issued by the Moscow publishing house Pantheon on the poet Valerii Briusov's recommendation.[7] This edition was printed as an elegant facsimile, with title page, vi-

82

covers, gold, silver, wooden, filigree and enamel artifacts, and illuminated manuscripts.[16]

Along with translations of French and Italian art tracts, Efros, throughout the 1920s, continued to translate from the old Hebrew texts and to review both translations from and commentaries on Yiddish literature. In 1911 he ran articles on the newly published Russian translations of works by Israel Zangwill, Shalom Aleichem and Y. L. Peretz in the newspaper *Utro Rossii* (Morning of Russia);[17] in 1921 he translated *The Wail of Jeremiah* and wrote an essay on its structure;[18] in 1923 he published a collection of Biblical lyrics in translation;[19] and in 1926 he translated part of the Book of Judges.[20] During the 1920s, Efros was deeply involved in diffusing the Jewish ideal, although he was not an enthusiastic Zionist, and one important avenue in his propagation was that of higher education and advanced research.

In the fall semester of the academic year 1920-21, Efros took charge of three courses at the Jewish People's University in Moscow: an introduction to Jewish folk creativity, Jewish creativity over the last decade, and Biblical poetry. At the university, the critic M. G. Fabrikant (1887-1965) also taught an introduction to the study of Judaica and Hebrew archaeology of the Biblical period.[21] Another Jewish critic and philosopher, Matvei Kagan, taught Jewish philosophy there, turning the university into a modest affiliate of RAKhN[22] (the Russian Academy of Artistic Sciences). Founded in Moscow in 1921, RAKhN was a large and complex Soviet institution that sought to establish – scientifically – a history, philosophy, and criticism of art, and Efros was one of its associates. This tentative development of a system of Russian Jewish art criticism at the Jewish People's University reflects, or parallels, the general development of Russian art criticism. This is true, for example, for the debate surrounding the investigation into national sources (whether primitive ones, as in the avant-garde,[23] or national and ethnic ones, in the case of the Realistic artists). Efros knew that the rediscovery of the Jewish folk tradition might well lead to the discovery or establishment of a Jewish art criticism, even though he had serious reservations about this deduction, as he indicated in his major article of 1918, "Aladdin's Lamp":

> The *lubok* and the gingerbread, the toy and the cotton print – for the contemporary observer this is an entire program of practical aesthetics. Any 'Introduction to the Art of Today' just has to have a special chapter that takes this influence into account. Nowadays, whoever the artist, we cannot help seeing characteristics in which we recognize the qualities and customary elements that distinguish folk art. This is quite logical since our age is

marked by the search for a synthetic form: here simplicity borders on schematicism, expressivity on exaggeration. This conditions our aspiration towards artistic primitivism. But in uniting with the national traits of each country, this programmatic primitivism assumes – inexorably – the physiognomy of an artistic 'Neo-Folkness' . . . .

> True, we have come to this aesthetic of folk creativity last and in the wake of everyone else. It is also true that, vis-à-vis the aggregate of other races, this makes us look very awkward inasmuch as our artistic-cum-popular zeal has manifested itself very late; and, obviously, in the world art market the apology of folk art is already becoming *demodé*. Still, there is a difference between what was and what is – between those of us pacesetters who are serving up the latest flashy trend, and those of us who are the rag-and-bone men of today, who clasp to their breast some piece of junk like an old lamp that we take to be Aladdin's Lamp. But in the role of pacesetters we must appear quite ridiculous to the art community at large – local yokels shouting with joy, jumping up and down like barbaric priests, in front of a *lubok* pattern or gingerbread ornament. Nevertheless, with all due respect, we state that we will give up our entrance ticket to nice society, if, in order to keep it, we have to deny ourselves the tears of joy and shouts of delight that we experience when we look at the meek beauty that gives flowered patterns to the *pinkos* [diary] or wildly voluted spirals to the tombstone. We state further that our entire artistic future lies precisely in this; that we are now ready to begin a new, unprecedented epoch in Jewish plastic creativity; and that we would give anything to apprehend this new world of national beauty more firmly, more greedily, more fervently. If we have something to fear, then it is, so to speak, the *naiveté* of the Jewish artist. Hearing the inevitable street cry – 'Anyone want to change old lamps for new?!' – he may well give up a precious piece of Aladdin junk in exchange for some fashionable, gaudy pot.[24]

As we see from this forthright discussion, Efros welcomed artistic innovation despite his grudging recognition of the strong Jewish tradition. However, Efros also implied that, for him, this artistic tradition concealed its real aesthetic, intrinsic value. For the moment, the lamp justified its existence simply because it had been made by a Jew, but the critic's task was to find the formal language that characterized the Jewish artifact. Efros felt that the new generation of Russian Jewish artists, especially those of the avant-garde, could help locate and develop this inner principle. He affirmed:

> Either our artistic renaissance will not occur at all or

КНИГА
РУФЬ

ПЕРЕВЕЛ
С ДРЕВНЕ-
-ЕВРЕЙСКАГО
АБРАМ
ЭФРОС

ГРАВЮРЫ
В. ФАВОРСКАГО

ИЗДАНИЕ М. и С. САБАШНИКОВЫХ

МОСКВА

MCMXXV

99

will arise from those two roots which nurture the whole of contemporary art – Modernism and folk creativity . . . Modernism and folk art! These two faces of Janus incite every nation to undertake a double task and always at one and the same time. The face of Modernism is turned outwards, that of folk art inwards. As they elaborate and give new artistic forms to the aesthetic program of Modernism, the Futurists, Cubists, Non-Objectivists . . . and Neo-Classicists of every nationality continue to work for a single, common artistic cause and on a universal scale. They are like masons who, while laboring in different parts of a building, are in constant communication through the alternate blows of their hammers.[25]

Efros then concluded:
But, at the end of the day, when each nation carries home the fruits of its labors. . . there arises . . . a unique combination of forms in which the national blood pulsates and its artistic compassion sings. Here is a folk art indeed, a pure and unadulterated crystallization of the national plasticity of form. And this is the super-regulator of artistic creativity in our time.[26]

In the context of the avant-garde, Efros emphasized that Jewish artists were at the spearhead, and that even the most radical tendencies were indebted to them. He explained this by referring to the extreme principles of the Talmudic argumentation that was to be conducted to the end "beyond measure."[27] But whereas Efros maintained that this Jewish presence in the avant-garde was a cause for celebration, Syrkin complained that many young forces had been "devoured" by the "Moloch" of contemporaneity.[28] Syrkin declared in 1916:
How many young, fresh and beautiful talents fly directly into the brightest, most unbearable light – just like butterflies – and add fuel to its furious heat with their burning bodies! What a racket, what a babble, what perdition! From every part false prophets summon fervently . . . . Must we also mention just how many Jews have sacrificed themselves for this![29]

One characteristic that Efros, Syrkin and Tugendkhold attribute to the Jewish artist is his eclecticism. Syrkin associated this element, specifically in the context of ancient Hebrew art, with the Diaspora:
At first in the homeland and then wherever fate cast them, they adapted the art of their environment to

their own uses – and they did this willingly, without the slightest resistance.[30]

In his article on Chagall, also of 1916, Tugendkhold maintained a similar argument – which he felt was valid whether for ancient times or for the contemporary work of Bakst:

> Jewish art could not help but develop the capacity to transform a foreign concept of beauty. With its nomadic history, Jewish art assimilated elements of Phoenician, Assyrian, Hellenistic and Arabic cultures. Hence, its 'national' weakness and ancient, racial finesse.
>
> In this sense, Bakst's creativity is, beyond doubt, 'national.' It is decorative by nature, it is eclectic without being archaeological; sensually it imbibes all cultures; in color it is oriental and spicy, in linear content it is classically refined. It is the product of an ancient, millennial concoction.[31]

Many critics of the 1910s regarded Jewish art as a "millennial concoction," although few tried to identify its more prominent and decisive ingredients. Lavrsky, whose pioneering monograph *Iskusstvo i evrei* (Art and Jews) appeared in Moscow in 1915, did, however, grapple with the problem of eclecticism in Jewish art, attempting to clarify the reasons for it and to determine its future consistency. Adducing the customary conditions that discouraged the creation of a Jewish visual art (the Biblical ban on the graven image, the Jewish people's constant displacement, etc.), Lavrsky argued that, even in new and favorable circumstances, a Jewish art could not be created overnight. That artists were now living and working in Palestine did not mean that a national art would arise; and, in any case, a national art did not depend simply upon the depiction of national types. He wrote:

> Even at the highest point of their cultural flowering, Jews not only did not create anything of brilliance and distinction, but they also failed to apprehend the art of the East, let alone the art of Greece.[32]

Lavrsky concluded, therefore, that a national Jewish art had not existed and perhaps would never exist. Yet the fact that critics were now writing on Jewish art indicated that there was enough evidence to assume that such a phenomenon might soon manifest itself. Lavrsky also pointed to the increasing number of professional Jewish artists in Russia, which he felt augured a national consolidation of forces, even though these artists were linked by their eclectic assimilation of Russian/European ideas and not by any deep sense of Jewish allegiance.

Efros also tried to define this Jewish eclecticism and to provide a basic pattern whereby it could be turned into a style, particularly through the application of folk motifs:

> For example, I would like Jewish artists to see just how researchers of Russian art inspected An-Sky's documents – they were quite baffled. That was really instructive! 'What eclecticism . . . and yet it's still "Jewish" – such was the aggregate of their judgements. Exactly: eclectic and at the same time Jewish. Can we really deny it?
>
> But that's just the point: as always, the whole is greater than the sum of its parts. In placing all the component elements together, our folk creativity obtains not only their total, but also a *certain imminent*/greatness, and this changes *quantity* into *quality. Therein* lies the secret and the ultimate meaning of our folk aesthetic. It creates the physiognomy which cannot be annulled by any ethnic analysis or division. The secret of the national artistic genius lies surely in the ratio mix alone or in the *means* of combination or in the *degree* to which these same common elements are reprocessed.[33]

The cohesiveness of style that Efros advocated in traditional Jewish art is something he also associated with Jewish Modernism:

> Our first imprimatur is our modernism, our leftism, and our youth; our second imprimatur is our orientation towards the people, our traditions, and our old age.[34]

This endeavor to balance and integrate two aesthetic or ideological poles makes Efros' position close to that of the Russian avant-garde artists and theoreticians – the archaists and innovators, the inhabitants of some distant Atlantis projected into the future.[35] Consequently, Efros was very careful in his selection of artistic candidates, since he identified this double principle with only a few modern Jewish artists, specifically with Altman, Chagall and Falk. As the following passage makes clear, Efros was extremely pragmatic and programmistic in evaluating these three painters:

> On the other hand, Chagall's centrifugal movement compels us to ask the question as to how long this Jewish tendency will last in our artist. It appears to me – and I think not mistakenly – that Chagall's 'Jewishness' is merely an episode in his artistic development and he will not continue with it . . . . He's fond of his dear Liozno, but finds it too crowded, and he's always expanding it in every possible way so that it will become a '*mestechko* in general,' or even the entire earth; and thanks to this 'in general' he seeks to expand his *concept* of the *mestechko* Jew . . . .
>
> The voice of Falk's blood is to be heard, I think, in the quality of his landscapes and portraits which is also characteristic, for example, of Levitan . . . . Just

as Russian nature is abstracted in Levitan, so – more or less – Falk elaborates the traditions of Cézanne just as abstractly and as elegiacally. The Russian Cézannists (Kuprin, Mashkov and Konchalovsky . . . ) are so much more 'tangible', stronger in their reality, healthier and more fertile, than these melancholic, universalized landscapes of Falk.

Altman . . . occupies a central position . . . in the context of the nationalization of Russian-Jewish artists. His Jewishness is not a component from which he tries to liberate himself (as Chagall does) and not a seven-sealed mystery which he tries to break open (as Falk does). For Altman, Jewishness is a goal, desired and sought after, which he follows from art as a whole or from the foreign art of other peoples. . . . Altman resolves his task emphatically and consciously – to fuse his national and artistic elements into one integral creation.[36]

In this text on Altman, Chagall and Falk, Efros reveals a clear capacity to combine the authentic and perhaps conservative values of the Jewish past and the contemporary, "fashionable" concerns of cosmopolitan Jewish society. In fact, Efros was here attempting to construct a new image of Jewish art, one that would crystallize traditions within this newly defined, immediate Russian Jewish context – symbolized for him in Altman's sculpture *Head of a Young Jew* (1915):

> . . . this really typical head of a *mestechko* Jew is what Altman had produced – and without beating about the bush. It bears the imprint of a truly convincing, triumphant beauty in which even the traditionally despised curls, here rendered precisely as curls, are beautiful in their distinctive, artistically justified charm.[37]

No doubt, Efros hoped to recognize and disseminate his ideas about this new synthetic aesthetic of modern Jewish art through his activities in the Jewish Society for the Encouragement of the Arts, especially through his co-organization of the "Exhibition of Pictures and Sculptures by Jewish Artists" held in Moscow in 1917.[38] This was, indeed, a major undertaking, and the participation by several Modernists (Chagall, Tchaikov, Lissitzky, Nis-Goldman, Isaac Rabinovich, et al.) was probably facilitated by Efros' own demands, even though the exhibition was supposed to "reflect all artistic leanings of Russian Jewry irrespective of epoch, aesthetic party and sect."[39]

Efros maintained his endeavor to formulate a theory of contemporary Jewish art even in later years, although in more guarded terms. Judging from his writings of the 1920s-30s, Efros, if and when he treated the Jewish question, continued to pay particular attention to Altman, Falk and David Shterenberg.[40] However, in

100

deference to him, we should also mention that Efros did not desert Chagall, and after his important monograph of 1918 (co-authored by Tugendkhold),[41] he even wrote a long entry on Chagall for the *Greater Soviet Encyclopedia* of 1934.[42] One of the last professional evaluations of Chagall by a Soviet critic, the text can be read as a brave attempt to rescue or at least justify Chagall's art within the contemporary context. Regarding Chagall's Jewishness, Efros censured the artist who

> derives from a petit-bourgeois, Jewish milieu in the town of Vitebsk. . . and whose perplexing pictures elicited indignation in the average viewer, but delight among the artistic bohemia and leftist critics of those years.[43]

Nevertheless, Efros concluded that Chagall "has not broken his ties with the Soviet public."[44]

Very different in his understanding and appreciation of contemporary Jewish art was Tugendkhold (fig. 100). True, Tugendkhold was much less active than Efros in this sphere and he favored a broader diapason of critical themes (especially French Post-Impressionism), but occasionally he touched on the Jewish question – even if his arguments were rather restrained and traditional. From the beginning, Tugendkhold concentrated on Jewish content rather than on Jewish form, a predilection that, on the contrary, one might have expected from the *littérateur* Efros, who was trained as a poet and translator rather than an art critic. Still, it was Tugendkhold who, in 1916, observed certain parallels between Chagall's painting and Bialik's poetry – and even Béranger's *Le Juif Errant*[45] (The Wandering Jew). Tugendkhold's concern with the content of Chagall's painting is evident in his striking analysis of the pictorial "subtext." For example, Tugendkhold affirmed that Chagall's art came directly from the traditional religious interdiction against representing human and animal forms:

> [Chagall's] images contain no human being, no forbidden image, and no likeness of God (he does not paint individual portraits), but they do have people and animals in them. His people are poor, suppressed by the Orthodox behests, by apocryphal fears, by a strict puritanism. His animals are meek, sentimental, looking like gazelles or, on the contrary, with the faces of beasts. Just as Gogol goes in for pigs' snouts, so the curious 'snouts' of oxen and calves peer into Chagall's *intérieurs* – thereby appearing like the demonic symbols of sinful temptation that once upon a time inspired Aaron to cast the idol of the Golden Calf [of] Mt. Sinai. There is something sodomic and erotic remindful of Bosch and Goya in these bestial faces of Chagall.[46]

Tugendkhold's analogies may bring to mind the vocabulary of the European Decadents, e.g., of René Gourmont and Briusov. But although Tugendkhold was certainly interested in Symbolism and Post-Symbolism, his subsequent approach to post-Revolution Jewish art was more superficial and matter-of-fact, relating to content but without morbid or erotic interpretations. In fact, Jewishness was never central to Tugendkhold's research and, in general, his point of view can be regarded as an exact counterpart to that of Efros, for he merely "sovietized" the ethnographical research initiated by Stasov and elaborated on by An-Sky. After the Revolution and until his death in 1928, Tugendkhold undertook many relevant projects: for example, while a journalist and critic,[47] he was also active within the RAKhN; in 1927 he realized his ambition of establishing a special department for the study of the art of the nationalities;[48] and a concrete result of his measures was the organization of the large exhibition in Moscow, also in 1927, called "The Jubilee Exhibition of the Art of the Peoples of the USSR." Divided into sections for art, literature, and the handicrafts, the Jubilee Exhibition[49] included several Jewish artists (e.g., Altman, Yehuda Pen and Solomon Yudovin) although they were categorized as Russian, Ukrainian, White Russian, etc., and not as Jewish.

The art of the nationalities remained critical for the Soviet Union from the late 1920s onwards – as Chagall mentioned in his obituary for Tugendkhold.[50] Naturally, we might expect Jewishness to have been discussed or at least raised by Tugendkhold in the context of the nationalities, but he never broached the subject. Even in his article "The Art of the USSR and the National Element" of 1925, Tugendkhold avoided all reference to it, although this was an ideal opportunity for him to apply his basic thesis – the center's imperialism vis-à-vis the provinces' servility – to the Jewish question:

> The capital degrades the provinces, the metropolis degrades the colonies. The provinces feel the fear of being out of step just as all the petit-bourgeoisie does.[51]

Curiously, Tugendkhold excludes the Jews from the peoples to whom the October Revolution had granted the right to "national self-determination, to their own government, own language, and own school."[52] Moreover, according to Tugendkhold, the Revolution affirmed the free cultural development of those national minorities and ethnographic groups that did not even have their defined territory.

Evidently, much research has yet to be carried out on the fate of the new ethnographical "on-site" museums founded after the Revolution and then dismantled, which are mentioned in Tugendkhold's article of 1925:

> These are museums of local culture, local discoveries, local cottage industries. One really exceptional phenomenon that we meet as we familiarize ourselves with the USSR is the new, enormous ethnographical department in the former Alexander III Museum (now the Russian Museum) in Leningrad and also the new Central Museum of Folk Studies in Moscow, arranged in the form of an ethno-park along the lines of the Stockholm Park.[53]

Undoubtedly, some of these local museums contained Jewish culture sections. But since many of these institutions, established just after the Revolution, were short-lived and since their archives were subsequently dispersed among different depositories or were lost, detailed documentation remains a primary problem. Did Tugendkhold know that, traditionally, the acknowledgement of a Jewish ethnic group in another nation often proved to be a reason for civil discrimination? Perhaps, therefore, Tugendkhold avoided mentioning Jews as a separate nationality? Unfortunately, these questions must remain unanswered. Still, when we read the catalog of "The Jubilee Exhibition of the Art of the Peoples of the USSR," we find occasional Jewish entries although, as indicated above, they are subsumed under other national sections (this is true both for individual Jewish artists and for Jewish organizations such as OZET [Society for the Agricultural Employment of Working Jews]). For example, a section on the Belorussian Jewish State Theatre carries the names of Rabinovich, Ryback and Tchaikov,[54] while the Belorussian graphics and painting section contains references to Pen, Yudovin, Volshtein, et al.;[55] Altman, Viktor Midler, Alexander Niurenberg, Ryback and Alexander Tyshler were grouped together under OZET.[56] Furthermore, the literary section contained 120 books in Russian and Hebrew, both by new proletarian writers such as M. Taits and by classical masters.[57]

The Jubilee Exhibition foreshadowed what would later be identified as the Socialist Realist approach to the national culture problem. On one hand, there was the pseudo-ethnographical industrialization of handicrafts; on the other, there were the fine arts with their "Socialist content in a national form." It was precisely in this exclusive context that Tugendkhold openly referred to Jewish painters and designers, thereby welcoming them into the pantheon of Soviet Realist artists. Describing two works on show (E. Shekhtman's *Sufferers of the Pogrom* and V. Kasian's *After the Pogrom*), Tugendkhold emphasized their thematic value, their message, their "homeless, tormented, immobilized, suffering people."[58] He argued that this Realism constituted an epic genre and that this was the most telling expression of the Jewish ethos.

Unfortunately, Tugendkhold's affirmation had little to do with the complex consistency of modern Jewish art. By the early 1930s, at least, every Soviet critic was obliged to argue that Realism was the most effective artistic expression for any national movement, whether Russian, Chinese or Jewish. By the time Socialist Realism was advocated exclusively in 1934, Arkin, Efros, Lavrsky, Syrkin and Tugendkhold had long ceased to deal with the question of Jewish style. The October Revolution had betokened much for the distraught minorities: the Jewish Modernists – Altman, Tchaikov, Ryback – aspired to produce an artistic rebirth by fusing the imprimaturs of leftism and tradition, and critics, too, felt that a meaningful theory and aesthetic of Jewish Modernism could be defined. But the guiding light of Aladdin's lamp was, as Efros feared, too weak to illuminate Stalin's domain, and the "certain imminent greatness"[59] that so many Jewish intellectuals had hoped for did not come to pass.

1 David Efimovich Arkin was born in Moscow in 1899. He entered Moscow University in 1916 and studied industrial design in Berlin, Leipzig and Dresden in 1923-24. In 1925 he co-organized the Soviet contribution to the "Exposition Internationale des Artes Décoratifs" in Paris. From 1922 through 1932 he worked for the journal *Ekonomicheskaia zhizn* (Economic Life), and in 1930-31 he was a professor at Moscow University. From 1931 through 1934 he taught at the Moscow Architectural Institute. Among his major publications are: *Iskusstvo bytovoi veshchi* (The Art of the Everyday Object), Moscow: Izogiz, 1932; *Keramika Frikh-Khara* (The Ceramics of Frikh-Khar), Moscow: Gizlegprom, 1934; and *Obrazy skulptury* (Images of Sculpture), Moscow: Iskusstvo, 1961. He died in Moscow in 1957.
2 Ieremii Isaevich Ioffe (1888-1947) is now remembered for his two major books on modern art: *Krizis sovremennogo iskusstva* (The Crisis of Contemporary Art), Leningrad: Priboi, 1925; and *Sinteticheskaia istoriia iskusstva* (A Synthetic History of Art), Leningrad: Ogiz-Izogiz, 1933.
3 D. Arkin, "Falk i moskovskaia zhivopis" (Falk and the Moscow Painting) in *Russkoe iskusstvo*, Moscow-St. Petersburg, 1923, no. 2-3, pp. 21-32. Ya. Tugendkhold, "K proizvedeniiam R. Falka" (On the Works of Robert Falk) in *Krasnaia niva*, Moscow, 1924, no. 17, p. 149.
4 N. Lavrsky, *Iskusstvo i evrei* (Art and the Jews), Moscow: Zhizn, 1915. I discuss this book later in my essay.
5 Abram Markovich Efros was born in Moscow on 21 April 1888. He attended the law school of Moscow University and, beginning in 1910, took courses in art history. In 1910-11 he travelled in Austria, Germany, Switzerland and Italy. During the 1910s, Efros contributed many articles on Russian and Jewish art to the Russian press and translated into Russian a variety of texts from French, Italian and Hebrew. After the October Revolution, he held many organizational positions, e.g., in the Tretiakov Gallery, within Narkompros (People's Commissariat for the Enlightenment). In the 1920s he worked closely with the Chamber Theatre and the Moscow Art Theatre. Efros was a primary member of RAKhN (the Russian Academy of Artistic Sciences) throughout the 1920s. Until his death in 1954, he continued to translate and to publish although his interests diversified, encompassing the Italian Renaissance, Russian Romanticism, and the drawings of Alexander Pushkin.
6 At the time of writing, the two published collections of Efros' writings at our disposal avoid any reference to his Jewish material, both in the introductions and in the biographical and critical essays. Even the bibliographical lists are far from being complete in this regard. See *A. M. Efros. Dva veka russkogo iskusstva* (Two Centuries of Russian Art), ed. M. Tolmachev, Moscow: Iskusstvo, 1969; *A. M. Efros. Mastera raznykh epoch* (Masters of Different Epochs), ed. M. Tolmachev, Moscow: Sovetskii khudozhnik, 1979. In my article I do not touch upon the subject of Efros and the Jewish theatre. This has been discussed in many other sources, including the present catalog.
7 A. Efros (translation and commentary) and V. Rozanov (preface), *Pesn pesnei Solomona* (The Song of Songs of Solomon), St. Petersburg: Pantheon, 1909 (second edition appeared in 1910).
8 W. Stassof and D. Gunzburg, *Drevne-evreiskii ornament po rukopisiam* (Ornementation des anciens manuscrits hébreux de la Bibliothèque Impériale Publique de St. Pétersbourg), St. Petersburg: Gunzburg, 1886. The discrepancy in the spelling of

the names Stasov (Stassoff/Stassof) and Guenzburg (Gint-s burg/Gunzburg/Ginzburg) is explained in part by differences in systems of transliteration. The English-language transliteration of the Russian names is Stasov-Guenzburg according to the *Encyclopedia Judaica* and these are used in the above text. The French edition of the book on Jewish ornament (1905) and the 1886 St. Petersburg edition, however, render it "Gunzburg" and this has been left for the sake of bibliographical accuracy.

9   Vladimir Andreevich Favorsky (1886-1964) was especially concerned with the concept of the book and wrote many articles on this subject. See, for example, *Ob iskusstve, o knige, o graviure* (On Art, On the Book, On Engraving), ed. E. Levitin, Moscow: Kniga, (1986). This collection contains Favorsky's texts on book illustrations (pp. 93-116), on style (pp. 117-26), and on ornament (pp. 187-89).

10   See, for example, A. Efros, "V. Favorsky i sovremennaia ksilografiia" (V. Favorsky and Contemporary Xylography) in *Russkoe iskusstvo*, 1923, no. 1, pp. 37-54; partially republished in Yu. Molok, *Kniga o Vladmire Favorskom* (A Book on V. Favorsky), Moscow: Progress, 1967, pp. 23-27. Efros maintained a life-long interest in the work of Favorsky, making many references to him in subsequent publications. For example, he devoted a chapter to Favorsky in his book *Profili*, Moscow: Federatsiia, 1930, pp. 153-76, and published an article on his frescoes, "Les fresques de V. Favorsky," *Le Journal de Moscou*, Moscow, no. 39, 27 September, p. 4.

11   A. Efros (translator and author of postface, pp. 35-42), *Kniga Ruf. Graviury V. Favorskogo* (The Book of Ruth, Engravings by V. Favorsky), Moscow: Sabashnikovy, 1925.

12   Unfortunately, biographical information on Syrkin is not available. In addition to the publications mentioned in this text, the following also deal with Jewish art in Russia: "Drevnie dereviannye sinagogi v Polshe i Litve" (Ancient Wooden Synagogues in Poland and Lithuania), *Novyi voskhod*, St. Petersburg, 1910, no. 11, pp. 27-30; "Doklad o evreiskom iskusstve v Evreisko-Istoriko-Etnographicheskom Obshchestve" (Report on Jewish Art in the Jewish Historical and Ethnographic Society), ibid., 1911, pp. 37-40. Syrkin was the editor of *Novyi voskhod*.

13   Yakov Alexandrovich Tugendkhold was born in Moscow in 1883. After being arrested for illegal activities at Moscow University in 1901, he went to Munich the following year, where he attended law school, and to Anton Asbe's (1862-1905) private art studio. In 1905 he travelled to Paris and in 1910 he became the Paris correspondent for the St. Petersburg journal *Apollon*. During 1910 he wrote extensively on French Impressionism and Post-Impressionism, including monographs on Degas and Gauguin. After the Revolution he assumed various organizational positions in agencies such as Politprosvet (Political Enlightenment) and GUS (State Scientific Council). He died in Moscow in 1928, and his major work on post-revolutionary art – *Iskusstvo oktiabrskoi epokhi* (Art of the October Epoch) – was published two years later (Moscow: Akademiia).

14   A. Efros, *Portret Natana Altmana* (A Portrait of Nathan Altman), Moscow: Shipovnik, 1922, p. 16.

15   Ya. Tugendkhold, "Mark Shagal" in *Apollon*, Petrograd, 1916, no. 2, p. 13. The text was then republished in A. Efros and Ya. Tugendkhold, *Iskusstvo Marka Shagala* (The Art of Marc Chagall), Moscow: Gelikon, 1918.

16   M. Syrkin, "Evrei i iskusstvo: I Starye vremena. Okonchanie" (The Jews and Art: Ancient Times. Conclusion), *Evreiskaia nedelia*, Moscow, 1916, no. 26, p. 40.

17   A. Efros, "Izrael Zangvill, Komedii Getto. Mechtateli i "fantazery Getoo" (I. Zangwill. Comedies of the Ghetto. Dreamers and Fantasists of the Ghetto) in *Utro Rossii*, Moscow, no. 5, 8 January, p. 5; "Sholom Aleikhem: *Sobranie sochinenii*. T. V. Neunyvaiushchie," ibid., no. 86, 16 April, p. 5; "Pavel Geize. Deti veka. *Sobranie sochinenii*," ibid., no. 110, 14 May, p. 5; "Leon Perets. *Sobranie sochinenii*, T. I. Iz ust naroda," ibid., no. 237, 15 October, p. 5; "D. Kokotsov: Vechnyi potok. Vtoraia kniga stikhov" (D. Kokotsov. The Eternal Stream. The Second Book of Poetry) and "Almanakh molodykh pisateli *Khmel* Kn. I" (Almanac of Young Writers. Khmel), ibid., no. 243, 22 October, p. 5.

18   A. Efros' translation of *The Wail of Jeremiah (Plach Ieremii)* was scheduled for publication in Moscow in 1921, but it remained in manuscript form. See Tolmachev, 1979, op. cit., p. 314.

19   A. Efros (translator), "Bibleiskaia lirika" in *Vostok*, Leningrad-Moscow, 1923, book 2, pp. 21-30; pp. 19-21 also carry Efros' preface.

20   A. Efros, *Skazaniia o Samsone (Kniga Sudei XIII-XVI)* (The Tale of Samson – Book of Judges XIII-XVI). Manuscript. See Tolmachev, 1979, op. cit., p. 316.

21   See the booklet issued by Narkompros (People's Commissariat for Enlightenment) in Moscow in 1921(?), *Evreiskii narodnyi universitet. Ocennii semestr 1920-21 (III akademicheskii god)*. This booklet contains the breakdown of the courses offered at the university, which include public economics, art, literature and history.

22   In May 1921, a scholarly commission was organized through the Narkompros to analyze the problem of artistic synthesis. The commission was made up of historians, critics, artists and natural scientists (physicists, psychologists, biologists and psycho-physiologists). In October 1921, RAKhN was established formally. In 1925, RAKhN changed its name to GAKhN, State Academy of Artistic Sciences, with Petr Kogan as its president. RAKhN was divided into three sections: 1) Psycho-physiological – directed by Wassily Kandinsky; 2) Philosophical – directed by Gustav Shpet; 3) Sociological – directed by Vladimir Friche (see A. I. Kondratiev, "Rossiiskaia Akademiia Khudozhestvennykh Nauk," *Iskusstvo*, Moscow, 1923, no. I, pp. 407-9; P. S. Kogan, "Gosudarstvennaia Akademiia Khudozhestvennykh Nauk" in *Pechat i revoliutsiia*, Moscow, 1927, no. 7, pp. 293-99). After 1930 GAKhN lost its autonomy and in 1936 it was fused with GAIS (State Academy of Art History).

23   For commentary on the parallels between primitive art and Russian Modernism, see *Primitiv iego mesto v khudozhestvennom kulture novogo i noveishego vremeni*, ed. V. Prokofiev, Moscow: Nauka, 1983. Of particular importance in this volume is A. Kamensky's article on Chagall (pp. 160-201) – "Skazochno-groteskovye motivy v tvorchestve Marka Shagala."

24   A. Efros, "Lampa Aladina. (K vykhodu v svet kapitalnogo izdaniia S. A. An-skogo *Evreiskaia narodnaia khudozhestvennaia starina*)" (Aladdin's Lamp. [On the Publication of S. A. An-Sky's Major Work *Jewish Popular Artistic Antiquities*]) in *Evreiskii mir*, Moscow, 1918, book I (eds. A. Sobol and E. Loiter), pp. 297-310. These quotations are from pp. 299-300.

25   Ibid., pp. 301-2.

26   Ibid., p. 303.

27   Ibid., p. 303.

28   M. Syrkin, "Mark Shagal," *Evreiskaia nedelia*, 1916, no. 20, p. 41.

29   Ibid., p. 42.

30  Syrkin, "Evrei i iskusstvo," op. cit., p. 40.

31  Tugendkhold, "Mark Shagal," op. cit., p. 14.

32  N. Lavrsky, *Iskusstvo i evrei* op. cit., p. 18.

33  Efros, "Lampa Aladina," op. cit., p. 309. Efros is here referring to the contemporaneous debate over the "authenticity" of the Neo-Russian style at the end of the nineteenth and early twentieth century. For information on this issue see: E. Kirichenko, *Arkhitekturnye teorii XIX veka v Rossii* (19th-Century Architectural Theories in Russia), Moscow: Iskusstvo, 1986, especially p. 196 et seq. In encouraging Jewish artists not to repeat the vulgarities of the Neo-Russian style, Efros may have had in mind the main gate and the fence outside the St. Petersburg synagogue. According to *Novyi voskhod*, St. Petersburg, 1910, no. 10, p. 25, they were designed by Ivan Ropet (the pseudonym of Ivan Petrov), who had been recommended by Stasov. Ropet, a leading exponent of the Neo-Russian style, designed the gate and fence on the basis of materials from the Stasov/Guenzburg *Ornement Hébreu*, which incidentally Ropet had also designed in the first Russian edition of *Dreune-evreiskii ornament po rukopisiam*, 1886 (see note 8 above).

34  Efros,"Lampa Aladina," op. cit., p. 310.

35  " . . . and I wondered: fairy tales, an elder's memory or not? Or a child's clairvoyance? In other words, I wondered: was the flood and perdition of Atlantis over or was it yet to be? More than likely I was inclined to think it was yet to be. I was on a bridge and had fallen into a reverie."
V. Khlebnikov, *Sobranie sochinenii*, Leningrad: Sovetskii pisatel, 1930, vol. 4, p. 286.

36  Efros, "Zametki ob iskusstve," *Novyi put*, Moscow, 1916. The first part of this article is called "Tema," the second, "Shagal, Altman, Falk." The article appeared in no. 48-49, pp. 58-64. This quotation is from p. 63.

37  Ibid., p. 64.

38  *Vystavka kartin i skulptury khudozhnikov evreev*, the exhibition catalog, was published by the Jewish Society for the Encouragement of the Arts in Moscow in 1917. The cover was designed by Lissitzky. For the review of this exhibition see Rosstsii (Efros),"Zhizn iskusstva" in *Russkie vedemosti*, Moscow, 16 April 1917 no. 84, p. 7.

39  Ibid., unpaginated. Author not indicated.

40  In 1930, for example, Efros included versions of his previous texts on Chagall, Altman and Shterenberg in his book *Profili*, op. cit. The collection also contained his essays on Favorsky, Rozanova, et al.

41  Efros and Tugendkhold, *Iskusstvo Marka Shagala*. See note 15. There was also a German translation, *Die Kunst Marc Chagalls*, Potsdam: Kiepenheuer, 1921.

42  Efros' entry on Marc Chagall appeared in *Bolshaia sovetskaia entsiklopediia*, ed. O. Shmidt, Moscow: Ogiz, 1934, vol. 61, pp. 787-88.

43  Ibid., p. 787.

44  Ibid., p. 788.

45  Tugendkhold, "Mark Shagal," op. cit., p. 17.

46  Ibid., p. 15.

47  From 1922 through 1926 Tugendkhold was art editor for the newspaper *Izvestiia*. Shortly before his death in 1928 he was art editor for *Pravda*. For further information see G. Sternin, "Yakov Alexandrovich Tugendkhold" in *Sovetskoe iskusstvoznanie*, Moscow, 1978, vol. 2 for 1977, pp. 291-310.

48  While a member of GAKhN, Tugendkhold was especially interested in industrial design and the popular arts and crafts. To this end he formulated a special Section for the Study of the Art of the Peoples of the USSR in 1928. For information on this see *Bulletten GAKhN*, Moscow, 1927-28, no. 8-9, pp. 58-60. Also see B. Sokolov, "Ya. A. Tugendkhold i iskusstvo narodov SSSR," *Iskusstvo*, Moscow, 1928, book 3-4, pp. 236-39.

49  *Yubileinaia vystavka iskusstva narodov SSSR*, catalog of the exhibition, Moscow: GAKhN, 1927. The three respective sections were actually located in three different places and each had a separate catalog (according to the inside cover of the above catalog), i.e., Visual Arts, Theatre and Movie Section (at the Vkhutemas Building), Creative Literature of the Nationalities Section (at the Herzen House on Tverskoi Boulevard), and Folk Creativity and Industrial Design Section (at the Central Museum for Folk Studies).

50  M. Chagall,"Pamiati Ya. A. Tugendkholda" in *Iskusstvo*, 1928, p. 238.

51  Ya. Tugendkhold, "Iskusstvo SSSR i natsionalyi element," *Novyi mir*, Moscow, 1925, no. 8, pp. 119-24. This quotation is from p. 120.

52  Ibid., p. 122.

53  Ibid., p. 123.

54  *Yubileinaia vystavka*, op. cit., entries 1366-1405 on pp. 28-29.

55  Ibid., pp. 16, 20-23.

56  Ibid., pp. 17-18.

57  P. Kogan, "Kniga na vystavke iskusstva narodov SSSR" in *Pechat i revoliutsiia*, Moscow, 1927, book 8, pp. 36-41.

58  Ya. Tugendkhold,"Iskusstvo narodov SSSR" in *Pechat i revoliutsiia*, 1927, book 8, pp. 42-61.

59  Efros, "Lampa Aladina," op. cit., p. 109.

All measurements are given in mm., height precedes width.

☐ Illustrations appearing also in articles, in larger scale.

* Shmeruk = *Jewish Publications in the Soviet Union, 1917-1960* (in Hebrew), ed. Kh. Shmeruk. "Galuyot" series. Jerusalem: The Historical Society of Israel, 1961.

* Ratner-Kvitni = *Dos Yidishe Bukh in FSSR far di Yoren, 1917-1921* (The Jewish Book in FSSR during 1917-1921). Kiev, 1930.

17

## Copies of Jewish ornamental motifs

**1**
Unknown artist, end of 19th century, Shklov
Deer, decorative motif for a tombstone
Pencil on paper, 185×422
*Boris and Lisa Aronson Collection*

**2**
Unknown artist, end of 19th century, Shklov
Eagle, tracing of a decorative motif for a tombstone
Pencil on paper, 225×380
*Boris and Lisa Aronson Collection*

**3**
Unknown artist, end of 19th century, Shklov
Decorative motif for a tombstone
Pencil on paper, 212×337
Inscribed, upper right (Russian):
"Why Don't You Give Me Paper to Write On,"
and numerical calculations
*Boris and Lisa Aronson Collection*

**4**
Unknown artist
Eagle, rubbing from a tombstone,
end of 18th century(?)
Pencil on wax paper (contours reinforced), 304×364
*Boris and Lisa Aronson Collection*

**5**
Unknown artist
Griffin and unicorn, tracing of a decorative motif for a tombstone, end of 19th century
Pencil on paper, 177×378
*Boris and Lisa Aronson Collection*

**6**
Unknown artist
Rubbing of a tombstone
Pencil and watercolor (for reinforcing) on paper, 208×400
*Boris and Lisa Aronson Collection*

**7**
Unknown artist
Decorative motif
Pencil, watercolor, and silver powder on paper, 113×154
*Boris and Lisa Aronson Collection*

**8**
Unknown artist
Decorative motif
Pencil and watercolor on paper, 98×137
*Boris and Lisa Aronson Collection*

**9**
Unknown artist
Decorative motif
Pencil and watercolor on paper, 148×111
*Boris and Lisa Aronson Collection*

**10**
Unknown artist
Decorative motif
Pencil, india ink, and watercolor on paper, 145×98
*Boris and Lisa Aronson Collection*

11
Unknown artist
(signed illegibly)
Copy of an 18th century (?)
Torah ark decoration
Black chalk and watercolor on
paper, 210×335
*Boris and Lisa Aronson
Collection*

16
Unknown artist
(Lissitzky?, Ryback?)
Copy of a decorative motif,
c. 1916
Black chalk and pencil on
paper, 223×217
*Boris and Lisa Aronson
Collection*

12
Unknown artist
Decorative motif with
inscription (Hebrew):
"Abounding in Kindness
and Faithfulness/
at the Pleasure of His Lord."
Copy of an 18th century (?)
wall painting from a synagogue
Pencil and watercolor
on wax paper, 311×230
*Boris and Lisa Aronson
Collection*

17
Unknown artist (Lissitzky?)
The Garden of Eden serpent
Copy of a decorative motif for
a Torah crown or a tombstone
Black chalk and watercolor on
paper, 355×220
*Boris and Lisa Aronson
Collection*

13
Unknown artist
Decorative motif
Ink and wash on paper,
264×203
*Boris and Lisa Aronson
Collection*

14
Unknown artist
Lion, tracing from a tombstone
Pencil on paper, 197×320
Verso: a deer
*Boris and Lisa Aronson
Collection*

15
Issachar Ber Ryback (?)
Lion, rubbing from a
tombstone, c. 1916
Inscribed verso (Yiddish):
"Issachar Ber Ryback Folk
Art Tombstone Carvings
1913-1917 14"
Pencil on paper, 222×355
*Boris and Lisa Aronson
Collection*

18
Illustration for Alexei
Kruchenykh's *Vzorval*
("Explodity"), 1913
Lithograph on paper, 176×112
*Michail Grobman Collection,
Tel Aviv*

23
The in-laws on a bench,
costume design for
*The Dybbuk*, Act II,
Habimah Theatre, 1920
Pencil and gouache on paper,
349×219
*Collection of Nahum Zemach,
founder of the Habimah
Theatre, Israel Goor Theatre
Archives and Museum,
Jerusalem*

19 □
Stage design for *The Dybbuk*,
Act I, Habimah Theatre, 1920
Pencil, india ink, gouache, and
tempera on paper, 265×405
Verso: pencil study for the
same set
*Tel Aviv Museum Collection
Lent by Habimah Theatre,
Tel Aviv*

24
The frog, costume design for
*The Dybbuk*, Act II,
Habimah Theatre, 1920
Pencil, wash and gouache on
paper, 328×199
*Collection of Nahum Zemach,
founder of the Habimah
Theatre, Israel Goor Theatre
Archives and Museum,
Jerusalem*

20
Stage design for *The Dybbuk*,
Act II, Habimah Theatre, 1920
Gouache, india ink, and
collage on paper, 263×354
*Israel Theater Museum
Haaretz Museum, Tel Aviv*

25 □
Tubercular beggar, costume
design for *The Dybbuk*, Act II,
Habimah Theatre, 1920
Pencil, gouache, and wash on
paper, 362×178
*Collection of Nahum Zemach,
founder of the Habimah
Theatre, Israel Goor Theatre
Archives and Museum,
Jerusalem*

21
Third *batlan* (bum), costume
design for *The Dybbuk*, Act I,
Habimah Theatre, 1920
Pencil and gouache on paper,
349×177
*Collection of Nahum Zemach,
founder of the Habimah
Theatre, Israel Goor Theatre
Archives and Museum,
Jerusalem*

26 □
The hunchback, costume
design for *The Dybbuk*, Act II,
Habimah Theatre, 1920
Pencil and gouache on paper,
351×251
*Collection of Nahum Zemach,
founder of the Habimah
Theatre, Israel Goor Theatre
Archives and Museum,
Jerusalem*

22
The *melamed* (teacher), the
bridegroom and his father,
costume design for
*The Dybbuk*, Act I,
Habimah Theatre, 1920
Pencil gouache and wash on
paper, 223×309
*Collection of Nahum Zemach,
founder of the Habimah
Theatre, Israel Goor Theatre
Archives and Museum,
Jerusalem*

27
Cover illustration for *Got der
Fayer* (God the Fire)
by Yehezkiel Dobrushin
Moscow: Yungwald, 1922
India ink and colored ink on
paper, 232×228
Signed and dated, lower left
(Yiddish): "Nathan Altman 22"
*Boris and Lisa Aronson
Collection*

28
*Got der Fayer* (God the Fire)
by Yehezkiel Dobrushin
Moscow: Yungwald, 1922
30 pages, 175×115
Shmeruk*, 1461
Cover
*Jewish National and University
Library, Jerusalem*

30₃
Lions

29
*Shtam/Azkore*
(Trunk /Memorial)
by D. Hofstein and
A. Kushnirov
Moscow: Shtrom, 1922
15 pages, 228×153
Cover
*Lent by Feige and Levia
Hofstein, Ramat Aviv*

30₄
Fantastic Animals

30
*Jüdische Graphik*
(Jewish Graphics)
German edition with text by
Max Osborn
Berlin: Razum-Verlag, 1923
32 pages, 485×362,
edition of 250
10 illustrations
*Israel Museum*

30₅
Program for an Evening
Concert

30₁
Eve and the Serpent

30₆
Pigeons

30₂
Recumbent Deer

30₇
Logo of Achinar Publishers,
named after Bialik

30₈
Candelabrum

33
Stage design for the
Jewish Chamber Theatre(?)
Moscow, c. 1920
Pencil on paper, 169×220
*Boris and Lisa Aronson
Collection*

30₉
Flower Vase

34
Stage design for the
Jewish Chamber Theatre(?)
Moscow, c. 1920
Gouache over pencil on
paper, 223×178
*Boris and Lisa Aronson
Collection*

30₁₀
Ex Libris for M. P. Persitz

35
Stage design for the
Jewish Chamber Theatre(?)
Moscow, c. 1920
Wash and watercolor over
pencil on paper, 224×313
*Boris and Lisa Aronson
Collection*

31
*Evreiskaia Grafika*
(Jewish Graphics)
Russian edition with text by
Max Osborn
Berlin: Petropolis, 1923
21 pages, 485×362
Cover and 10 illustrations
*Museum of Jewish Art,
Jerusalem*

36
*Uprooted Flower*, illustration
for a poem by Z. Schneur,
1920
Woodcut on paper, 358×278
Reproduced on page 19 of
item 174
*Boris and Lisa Aronson
Collection*

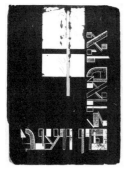

32
*In Tavel fun Vent*
(On the Tablet on the Wall)
by David Hofstein
Berlin: Farlag Funken, 1923
64 pages, 259×187
Cover
*Uzi Agassi Collection,
Raanana*

37
*Shtetl* (Small Town)
Woodcut on paper, 1920 ,
192×255
Signed, lower right:
"B. Aronson"
Reproduced on page 44 of
item 174
*Boris and Lisa Aronson
Collection*

38
Untitled
Woodcut on paper, 1920 ,
515×383
Inscribed and signed, lower
center: "B. Aronson
Berlin 921"
Reproduced on page 57 of
item 174
*Boris and Lisa Aronson
Collection*

39
*Mourning*
Woodcut on cloth, 1920 ,
125×170
Reproduced on page 95 of
item 174
*Boris and Lisa Aronson
Collection*

40
Illustration for *Sleeping
Beauty*, c. 1919
India ink on paper, 220×185
Inscribed on back of support
(Yiddish): "Tyshler,
The Sleeping Princess"
Stamped by publisher:
"Yidisher Folks Farlag
Kiev-St. Petersburg Kooperativ
Geselshaft"
*Boris and Lisa Aronson
Collection*

41
Illustration for the Book of
Ruth, c. 1920
Black chalk and pencil on
paper, 220×151
*Boris and Lisa Aronson
Collection*

42
Illustration for the Book of
Ruth, c. 1920
Black chalk on paper, 220×178
Inscribed on back of support
(Yiddish): "Tyshler Ruth"
Stamped by publisher:
"Yidisher Folks Farlag
Kiev-St. Petersburg Kooperativ
Geselshaft"
*Boris and Lisa Aronson
Collection*

43
Illustration for the Book of
Ruth, c. 1920
Black chalk on paper, 220×178
Inscribed on back of support
(Yiddish): "Tyshler Ruth"
Stamped by publisher:
"Yidisher Folks Farlag
Kiev-St. Petersburg Kooperativ
Geselshaft"
*Boris and Lisa Aronson
Collection*

44
Illustration for the Book of
Ruth, c. 1920
Black chalk on paper, 220×178
Inscribed on back of support
(Yiddish): "Tyshler Ruth"
Stamped by publisher:
"Yidisher Folks Farlag
Kiev-St. Petersburg Kooperativ
Geselshaft"
*Boris and Lisa Aronson
Collection*

45
*Temerl* (Little Tamar)
by Moshe Broderzon
No. 4 in the "Kinder Bibliotek"
(Children's Library) series
Moscow: Khaver Farlag,
[1917]
9 pages, 136×345
Shmeruk*, 2406;
Ratner-Kvitni*, 119
Cover and 9 illustrations
*Jewish National and University
Library, Jerusalem*

45<sub>4</sub>

45<sub>5</sub>

45<sub>1</sub>

45<sub>6</sub>

45<sub>2</sub>

45<sub>7</sub>

45<sub>3</sub>

45<sub>8</sub>

46
*Kinder* (Children)
by Aharon Reuveni
No. 13, in the "Shul Bibliotek"
(School Library) series
Kiev: Kiever Farlag, 1918
23 pages, 167×130,
edition of 5000
Shmeruk*, 2707;
Ratner-Kvitni*, 354
2 illustrations
*Jewish National and University
Library, Jerusalem*

47₂

46₁

47₃

46₂

47₄

47
*Lemel Nasher* (Greedy Lemel)
by Leib Kvitko
Kiev: Kiever Farlag, 1919
14 pages, 118×165,
edition of 5000
Shmeruk, 2615*;
Ratner-Kvitni*, 609
6 illustrations
*Jewish National and University
Library, Jerusalem*

47₄

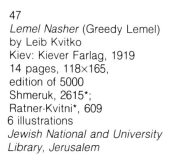

47₅

47₁

47₆

48
*Finf Arbeslakh*
(Five Chick Peas)
by Hans Christian Andersen
Kiev: Anhoyb Farlag, 1919
12 pages, 200×260
Ratner-Kvitni*, 562
Front and back covers, and
8 illustrations
*Jewish National and University
Library, Jerusalem*

48₄

48₅

48₁

48₆

48₂

48₇

48₃

48₈

49
*Margaritke* (Daisy) by Hans
Christian Andersen
Kiev: Anhoyb Farlag, 1919
8 pages, 196×312
Ratner-Kvitni*, 559
Cover and 7 illustrations
*Jewish National and University
Library, Jerusalem*

detail of 49₄

49₁

49₂

49₅

49₃

detail of 49₅

49₄

49₆₋₇

detail of 49₆₋₇

50
*Baginen* (Beginning), Vol. 1
Kiev: All-Ukrainian Literary
Committee, Jewish Section,
June 1919
126 pages, 245×164,
edition of 5000
Shmeruk*, 3545
Front and back covers, title
page, and 11 illustrations
*Uzi Agassi Collection,
Raanana*

50₃

51
Cover illustration for
David Hofstein's
*Bay Vegen* (On the Way)
Kiev, 1919
India ink on paper, 172×115
Shmeruk*, 1532
*Boris and Lisa Aronson
Collection*

52
Design for the emblem of the
Yidisher Folks Farlag
publishing company, c. 1919
India ink on paper, 220×176
Inscribed verso (Yiddish):
"Tchaikov Fraie,"
and an illegible word
Stamped by publisher
*Boris and Lisa Aronson
Collection*

50₁

53
Drawing for illustration, page
36 in Peretz Markish's
*Shveln* (Doorways), Kiev,
c. 1919
India ink on cardboard, 99×88
*Boris and Lisa Aronson
Collection*

50₂

54
Drawing for illustration, page
98 in Peretz Markish's
*Shveln* (Doorways) Kiev,
c. 1919
India ink on cardboard, 98×70
*Boris and Lisa Aronson
Collection*

55
*Shveln* (Doorways)
by Peretz Markish
Kiev: Yidisher Folks Farlag,
c. 1919
168 pages, 205×130
Shmeruk*, 1844;
Ratner-Kvitni*, 484
Cover, title page, and
13 illustrations
*Lent by Esther Markish, Kiron*

58₁

56
Illustration for the book (?)
*Zomer oyfn Shpatzir*
(A Summer Walk), c. 1919
India ink on paper, 202×210
Inscribed verso (Yiddish):
"Tchaikov A Summer Walk"
Stamped by publisher:
"Yidisher Folks Farlag
Kooperativ Geselshaft"
*Boris and Lisa Aronson
Collection*

58₂

57
Illustration for the Book of Job,
c. 1919
India ink and watercolor on
paper, 365×315
Inscribed, lower right
(Yiddish): "Chapter b., c."
Inscribed, lower left: "Tchaikov"
*Boris and Lisa Aronson
Collection*

58₃

58
*Dos Kelbel* (The Calf)
by Mendele Mokher Seforim
Kiev-St. Petersburg: Yidisher
Folks Farlag, 1919
16 pages, 200×270
Edition of 5000
Shmeruk*, 2543;
Ratner-Kvitni*, 832
(Also published by Kultur Lige,
Warsaw, 1921;
Ratner-Kvitni*, 832;
First edition of 3500 copies,
June 1921; second edition of
4500 copies, 1921)
Identical cover, title page, and
7 illustrations
*Jewish National and University
Library, Jerusalem*

58₄

58₅

58₆

58₇

59

*In Fayerdiken Doyer*
(In the Burning Epoch),
a collection of revolutionary
lyrics
Kiev: Melukhe Farlag, 1921
64 pages, 175×135
Shmeruk*, 1113
Cover
*Lent by Feige and Levia
Hofstein, Ramat Aviv*

60

*Vocal Suite* by M. Milner,
10 children's songs by Y. L.
Peretz, for voice and piano
Kiev: Melukhe Farlag, Kultur
Lige, 1921
23 pages, 324×250
Shmeruk*, 1084;
Ratner-Kvitni*, 801
Cover
*Jewish National and University
Library, Jerusalem*

61

*Knaknisl un Moyzenkayser*
(The Nutcracker and King Rat)
by Ernest Theodore Hoffmann,
translated from German
by L. Reznik
Kiev: Kooperativer Farlag,
Kultur Lige, 1922
84 pages, 225×168
Cover
*Gift of Zusia Efron, Jerusalem
Israel Museum, 1986*

62

Drawing for illustration,
page 18 in Peretz Markish's
*Der Galaganer Hon*
(The Arrogant Rooster)
Berlin, 1922
India ink and white gouache
on paper, 156×205
Inscribed, lower right
(Yiddish): "For Chapter X"
Inscribed, lower left: "N 14"
*Boris and Lisa Aronson
Collection*

63 □

*Der Galaganer Hon*
(The Arrogant Rooster)
by Peretz Markish
Berlin: Klal Farlag, 1922
30 pages, 294×225
Cover and 26 illustrations
*Uzi Agassi Collection,
Raanana*

63₁

63₂

63₃

63₄

63₉

63₅

\*

63₁₀

63₆

**64**
*Di Kupe* (The Pile)
by Peretz Markish
Kiev: Kultur Lige, 1922
36 pages, 181×134
Shmeruk\*, 1847
Cover
*Lent by Esther Markish, Kiron*

63₇

**65**
*In Shturm fun Geshikhte*
(In the Storm of History)
by David Kaigen
Berlin: Yidisher Literarisher
Farlag, 1923
284 pages, 185×128
Cover
*Uzi Agassi Collection,
Raanana*

63₈

**66** ☐
*Bereishit* (In the Beginning)
Moscow-Leningrad, 1926
204 pages, 231×159
Shmeruk\*, 315
Cover
*Uzi Agassi Collection,
Raanana*

67
Lion, copied from the zodiac
painting on the ceiling
of the Mohilev synagogue,
White Russia, 1916
Black chalk and watercolor on
paper, 220×245
*Boris and Lisa Aronson
Collection*

68
Lion, copied from the wall
painting above the Mohilev
synagogue's portal,
White Russia, 1916
Black chalk and pencil on
paper, 355×223
*Boris and Lisa Aronson
Collection*

69
Sagittarius, copied from the
zodiac painting on the ceiling of
the Mohilev synagogue,
White Russia, 1916
Black chalk and watercolor on
paper, 220×233
*Boris and Lisa Aronson
Collection*

70 ☐
Peacock, based on a wall
painting on the west side of
the Mohilev synagogue
ceiling, White Russia, 1916
Black chalk, watercolor, and
gouache on paper, 223×267
*Boris and Lisa Aronson
Collection*

71
Sea horse and bird, based on
a painting in the Druya
synagogue, Lithuania, 1916
India ink, watercolor, and
pencil on paper, 208×270
*Boris and Lisa Aronson
Collection*

72
*Sikhes Kholin* (Small Talk)
(*Legend of Prague*)
by Moshe Broderzon
Moscow: Shamir (originally
Nashe Iskusstvo), 1917
Shmeruk*, 2405;
Ratner-Kvitni*, 118
Hand-colored lithograph on
paper, 228×3855
Title page, 15 illustrated
pages and colophon, 7/110
Scroll-form in a wooden box
carved by the artist
*Gift of Marianna and Walter
Griessmann, London, for
Teddy Kollek's 70th birthday
Israel Museum, 1982*

74₁

72₁ □
Title page

74₂

72₂
Colophon

74₃

73 □
Cover page illustration for
Moshe Broderzon's
*Sikhes Kholin* (Small Talk)
(*Legend of Prague*)
Moscow, 1917
Linoleum cut on paper,
180×186 (trimmed margins)
*Lent by Sheine Miriam
Broderzon, Holon*

74₄

74
*Sikhes Kholin* (Small Talk)
(*Legend of Prague*)
by Moshe Broderzon
Moscow: Shamir (originally
Nashe Iskusstvo), 1917
Shmeruk*, 2405;
Ratner-Kvitni*, 118
Lithograph on paper (the title
page is hand-colored), 228×295
□ Title page, 15 illustrated
pages and colophon, 52/110
*Israel Museum, 1961*

74₅

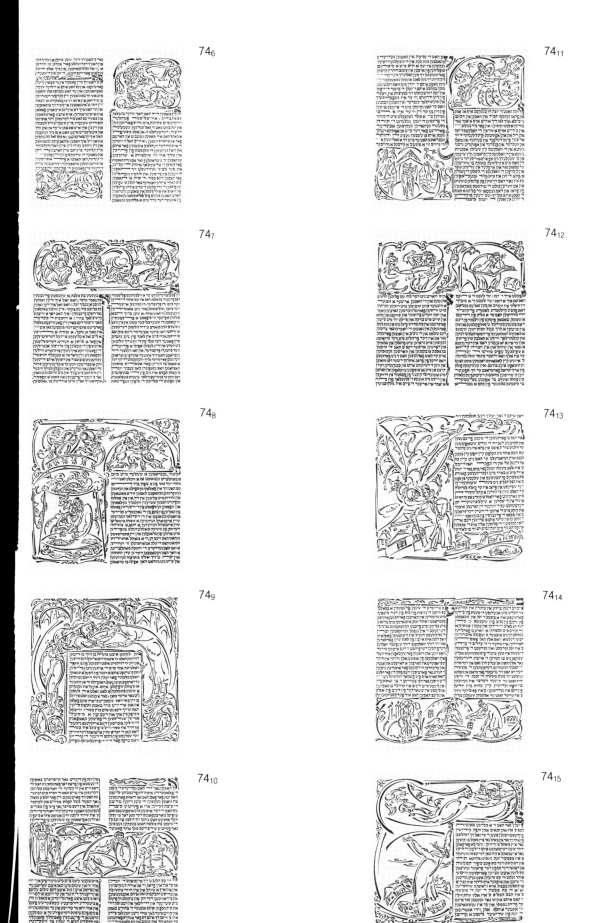

74₆

74₁₁

74₇

74₁₂

74₈

74₁₃

74₉

74₁₄

74₁₀

74₁₅

74
Colophon

77₃

77

75 □
Vitebsk synagogue, 1917
Hand-colored linoleum cut on
paper, 340×540
Inscribed and dated, left
(Russian): "Vitebsk synagogue
1917 Linoleum Cut"
*Boris and Lisa Aronson
Collection*

77₄

77

76
Safrut emblem on back cover of
*A Jewish Anthology*, edited by
V. P. Khodasevich and
L. B. Jaffe
Moscow: Safrut, [1917]
192 pages, 248×169
*Michail Grobman Collection,
Tel Aviv*

77₅

7

77
"Shlomo Hamelekh" (King
Solomon) by C. N. Bialik
*Shtilim* (Saplings), no. 6-7,
October 1917
Pages 2-16, 258×195
Shmeruk*, 341
11 illuminated captions and
one illustration
*Jewish National and University
Library, Jerusalem*

77₆

77

77₂

77₇

77

77₁₀

78 □
Emblem of "Yidish Ferlag,"
1917, in *Kunst-Ring,
Literarish-Kinstlerisher Almanakh*
(Art Circle Literature-Art
Almanac)
Edited by K. Zingman, Vol II,
second edition, [Berlin, 1922?]
222 pages, 184×150
Shmeruk*, 3833;
Ratner-Kvitni*, 631
*Chimen Abramsky Collection,
London*

79
*Yingl Tsingl Khvat* (The
Mischievous Boy) by Mani Leib
Kiev-St. Petersburg: Yidisher
Folks Farlag, 1919
12 pages, 258×208
Shmeruk*, 2538;
Ratner-Kvitni*, 593
Cover, title page, and
10 illustrated pages
*Uzi Agassi Collection,
Raanana*

79₁ □

79₂

79₃

79₄

79₅

79₆

79₇

79₈

79₉

79₁₀

80 □
Yidisher Folks Farlag emblem in
*Shriften* (Writings), Vol. II, by
H. D. Nomberg
Kiev-St. Petersburg: Yidisher
Folks Farlag, 1919
134 pages, 195×129
*Jewish National and University
Library, Jerusalem*

81 □
Kiever Farlag emblem in
*Royte Blitn* (Red Blossoms)
by D. Hofstein
Kiev: Kiever Farlag, 1920
31 pages, 159×116
Shmeruk*, 1533
*Lent by Feige and Levia
Hofstein, Ramat Aviv*

detail of 79₉

82 ☐
*Az Ikh Volt Gehot ot Dos Vos
Ikh Mayn*
(If I Had Just What I Wanted),
sheet music for voice and
piano by Joel Engel
Moscow: Society for Jewish
Folk Music, 1919
6 pages, 350×260
Title page
*Central Library for Music and
Dance, Archives of Menashe
Ravina, Tel Aviv*

83
*Dem Zeydns Kloles*
(Grandfather's Curses)
by Tzadok Dolgopolski
A one-act children's comedy
from the "Yidishe Teatrale
Bibliotek" (Jewish Theatre
Library) series
Moscow: Tsentraln Yidishn
Komisariat, 1919
32 pages, 143×380. Shmeruk*,
2439; Ratner-Kvitni*, 575
Front and back covers, and
2 illustrations
*Jewish National and University
Library, Jerusalem*

83₁

83₂

84
*Shabes in Vald*
(Sabbath in the Forest)
by Jacob Fichman
From the "Shul Bibliotek"
(School Library) series
Kiev: Kiever Farlag, 1919
18 pages, 157×118
Shmeruk*, 2574
3 illustrations
*Jewish National and University
Library, Jerusalem*

84₁

84₂

גאהט ליפא אריין און וואלד מיט גרויס פהד. גאהט

84₃

85 ☐
*Andersen's Mayselekh*
(Andersen's Fairy Tales)
by Hans Christian Andersen,
translated into Yiddish
by Der Nister (Pinkhes
Kahanovich)
Kiev: Kiever Farlag, 1919
190 pages, 217×145,
edition of 2000
Cover
*Jewish National and University
Library, Jerusalem*

86 ☐
Illustration 1 for *Had Gadya*,
*Gekoyft der tate far tsvay
gilden ayn tsigele*
(Father Bought a Kid for Two
Zuzim), c. 1918
Watercolor, gouache, india ink,
and pencil on paper, 279×228
*Salome and Eric E. Estorick
Collection*

87 □
Illustration 1 for *Had Gadya*,
*Dezabin abba bisray zuzay*
(Father Bought a Kid for Two
Zuzim), 1918-19
Gouache, india ink, and pencil
on paper, 280×229
*Tel Aviv Museum*

90₂
*Then Came a Cat and Ate the
Kid*

88
Illustration 7 for *Had Gadya*,
*Veyoso toyro veshoso lemayo*
(Then Came an Ox and Drank
the Water), 1918-19
Gouache, india ink, and pencil
on paper, 280×229
*Tel Aviv Museum*

90₃
*Then Came a Dog and Bit the
Cat*

89 □
Illustration 10 for *Had Gadya*,
*Veyoso Hakodosh borukh hu
veshokhat lemalakh hamoves*
(Then Came the Holy One,
Blessed Be He, and Slew the
Angel of Death), 1918-19
Gouache, india ink, and pencil
on paper, 280×228
*Tel Aviv Museum*

90₄
*Then Came a Stick and Beat
the Dog*

90 □
Title page and 10 illustrations
for *Had Gadya*
Kiev: Kultur Lige, 1919
Color lithograph on paper,
279×258
Shmeruk*, 2520;
Ratner-Kvitni*, 581
*Israel Museum, 1976*

90₅
*Then Came a Fire and Burnt
the Stick*

90₁
*Father Bought a Kid for Two
Zuzim*

90₆
*Then Came Water and
Quenched the Fire*

90₇
*Then Came an Ox and Drank the Water*

92
*Der Milner, di Milnerin un di Milshtayner* (The Miller, His Wife and Their Millstones) by Uncle Ben Zion (Ben Zion Raskin)
From the "Kinder Gortn" series
Kiev: Yidisher Folks Farlag, 1919
16 pages, 158×110
Shmeruk*, 2723
Cover and 11 illustrations
Also published by Kultur Lige, Warsaw, 1922
*Jewish National and University Library, Jerusalem*

90₈
*Then Came the Butcher and Slew the Ox*

92₁

90₉
*Then Came Death and Took the Butcher*

92₂

90₁₀
*Then Came the Holy One Blessed Be He, and Smote the Angel of Death*

92₃

91
*Had Gadya*
Warsaw: Kultur Lige, 1923
12 pages, 181×177, edition of 1000
Shmeruk*, 2520
Cover (in color), title page, and 10 black-and-white illustrations
*Jewish National and University Library, Jerusalem*

92₄

92₅

92₁₀

זיצן זיי אלע אַוועק אַהיים צו דעם מילנער
און דער מילנערין, וואו זיי לעבן נאָך
עד-היום.

92₆

92₁₁

92₇

93
*Hatochen, Hatochenet Veavnei Hareihaim* (The Miller, His Wife and Their Millstones)
by Ben Zion Raskin (Uncle Ben Zion) (in Hebrew)
Warsaw: Tarbut, 1922
16 pages, 210×169
Cover, identical title page, and 11 illustrations
*The Feinstein Library of the Ruth Youth Wing, Israel Museum*

· הטוחן ·
· הטוחנת ·
· ואבני הרחים ·

92₈

94
*Der Ber* (The Bear)
by Uncle Ben Zion (Ben Zion Raskin)
From the "Kinder Gortn" series
Kiev-St. Petersburg: Yidisher Folks Farlag, 1919
12 pages, 198×160
Shmeruk*, 2721
Title page and 8 illustrations
*Uzi Agassi Collection, Raanana*

דער
ב ע ר

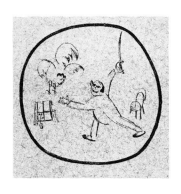

92₉

94₁

פֿאַרבײַ איז בנציון אַ בעלף-קינטשעסטער בער.
האָט אים אַן אֵלטער ייִנג נעבעך אַרבעט די יאָרהיים
און דערפֿאַר מעג דער בער מאַכן פֿאַר דעם
עולם. ער פֿרעג נעמען דעם יונג ווייטל איז
זיי ציונער, גיין אַרויף די טרעפֿשטעפֿע אין
און קליינען נעמט פֿאַר דעם זײַן.

94₂

אײַנמאָל: דער בער האָט אַנגעקלונגן אַ זאַק מיט
געלט. איז דער ייך אױרעק און שאָען שיינינג, געקומען
אַ שפריינגר אַרום געלונען אַ האָק אין שאָען.
האָקט דעם בער אַ טום.
דער בער האָט געגומען יאָמערן, געבאָמט זיך שאָפ-
האָקנט טום אין די זײַן און אַוועקגעשפרינגט:

שפרינגט עק, שפרינגט עק: שפרינגט מיר יאָמערע.
ביי עק האָט באָגעגען אַרום וועג אַ קאַץ.
וועגנט זיך דער בער צו דער קאָץ:
קעגעדיק קאָץ, שאַרני מיר מיין טום.
מאַרשטעף מיר מיין פעל.
דער ביױער זײַן האָט מיר אַנטראָקטם:
אַן וויל נים.

94₃

איז דער בער אוועקגעשפרינגט װײַטער.
שפרינגט עק און שפרינגט עק: שפרינגט יאָמערע.
ביי עק האָט באָגעגען אַרום וועג אַ הונט.
וועגנט זיך דער בער צו דעם הונט:

הענעדיק הונט, שאַרני מיר מיין טום. מאַרשטעף
מיר מיין פעל.
דער ביױער זײַן האָט מיר אַנטראָקטם:
אַן וויל נים.

94₄

איז דער בער אוועקגעשפרינגט װײַטער.
שפרינגט עק און שפרינגט עק: שפרינגט יאָמערע.
ביי עק האָט באָגעגען אַרום וועג אַ חויר.
וועגנט זיך דער בער צו דעם חויר:

חויר, חויר: שאַרני מיר מיין טום.
מאַרשטעף מיר מיין פעל.
דער ביױער זײַן האָט מיר אַנטראָקטם:
אַן וויל נים.

94₅

איז דער בער אוועקגעשפרינגט װײַטער.
שפרינגט עק און שפרינגט עק: שפרינגט יאָמערע.
ביי עק האָט באָגעגען אַרום וועג אַ שעפס.
וועגנט זיך דער בער צו דעם שעפס:

שעפסעלע שעפס, שאַרני מיר מיין טום.
מאַרשטעפ מיר מיין פעל.
דער ביױער זײַן האָט מיר אַנטראָקטם:

94₆

דער שעפס האָט זיך אַרוקגעשטעל־ט, געגומען ציהקן
וואָל אוז זיך.
ציהט די וואָל, רײַט פאָרום און פקקט סאָר
זיך אין דער שפרי: מם־עץ, הפל־עץ

מרגום דער בער דעם שעפס:
שעפס, שעפס, װאָט זאַטסטו דאָרם. װאָט
רעדסטו דאָרם?

94₇

— אַן בער בער, אַך זאַב.
דין טאָאוע האָט מיין טאָען אױסגעגומען.
דין טאָאוע האָט מיין טאָען אױסגעגומען.
אױ, שעטסל, ציה זאַל מיר זיך.
ציה װאָל, דריי אַריס פאַדים:
— ניין, שעפט שעפס, איך מין ניט אַ מאַרשטער בער.
ניט מיין טאָען גלירן, ניט מיין טאָען גלירד.
איך זײַן דאָר אַ גערטלעטאָער בער.
מיר װאָלין שוין בשלום לעבן.
מאַרני מיר טאָען מיין טום.
מאַרשטעפ מיר טאָער מיין פעל.
דער ביױער זײַן האָט מיר אַנטראָקטם:
דער שעפס האָט מאַרניס דעם בערס טום.
מאַרשטעפט דעם בערס פעל.

94₈ ☐

דער בער אַנגעדאָנקט דעם שעפס,
און די מעטאָריע איז אַרום.

95 ☐
*Di Hun Vos Hot Gevolt Hoben
a Kam* (The Hen That Wanted
a Comb) by Uncle Ben Zion
(Ben Zion Raskin)
From the "Kinder Gortn" series
Kiev-St. Petersburg: Yidisher
Folks Farlag, [1919]
16 pages, 110×150
Shmeruk*, 2722
Cover and 9 illustrations
*Uzi Agassi Collection,
Raanana*

95₁

דער האָן איז געגומען אַ שוריער און די הון אַ הון קודקט.

95₂

אַוועקגעפאָרן!

95₃

100
*Ivashke* (Little Ivan),
illustration for *Ukraynishe
Folkmayses* (Ukrainian
Folktales) (opposite page 34),
c. 1922
India ink on paper, 304×227
Inscribed, lower right
(Yiddish): "Little Ivan"
*Boris and Lisa Aronson
Collection*

96
*A Henetske* (A Glove),
illustration for *Ukraynishe
Folkmayses* (Ukrainian
Folktales) (opposite page 4),
c. 1922
India ink on paper, 285×220
Inscribed, lower right
(Yiddish): "Ukrainian Folktales
L. Kvitko"
Inscribed, lower left (Yiddish):
"1 A Glove"
*Boris and Lisa Aronson Collection*

101
*Der Kater* (The Cat),
illustration for *Ukraynishe
Folkmayses* (Ukrainian
Folktales) (opposite page 56),
c. 1922
India ink on paper, 308×230
Inscribed, lower right
(Yiddish): "8 The Cat"
*Boris and Lisa Aronson
Collection*

97
*A Kneidl* (A Dumpling),
illustration for *Ukraynishe
Folkmayses* (Ukrainian
Folktales) (opposite page 8),
c. 1922
India ink on paper, 303×231
Inscribed, lower right
(Yiddish): "2 A Dumpling"
*Boris and Lisa Aronson
Collection*

102
*Dos Gildene Shikhele*
(The Golden Shoe), illustration
for *Ukraynishe Folkmayses*
(Ukrainian Folktales) (opposite
page 64), c. 1922
India ink on paper, 296×225
Inscribed, lower right
(Yiddish): "9 The Golden Shoe"
*Boris and Lisa Aronson
Collection*

98 □
*Dos Fligendike Shif*
(The Flying Ship), illustration
for *Ukraynishe Folkmayses*
(Ukrainian Folktales) (opposite
page 80), c. 1922
India ink on paper, 295×224
Inscribed, lower right
(Yiddish): "10 The Flying Ship"
*Boris and Lisa Aronson
Collection*

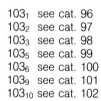

103₁   see cat. 96
103₂   see cat. 97
103₃   see cat. 98
103₅   see cat. 99
103₆   see cat. 100
103₉   see cat. 101
103₁₀  see cat. 102

103 □
*Ukraynishe Folkmayses*
(Ukrainian Folktales),
translated into Yiddish by
Leib Kvitko,
FSSR, Jewish Section in the
Commissariat
for Public Education, 1922
88 pages, 215×160
Front and back covers,
10 illustrations
*Elaine and Arthur Cohen
Collection, New York*

99
*A Klug Meydl* (A Wise Girl),
illustration for *Ukraynishe
Folkmayses* (Ukrainian
Folktales) (opposite page 24),
c. 1922
India ink on paper, 307×228
Inscribed, lower right
(Yiddish): "4 A Wise Girl"
*Boris and Lisa Aronson
Collection*

103₄

103₇

103₈

104 ☐
*Yingl Tsingl Khvat* (The Mischievous Boy) by Mani Leib
Warsaw: Kultur Lige, 1922
10 pages, 244×194
(2 editions of 2000 each, one large and one small)
Cover, title page, and 10 illustrated pages
*Jewish National and University Library, Jerusalem*

105 ☐
Illustration for "Shifs Karta" (Boat Ticket)
in Ilya Ehrenburg's *Six Stories with Easy Endings*
Moscow-Berlin: Helikon, 1922
India ink and collage on paper, 435×241
*Boris and Lisa Aronson Collection*

106
*Six Stories with Easy Endings* by Ilya Ehrenburg
Moscow-Berlin: Helikon, 1922
165 pages, 194×136
6 illustrations
*Uzi Agassi Collection, Raanana*

107
*Rabbi*, a play by Olga Forsch
Berlin: Skythen, 1922
64 pages, 199×140
Cover
*Chimen Abramsky Collection, London*

108 ☐
*Vaysrusishe Folkmayses* (White Russian Folktales), translated into Yiddish by Leib Kvitko
FSSR, Jewish Section in the Commissariat for Public Education, 1923
102 pages, 208×145
Front and back covers, 14 illustrations
*Jewish National and University Library, Jerusalem*

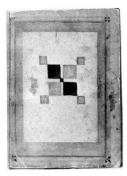

108₁

108₆

108₁₁

108₂

108₇

108₁₂

108₃

108₈

108₁₃

108₄

108₉

108₁₄

108₅

108₁₀

108₃

111

ראמאנטיש

109
*Bilder* (Pictures), c. 1914,
illustration for Zussman
Segalovitch's *Bloykayt*
(In Blue), Kiev, 1919
India ink on paper, 135×133
Verso: drawing of a figure and
a date (1914?)
Inscribed on back of support
(Yiddish): "In Blue" and "Elman"
*Boris and Lisa Aronson
Collection*

112
Stage design for *Jacob's
Dream*,
Habimah Theatre, 1925
Gouache and collage on
paper, 270×389
*Israel Theater Museum,
Haaretz Museum, Tel Aviv*

110
*Fun Der Vaytns* (From Afar),
c. 1914
Possibly cover illustration for
Zussman Segalovitch's
*Bloykayt* (In Blue), Kiev, 1919
India ink on paper, 218×140
Inscribed on back of support
(Yiddish): "From Afar"
*Boris and Lisa Aronson
Collection*

113
Stage design for *Jacob's
Dream*,
Habimah Theatre, 1925
Gouache and watercolor on
paper, 279×426
*Israel Theater Museum,
Haaretz Museum, Tel Aviv*

111
Bloykayt (In Blue)
by Zussman Segalovitch
Kiev: Yidisher Folks Farlag,
1919
154 pages, 207×132
Shmeruk*, 1931;
Ratner-Kvitni*, 487
9 illustrations
*Jewish National and University
Library, Jerusalem*

114
Portrait of the actor Binyamin
Zuskin in *Travels of Benjamin III*
Jewish State Theatre,
Moscow, 1927
Pencil and black and white
chalk on paper, 339×226
*Lent by Ala Perlman-Zuskin,
Neve Monoson*

## Isaac Binitch Rabitchev
### 1894-1961

**115**
Illustration for *Klezmer*
(Band) (?), c. 1920
India ink over pencil on paper,
254×207
Inscribed verso, upper right
(Yiddish): "Band"
Verso stamped by publisher:
"Yidisher Folks Farlag"
*Boris and Lisa Aronson
Collection*

**116**
Illustration for *Klezmer*
(Band)(?), c. 1920
India ink on paper, 274×212
Inscribed verso, upper right
(Yiddish): "Rabitchev Band"
Verso stamped by publisher:
"Yidisher Folks Farlag"
*Boris and Lisa Aronson
Collection*

**117**
Illustration for *Klezmer*
(Band)(?), c. 1920
India ink on paper, 274×211
Inscribed verso, upper right
(Yiddish): "Rabitchev Band"
Verso stamped by publisher:
"Yidisher Folks Farlag"
*Boris and Lisa Aronson
Collection*

## Isaac Rabinovich, 1894-1961

**118**
Stage design with figures for
*God of Vengeance*
by Sholem Asch
Jewish Chamber Theatre,
Moscow, 1921
Pencil on paper, 264×402
*Lent by Natalia
Mikhoels-Vovsi, Tel Aviv*

## Issachar Ber Ryback
### 1897-1935

**119** ☐
Drawing based on the ceiling
of the Mohilev synagogue,
White Russia, c. 1916
Watercolor and india ink over
black chalk on paper, 645×480
Signed, lower center (Yiddish):
"Issachar Ber Ryback"
Inscribed, lower center
(Russian): "The Mohilev
synagogue ceiling"
*Purchased through a donation
from Mr. and Mrs. Ludwig
Bravmann, Riverdale, New
York, to American Friends of
the Israel Museum, 1986*

**120**
Goat, 1917 (?)
Black chalk on paper, 106×165
Signed and dated, lower right
(Hebrew): "I. R. 1917"
*Ryback Museum, Bat Yam*

**121**
*Horse and Wagon*, 1917 (?)
Black chalk on paper, 107×165
Signed and dated, lower right
(Hebrew): "I. R. 1917"
*Ryback Museum, Bat Yam*

**122**
From the "Pogrom" series,
1918
Pencil, india ink, and
watercolor on paper, 330×450
Signed, inscribed and dated,
lower left (Yiddish):
"Issachar Ber Ryback,
Kiev, 1918"
*Mishkan Le'omanut, Museum
of Art, Ein Harod*

123
From the "Pogrom" series,
1918
Pencil, india ink, and
watercolor on paper, 369×546
Signed, inscribed and dated,
lower left (Yiddish):
"Issachar Ber Ryback,
Kiev, 1918"
*Mishkan Le'omanut, Museum
of Art, Ein Harod*

128
Cemetery, c. 1921
Oil on canvas, 515×677
Signed, lower right (Yiddish
and Latin):
"Issachar Ber Ryback"
*Ryback Museum, Bat Yam*

124
From the "Pogrom" series,
1918
Pencil, india ink, and
watercolor on paper, 368×545
*Mishkan Le'omanut, Museum
of Art, Ein Harod*

129
Title page for Miryam
Margolin's *Mayselekh far
Kleyninke Kinderlekh*
(Little Tales for Little Children),
c. 1922
Petrograd, 1922
India ink on paper, 265×350
*Marianna and Walter
Griessmann Collection,
London*

125
From the "Pogrom" series,
1918
Pencil, india ink, and
watercolor on paper, 499×650
Signed, inscribed and dated,
lower left (Yiddish):
"Issachar Ber Ryback,
Kiev,1918"
*Mishkan Le'omanut, Museum
of Art, Ein Harod*

130
*Yingele Tsingele* (Mischievous
Boy), illustration for Miryam
Margolin's *Mayselekh far
Kleyninke Kinderlekh*
(Little Tales for Little Children),
c. 1922
Petrograd, 1922
India ink on paper, 268×352
Signed and inscribed, lower
right (Yiddish):
"Ryback, Mischievous Boy"
*Marianna and Walter
Griessmann Collection,
London*

126
From the "Pogrom" series,
1918
Pencil, india ink, and
watercolor on paper, 491×642
Signed, lower right (Yiddish):
"Issachar Ber Ryback"
*Mishkan Le'omanut, Museum
of Art, Ein Harod*

131
*Di Hun*, (The Hen), illustration
for Miryam Margolin's
*Mayselekh far Kleyninke
Kinderlekh* (Little Tales for
Little Children),
c. 1922
Petrograd, 1922
India ink on paper, 268×352
Signed and inscribed, lower
right (Yiddish):
"Ryback, The Hen"
*Marianna and Walter
Griessmann Collection,
London*

127
*Oyfgang* (Sunrise),
first collection
Kiev: Kultur Lige, 1919
132 pages, 241×156
Shmeruk*, 3491;
Ratner-Kvitni*, 629
Cover
*Jewish National and University
Library, Jerusalem*

132
*A Shlang* (A Snake),
illustration for Miryam
Margolin's *Mayselekh far
Kleyninke Kinderlekh*
(Little Tales for Little Children),
c. 1922
Petrograd, 1922
India ink on paper, 268×352
Signed and inscribed, lower
right (Yiddish):
"Ryback, A Snake"
*Marianna and Walter
Griessmann Collection,
London*

134₁

133
*Alter der Fisher* (Alter the
Fisherman), illustration for
Miryam Margolin's *Mayselekh
far Kleyninke Kinderlekh*
(Little Tales for Little Children),
c. 1922
Petrograd, 1922
India ink and collage on
paper, 267×357
Signed and inscribed, lower
right (Yiddish):
"Ryback, Alter the Fisherman"
*Marianna and Walter
Griessmann Collection,
London*

134₂

134₃

134
*Mayselekh far Kleyninke
Kinderlekh*
(Little Tales for Little Children)
by Miryam Margolin
Petrograd: Jewish Section of
the Commissariat
for People's Education, 1922
23 pages, 205×270,
Shmeruk*, 2539
Front and back covers, and 10
illustrations
*Jewish National and University
Library, Jerusalem*

134₄

134₅

134₉

134₆

134₈

134₇

134₁₀

135
*Kinder Velt* (The Child's World)
by B. Smoliar
Berlin: Shveln [c. 1922]
16 pages, 308×235
Title page and 14 illustrations
*The Feinstein Library of the
Ruth Youth Wing, Israel
Museum*

135₅

135₁₀

135₁

135₆

135₁₁

135₂

135₇

135₁₂

135₃

135₈

135₁₃

135₄

135₉

135₁₄

די פייגל דאַרט שפרינגגען און שטיפן,  דער וואַלד איז די שטאָט פון די ביימער,

זיי זיצן ניט אייַן אויף קיין אָרט,  דאָרט וואַקסן די ביימער זיך שטיל,

פּונקט ווי בייַ אונז דאָ די קינדער,  זיי שטייען ווי נאָהענטע שכנים,

אַזוי איז אין וואַלד בייַ זיי דאָרט.  און יעדערער וואַקסט ווי ער וויל.

136₂

136
*Shtetl, Mayn Khoyever Heym,*
*a Gedenknish*
(Small Town, My Destroyed
Home, A Recollection)
Berlin: Farlag Shveln, 1923
30 pages, 339×500,
edition of 50
Front and back covers, title
page, and 30 illustrations
*Israel Museum*

136₄
*In Shul* (In the Synagogue)

136₁
Title Page

136₂
*Shul* (Synagogue)

136₃
*Shul Gas* (The Synagogue
Street)

136₅
*In Heder* (In the Classroom)

136₆
*In Zal* (In the Living Room)

136₇
*Der Shadkhan* (The Matchmaker)

136₈
*Mekhuteniste* (Mother-In-Law)

136₉
*Kale Matones* (Bride's Gifts)

136₁₄
*In A Haysn Tog* (On a Hot Day)

136₁₀
*Di Khupe* (The Wedding Canopy)

136₁₅
*Der Vaserfirer* (The Water Carrier)

136₁₁
*Klezmer* (Band)

136₁₆
*Der Shnayder* (The Tailor)

136₁₂
*Likht Benshn* (Blessing the Candles)

136₁₇
*Der Glezer* (The Glazier)

136₁₃
*Kidush* (Santification)

136₁₈
*Der Shuster* (The Shoemaker)

136₁₉
*Der Shlayfer* (The Knife-Sharpener)

136₂₄
*Farnakht* (Evening)

136₂₀
*Der Fishmark* (The Fish Market)

136₂₅
*Simkhes Toyre* (Rejoicing of the Law)

136₂₁
*Oyfen Mark* (Market)

136₂₆
*Nokh Sukis* (After Succot)

136₂₂
*Der Shokhet* (The Ritual Slaughterer)

136₂₇
*Di Levaya* (The Funeral)

136₂₃
*Di Tzig* (The Goat)

136₂₈
*Oyf Bays Oylem* (In the Cemetary)

136<sub>29</sub>
*Der Rov* (The Rabbi)

137<sub>2</sub>

136<sub>30</sub>
*Der Rebbe* (The Grand Rabbi)

137<sub>3</sub>

137<sub>4</sub>

137 ☐
*Foyglen* (Birds) by Leib Kvitko
Berlin: Farlag Shveln, [1922]
15 pages, 240×310
Front and back covers, and
14 illustrations
*Jewish National and University
Library, Jerusalem*

137<sub>5</sub>

137<sub>1</sub>

137<sub>6</sub>

137₇

137₁₂

137₈

נאָר פֿון בװײַסטער דיים: סת פֿיקס:
פֿיקס: פֿיקס: טרײַס רעד מעסטר:
,הער מיך ארײַן דאַרֿ פֿיקאָקעלֿ: מיק!

137₁₃

די פֿים: דיינע פֿים —
ן — די מאַטײם:
כלדאַרֿ סיט ראָב דאַ אינערשמאָקן מ די אָשרין ור ד געלֿעבסט:
רעקסט נאָך ורזם: װארס סין אריך פֿן אנרטרים אָשרטשעמם:

137₉

און ארײַ זיך מיט א זומל/
װאַט רעם סיך פֿן דירבעט גלעטמ:
שטאַלֿן פֿן מ מוי רעהַרַט:

138 □
*Gringroz* (Green Grass)
by Leib Kvitko
Berlin: Yidisher Literarisher
Farlag, 1922
210 pages, 186×130
Cover, identical title page, and
10 illustrations
*Jewish National and University
Library, Jerusalem*

137₁₀

138₁

137₁₁

138₂

138₃

139
*Build Communist Life in the Fields of Russia*, c. 1926
Color lithograph, 965×680
Moldovan Family Collection, New York

138₄

140
*Karl un Mizra* (Karl and Mizra)
by Leib Kvitko
From the *Pionern Bikhl* (Pioneer Book) series
Kharkov: Knihaspilka, 1927 (?)
12 pages, 257×322
Shmeruk*, 2636
Cover and 5 illustrations
*Jewish National and University Library, Jerusalem*

138₅

140₁

138₆

140₂

138₇

140₄

איבער דער נאָרמע, אום דערמיט זיי אויסמאַטצרן און אָפּצוואַכן —
אַז מע אַרבעט איבער די קוויכעס קאָן מען דאָך שוין אף קיין מיטינ-
גען און זיצונגען ניט גיין. האָט׳ס געטראָפֿן, ווען קאַרל האָט דעם
אוילעם אַגיטירט, אַז אַן עק זאָל נעמען, שטרייקן זאָל מע׳. — האָט אים

דער פֿאַרוואַלטער דעמאָלט באַמערקט און אים געשיקט אַוועקפֿירן דעם
הויב-קראַן צום דאַק. ס׳האָט שוין שטאַרק געטונקלט און קאַרל איז מיד
געוואָרן, קוים געשלעפּט זיך. האָט ער זיך שלעכט פֿאַרדרייט אין די הויב-
קייטן, אַ פֿאַלשן קער געטאָן און זיך שיר-שיר, — און געבליבן הענגען אין-
דערלופֿטן בײַ אַ פֿוס. ס׳איז געוואָרן אַ ראַש און גערודער, די אַרבעטער

141 ☐
*The Mikveh* (Ritual Bath), 1910
Pen and ink on brown paper,
231×268
Signed, lower right: "Chagall"
Inscribed, lower right (Russian):
"The Ritual Bath, 1910"
*Gift of Mr. and Mrs. Daniel
Saidenberg, New York,
to America-Israel Cultural
Foundation, 1971
Israel Museum Collection*

142
*Old Rabbi Reading the Torah*,
c. 1914
Pencil on paper, 180×230
*Gift of Cecil de Rothschild,
Tel Aviv Museum*

143
*The Magician*, 1915
India ink, wash, and white
gouache on paper, 225×180
Signed and dated, lower right:
"Marc Chagall 1915"
*Permanent loan from Dr. and
Mrs. A. Lejwa, New York,
to America-Israel Cultural
Foundation, 1971
Israel Museum Collection*

144
*A Mayse mit a Hon, Dos
Tsigele* (A Story about a
Rooster, The Little Kid) by
Der Nister
[Petrograd]: Vilner Farlag fun
B. A. Kletzkin, 1917
30 pages, 160×110
Shmeruk*, 2548;
Ratner-Kvitni*, 128
Cover and 8 illustrations
*Jewish National and University
Library, Jerusalem*

144₁

144<sub>2</sub>

144<sub>7</sub>

144<sub>3</sub>

144<sub>8</sub>

144<sub>4</sub> ☐

145 ☐
*The Traveller*, 1917
Gouache and graphite on
paper, 381×487
Signed and dated, lower
center: "M. Chagall 1917"
Inscribed, upper left (Russian):
"Coachman"
*Permanent loan from the Art
Gallery of Ontario, Toronto,
Sam and Ayala Zacks
Collection*

144<sub>5</sub>

146
*Ba'al Hamakhshoves* (The
Thinker) (Dr. I. A. Eliashev), 1918
Pencil on paper, 338×247
Signed, lower right:
"Marc Chagall"
Inscribed and dated, upper
right (Yiddish and Russian):
"The Thinker"
Received from IRSO (Jewish
Restitution Successor
Organization) *Israel Museum,
1955*

144<sub>6</sub> ☐

147
Portrait of Alia Eliashev, 1919
Pencil on paper, 330×235
Received from IRSO (Jewish
Restitution Successor
Organization), *Israel Museum,
1955*

148

148
*The Promenade*
(sketch for a banner), 1919
Pencil, watercolor, and
gouache on paper, 318×225
Signed, dedicated, and dated,
lower right (Russian):
"Souvenir to Vitebianiko Puni,
1919"
*Israel Museum, 1971*

149
*Kunst-Ring Almanakh*
(The Art Circle Almanac),
edited by K. Zingman, Vol. I,
second edition [Berlin, 1922?]
70 pages, 222×145
Shmeruk*, 3833;
Ratner-Kvitni*, 145
2 illustrations by Chagall (also
others)
*Chimen Abramsky Collection,
London*

149₁

149₂

150 ☐
*Troyer* (Mourning)
by D. Hofstein
Kiev: Kultur Lige, 1922
23 pages, 345×253
Shmeruk*, 1537
Cover, title page, and
6 illustrations
*Lent by Feige and Levia
Hofstein, Ramat Aviv*

150₁

150₃

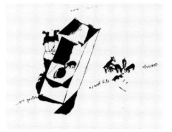

150₄

150₅

150₆

151 □
*Shtrom* (Stream), no. 1
Moscow: Shtrom, 1922
82 pages, 255×155
Shmeruk*, 3876
Cover
*Jewish National and University
Library, Jerusalem*

152
*The Grandfathers*, plate 3
from the series *My Life*
Berlin: Paul Cassirer, 1923
Etching and drypoint on
paper, 280×215
*Israel Museum, 1950*

153
*The Dining Room*, plate 10
from the series *My Life*
Berlin: Paul Cassirer, 1923
Etching and drypoint on
paper, 215×275
*Israel Museum, 1950*

154
*The Wedding*, plate 16 from
the series *My Life*
Berlin: Paul Cassirer, 1923
Etching and drypoint on
paper, 145×160
*Israel Museum, 1950*

155
*The Father's Grave*, plate 20
from the series *My Life*
Berlin: Paul Cassirer, 1923
Etching and drypoint on
paper, 146×203
*Israel Museum, 1950*

156
*Dos Pantofele, An Egiptish
Maysele* (The Slipper, An
Egyptian Tale) by Itzik Kipnis
Kiev: Kultur Lige, 1923
12 pages, 165×125
Shmeruk*, 2676
3 illustrations
*Jewish National and University
Library, Jerusalem*

156₁

156₂

156₃

157
*Dos Tsigaynerl* (The Little
Gypsy) by Itzik Kipnis
Kiev: Kultur Lige, 1923
10 pages, 165×125, edition of
1000. Shmeruk*, 2677
Cover and 3 illustrations
*Jewish National and University
Library, Jerusalem*

158
A flag for Simhat Torah,
Eastern Europe,
18th-19th century
Woodcut on paper, 186×217
*Israel Museum, 1958*

1601

159
*L'Ornement Hébreu*
by Baron David Gunzburg and
Vladimir Stassof
Berlin: S. Calvary & Co., 1905
20 illustrated pages
(originally 36), 595×467
*Israel Museum*

1602 ☐

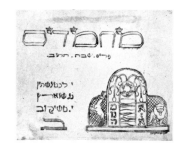

1591 ☐

1603

1592 ☐

1604

160
*Makhmadim*, no. 2 (Sabbath)
Paris, 1912
Artists: Y. Lichtenstein,
M. Shwarz, J. Tchaikov
6 pages, 240×203
8 illustrations
Hectography
*Israel Museum*

1605 ☐

160₆

161₂ ☐

160₇

161₃

160₈

162
*Makhmadim*, no. 5 (Shavuot)
Paris, 1912
Artists: B. Ravitzky, Y.
Lichtenstein, Arie, M. Shwarz,
Pastin (?), J. Tchaikov
6 pages, 252×261
7 illustrations
Hectography
*Israel Museum*

161
*Makhmadim*, no. 4 (Passover)
Paris, 1912
Artists: J. Tchaikov, Y.
Lichtenstein, Arie, M. Shwarz
6 pages, 214×241
3 illustrations
Hectography
*Israel Museum*

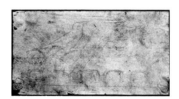

162₁

161₁ ☐

162₂ ☐

160

162₃

163
Leonid Pasternak, 1862-1945
*Jüdische Volkslieder*
(Jewish Folk Melodies)
(Musical Arrangements by
Joel Engel)
Moscow: P. Jurgenson, c. 1912
35 pages, 305×233
Title page
*Jewish National and University
Library, Jerusalem*

162₄ □

164
A letter from S. An-Sky to
Abraham Rechtman,
Secretary of the Jewish
Ethnographic Expedition, 1913
*Pavilion of Ethnography and
Folklore, Haaretz Museum,
Tel Aviv*

162₅

165
Moisei Maimon
Cover for E. Schkljar's *Farn
Obschejd* (Before Leaving),
Sheet music for voice and
piano
St. Petersburg: Society for
Jewish Folk Music, 1914
4 pages, 340×270
*Central Library for Music and
Dance, Archives of Menashe
Ravina, Tel Aviv*

162₆

166 □
*History of the Jews in Russia*,
vol. I, in *History of the Jewish
People,* edited by M.
Wischnitzer and others
Designed by Rachel
Bernstein-Wischnitzer
Moscow: Mir, 1914
Decorative opening page
532 pages, 268×178
*Lent by Zusia Efron,
Jerusalem*

162₇

167
*Dos Yidishe Etnografishe
Program* (The Jewish
Ethnographic Program)
by S. An-Sky
Petrograd, 1914
238 pages, 247×158
*Jewish National and University
Library, Jerusalem*

222

168 □
Leonid Pasternak, 1862-1945
Portrait of S. An-Sky, 1919
Black chalk with
red and white touches
on cardboard, 608×406
Signed and dated (in
Russian): "Moscow 18/6 19"
*Israel Museum, 1963*

170₁
Tombstone from Vinnitsa,
1859

169
Catalog of the *Jewish
Exhibition of Sculpture,
Graphics and Drawings*
Originally with cover
illustration by Joseph Tchaikov
Kiev: Kultur Lige,
February-March 1920
30 pages, 160×110
*Jewish National and University
Library, Jerusalem*

170₂
Tombstone from
Staro-Konstantinov, 1850

170
Solomon Yudovin, 1892-1954
Yidisher Folks-Ornament
(Jewish Folk Ornament),
Vitebsk: 1920
Linoleum cut on paper, 92×175
Covers, inside cover and
26 illustrations
*Elaine and Arthur Cohen
Collection, New York*

170₃
Tombstone from Proskurov,
1794

170₄
Tombstone from Dubno, 1852

Inside cover

170₅
Tombstone from Olyka, 1791

170₆
Tombstone from Kremitz,
(date unknown)

170₁₁
Tombstone from Zhitomir,
1846

170₇
Tombstone from Polonya,
1730

170₁₂
Tombstone from Bar, (date
unknown)

170₈
Tombstone from Vinnitsa,
1795

170₁₄
Tombstone from Radziwillow,
(date unknown)

170₉
Tombstone from Radziwillow,
1800

170₁₅
Tombstone from Zhitomir,
1830

170₁₀
Tombstone from
Staro-Konstantinov, 1849

170₁₆
Tombstone from (place
unknown) (date unknown)

170₁₇
Sketch for a tombstone
acquired from a family of
tombstone cutters, inherited
from their parents... Shklov,
(date unknown)

170₂₃
Torah Crown finial from Lutzk

170₁₈
Sketch for a tombstone
acquired from a family of
tombstone cutters inherited
from their parents... Shklov,
(date unknown)

170₂₄
Torah Crown finial from
Kremenitz

170₁₉
Sketch for a tombstone
acquired from a family of
tombstone cutters, inherited
from their parents... Shklov,
(date unknown)

170₂₅
Torah shield from Dubno

170₂₁
Finger bowl ("Mayim
Akhronim")

170₂₆
Reader's lectern from the
Great Synagogue,
Szepetowka

170₂₂
Torah Shield

170₂₇
Signs and letters from a
prayer book
written on parchment from
Dubno, 1841

170₂₈
Signs and letters from a
prayer book
written on parchment from a
Dubno, 1841

173₁

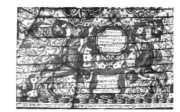

170₂₉
Back cover

173₂

171
Joseph Tchaikov, 1888-1896
*Skulptur* (Sculpture)
Kiev: Melukhe Farlag, 1921
15 pages, 131×92
Ratner-Kvitni*, 803
*Uzi Agassi Collection,
Raanana*

173₃

172
Catalog of an exhibition of
Nathan Altman, Marc Chagall
and David Shterenburg
Organized by Kultur Lige,
Moscow, March-April 1922
135×216
*Institute of Modern Russian
Culture, Texas, USA*

173₆

173₄  see cat. 67
173₅  see cat. 68
173₇  see cat. 71

173
*Rimon*, A Hebrew Magazine of
Art and Letters, no. 3
Berlin, 1923
Literary editors:
M. Wischnitzer and M. Kleinman
Art editor: Rachel
Bernstein-Wischnitzer
52 pages, 356×240
Illustrations from article by El
Lissitzky  (translated in Appendix)
*Israel Museum*

174
*Contemporary Jewish
Graphics* (in Russian)
by Boris Aronson
Berlin: Petropolis, 1924
116 pages, 323×258, 109/300
*Israel Museum*

# Appendix

# Paths of Jewish Painting*
## I. Ryback and B. Aronson

The first experiments by Jewish painters in quest of a Jewish art were made in Russia. The most outstanding expression was achieved by Chagall, Falk and Altman, who perceived the modern abstract form in an idiosyncratic manner.

Nathan Altman is one of the artists in the forefront of Russian Romantic Impressionism. He promptly rid himself of certain backward elements in Russian painting and turned to the achievements of the French artists. Altman's work aroused admiration in the Russian artistic world (e.g., *Portrait of Anna Akhmatova*, 1914). In Akhmatova's portrait we find a rational, intellectual analysis of the achievements of the Western world, having passed through the prism of Russian painting perceptions.

On the other hand, his canvasses are more graphic than painterly. In his still lifes, he seeks to discover the essence of things. In Altman, two moments have converged: that of the modern Jewish painter-innovator alongside the remnants of time-worn naturalistic painting traditions, which have hindered his quest for a specific Semitic structure. But Altman possesses an intellectual rationality, which has overpowered the modern Jewish innovator. He began looking for the elements through which he could uncover his specific self and, not by chance, began to study Jewish folk creations. The result of such searchings was a cycle of Jewish graphics (in the exhibition "Mir iskusstva," 1914). Lamentably, folk creation was not individually or poetically recreated there but simply copied.

To a larger extent, the Jewish perception has been reflected by Robert Falk. This was demonstrated clearly in his works of the Crimea period (1916-1917), *Portrait of a Tatar, Still Life*, and others. In Falk, the national is expressed in the synthesizing of tone and coloration. In many of his still lifes and landscapes we feel the synthesis of red, black, or blue. Such perception is possible only by a Jew.

A special place is occupied by Marc Chagall. We say a special place because contrary to Falk and Altman, Chagall, in an abstract form, partially uncovered both his own painting style and national substance. Chagall is in certain details already a product of Jewish culture. Through painting values he reflects the forms of his people's life. Residing in Paris, in the very hub of the search for the newest forms which have swallowed many a personality, thanks to his perceptions, Chagall preserved his individuality. He took up all modern achievements, including Futurism, and succeeded to incarnate them in a specific manner. One sees this in Chagall's best canvas, *Jew in Prayer* (1914), which is entitled to occupy an outstanding place among the great achievements of modern painting. That painting may serve as a cornerstone of the revival of Jewish art. Nowhere else are concentrated the generations-old culture, the accumulated experience and the freshness and sharp wit of the Jewish world view. The portrait achieves the monumentality of an arabesque. *Jew in Prayer* possesses a picturesque-constructive national pathos and is entitled to occupy the first place in a Jewish museum. Also characteristic is Chagall's *Shtetl Landscapes* cycle, particularly *In the Neighborhood of Vitebsk*. The simplification of form and the primitiveness of perception are outstanding.

But for all that, one cannot excuse Chagall for the fact that a great number of his literary-anecdotal canvasses lack construction and composition.

In Chagall's painting his indebtedness to the shtetl is manifest, enabling him to poetically recreate Jewish folk creations. His childhood fascination with tombstones, synagogue ornamentation, and the works of Jewish primitives, later served as his material and has helped him discover his national "identity."

Chagall's achievements in the field of graphics are also interesting. The very essence of graphics – the rhythmic effect of black-and-white – is prominently and convincingly demonstrated. In his graphics we also see the influence of the Galician Jewish wood-primitives. Of all the Jewish artists, Chagall is the only one to have understood, appreciated and partially recreated, poetically, the Jewish plastic folk-trait. To the question, how has Chagall demonstrated his picturesque material, we may respond: being a product of Jewish culture, Chagall has also demonstrated his national form. That is his great merit, and he's thus the first one entitled to bear the name "Jewish artist."

Besides the Jewish artists cited, there are a great number of Jewish painters striving to discover their national art. In many towns and shtetls "collectives" of Jewish artists have been formed endeavoring to depict life through a national medium. An interesting phenomenon is the artist Sakal, who came out of that group.

Jewish folk art demonstrates most clearly that our people were always alive in the organic, painting sense. The accumulated painting energy that had no outlet for expression in plastic form has been reflected only in the written word in Jewish culture. The artistic word, having incarnated plastic perception, thus acquired all the elements of plastic art. When a Jewish artist sets out to reflect his national material, he must absorb the cultural values of his people amassed over the generations. In the background of the utmost achievements of Western art is the Jewish artist, thanks to his freshness and his passionate and naive perception.

Jewish art is here. It is awakening!

*Article appeared in *Oyfgang*, Kiev: Kultur Lige, 1919, excerpts from pp. 119-124. Translated from the Yiddish by Reuben Szklowin.

## Introduction from the Catalog of the "Jewish Exhibition of Sculpture, Graphics and Drawings," February-March, 1920*

With this exhibition, the art section of the Kultur Lige inaugurates the first show of Jewish art in Kiev for the general public.

The art section of the Kultur Lige is composed of young Jewish artists of wide-ranging perspectives who are united in their efforts to place a sovereign national stamp upon their act and to participate fully in modern Jewish cultural life. Without rejecting world trends, modern Jewish art seeks the sources from which emerge the natural pathways of Jewish art, while striving to discover uniquely Jewish forms of expression.

This is the first public appearance of the art section of the Kultur Lige; with this exhibition it may begin to resolve its problems.

Two principal goals confront the art section: 1) To acquaint the Jewish masses with Jewish and general art. 2) To create a Jewish artistic milieu which provides the Jewish beginner with both the possibility and impetus to broaden, deepen and bring to fruition the distinctiveness of Jewish plastic expression. To fulfill this task the art section has established art studios and a museum, and it will organize periodic exhibitions.

This premier exhibition must not be considered in any way as a final tally. We offer no conclusions, we offer only beginnings, the first sproutings, more or less ripe, which have grown up in the soil of Jewish creativity.

Unfortunately, this inaugural exhibition is not a complete one. A number of Jewish artists who have direct ties to Jewish art live outside of Kiev, in Russia, or in foreign lands, and thus could not be included. For this reason, there is no section devoted to oil painting because a large number of the most characteristic works of modern Jewish art by young Jewish painters of the art section are absent from Kiev, and due to clear foreign hindrances we have not been able to bring them to the exhibition. The art works in this category will have to await their own special showing. For reasons of unity and completeness in the present exhibition, we are forced to limit ourselves, this time, to sculpture and the graphic arts.

Jews have been active sculptors for about fifty years. Sculpture was developed in the great cultures by the pagan and Christian artists of Egypt, Assyria, Greece, India, China, and later France and Italy, and it has been closely associated for the most part with religious cults foreign to the Jewish spirit. An architectural creation which took its first steps alongside architecture, sculpture was always closely tied to place and therefore it could not be developed by Jews – a people who led a "nomadic" existence. Jewish sculptors made their appearance just at the time when sculpture was in a state of decay in Europe. It was a period when pseudo-classicism, Academicism and Impressionism reigned. The Jewish sculptors of that time did not raise questions about national form. Such artists as Antokolski (a member of the Wanderers), Bernstrom (an academic sculptor), and the Impressionists Glitsenstein and Aronson, worked devotedly in whatever school they received their artistic training. The language of sculpture was foreign to them, with a value all its own. For them, art was only a means to express their distinct social and literary thoughts. Among the innovators were the sculptors living in

Paris, such as Epstein, London and Nadelman, who managed only to absorb foreign forms before transforming themselves into petty officials of cosmopolitanism and abstraction.

Only in the past ten years has the search for a specific national form in sculpture begun. The Frenchmen Bourdelle and Maillol, the German Metzner, the Serb Mestpovic, and the Russian Konyenkov, all returned to the ancient sources of national creation in the domain of sculpture and thanks to their accomplishments in the area of specific national form, created new sculptural possibilities. Such a self-conscious approach to Jewish sculpture is evidenced in the "Semitic searchings" of Zadkine and Indenbaum. But they understand national form only from a strictly ethnographic point of view. Modern sculptural form, however, is essentially symbolic, and the symbolic does not reveal any external subjective particularities. The modern artist composes formally upon life on the strength of his specific plastic material and perspective of art. And when the Jewish artist draws his plastic world-view from the accumulated folk strength, from folk instincts and from folk culture, then his work is, as a matter of course, national and Jewish.

New Jewish sculpture seeks the modern national form in which to express the Jewish spirit of creativity.

The first steps in this direction have already been made.

Even in the domain of graphics, the endeavor to reach pure national form began only recently.

Our graphics stem from several sources: 1) Engravings from the period when Jewish communities thrived in Spain, Italy and Holland; 2) Primitive engravings from Galicia and Lithuania; 3) The picturesque graphics which are a result of research by the modern painter, and which are based on the play of black and white.

Up until the last decade, our folk creations in this domain were almost entirely unknown to Jewish painters. Struck, Heine, and others, were, in the best of cases, only virtuosos in the techniques of graphic art. Lilien brought absolutely nothing into Jewish art; his foreign-Jewish motifs were expressed through the techniques of the German School.

The first source of our graphics is the Hebrew letter and the ornaments of old Jewish prayer books and religious articles. As the folk *niggun* (spiritual song) is sung without words, so the finest nuances and rhythms of the Jewish folk soul are often expressed in old Jewish graphic ornaments.

Modern Jewish artists, who self-consciously seek specifically national graphic art forms, like Altman, Lissitzky, Chagall and others, find, in fact, a rich selection in our ancient symbols – in *Sifrei Torah* (Torah Scrolls), *Megillot*, the title pages of prayer books, *Simhat Torah* flags, etc.

Modern Jewish art seeks to recreate our artistic inheritance in national forms, in which it expresses the accomplishments of modern art.

The collected primitive folk art effort thus becomes the basis of a higher Jewish art form, which joins the latest universalist quests with the creative skills of the folk masses.

*The excecutive committee of the exhibition included: Issachar Ber Ryback, Chairman; Yosef Elman, Secretary; Joseph Tchaikov, Bal-Makhshoves, and Yehezkiel Dobrushin, Honored Members; Boris Aronson, Administrator.
*Catalogue published by Kulture Lige in Kiev, 1920. Author unknown. Translated from the Yiddish by Seth L. Wolitz.

# Sculpture*
## Joseph Tchaikov

*Pure plastic form is deeply national
and the direct approach to art creates its own
form.*

*Steel-cement, technique and
electricity will introduce
the new in art.*

*There is no new sculpture.*

Jewish self-reliance in representational art has awakened at a time of electrical and industrial technology, and the use of iron and cement construction.

These new proofs of human genius have endlessly revolutionized our lives and are destroying the old dogmas of our humanistic creations.

With ever greater speed, the new conquests of mankind press upon nature, which always seeks to put up a stiff resistance to man.

Art, as always, acts as the summation of these events.

All perspectives found in representational art place in doubt our continued success, for the break with the past is evident.

What then can committed Jewish artists say, and are they now a necessity?

Art is undergoing a period of analysis; its representational, scientific attainments are timeless and for all mankind.

The Jewish artist in the plastic arts, no matter to what culture he is drawn (putting aside the question of taste), cannot be found in a normal relationship with all peoples and periods.

The specific material expresses the form and the form expresses the artist and vice versa.

Although the Jewish artist has not yet shown his volitional line in modern plastic creativity, within the culture and art of all nations he will proffer his synthesis through the prism of his specific material.

National creativity does not express itself in ethnographic contents, as in our sculpture by Antokolski, Ginzburg, Glitsenstein, and others. The Academicians, Peredvizhniki (Wanderers), and the Impressionists produced no Jewish sculpture.

If we notice nationality among these schools, it is found only in traditions and temperament.

The Jew has no particular tradition, because he is a newcomer to the plastic arts. We have only just begun to collect our thoughts regarding the foundations of our movement and in what direction our path must be marked. This is strictly in the area of plastic form, which lifts our spirit, like a song without words.

We also hold as untrue the approach of the young leftist artist who wishes to resolve this problem according to our history and folkloric ("folks-primitive") accomplishment. This only leads to stylization and stylization is aestheticism, i.e., a lie concerning our present day and a caprice of individualism which functions in the service of beauty.

Art must be alive, i.e., inventive, and must bore into the body of the dawning day.

In this way, we shall create a Jewish sculpture.

*Excerpts from the book *Sculptur*, Kiev: Kultur Lige, 1921. Translated from the Yiddish by Seth L. Wolitz.

# The Victory Over Art*
## El Lissitzky

### IV

In 1913, Kasimir Malevich exhibited in St. Petersburg a white canvas on which was painted a black quadrant. This was the foundation of Suprematism. What type of universal perspectives and relationships are expressed in Suprematism? The bearer of a colored whirlwind, the artist, the painter has removed from his winged path all the supports upon which he had hung his colors. He gave his color independence. He made the painting objectless. He has gone forth to pure creation. The Suprematists stated: as the flower which grows out of the earth is distinctly colored, clearly defined, affects nothing and describes nothing more than itself, so should the painting sprout from the painter. The painting must not be a reproduction but a work. The modernity of Suprematism in contrast with other kinds of objectless art (Kandinsky, abstract painting in Germany, Simultanism in France) appears in its organization and in the new, painterly expression of space which it has provided. The way to infinity which proceeded through perspective was brought to its culmination by Suprematism: it chopped down the arched, blue sky and went off into white infinity. Suprematist color masses swim like planets in white space. Only in this way could it totally banish illusoriness from the painting. It removed beauty and put in its place another measuring device – economy.

### V

Malevich maintained that with the quadrant he had brought an end to painting. It was brought to point zero. But when we did further research into our work, we said, yes, the road of painterly culture is becoming shorter, narrowing to the quadrant. On the other side a new culture is beginning to sprout. Yes, we salute the brave man who cast himself into the abyss in order to resurrect the past in a new form. Yes, if the painterly line used to descend like 6 5 4 3 2 1 to zero, then a new line ascends on the other side of zero to 1 2 3 4 5 6 and we perceive that a new painterly work which was growing out of us, is no longer a [mimetic] painting. It describes nothing; it constructs only volumes, planes and lines for its own sake; in order to create a system of the new composition of the real world. To the new structure we gave a new name – Proun [Proup].

We have dubbed the name of the way station, Proun, on the road to creating the new form, which grows out of the earth that is fertilized with the corpses of the [mimetic] representation and its artist. [Mimetic] representation has fallen together with the old world which created it for itself. The new world will not need any [mimetic] representations. If it needs a mirror, it has photography and cinema. In the new world, the creator, "the artist," will create the world itself and not describe it. Proun– this is the way by which we will arrive at the new composition. If science and the engineer have come, at present, to create their realities by mathematical tables, by drawings of projects, we do not categorically consider this the only way. We believe more in creative intuition, which creates its method, its system outside of mathematics and drawings but according to laws which are also as organic as the shape of a flower. Proun does not compose, it constructs. This is the basic difference with [mimetic] representation. Composition is a discussion in the given plane with many variants; construction is a confirmation of someone for the given necessity. Proun has no single axis which is perpendicular to

the horizontal, as in a traditional painting. It is constructed and brought to an equilibrium in space. And as a structure, one must inspect it from every side, from top to bottom. The canvas has become kinetic. Proun is made of material and not of any aesthetic. We have taken from the richest gold mines of color the absolutely purest or subjective quality. Yellow, green, blue – these are blond and brunette shadows on the spectrum. We do not need any individuated ones, only general ones. We have taken color from black to white. And the contrast or accord of two blacks or two whites or of two pigments between black and white serve for us as a contrast or an accord of two materials such as granite and wood, or iron and concrete. Color has become for us the barometer of the material.

### VI

Just as we were victorious over religion, so are we fighting with our new accomplishments for victory over art.

We are far removed from the period of the hunter who chased the animal and captured it: he depicted it. Remote, too, is the epoch of the shepherd who sat by an oven and abstracted nature: he embellished it. We live in a period of iron and concrete, a dynamic period: we do not depict or embellish, we hunt and create. We abandon on the one hand the artist with his [mimetic] representation, and on the other, the engineer with his project. We go forth to create in space and in time the elements of the first, second, and third dimension in order to grow with nature according to the laws of the universe. We are the footsteps of our movement which is unceasing and also incomprehensible as is the way of the lunatic from whom all withdraw in embarrassment.

*Article appeared in *Ringen* 10, Warsaw, 1922, excerpts from pp. 32-34. Translated from the Yiddish by Seth L. Wolitz.

# Memoirs Concerning the Mohilev Synagogue*
## El Lissitzky

It happened between 19- and 1916. If one counts the calendar years, it certainly does not seem like long ago, but if reckoned by life itself, it seems light years away.

Some pioneering Jewish painters earned a living by going to the very psychological limits of the Pale of Settlement; i.e., they perceived that when one moves crayon or charcoal over paper or a paintbrush over canvas, a picture emerges. A new generation suddenly became "artistic." Art circles cropped up, and from art circles, they became "schools." But above all else there were problems.

Groups of *heder* children, indeed, a whole generation including even talmudic students, were thoroughly soured by years of doing textual analysis only.

Quickly taking pencil and brush in hand, we began to dissect at once not only Nature, but ourselves as well. Who were we? And where did we belong among the nations of the world? And what was our culture about? And how should our art be? It was all worked out in a few towns in Lithuania, White Russia, and the Ukraine. From there it circled around to Paris and came to an end – at that time we thought it was the beginning – when this movement arrived in Moscow for the "First Exhibition of Jewish Artists in the Year 1916."

Seeking to find ourselves and the shape of our time, we tried to peer into the old mirrors in order to penetrate deeply into the so-called "folk creations." At the beginning of our era, this path was trodden by almost all nations. My own case in point followed this same logic when, suddenly one summer, I let myself return to "the folk." I was joined by Ryback.

Many tales were circulating about the Mohilev synagogue, and we were drawn to them. We first moved to Kapust. We had been told that the Kapust synagogue was of the same type as the one in Mohilev, and was painted by the same master. All we found in Kapust were bits of charcoal and charred bricks from the foundation, and some rotted logs which someone had planned to use for a new synagogue. The old one had burned down. In fact, the entire town had gone up in flames, and not the slightest trace of its past remained.

We pressed on and arrived at Mohilev. From a distance, by the Dnieper River, we could see a tall black object that looked like a granary – not a large building – which turned out to be a synagogue. But it seemed like only the outskirts of town, so this could not be *the synagogue*. We followed the river bank into the town seeking the synagogue. They sent us off to a somewhat "beautiful" new stone synagogue with boudoir lamps and freshly painted cornices and walls, just like in a provincial "diorama."

Within a few hours we found it. The synagogue stands on the banks of the Dnieper, but set so that it is completely hidden. It is remarkable! Synagogues were usually placed in such a way that they would dominate the surrounding valleys. This was true of Druya, Dubrovna, and other small towns: the synagogue with its imposing mass, and especially its high roof, gives the entire town its characteristic contours, just as the character of old European cities is recognizable by its towers and cathedrals.

The synagogue style of the Mohilev type (crisp and well-ordered; I would say classical) is of the same order as the church basilicas; i.e., there is a prominent middle section with windows in the upper part, and two lower wings to the north and south sides. However, in contrast to the churches, the side sections are not open, but strictly separated from the center, men's section of the synagogue. The women's section is in the wings and only a small eye-level aperture joins it with the men's section. This is an old style. Only by this means was it possible for us to observe the paintings of the innermost part of the oldest synagogue in Worms, Germany (from the thirteenth century). There, too, the men's and women's sections were one level, and in the wall between them was a tiny window. An old Jewess used to stand at that window and follow aloud the prayers of the cantor, and soon after, the other women worshippers would repeat the prayers. In the Jewish cemetery of Worms there is a fourteenth-century tombstone of four women prayer leaders.

The women's gallery was a later idea. In Mohilev there is also a gallery for women. Both the side wings are occupied: one is for the beadle, a turner, who one day will certainly burn down the synagogue with his wood shavings and little stove. In the second wing is the religious elementary school (*heder*). But the entire character of the synagogue belongs to the upper middle section with the tall pointed roof and the two compressed wings on the sides, closely drawn up, with sloping roofs and tiny windows.

The synagogue was closed at noon. We sought out the beadle and he opened it for us.

This was truly something special, like those surprises in store for me when I first visited a Roman basilica, a Gothic chapel, Baroque churches in Germany, France and Italy; or like a crib, bedecked with a fine veil embroidered with flies and butterflies, in which the infant suddenly awakes in surroundings sprayed with sunlight; such, perhaps, is how it looks inside the synagogue.

The walls – made of oak logs – rung when struck. Above them, the ceiling looks like a tent of wooden planks. All the rivets are exposed – no deception, no fantasy. The work is by a cartwright from top to bottom, but the entire shape was organized by the painter with just a few basic colors, so saturated that an entire vast world lives here, blossoms forth and fills up this none-too-large cube.

The interior of the synagogue is embellished, from the backboards of the benches to the entire length of the walls and up to the very top of the "tent." The synagogue, quadrangular on the ground floor, rises to an octagonal tent ceiling, exactly like a skullcap. Three-cornered boards mask the passage from four corners to eight corners. The ceiling panels are organized with a striking sense of composition. This is something entirely contrary to the laws of primitivism; rather, this is the fruit of a great culture. Where does it come from? The master of this work, Segal, says in his inscriptions with the most noble insprration, ". . . for a long time I have been travelling about the living world. . . ."

They say he painted three synagogues: in Mohilev, Kapust and Dolhinov (others name other places). When he had completed his work, he fell from the scaffolding and died. Each town tells this same tale but with a slight difference; the Mohilever Jews say he died in Mohilev, the Kapuster, in Kapust, and the Dolhinover in their town. His synagogues in the latter two towns are burnt down, the Dolhinov long ago. My father used to relate that he remembered it had a gigantic fresco of Jacob's burial, with a chariot, a horse, the children of Jacob, Egypt, etc. We could not compare it with anything today. The story illustrates the esteem in which the artist was held. So great was his work that his later life could only denigrate him. Having completed the work, his soul had no more need to remain in his body.

The focus of the whole building is the ceiling. On the western side, above the entrance, are gigantic lions with peacocks below. The lions hold two shields with inscriptions, the lower one being the master's memorial to himself. On the three-cornered northern and southern planks of the tent, like a frieze, are placed side by side carnivores and their prey, underwater and on the earth. In the sky above, stars burst forth in flowers. In the water, a fish is being seized by a bird. On the earth, a fox carries a bird in his mouth. A bear climbs a tree looking for honey. Birds carry snakes in their beaks. The fleeing and running figures are really people. Through their quadruped or feathered guises, they stare with human eyes. This is a remarkable characteristic of Jewish folk art. Isn't that a rabbinic face on the lion's head in the zodiac painting in the Mohilev synagogue?

Above the frieze, a voluminous, fully developed line ornament bursts forth, capturing the entire ceiling within its ring. Further up, there is a row of stamps of a somewhat oriental design – perhaps from a Mauritanian assemblage – composed of a complicated entwining of rope, a motif which brings to mind Leonardo da Vinci's drawing for the stamp of his academy. And I remember I saw in Milan, in the Castello, a room whose ceiling is also attributed to Leonardo, which made use of a comparable rope ornamentation.

Above them, arranged in a row, stand the twelve zodiac signs in rondels all linked to one another. The zodiac pictures are very unusual, and some of the drawings are remarkably laconic and vigorous. The archer in the zodiac, for example, is depicted with one hand holding the bow, the other hand drawing on the string. The latter is the "strong" hand, the "punishing hand" of the Bible. In the very center of the "skullcap" surmounting everything; is a three-headed eagle, a fusion of the Polish and Russian eagles.

On the eastern side, above the Holy Ark, there are lions again, but here they hold the Tablets of the Law, and dangling from them a large, sacrificial fowl seizes the Holy Ark. On the sides are two panoramas. On the left, or the north wall, is an imaginary representation of Worms, a seemingly cursed town in the clutches of a dragon, and with a Tree of Life. On the other side, the northwestern side, is Jerusalem and the Tree of Knowledge.

On the three-cornered board that covers the passage from the wall to the ceiling, on the northwestern side, is the legendary wild ox. On the northeastern side is a wild goat; on the third plank, in the southeast, is the Leviathan; and on the fourth plank, to the southwest, is an elephant with a saddle on his back.

On the walls, there are boards with inscriptions, holy objects from King Solomon's Temple, additional ornaments, and all kinds of living creatures.

This painter's wealth of forms seems inexhaustible. One can see how it all poured out as from a horn of plenty, how the hand of the virtuoso neither tires nor resists the rapid flow of thoughts. On the back side of the Holy Ark, I discovered the first brush sketch, the "outline" of the entire picture, which serves as the basis for further elaboration in color. This particular "outline" was cast on the wall by a master of remarkable discipline whose brush is completely subordinated to his will.

The coloration of the painting is amber-pearl with brick-red rays. It is not to be grasped; it lives and moves because of its own specific lustre. On all four walls there are windows on the uppermost reaches. The sunlight flows around and around at each hour on each wall with a different light effect, especially on the sloping parts of the ceiling. This provides the whole work with a continuous play of light. The painting, with all its transparency, is very thick: from the heaviest pigments –ochre, lead-white, cinnabar and green, to the lightest color tones– blue and violet.

Where does this stream come from? How did this cloud burst and precipitate such a salubrious downpour?

Let the researchers seek and clamber about in the sea of art history. I can only describe my own observations. There is always a small library in the synagogue. On the bookshelves of the old synagogues are talmudic texts and other books of the oldest printings with highly ornate title pages, some illustrations and tailpieces. In their time, these few pages played the same role that the illustrated journals do today: they made known the latest art forms. Indeed, I once saw a tombstone with such a bas-relief: a standing bear with a flowering ornament in its front paws. In the attic of the Druya synagogue, I saw this same tailpiece in a book that was published by a reknowned Amsterdam house in the sixteenth or seventeenth century. There can be no doubt that the sculptor of the tombstone had been "instructed" by the same tailpiece.
A second example is the wood carving and the entire composition of the multi-layered Holy Ark in the Renaissance-Baroque title page style of Jewish books. For the Jewish wood carver these title pages served as models just as the architects used the works of Vitruvious and Palladio.

A further question remains concerning the national meaning of this painting, but we will leave this to the psychologists and ethnographers. We will only draw their attention to the relationship of the profusion of designs on the walls and ceilings in the Mohilev synagogue with the contemporary forms of other nations which one would do well to consider earnestly. The Italian Fioravanti constructed the Uspensky Cathedral in the Kremlin, and his compatriot Aliezio, the Kremlin walls. The Phoenician Hiram built Solomon's Temple. There is no end to such examples.

At present, therefore, when printed literature, newspapers, journals, one's own theatre, painting, music, etc., serve as symbols of a cultured folk, we, too, have it all; we too, are a cultured people. Only a brilliant genealogical chart is lacking. If, however, this compels one to begin to creep back towards antiquity and if it is only with this intention one shows an interest in "folk" creativity then this type of culture is surely not necessary.

And if, at present, when the technical means to repeat a performance are so available and printing presses work so quickly, these artifacts will receive the broadest distribution, and will infect the "art teachers," who will begin to powder and stylize this uniquely arranged face. (They will hack it to pieces.) This unstable "vinaigrette" will then be stirred up as a new art culture, but we would be better off without this culture; it is unnecessary.

What is called art is created when one is not aware that what one is doing is art. Only then does it remain as a monument of culture. Today art is created by those who battle against it.

To us, the living dog is dearer than the dead lion. We know that when the dog dies, it becomes a lion.

*Article appeared in *Rimon/Milgroim*, no. 3, Berlin, 1923, pp. 9-13.
Translated from the Yiddish by Seth L. Wolitz.

# Contemporary Jewish Graphics*
## Boris Aronson

### Chapter Three

Hebrew is one of the most ancient scripts. It has retained its simple, geometrical form, which is akin to Assyro-Babylonian cuneiform. The form of Hebrew script remained inviolable because it was transmitted in a traditionally precise manner due to the prescribed manuscript shape of sacred books, which were, and still are, written by professional scribes (sofer).

Jewish law requires that Torah scrolls be written on parchment, with a quill pen and specially prepared ink, by a worthy man who comes from a line of professional scribes. No innovations were ever admitted in the script. That is why book printing neither affected the purity of the style of Hebrew letters, nor replaced the manuscript. Neither time nor personal taste has made its impression on the written page. The Torah scroll (the arrangement as well as the distance between letters and the "accentuation" of the page) remains absolutely unchanged.

But the Hebrew script is by no means monotonous. There were many variations within the confines of the same line. This is because the commentaries (Rashi or Kontres script) were added to the main script (Panim Ketav). But in all its variations, the Hebrew letter retained its unique character. As in every ancient alphabet, the abstract, graphic character of the Hebrew letter arrests attention. Neither the applied meaning of the letter, nor its sense or its hidden sound, but only its intrinsic, graphic meaning is apparent. The Hebrew letter is already a graphic element which preserves its uniqueness everywhere, namely, its geometrical simplicity, its reserved character, its completeness and unusual capacity to be connected to its neighbor, forming the complete, viscous arabesque of the line.

The scribe could be free in invention only in those manuscripts in which he was not bound by immutable law. Numerous scrolls (megillot), bills of divorcement, Passover haggadot, daily and festival prayer books (siddurim and mahzorim), Pentateuchs in Yiddish translation (taitch-humashim), synagogue diaries (pinkossim), which do yield in their quality to the art of medieval monks, all display to what extent a Jew is fond of expressing humor and sparks of fantasy. The Hebrew letter represents by itself that rudiment out of which it is possible to develop the ornamental pattern. Kabbalistic sheets, amulets, the Tablets of the Law, mathematical, physical, and astronomical tables (calendars and signs of the zodiac), large wall prayer-sheets (made for women who could not memorize them), all are patterned and symmetrical, woven into complex compositional networks.

In contrast to the rigid structure of the geometrical Latin letter (which despite its geometrical form does not possess viscosity and tenacity), the Hebrew letter is surprisingly fluid and flexible. It can be expanded to fill any space, adding rhythmic wealth rather than disturbing the unity of the line, as is the case with Latin letters. The same quality of expansion gives the whole manuscript compactness and the unity of a "scroll."

The Hebrew written or printed page, in its total appearance, constitutes a textual part of the most characteristic oriental ornament, in which the blank space between the lines has no less significance than the areas covered with ink drawing.

The next stage in the development of the black-and-white pattern came with the filling in of margins with calligraphically-patterned flourishes, as in scrolls. Capital letters were embellished with ornamentation, sometimes in the form of variations of the letter itself. Allegorical beasts appeared very late, in the twelfth through thirteenth centuries, because their representations had been considered sinful before this time. In view of the general prohibition against depicting living creatures, Jewish art had certain features that distinguished it from the art of other peoples; moreover, it made a powerful impression (maybe more psychological than active) on the development of the visual art of other nations.

Jews have never had a naturalistic art. Jewish art is of a religious, sublime, and abstract character, for it has never realized and materialized its observations, but has created out of fantasy. Jewish artists did not stress the true features of the animals they represented, perhaps because these animals were not familiar to them, but were rather symbolic images, which these artists took from fairy tales, legends, and poetic fables.

This is how we can explain the surprising unity of Jewish ornaments, their abstract, two-dimensional graphic character, whether in metallic works or in carving. Jewish artists perceived the lion's tail and mane or the deer's antlers as if they were graphic elements together with flowers, letters and clasped hands (which symbolize benediction). In this sense, Jewish folk art differs from the Persian, Egyptian, and Assyro-Babylonian, which emphasize the contrast between the mobile animal world and static grass and trees.

Jews also lacked a basis for monumental art, the tradition of the art guilds, as well as the immediate connection between religious thinking and plastic art. The absence of a traditional plastic art is apparent in that each work of Jewish art is independent and unique, so its images are created each time anew; that is why they have so much enthusiasm and genuine creativity, so much inspiration and exultation. When we speak of creating a national art and defining its character, we must first of all turn to graphic art. The main feature of Jewish folk art is its two-dimensional quality. Again, this has been dictated by religious prohibitons against three-dimensional artistic representations. Synagogue decorations, stone and wooden tombstones, carved Torah arks, altars, Torah crowns, Torah rollers, sacred utensils, candlesticks, prayer shawls, embroidered skullcaps, book-supports, eastern wall samplers, (mizrohim), wall samplers with signs of the zodiac, Passover haggadot, Passover plates, spice boxes, braided candles, phylactery bags, synagogue diaries, marriage contracts, bills of divorcement, bridal canopies, Hanukkah lamps, Succot booths and citron boxes, rings for palm branches (lulavs), myrtle holders (hadassim), Simhat Torah flags, Purim rattles, Hanukkah spinning tops, snuff boxes, embroidered bridal veils, illustrated tales about holy men, Galician cakes, Hasidic cushions, Galician, Podolian, Volynian, Polish and Lithuanian lubki, festive attire – each has its own independent character.

If one speaks of a national style, it may not apply to the majority of the above-named objects; for they have so much eclecticism, borrowings from the Empire, or the Baroque. Yet there is an inner impulse which unites all Jewish art and stamps it with a particular imprint. Some details, certain features, and trifles (which almost become law with artists) impart to each object the mark of refined taste and even wry humor. It is noticeable not so much in individual items as in the whole. Jews do not have a systematic culture, traditional art, cultural continuity, or museums. But the uniquely Jewish relation to material has been the deep-rooted starting point which united artists remote from each other, whether creating White Russian silver or Galician *lubki*. We probably cannot define precisely the features of folk plastic genius and its formal basis – indeed, a Hebrew style has not yet been created; but in spite of its having formal dependence, folk art has deepened certain features which were borrowed from alien cultures, adding to them a new, specific character.

## Chapter Four

One of the expressions of the modern aspiration for a style is the development of an interest in national art. It is accompanied by an increased interest in primitive folk art, both contemporary and past. With some artists, it has been expressed through an interest in the Archaic (Maillol), the African (Picasso), or the decorative rhythm of the Persian miniatures (Matisse), while with others the simplification of reality (Gauguin, Rousseau) was stressed. Still other artists expressed it by collecting and studying primitive folk art: *lubki*, icons and miniatures.

In Russia this movement was especially powerful, deeply touching all branches of art and affecting artistic thinking. After the movement of the Peredvizhniki (Wanderers), in which the focus was content and theme, the artists turned towards the exterior, formal elements of a picture – its beauty. The painting or sculpture was first of all meant to be an object of beauty (art for art's sake), not the bearer of moral or philosophical messages.

The artists who belonged to the Mir iskusstva (World of Art) group, sought new motifs in folk wood carvings, embroidery, icons, antique carpets, and figured treacle cakes (*pryaniks*). As a source of stylization these objects were collected by the artists, who saw in them a basis for purely ornamental and decorative formation of their art. Inaugurated by Stasov and having its origin in Vasnetzov's art, this quasi-nationalistic direction was adopted by Bilibin and Stelletzky, based on folk prototypes vividly replicated by both Rerikh and Goncharova. Every folk object became a fashion; whether it was a colorful shawl, national women's dress (*sarafan*) or a *troika* (three horses harnessed abreast) pattern on a kitchen towel, everything had an expressive folk character.

Not only was visual art studied then, but also folktales, and music and song, which composers adapted to their compositions. This period can be characterized not only by a "bookish," salon-like or narrowly professional interest in this movement, but mostly by a vivid, cultural and practical activity, which is expressed in the founding of craft schools, in the organizing of craftsmen's works as well as in the mounting of exhibitions. This movement did not have the so-called narodnichesky (populist) character [the character of the "the intelligentsia's view of simple folk"; [Aronson here draws a contrast between the Wanderers' interest in folk art and in that which is expressed by the Mir iskusstva (World of Art) group – translator's note], but was evoked by a real artistic interest, by a wish to find a solid basis in the search to define a national style and by an aspiration to find one's own style. Not only Russians, but also Ukrainians, Georgians, Tatars and all other nations that inhabit Russia, shared a wide interest in collecting their national folk art.

This trend had special significance for Jews. This age has awakened in Jews an aspiration to their own style. It is connected with a revival of interest in visual art as well as with an awakened desire to lay a foundation for their own museums, and to collect folk art in all of its forms and all the monuments of religious customs and modes of life up to the recent past. In the Pale of Jewish Settlement, in Lithuania, White Russia, Poland, and Galicia, the artists collected, photographed, copied and drew synagogues and their wall decorations, ritual objects and tombstones – any subject that had some relation to Jewish folk art. Often the same person (e.g., An-Sky Rapoport) collected tales and parables, folksongs and motifs, *lubki* and manuscripts. The initially ethnographic character of these finds was replaced by an aesthetic attitude. Along with collectors there appeared researchers, who longed to discover and study the formal basis of Jewish style.

Not only national pride, but also the significance of Jewish folk art, as well as its distinctive features, inspired the artists to new thoughts and inventions. The Jewish populist art movement can be divided into three periods: *imitation and copying; stylization*, and finally *individualization* [Aronson's emphasis]. We should note that often one artist cannot be confined exlusively to one period, but his creation taken in total view may represent an original picture of the general evolution.

Lissitzky approached the task of copying artifacts from a professional viewpoint; he exactly reproduced the synagogue decorations in Mohilev, Shklovsk, Druya and Kapust. Similarly, Ryback worked on copying the tombstones in Orsha, in the provinces of Podolia and Volynia, while Elman worked on copying silver objects and synagogue carvings. Each of these artists became a researcher in the formal principles of the popular style.

But when artists of this type wish to do something of their own, they cannot avoid copying folk art exactly. Thus Lissitzky publishes *Sikhes Kholin*, which is an imitation of a scroll; in other words, a scribe writes a text for him, imitating the style and form of the scrolls, which are to be kept in special wooden cases. For this edition, Ryback makes a book cover which is a copy of a Galician *lubok*, adding to this a figure of a deer which he had previously copied from a tombstone, as well as Hebrew letters from an antique scroll. For Tchaikov as well, a scribe writes a text of the Song of Songs. He even includes the entire first sheet of the popular folk edition in his own portrait.

The first period of copying the folk style was of short duration. Elements of folk art were perceived cursorily and formal origins remained undiscovered. The artists were looking only for some exterior features which eventually could help them to create a new, nationalistic visual art.

The second period, that of stylization, was more fruitful. Elements of folk art were adapted to a modern idiom. Lissitzky edited *Had Gadya* as a stylized *lubok*, in which folk spontaneity was transformed into Jewish stylish beauty. Elements that had no prototype in Jewish folk art (cats, dogs) were freely interpreted without adding specific Jewish features. Lissitzky also created works for the publishers, Folks Farlag and Kultur Lige, in which he incorporated traditional Jewish motifs such as columns, deers, lions and candlesticks.

Similarly, Ryback modernized the folk *lubok*, with careful attention to every element of composition and content, as if wishing to preserve the very dust of ages, while distorting facial features, deliberately individualizing and stressing obviously Jewish details: earlocks, beards and *lapserdak*, (the long, torn Hasidic coat).

Artists such as Goldfein, Elman and Tchaikov work under the impact of Mir iskusstva. Tchaikov, however, reveals some features of individualization and therefore is unlike his colleagues, who are united by the general stamp of their school.

Supported by the press and receiving a response across broad circles of the intelligentsia, young artists developed an activity which eventually would leave significant marks on the history of Jewish cultural life. They founded museums and schools, they engaged in debates, organized lectures and exhibitions. There was a rekindled interest in everything national, not only in Russia, but also in Germany, Austria, and Czechoslovakia. Thus they rekindled an interest in everything national; but this interest is expressed principally in the themes either of Zionist slogans, or of tendentious literary lines of thought. The graphic art of Lilien, Steinhardt, Zuckerman, or Budko is not of high quality, for these artists could not liberate themselves from tedious motifs such as palm trees, Stars of David, or of emaciated, tired faces of Old Jews and exalted, elongated faces of youths. German stylistic influences are also reflected in the works of Elman and Tchaikov.

Another characteristic feature of this period of stylization is its graphic quality. For stylization, linearity played an important role. However, this linearity may be of naturalistic rather than ornamental character. So, for example, Tchaikov is preoccupied not with the rhythm of line but with its anatomical place, not with the composition of color patches but with the filling of space by figures. On the other hand, in the art of Lissitzky, patches of color are essential. His highly deliberated illustrations perfectly fit their texts. He was the first to reveal a cultural understanding of the graphic tasks and formal elements of Jewish folk art. His use of stylistic folk elements was always skillful and intelligent.

In general, the period of stylization had only a superficial connection to folk art. Feeling a lack of formal Jewish elements, which could be counted on one's fingers – lions, candlesticks, signs of the zodiac, Torah scrolls, prayer shawls, deer, Stars of David and symbolic palms of hands – the artists began to stylize other accessories of Jewish life such as earlocks, beards, skullcaps, prayer shawls, phylacteries, walking sticks, *kartuz*, (visored, peaked caps), and Sabbath lamps. Mercilessly exaggerating the objects and features of Jewish life in order to attach significance to insignificant things (to make something monumental out of something small and barely visible), the artists of this period broadened the formal horizons of Jewish art. Such are Ryback's drawings, which are constructed from folk themes traditionally accepted as Jewish. He exaggerates the asymmetry of facial features, the curly earlocks and protruding ears, all in order to create a prescription for the so-called conscious "national action."

In a similar manner, just as the symbols of "boyar's" Russia of the fourteenth to seventeenth centuries – *kokoshniks* (women's top hats) and sarafans, weapons and brocade, Kremlin walls and church domes – served as motifs in the nationalist stylization of Bilibin's art, so the shtetl Jew, his fences, his miniature goats, carved wooden houses and curved staircases became the hallmarks for stylizing Jewish folk art.

## Chapter Five

The period of individualization produced two masters, opposites in character creation: Altman and Chagall, revealing two aspects of art: reason and intuition.

Deliberate mastery and intellect are Altman's. He invents nothing, discovers nothing. The inventions of others become his possession. He organizes ideas, and knows how to classify the essentials. The mature realism, deliberation and presence of mind in his painting and graphics converts each of his works into a model of brilliant mastery. Altman's eclecticism is cultural and deep; he is the European who imparts a gloss and brilliant skill to the national, visual art. It was he who discovered the formal principle of folk creation - not its literary content, but the essence of its composition: the proportion and interplay of black and white, the traditional dependence of line on color patch, its unity and completeness, the patterned sameness of the elements in the folk artifact. And using his achievements, he found independent, new Jewish forms of perception. In *Illustrations to the Bible*, he uses techniques found in Jewish art (especially in chase silver works), namely chiaroscuro and a gradual decrease in the intensity of color patch, most typical of Oriental *lubki*. In spite of the fact that his lions look more like pigs, they are perceived as purely Jewish, because formally they are Jewish. What is important is not the subject, but the relation of black and white patches, the figures' weight and form. The understanding of the essence of the formal side of Jewish art gives Altman a key for creating forms, reminiscent of Jewish folk creation. Even when he introduces into Jewish graphics new objects such as a human figure or a tree, they are nonetheless perceived as Jewish elements of art along with the more traditional ones like lions or deer (e.g., a drawing of Eve and the Serpent). He neither copies nor uses the antique objects of folk art, but creates out of their elements independent compositions of his own.

Altman is a graphic artist by nature and his inclination is towards design. The three-dimensional distribution of light does not interest him and, even when he uses Cubist elements, it is solely in the service of pure ornamention. The correlation of black and white is the same in all of his works and aims at underlining and emphasizing contrasts. The clever adaptation of essential features of folk art, understood in its formal aspect, and its skillful transformation into a new art not only makes Altman's graphic works interesting from the national point of view, but also establishes him as an artist of distinction in the general European context.

Abstraction of plastic sensation and the systematic pursuit of exclusively formal tasks are completely absent in the works of Chagall, who personifies the second aspect of Jewish art, namely its primitive spontaneity. Chagall is complete and immediate. He perceives life with sensuous exaltation. Neither European culture, artistic traditions, nor training and skill diminish his organic Hasidic pantheism, with its canny naiveté. Eclecticism is alien to Chagall because he is occupied with his own personality, disclosing his private sensations, revealing his unique relation to his surroundings. Out of his integral pictorial perception emerge things and people suffused with a Chagallian atmosphere. This emotional perception animates the objective world, disclosing the essence of an object and transforming it into a symbol. Chagall is on intimate terms with the world view that characterizes folk creation. Nevertheless, he does not imitate and counterfeit traditional elements, but uses them in order to transmit his own experiences in his native shtetl. An object which he discovers immediately becomes a new Jewish motif. In his creation, stylization is totally absent, but the completeness of his perception, the unity and organic richness of his images flow out into something akin to a style; images emerge which are imbued with the character of independent national monuments. Thus a Jew with a *lulav* seems to be mystical, rendered with a calm linear fluidity that expresses everything Jewish that is inexpressible in words. Just as Japanese engravings of actors have a linear pliancy, pointedness and elasticity of line, which are all associated with specific Japanese national features, so the lines and color patches of Chagall's Jew have a dominant Jewish look. In the same manner, another work by Chagall, *Boy with a Guitar*, is an example of the play of blotches of color, which are distributed so uniquely, that taken together they could serve for constructing an outline of an archetypal Jewish boy.

Chagall uses hatching, weaving masses out of fine lines and the play of white surfaces in his graphic work, which stands in contrast to Altman's work where everything is constructed on black.

Goats and fences, motifs of Jewish life (which would take pages to enumerate) are discovered only by Chagall and belong only to him. Young artists have grown up on the elements of his art and, therefore, Chagall's influence is traceable in the work of each of them. And if the elements of Chagall's art became the banner of the artistic revival, and if they became a cliché, Chagall should not be blamed. Because these elements, later to become a synonym for Jewish life, are indeed discovered and created by Chagall. But, what is important, is that they never had an independent function in his art, forever remaining just the parts of his integral organic creation. His multifaced images, his all-comprehending scope (which rejects nothing, however small), his enchanted, spontaneous world, all comprise the monumentality of Chagall's creative personality.

### Chapter Six

Mir iskusstva (the search for a national style in Russia) played an important role in creating the general atmosphere out of which Jewish stylization grew (the origins of which are the rich treasury of folk art).

New idols came from the West in the forms of the Cubist masters, with their program in which the theoretical essence of art turned out to be more important than its materialized design. The new aspiration of Russian cultural life was closely associated with Cubism and its branches: Futurism, Expressionism, Suprematism, Dadaism, and Constructivism.

In contrast to external aesthetic beauty, emphasis was placed on analysis, science, the rhythm of nervous urban life, pathos of mechanics, construction and engineering skill. In the Constructivism of Lissitzky and in the craftsmanship of Shterenberg we see the aspiration to a minimum of means by the simplest forms: lithographic stone, paste, and moveable type.

Time individualized these tasks. Egoism was the psychological origin of Cubism. The evolutionary transmission of the collective experience was replaced by the revolutionary search for new correlations. In this new direction a heroic character of the populist creation was forever lost.

The new ideology put forward just a few names in Jewish art. But the majority of Jewish artists, who paved the road towards aestheticism, while they still remained within the frontiers of national art, moved towards the tasks of pure formalism. Some of them used the new achievements in order to sharpen their "own" forms (Chagall, Ryback); others took from the Jewish style only its "apparent look," that is, the letters and the blackened coloration (e.g., Altman in his latest covers of Jewish books). The majority of Jewish artists withdrew from past ideology [or searches for a Jewish national style – translator's note] and instead began to solve problems of a purely formal character, which became an aim instead of a means for their own work.

As Anisfeld, Sorin, Brodksy and Bakst merged with the trend which created them, so Lipchitz, Shterenberg, and Lissitzky became inseparable parts of the Cubist movement. Slightly to the side stands Zack, who similarly rejected the national, but not for the sake of formal elements. He was able to find himself by tearing away from the Russians and Jews and adapting some features of the French tradition. Yet, he did not achieve an organic unity in his art, only the outer likeness of French prototypes.

Populist, national art cultivated inner integrality and organic unity of the pictorial mode. Cubism pushed forward the principle of division: separate problems of form, color and texture.

Contemporary Jewish artists, however, failed to forge a new style. Generally speaking, each national style contradicts the whole atmosphere in which the dynamism, mechanics and fragmentation of our age play such an important role. When they attempted to offer new Jewish interpretations of diverse subjects, populist artists found themselves at a loss. The patterns of the antique lion received a new look, but a new form was not found. Creation of style went against the direction of time. Yet style cannot be dependent on a premeditated program, effort or diligence; it comes as a natural consequence of surrounding conditions. The populist movement is important in awakening the historic consciousness and animating the relation between tradition and craft. Modernity, which comes close to the primitive, reverts back to the sources, to the real primitive figuration. Modernity is attracted by national folk art because of its even distribution of forms, wise self-limitation, static calm and simplification of means.

The Jewish populist movement has value in being an integral organization. The apparent unity of the artists of this group is not an occasional feature, but rather a deeply organic one. The significance of this movement is that it served as a natural reaction to the ideological movements of the whole modern epoch.

*From the book, *Sovremennaya Evreiskaya Grafika*, Berlin: Petropolis, 1924. Chapters 3, 4, 5, and part of 6. Translated from the Russian by Luba Freedman, Abridged by Malka Jagendorf.

# Biographies of the Artists

## Nathan Altman (1889-1970)

Born in Vinnitsa in the Podolia province, Altman studied painting and sculpture under K. K. Kostandi at the Odessa art school from 1903-07. In 1910, he exhibited there in the group show of the Society of South Russian Artists before leaving in December for Paris. While there he attended M. Vasileva's Académie Russe. It was also in Paris that he became acquainted with the old masters (Velásquez, Zurbarán, El Greco) and the contemporary artists (Picasso, Matisse, Léger, Delaunay). He began working in the Paris studio of an Odessa student, Baranov-Rossiné, where he was influenced by Futurism before moving onto La Ruche where he met Chagall, Archipenko, Zadkine, Shterenberg and Soutine. In the autumn of 1911, Altman returned to Vinnitsa in Russia where he taught drawing, did graphics, and painted his famous picture, *Jewish Funeral*. Altman arrived in St. Petersburg at the end of 1912. In 1913, he exhibited with the Mir iskusstva (World of Art) group. During the summer he lived in Gritsev, in the Volynia district, where he copied reliefs from Jewish tombstones and ornaments from synagogue textiles. This work was later published in his album, *Jewish Graphics* (Berlin, 1923). Through the year 1917, Altman illustrated books in St. Petersburg (his first: *Kiss the Sun*, by A. Volkovski), completed caricatures for satirical journals and showed his work at exhibitions with such groups as the Union of Youth, World of Art, 0.10, and Jack of Diamonds. In 1916, Altman did his first sculpture, *Self-portrait* (or The Portrait of a Young Jew) and his first stage design for the cabaret Comedians Halt. The same year Altman participated in the founding of the Jewish Society for the Encouragement of the Arts (JSEA) in Petrograd and exhibited in the show of Jewish artists.

Immediately after the Revolution, Altman became active in the organization of artistic education and culture at the state level. He was a member of IZO Narkompros, taught at Svomas, directed the Museum of Artistic Culture, and edited the journal, *Art of the Commune*. In 1918, he designed the outdoor decorations for Uritsky Square in celebration of the first anniversary of the Revolution. He also did agit-posters, sculptures, reliefs, and drawings of the revolutionary leaders, among them Lenin and Lunacharsky. Altman also took part in the 1918 "Exhibition of Painting and Sculpture by Jewish Artists" in Moscow. In 1919, he participated in the "First State Exhibition of Local and Moscow Artists" in Vitebsk. He moved to Moscow in 1921 to become head of the IZO Narkompros section. While in Moscow, Altman became involved in theatre design. In 1921, he did the sets for Mayakovski's *Mystery-Bouffe* at Meyerhold's First Theatre of the Russian Soviet Federal Socialist Republic (RSFSR). The next year was marked by his two famous Contructivist stage designs for Granovsky's production of *Uriel Accosta* at the GOSET, and Vachtangov's production of *The Dybbuk* at Habimah. In 1922, Altman exhibited at the "Show of the Three" (Altman, Chagall, Shterenberg), organized by Kultur Lige in Moscow. He also took part in the "First Russian Show," in Berlin's Van Diemen Gallery, which was repeated the following year in Amsterdam. While in Berlin, Altman published his album, *Jewish Graphics*, with a preface by Max Osborne, and designed covers for numerous books published by Helikon and Petropolis. Upon returning to Russia, he went back to work in theatre design, first in 1925 with his set for Shalom Aleichem's *Doctor*, a production by Granovsky at the GOSET followed by his costume designs and poster for Granovsky's film based on Shalom Aleichem's text, *Jewish Luck*. In 1926, Altman did the set for Granovsky's production of *The Tenth Commandment*, and in 1927, the stage design for *The Marriage of Trouhadec*, both at the GOSET. In 1928, Altman accompanied the GOSET on its European tour, remaining in Paris until 1931. Upon returning to the USSR, Altman conformed to the artistic demands of the regime. For the next decade he continued to be active in theatre and book design, and after World War II, he also did graphic work and sculpture. His exhibitions included one-man shows in Moscow (1938) and Leningrad (1939, 1941 and 1969). He also took part in major international exhibitions in Venice (1924), Dresden and New York (1926), Monza-Milano (1927), Berlin and Vienna (1928). Altman wrote many articles on art theory, theatre, film, sculpture, etc., during the early post-revolutionary years, and again during the late thirties and sixties. He died in Leningrad.

### Selected Bibliography:

A. Efros. *Portret Natana Altmana*. Moscow, 1922.
L. Lozowick, "The Art of Nathan Altman" in *Menorah Journal*, no. 12, 1926.
W. Georges, and I. Ehrenberg. *Natan Altman*. Paris, 1933 (Yiddish).
M. Etkind. *Natan Altman*. Moscow, 1971.

## Boris Aronson (1898–1980)

The son of a rabbinical family in Kiev, Aronson graduated, in 1916, from the State Art School in Kiev. He continued his studies at the School of the Theatre, also in Kiev, and there joined Alexandra Exter's studio. In 1918, he began working with Kultur Lige, acting as its manager between 1919-20. During this time, he also co-authored an article with Ryback entitled "Di Vegen fun der Yidisher Malarei" (Paths of Jewish Painting), published by Kultur Lige in the journal, *Oyfgang*. In 1920, Aronson participated in the Kiev group exhibition of Jewish artists while also serving on the exhibition's organizing committee. He is believed to have designed the costumes and decorations for Weiter's play, *The Dawn* (Fartog) (1919-20) at the GOSET in Moscow, while studying there with the painter Mashkov. He left Russia in 1922 for Berlin, where he studied with Hermann Struck, and participated in the "First Russian Show" at the Van Diemen Gallery. While in Berlin he also published two books, *Marc Chagall* and *Contemporary Jewish Graphics* (1924). Later that year Aronson immigrated to the United States, stopping first in Paris.

Once in New York, Aronson worked as a stage designer at Unzer Teyater in the Bronx (1924-25), and at Maurice Schwartz's Yiddish Art Theatre. His first solo show of designs, models and costume drawings was held in 1927 at the Anderson Galleries, New York. During the 1930s he worked in Broadway theatres. He continued to work as a stage designer and to exhibit his work until the late seventies. He died in New York.

### Selected Bibliography:

W. George. *Boris Aronson et l'art du Théâtre*. Paris, 1928.
*Boris Aronson – From His Theatre Work*, exhibition in the Vincent Astor Gallery, the New York Public Library at Lincoln Center, 31 March – 15 August 1981.
*Lexicon of the Yiddish Theatre*, ed. Zalman Zylbercwaig. New York: The Hebrew Actors' Union of America, 1931, vol. I, p. 90, (Yiddish.)
Fran Rich with Lisa Aronson, *The Theatre Art of Boris Aronson*. New York: A. A. Knopf, 1987.

## Alexander Grigorievich Tyshler (1898 – 1980)

Tyshler was born in Melitopol, the son of a carpenter. He studied from 1912 to 1917 at the Kiev art school with Ana Osipova. While visiting Alexandra Exter's studio, he met Shifrin and Rabinovich. Between 1917 and 1918 he worked primarily on graphics; The "Ruth" cycle of drawings; illustrations for Zhukovsky's poems; and for *Petukh*, a series of poems by Venegrov. Tyshler joined the Red Army in 1919 and the next year, in Melitopol, he worked on poster designs for the windows of the Russian Telegraphic Agency (ROSTA). The following year he exhibited in the group show of Jewish artists in Kiev, under his own name and Dzhin-Kzhikh-Shvil, his mother's maiden name. Tyshler moved to Moscow in 1921, where he was accepted by VKhUTEMAS. He created his first set designs in 1927 for *Fuente Ovejuna* by Lope de Vega, and *Botvin* by Vevyurko, both at the BelGOSET in Minsk. The following year he worked on the stage designs for *The Deaf* by D. Bergelson, and *62nd Division* by Y. Dobrushin, again at the BelGOSET, as well as for the production of *The Last* by Reznikov, at the Kharkov Jewish Theatre. In 1929, he designed the sets for two plays at the BelGOSET, *Jim Coopercop* by S. Godiner and a *Poem About an Ax* by Pogodin. Between 1927 and 1930, Tyshler was also known for his portraits of poor Jews, street vendors, jugglers, families, brides, and his childhood neighbors, while he continued to illustrate books. In the 1930s, Tyshler began working for the Gypsy Theatre in Moscow, and between 1935 and 1949, he worked on designs for the GOSET. During this period, he also illustrated books by Mayakovski, Kirsanov, Bagritsky, Shalom Aleichem, and Pushkin, and painted portraits of celebrities, such as Mikhoels, Akhmatova, Eisenstein and Brik. In the 1950s and 1960s, Tyshler designed sets for plays by Shakespeare, Shaw, Mayakovski and Arthur Miller at various Leningrad and Moscow theatres.

Tyshler exhibited his work at the "First Discussional Exhibition of the Association of Active Revolutionary Arts," Moscow (1924); at two of the OST exhibitions (Moscow, 1926 and 1927); at the "Jubilee Exhibition of USSR Art," organized by the State Academy of Artistic Science (Moscow, 1927); and at the exhibition of "Russian Drawing during the First Decade of the October Revolution," (Moscow, 1928). He continued to take part in major group exhibitions in the USSR until 1935, and again from 1956 to 1966. Solo shows of his work were held in 1956 in Leningrad, and in 1964 and 1966 in Moscow. Tyshler also took part in many international exhibitions during the late 1920s and early 1930s. During the 1930s, and again in 1965, Tyshler wrote a number of articles on his work in the theatre which were published in Soviet art and theatre magazines. He died in the Soviet Union.

**Selected Bibliography:**

F. Syrkina. *A.G. Tyshler*. Moscow: Sovetskii khudozhnik, 1966.

## Joseph Tchaikov (1888–1986)

Born in Kiev to a family of artisans, Tchaikov grew up in Pinsk, in the home of his grandfather, a scribe (*sofer*) who stimulated the child's interest in drawing. In 1908, Tchaikov was apprenticed to an engraver in Kiev. During this time he began creating metal medallions and bone and clay sculptures. The Russian sculptor Nahum Aronson recognized his talent and helped him obtain a scholarship from the Artisans' Society of Kiev. Tchaikov spent the years 1910-14 in Paris, where he studied with Aronson at the Higher School for Decorative Arts and at the Higher School for Fine Arts. In Paris, he associated with the Makhmadim, a group of Jewish artists who were searching for a Jewish national style. While there he also met Chagall, Soutine and Shterenberg and was first influenced by Rodin, and then by Archipenko, Lipchitz, Modigliani, Zadkine and Picasso. During his Paris period Tchaikov exhibited in the Salon d'Automne Russian group exhibition (1912), and in Kiev at the Spring Salon (1913 and 1915). During World War I, Tchaikov was mobilized to the Russian-German front, but later returned to Kiev where he met Lissitzky and Exter.

After the Revolution, Tchaikov worked simultaneously on developing a Jewish national style and post-revolutionary Soviet art. In 1918, Tchaikov participated in the "Twenty-Fourth Exhibition of the Moscow Society of Artists" and at the "Exhibition of Paintings and Sculptures by Jewish Artists," in Moscow. He illustrated Yiddish books for children between 1919 and 1922 and executed sculptures of Karl Liebknecht and Marx in Kiev. In 1920, he exhibited at the "Jewish Exhibition of Sculpture, Graphics and Drawings," in Kiev. His book on sculpture, written in Yiddish, was published in 1921 by Kultur Lige in Kiev. The following year Tchaikov taught sculpture at the Kiev Art Studio, and took part in the art exhibition organized there by Kultur Lige. In 1922-32, he taught sculpture at VKhUTEMAS and VKhUTEIN, while participating in the "First Russian Show" at the Van Diemen Gallery of Berlin. The show later traveled to Amsterdam.

During the early 1920s Tchaikov's style was Constructivist, containing themes of sport, acrobatics and the circus. By the end of the 1920s, he had joined the prevalent Social Realist trend. Tchaikov had a one-man show in the 1924 "First Discussional Exhibition of the Association of Active Revolutionary Art," organized by VKhUTEMAS in Moscow. Additional solo exhibitions of his work were held in 1948 and 1959, for the celebration of thirty-five years and forty-five years of his art, respectively. Additionally, Tchaikov took part in numerous group shows in the USSR and abroad until the late 1970s, including: "Drawings by Contemporary Russian Sculptors," sponsored by the Four Arts Society, Moscow (1925); "The First Exhibition of the Society of Russian Sculptors," also sponsored by the Four Arts Society in Moscow (1926); "The Second Exhibition of the Society of Russian Sculptors," and "Art of the People of the USSR," both in Moscow (1927); and other group shows in the Soviet Union, continuously until the late 1970s. In addition, he took part in a number of international exhibitions: Paris (1925), Monza-Milano (1927), Venice (1928), New York (1929), Venice, Berlin and Vienna (1930), Venice and Istanbul (1934), Paris (1937), New York (1939), and New York and Mexico (1959). His later sculptures included studies of athletes, portraits, and public monuments. Tchaikov wrote a number of articles on sculpture for Soviet magazines from 1936 to 1974. His book, *Lepka i formavka Skulptury* (Modeling and Forming Sculpture), was published in Moscow in 1953.

**Selected Bibliography:**

*Chaliastra*, vol. 2, Warsaw, 1922, p. 50 (Yiddish).
I. Schmidt. *Joseph Tchaikov*. Moscow: Sovetskii khudozhink, 1977.

# El Lissitzky (1890 – 1941)

Born in Pochinok, near Smolensk, Lissitzky began to study art with Yehuda Pen in 1903. In 1909, after failing to be accepted to the St. Petersburg Academy of Art, he went to Germany and enrolled in the Technische Hochschule of Darmstadt, where he studied engineering and architecture for five years. Lissitzky took part in the 1912 exhibition of the Union of Artists in St. Petersburg. Between 1912 and 1913 he visited Paris, where he met Zadkine, and also toured Italy. He returned to Russia in 1914, and attended the Riga Polytechnic Institute from 1915-17, where he concluded his studies as an architect. He also took part in the following exhibitions: "World of Art" (1916-17), "Exhibition of Pictures and Sculptures by Jewish Artists" at the Lemercier Gallery (1917, Moscow), "The Exhibition of Paintings and Sculpture by Jewish Artists" (1918, Moscow), and a group exhibition of Jewish artists (1920, Kiev). His interest in Jewish folk art was already manifest in 1916, when he, Ryback, and possibly Elman, went on an ethnographic expedition organized by the Jewish Historical and Ethnographic Society to explore the synagogues along the Dnieper River. It was not until after the Revolution that Lissitzky became actively involved in the development of Jewish art and culture. For the next seven years, 1917-23, he illustrated Yiddish books for children, while at the same time he actively participated in many of the post-revolutionary artistic developments. In 1918, Lissitzky joined IZO Narkompros. In May of 1919, at Chagall's invitation, he went to Vitebsk where he taught architecture and graphics at the Vitebsk art school. Commencing with Malevich's arrival at the school, in November 1919, Lissitzky became strongly influenced by Suprematism and developed his Prouns. He exhibited at the Unovis exhibitions in Vitebsk and Moscow (1920-21), took part in many of the activities around the revolutionary festival and designed agitprop posters. In 1920, he became a member of the Moscow INKhUK. He spent the years 1922-25 in Western Europe. In 1922, together with Ehrenburg, he published the journal, Object in Berlin and also illustrated Ehrenburg's book, Six Stories with Easy Endings. He expressed his concern about a Jewish national style in an article entitled, "The Victory Over Art" in the Yiddish journal, Ringen. During that same year, Lissitzky designed the catalog cover for and participated in the "First Russian Art Show" held in Berlin. In 1932, he published an article based on his expedition with Ryback – "Memoirs Concerning the Mohilev Synagogue," in the journals, Rimon (Hebrew) and Milgroym (Yiddish). While abroad, Lissitzky established contacts with Dada artists at the Congress in Düsseldorf, at De Stijl in Holland, and the Bauhaus in Weimar. In 1922-23 he published articles on his Prouns (in De Stijl, no. 6, 1922); collaborated with Mies van der Rohe on the magazine, G; designed Mayakovski's book of poetry entitled, For the Voice (Berlin: 1932); and published the portfolio, Victory Over the Sun (Hanover, 1932). In 1923, he also designed a Proun room for the "Great Berlin Art Exhibition." In 1924, Lissitzky worked with Schwitters on the magazine Merz, with Arp on Die Kunstismen, and with Stam on the journal, ABC. In 1925, he returned to the Soviet Union, where he taught for five years at the Moscow VKhUTEMAS. He continued his work in interior design, exhibition design, theatre, photography and photomontage. He also continued to exhibit in the USSR and abroad. Solo shows of his work were held in Hanover (1932), Berlin (1924), Dresden (1925), and the Dessau Bauhaus (1972). He died in Moscow.

## Selected Bibliography:

S. Lissitzky-Küppers. El Lissitzky. Dresden: VEB Verlag der Kunst, 1967.
Chimen Abramsky. "El Lissitzky as Jewish Illustrator and Typographer," in Studio International, October, 1966, vol. 172. pp. 182-85.
Alan C. Birnholz. El Lissitzky. Ann Arbor, Michigan: University Microfilms International, 1983.

# Yosef Elman

Little is known of Elman's life, but he is believed to have taken part in the ethnographic tour together with Lissitzky and Ryback, organized by the Jewish Historical and Ethnographic Society around 1915-16, during which time they concentrated on copying silver ceremonial objects and wood carvings in synagogues. Otherwise, the record of his work is limited to a frontispiece he designed, in 1919, for the Yiddish magazine, Eygns, and the illustrations he did for Z. Segalovich's book, Bloikeit, both of which were published in Kiev.

## Selected Bibliography:

B. Aronson. Sovremmenaya Evreiskaya Grafika (Contemporary Jewish Graphics). Berlin, 1924. pp. 68, 72.

# Robert Rafailovich Falk (1886-1958)

The son of a prosperous Moscow lawyer, Falk studied at K. F. Yuon's and I. I. Mashkov's studios from 1902 until 1905, when he entered the Moscow School of Painting, Sculpture and Architecture. There he studied with Arkhipov, Vasnetsov, and Pasternak, and took master classes with Serov and Korovin. In 1906, Falk participated in his first student exhibition entitled, "The Young Painter," and in 1909, he took part in the "Golden Fleece" exhibition. During the school year of 1909-10, he taught drawing in elementary schools, and then traveled to Italy. Upon his return to Russia, Falk participated in the first exhibition of the Jack of Diamonds group (December 1910 to January 1911) of which he was a founder along with Mashkov, Konchalovsky, Kuprin, Lentulov and Roshdestvenski. Between 1910 and 1917, Falk exhibited frequently in the Jack of Diamonds exhibitions, while at the same time taking part in the World of Art exhibitions. His work was featured in the 1917 "Exhibition of Pictures and Sculptures by Jewish Artists," at Lemercier Gallery in Moscow and the following year he helped to organize the Free State Art Studios (Svomas) in Moscow. From 1918 to 1925, he taught in Moscow at VKhUTEMAS and VKhUTEIN. Falk exhibited in various forums: a group show in Vitebsk (1919), in the "World of Art" exhibition (1921-22), and in the "First Russian Show" at Berlin's Van Diemen Gallery (1922), where he was a Jack of Diamonds representative. In 1925, his first one-man show was held at the Tretyakov Gallery.

Falk began his work in the theatre in 1925 with the stage designs for Granovsky's production, Night at the Old Market by Y. L. Peretz at the GOSET, and for Jacob's Dream at Habimah. In 1927, Falk designed the sets for the Voyage of Benjamin III, directed by Granovsky at the GOSET, and in 1930, he did the sets for Habimah's Berlin production of Uriel Accosta. Ten years later he did designs for the production of Solomon Maimon directed by Mikhoels at the GOSET, and the following year for Shalom Aleichem's Possessed Taylor, at BelGOSET in Minsk.

In addition to work at the GOSET and Habimah theatres, Falk was actively involved in Soviet artistic life. He participated in the eighth exhibition of AkHRR in Moscow and Leningrad (1926), as well as in the exhibitions of OMkH (1926, 1928). While dean of the Faculty of Painting at VKhUTEIN (from 1926 to 1928), a solo show of his works was organized in the House of the Scientists (1927). In 1927, he also exhibited with the Jack of Diamonds group at the Tretyakov Gallery. Falk actively took part in international exhibitions in Venice (1924, 1928) and in Paris (1925). In 1928, he accompanied the GOSET theatre on its European tour, staying in Paris until 1937. It was there that he met Altman and became close friends with Soutine. During his first year in France, Falk exhibited in a group show which included Altman, Chehonin and Janiz at the Gallery de l'Hirondelle and, in 1930, his one-man-show was featured at the Gallery Zac. It was also during this time that Falk worked with Granovsky on a film of Gogol's *Taras Bulba* (1935). After his return to the USSR, a solo show of his work was held at the Writer's House in Moscow (1939). During the war years he was evacuated to Samarkand, Central Asia, where he was influenced by oriental color and form. Following the war, Falk's work was exhibited in 1957, and again, posthumously in 1962-63 and 1965-67.

## Selected Bibliography:

D. Sarabjanov. *Robert Falk*. Dresden: VEB Verlag der Kunst, 1974.

# Isaac Binitch Rabitchev (1894-1961)

Rabitchev is known mainly as a stage designer and graphic artist. In 1923, he collaborated with A. Stephanova on the stage design for two of Granovsky's productions at the GOSET: *Carnival of the Jewish Masques* by Dobrushin, Oislender and Kushnirov, and *200,000*, by Shalom Aleichem. In 1924, he collaborated again with the Stephanova in designing the sets for *Three Jewish Raisins*, an adaptation by Dobrushin and Oislender, directed by Granovsky, Vulf and Mikhoels, at the GOSET. Rabitchev moved out on his own in 1921-32 when he created the stage designs for a play on the civil war entitled, *Partisans* by F. Arones, staged at the BelGOSET in Minsk. Simultaneously, Rabitchev took part in a number of art exhibitions in the Soviet Union and elsewhere. Beginning with the exhibition of Jewish artists held in Kiev in 1920, and then again in 1925, when he exhibited with the Society of Easel Artists (OST) in Moscow. In 1928, Rabitchev's work was included in the "Third Graphic Exhibition," in Moscow. Between 1932 and 1934 he participated in several group exhibitions of poster design in Moscow. One year later he took part in the show "Soviet Theater Artists during Seventeen Years." The following year, he exhibited in the show "Jewish Autonomous Region and Jewish National District in Paintings and Graphics," also in Moscow. We lose track of Rabitchev after 1936, when his name no longer appears in exhibition catalogs or among stage designers.

## Selected Bibliography:

B. Picon-Vallin. *Le Théâtre Juif Soviétique pendant les Années Vingt*. Lausanne, 1973.

# Isaac Rabinovich (1894–1961)

The son of a sign painter in Kiev, Rabinovich became interested in the theatre early in childhood, spurred both by his father and by the fact that actors from the Solovtsovsky Theatre lived in the neighborhood. Between 1906 and 1912 he attended the Kiev art school, where he studied with Prakhov and Didchenko. From 1912–1915 he was a member of Murasko's studio, where he met Shifrin. During this time Rabinovich also visited Alexandra Exter's studio. In 1911, he did his first stage design for a production of Hans Christian Andersen's fairy tales performed at Kiev's Bergone Theatre. In 1916, he took part in the group show "Koltso" in Kiev, where he exhibited his graphic works and paintings. Three years later, he did stage designs for the Solovtsovsky Theatre while also taking part in the outdoor decorations of Kiev and Kharkov for the May Day celebrations of 1919 and 1920. In 1921, he moved to Moscow and started to work for the GOSET, creating the stage designs for Granovsky's production of Sholem Asch's *God of Vengeance*. The next year he designed sets for Goldfaden's *The Witch*, also directed by Granovsky. While in Minsk, he designed the sets for Shalom Aleichem's *Holiday in Kasrilevka*, staged at the BelGOSET in 1926. Two years later he did the decorations for two GOSET plays – *The Trial is Going On* and *The Deaf*, and thereafter continued his Yiddish theatre work on the productions of *Earth* and *Four Days* (1930-31), as well as for the productions of *Tevye the Milkman* and *Prince Reubeni*, in 1939 and 1946.

Apart from his Yiddish theatre work, Rabinovich is considered a key figure in the development of Russian stage and film design. In 1922, he did the stage designs for Schiller's *Don Carlos* at the Moscow Comedy Theatre and, in 1923, for Aristophanes' *Lysistrata* at MHAT (Moscow Art Academic Theatre), for which he received an award at the Paris International Exhibition of Decorative Art (1925). He also did set designs for the film, *Aelita* (1924) (costumes by Exter) and carried on with production designs for the major Moscow theatres until the late fifties.

Rabinovich's works were shown in numerous group exhibitions in the USSR and abroad. His first solo show was organized by the Academy of Arts in Moscow in 1924. He took part in international exhibitions in Paris (1925), New York (1929), England (1930), New York (1934), Paris (1937), and again in New York (1939). He taught in the Department of Decorative Arts at VKhUTEMAS from 1926-30. In addition, between 1929 and 1957, he wrote a number of articles dealing with his work as a stage designer. A commemorative exhibition of his work was held in Moscow in 1961, a year after his death.

## Selected Bibliography:

F. Syrkina. *Isaak Rabinovich*. Moscow: Sovetskii Khudozhnik, 1972.

## Issachar Ber Ryback (1897-1935)

Ryback was born to a family with a Hasidic background in Yelizavetgrad, where he attended art school in 1907. From 1911-16, he studied at the Art Academy in Kiev. During this time he participated (with Lissitzky, and perhaps Elman) in an expedition, financed by the Jewish Historical and Ethnographic Society, through the surrounding Ukrainian villages, whereupon he collected *lubki* and copied tombstones. Ryback was also active in the Jewish Theatre Studio in Kiev, and knew Alexandra Exter, who introduced him to Cubism. From 1917, Ryback was employed by the Kultur Lige in Kiev, where he, together with Lissitzky, Tchaikov and others, founded the art department and taught painting and drawing to both children and adults. In 1919, he co-authored with Aronson the article, "Die Vegen fun der Yidisher Malerei" (Paths of Jewish Painting), which was published by Kultur Lige in the journal, *Oyfgang*. In the same year he moved to Moscow, where he studied at the Art Academy, taught art, and may have associated with the Constructivists. In 1920, Ryback served as chairman of the committee for the group exhibition of Jewish artists held in Kiev. In 1921, he moved to Berlin where he became a member of November Gruppe and participated in the exhibitions, "Juryfreien" and "Secession." While in Berlin, Ryback also illustrated Yiddish children's books and published two albums of lithographs: *The Shtetl* (1923) and *Jewish Types of the Ukraine* (1924). In 1925, he returned to the USSR and visited the Jewish settlements of the Ukraine, which resulted in his album, *On the Jewish Fields of the Ukraine* (Paris, 1926). At this time, Ryback also worked for the Jewish theatres in Moscow and Kharkov. In 1925, he created the stage designs for Y. L. Peretz's play, *In Folisch Oyf der Keit*; for the Loiters' production of *The Purimspiel* (Moscow); and for *In the Fire* by Daniel, in Kharkov. In 1926, he moved to Paris. There he produced the last of his albums, *Shadows of the Past* (1932). He exhibited throughout Europe between 1928 and 1934. Ryback died in 1953 on the eve of the opening of a major one-man retrospective of his work organized by Wildenstein in Paris. In 1962, his collection was donated for the establishment the Ryback Musuem in Bat Yam, Israel, where it is now on permanent display.

### Selected Bibliography:

R. Cogniat. "I. Ryback" in *Le Théâtre Juif Soviétique pendant les Anées Vingt*, B. Picon-Vallin. Lausanne, 1973.

## Marc Chagall (1887-1985)

Chagall commenced his artistic training in 1906 at the studio of Yehuda Pen in his native Vitebsk. In that same year he moved to St. Petersburg in order to attend the School of the Imperial Society for the Protection of Fine Art, directed by Nicholas Roerich. Between 1908-09, he studied at the Zvantseva art school directed by Bakst and Dobujinsky. Chagall remained in close contact with Bakst and, in 1910, helped him prepare the stage decoration for *Narcisse* and for Diaghilev's *Les Ballets Russes* (1910). In 1911, thanks to a monthly allowance from his patron Maxim Vinaver, Chagall left for Paris where he lived until 1914. While in Paris, Chagall exhibited at the Salon des Independants (1912 and 1913), and one year later his works were shown in Berlin's Der Sturm Gallery (1914). In that same year, while visiting in Vitebsk, World War I broke out, preventing him from obtaining a passport and returning to Paris. In 1915, he exhibited in "The Year 1915" in Moscow, and married Bella Rosenfeld. In 1916, he contributed to exhibitions of the Jack of Diamonds group in Moscow and contemporary Russian art, as well as the "Exhibition of Members of the JSEA" (1916) in Petrograd. The next year he participated in the "Exhibition of Pictures and Sculpture by Jewish Artists" at the Lemercier Gallery in Moscow (April 1917). Immediately after the Revolution, in 1918, Chagall was appointed Commissar of Art in Vitebsk. As Commissar, he organized the outdoor decorations for the celebration of the first anniversary of the Revolution, and founded an art school and a museum in Vitebsk. In the spring of 1919, Dobujinsky, Jean Pougny, and Pen together with Chagall taught at the Vitebsk art school, to which the Petrograd authorities sent a new director – Vera Ermolaeva. When Lissitzky and, in November, Malevich joined the school, Chagall withdrew. In 1920 and 1921, he worked for the GOSET in Moscow, where he painted the murals for the theatre and did the set designs for the opening production based on Shalom Aleichem's stories, produced by Granovsky. In 1922, Chagall exhibited in "The Show of The Three" (with Shterenberg and Altman) in Moscow. That year he left Russia.

Chagall stopped in Berlin for the next year where he exhibited two pictures in the "First Russian Show" in Van Diemen's Gallery (October, 1922). While in Berlin, Boris Aronson wrote a book about him, and also included him in another one – *Contemporary Jewish Graphics* (Berlin, 1924). Chagall published a portfolio of etchings entitled, *Meyn Leben*, before settling in Paris in 1923 at the invitation of Ambroise Vollard, who also commissioned him to execute a series of etchings for Gogol's *Dead Souls*. Slowly Chagall's work gained recognition in France, Germany and Switzerland. Fearing persecution from the Nazis when they invaded France, Chagall escaped, in 1941, to the United States where he lived for seven years. Bella Chagall died in New York, in 1944, and in 1948 Chagall returned to France where he worked in theatre, book illustrations, stained-glass windows and painting. Exhibiting internationally, Chagall earned a worldwide reputation as one of the leading modern artists. He died in 1985.

### Selected Bibliography:

F. Meyer. *Marc Chagall*. New York, 1964.

## Nisson Abramovich Shifrin (1892-1961)

Shifrin was born in Kiev, the son of a communications officer. He studied at the Commercial School from 1902-11, and then continued his studies at the Commercial Institute between 1911-16, where he graduated in economics while simultaneously attending university lectures on Greek philosophy and art history. During 1912, he often visited A. Murashko's art studio in Kiev and there associated with the artists of the "left," as well as the Jack of Diamonds group (P. Konchalovsky, R. Falk, I. Mashkov). Shifrin also met Rabinovich at Murashko's studio in 1914, and through him the Futurists Mayakovski, Kamensky, and Burliuk. He was further influenced by icon painting, primitivism, and the works of Cézanne, Picasso and Matisse. During the war years, while serving in the Russian army, Shifrin met the theatrical designer, A. Mikhailov. After the Revolution, however, Shifrin returned to his profession as a statistician in Kishodovsk and then Kiev.

In 1918, Shifrin finally left his occupation and joined Alexandra Exter's studio. His first works for the stage were set designs for the Leckoque operetta, *Green Island* and the Ehrenberg play, *Rubashka Blansh*. With his artist wife Margarita Genrikovna Genka, Shifrin joined the Agittrain of the Twelfth Army during the civil war, travelling to the front lines and dispensing Bolshevik propaganda. In 1920, Shifrin exhibited with a group of Jewish artists in Kiev, and in the following years he worked for the Kiev Jewish Theatre Studio, designing sets for plays by Sholem Asch, Shalom Aleichem, Y. L. Peretz and L. Andreev (including *200,000* and *God of Vengeance* directed by S. Semdor). At that time he also did the stage designs for plays by Molière and Cervantes, performed by the Russian Drama Theatre, and for Stravinsky's ballet, *Petrushka*. In 1922, Shifrin moved to Moscow where he continued his work as a stage designer, which he expanded through the use of painting and graphics. During the 1920s he became a member of the Society of Easel Painters (OST) and published two albums of his drawings in 1929 entitled *The Train Goes and We Run*; and *Transport, Work, Moscow is Built*. In the 1930s he was known for his book illustrations of Amundsen, Jack London and others. Following World War II, Shifrin continued to work in theatre design until his death in 1961. His autobiography, *My Work in the Theatre*, was published post-humously in Moscow in 1966.

### Selected Bibliography:

M. Pozharskaya. *Nisson Abramovich Shifrin.* Moscow: Sovetskii khudozhnik, 1971.

Compiled by Mirjam Rajner

Nisson A. Shifrin

Boris Aronson, Alexander Tyshler, Issachar B. Ryback

Issachar B. Ryback, Joseph Tchaikov, Boris Aronson

Marc Chagall

Isaac Rabinovich

El Lissitzky

Nathan Altman

# Chronology of Jewish Events

## History and Russian Culture

## Jewish Culture

### 1911

An-Sky leads a Jewish Ethnographic Expedition through the Ukrainian regions of Volynia and Podolia, financed by the Jewish Historical and Ethnographic Society of St. Petersburg.

### 1912 The Dobychina Bureau opens in St. Petersburg.

*Makhmadim*, probably the first Jewish art journal, is published in Paris.

### 1914 World War I begins.

An-Sky's book, *The Jewish Ethnographic Program* (in Yiddish), is published in Petrograd.

The Jewish Society for the Encouragement of the Arts (JSEA) is founded and operates until the summer of 1917, with branches in Petrograd, Moscow, Kiev, and Kharkov.

The Jewish Literary and Art Society (Y. L. Peretz Society) is founded by L. M. Aizenberg, V. S. Mandel, and State Duma member M. Kh. Bomash.

The Jewish Theatre Society is founded in Petrograd.

### 1916

The Jewish Historical Museum is founded in Odessa by S. Ya. Kirshinevsky.

The JSEA sponsors a Jewish art exhibition, "Exhibition of Members of the JSEA."

The Jewish Ethnographic Museum, based on the findings of An-Sky's expedition, opens in Petrograd.

### 1917 Revolution sweeps Russia. The Bolsheviks take control. All restrictions on Jews are lifted.
Narkompros (People's Commissariat for Enlightenment) is established under Lunacharsky's jurisdiction.

The Habimah theatre is founded in Moscow.

The JSEA mounts the exhibition "Pictures and Sculpture by Jewish Artists" at Moscow's Galerie Lemercier.

### 1918 World War I ends. A visual arts section – IZO – is established within Narkompros. David Shterenberg supervises the section, heading the Petrograd division, while Vladimir Tatlin directs the Moscow division.

The Svomas (Free State Art Studios) replace Petrograd's Academy of Arts and the old art schools in Moscow and the provincial centers.

The Museums of Painterly Culture (Artistic Culture) are established in Moscow, Petrograd, and other cities.

Chagall is appointed Commissar and Director of the Vitebsk art school.

Kultur Lige, a secular Yiddish cultural organization, is opened in Kiev.

Two Yiddish literary magazines, *Baginen* and *Eygns*, appear in Kiev.

The "Exhibition of Painting and Sculptures by Jewish Artists" is held in Moscow.

The Moscow Circle of Jewish Men of Letters and Artists is founded.

The Bolsheviks close the Jewish Ethnographic Museum. An-Sky reopens it until the 1930s.

The Jewish Chamber Theatre, founded by Granovsky, opens as a studio in Petrograd.

The Jewish Popular University operates in Moscow (until 1921).

## History and Russian Culture

**1919** Pogroms sweep the Ukraine.

**1920** In Vitebsk, Malevich and his students establish the Posnovis, which is renamed Unovis later this year.

The INKhUK (Institute of Painterly Culture) is organized in Moscow, with affiliates established soon afterwards in Petrograd, Vitebsk, and other cities.

The VKhUTEMAS (Higher State Art-Technical Studios) replace the Svomas.

**1921** The RAKhN (Russian Academy of Artistic Sciences) opens in Moscow under Petr Kogan's direction and with Wassily Kandinsky's assistance. It is renamed GAKhN (State Academy of Artistic Sciences) in 1925.

**1922** The Union of Soviet Socialist Republics (USSR) is established.
The AKhRR (Association of Artists of Revolutionary Russia) is formed in Moscow.

**1923**

**1924** The GINKhUK (State Institute of Painterly Culture) is founded in Leningrad.

**1925** The Society of Easel Artists (OST) is formed.

**1926** VKhUTEIN (Higher State Art-Technical Institute) replaces VKhUTEMAS.

**1927** INKhUK is closed. "The Jubilee Exhibition of the Art of the Peoples of the USSR," is organized by Tugendkhold in Moscow.

## Jewish Culture

Malevich replaces Chagall as Director of the Vitebsk Art Academy and Lissitzky becomes a professor there.

Nathan Altman, Art Commissar of Petrograd, designs the festivities for the first anniversary of the Russian Revolution.

Yudovin organizes an exhibition of folk art in Vitebsk.

Lissitzky and Shterenberg are teaching at the VKhUTEMAS.

The "Jewish Exhibition of Sculpture, Graphics, and Drawings" is organized by Boris Aronson, working for Kultur Lige, in Kiev.

An exhibition of painting and sculpture by Jewish artists is held in Moscow.

The Jewish Chamber Theatre moves from Petrograd to Moscow. Also becomes known as the Kamerny and the Yiddish State Theatre.

The Yiddish art and literary magazine *Shtrom*, appears in Moscow.

An exhibition of the works of Chagall, Altman, and Shterenberg is organized by Kultur Lige in Moscow.

Lissitzky writes "Memoirs Concerning the Mohilev Synagogue," published by *Rimon/Milgroim* in Berlin.

Altman publishes *Jüdische Graphik* in Berlin.

The Jewish Museum opens in the city of Samarkand.

The Jewish Printing Industry School is founded in Leningrad.

Boris Aronson's book *Contemporary Jewish Graphics* (in Russian) is published in Berlin.

The Ukrainian Academy of Sciences in Kiev, establishes the Department of Jewish Culture.

Compiled by Michal Sofer

# Glossary

**Bund**   Jewish Social Democratic Union in Russia, Poland, and Lithuania (founded in 1897).

**GOSET**   Russian abbreviation for the Jewish State Theatre from 1925. From 1919-25, it was known as the Jewish Chamber Theatre, popularly called the Kamerny (see Kamerny below).

**Habimah**   Hebrew theatre founded in Moscow (1917) following the Revolution. Relocated from the Soviet Union in 1926 to Israel, and presently the national theatre.

**JSEA**   Jewish Society for the Encouragement of the Arts. Opened in Petrograd in January 1916 until the summer of 1917. Also refered to in this catalog as Society for the Encouragement of Jewish Art.

**Kamerny**   Popular name for the Jewish Chamber Theatre. Founded by Granovsky as a studio at the end of 1918 in Petrograd, formally named in 1919, and relocated to Moscow in 1921 (see GOSET).

**Kultur Lige**   A secular Yiddish cultural organization, founded in Kiev, 1918.

**Makhmadim**   The Precious Ones. Coined by the Hebrew writer Shlomo Zemach. A group of Jewish painters at La Ruche in Paris concerned with Jewish art. Also published *Makhmadim* (1912), considered the first Jewish art journal in the twentieth century.

**Mir iskusstva**   World of art group. Russian art society founded in 1898 to advance the cause of "art for art's sake."

**Narkompros**   People's Commissariat for Enlightenment. Established in November 1917 under the directorship of A. Lunacharsky. Responsible for general education, the organization of exhibitions, cultural publications, etc.

**IZO Narkompros**   Department of Visual Arts in the People's Commissariat for Enlightenment. Opened in April 1918 under the general directorship of David Shterenberg.

**OST**   Society of Easel Painters. Founded in Moscow, 1925.

**OZET**   Society for the Agricultural Employment of Working Jews. Established by the Soviet Government in January 1925.

**Peredvizhniki**   Wanderers. A group of artists who rejected the dominant art and sought in the 1870s and 1880s to express their populist social humanism by depicting only contemporary Russian subjects.

**Poalei Zion**   Workers of Zion. First organized in Ekaterinoslav, 1900.

**PROUN**   Project for the Affirmation of the New. Lissitzky's name for his experimental paintings of volumetrical and spatial arrangements, many of which he created in Vitebsk.

**RADA**   Grand Council (Parliament). General name of the first Ukrainian democratic government.

**RAKhN**   Russian Academy of Artistic Sciences. Formed during the summer of 1921 in Moscow.

**Shamir**   Circle of Jewish National Aesthetic. Organized in January 1918.

**Unovis**   Affirmation of the New Art. The name Malevich gave to the Vitebsk art school after he became director in 1919, replacing Chagall.

**VKhUTEMAS**   Higher State Art and Technical Studios. Formed in November 1920 from the Moscow Svomas (Free Art Studios).

**VKhUTEIN**   Higher State Artistic and Technical Institute. The new name given to VKhUTEMAS (1927).

**Yevsektsia**   Jewish section of the propaganda department of the Russian Communist Party (1918-1930).

# List of Illustrations

30 El Lissitzky. Cover of *Andersen's Mayselekh* (Andersen's Fairy Tales), cat. 85.

31 El Lissitzky(?). Cover of *Oksn* (Oxen) by I. Kipnis. Kiev: Widervuks, 1923.

32 El Lissitzky. "Schifs Karta" (Boat Ticket), cat. 105.

33 Issachar Ryback. Cover of *Foyglen* (Birds), cat. 137.

34 Issachar Ryback. Cover of *Karl un Mizra* (Karl and Mizra), cat. 140.

35 Joseph Tchaikov. Cover of *Der Galaganer Hon* (The Arrogant Rooster), cat. 63.

36 Joseph Tchaikov. Cover of *Bereishit* (In the Beginning), cat. 66.

37 Marc Chagall. "The Mikveh" (Ritual Bath), cat. 141.

38 Marc Chagall. "Cain and Abel," 1912, gouache on paper. Ida Chagall Collection, Paris.

39 Marc Chagall. "Adam and Eve," 1912, oil on canvas. St. Louis Art Museum.

40 Yehuda Pen. "Morning's Lesson in the Talmud," before 1912, *Ost und West*, vol. 12, 1912, p. 738.

41 Marc Chagall. "The Pinch of Snuff," c. 1912-13, oil on canvas. Private collection.

42 Marc Chagall. "Jew in Prayer," c. 1912-13, oil on canvas. Israel Museum, Jerusalem.

43 Yehuda Pen. "Shamash," before 1912, *Ost und West*, vol. 12, p. 743.

44 Marc Chagall. "Jew in Red," c. 1914-15, oil on cardboard. Charles Im Obersteg Collection, Geneva.

45 Marc Chagall. "Jew in Green," c. 1914-15, oil on cardboard. Charles Im Obersteg Collection, Geneva.

46 Josef Israels. "Son of an Ancient People," c. 1889. Stedelijk Museum, Amsterdam.

47 Rembrandt van Rijn. "Old Man in an Armchair," 1654. Hermitage, Leningrad.

48 Marc Chagall. "Jew in Black and White," c. 1914-15, oil on canvas. Museum of Modern Art, Venice.

49 Marc Chagall. "Sukkoth" (Feast of Tabernacles), c. 1917, gouache. Private collection.

50 "Seder," *Haggadah* of Mantua, 1560, *Ost und West*, vol. 4, 1904, p. 279.

51 Marc Chagall. "The Traveller," cat. 145.

52 Marc Chagall. "Collage," strips of paper and gouache on paper. Artist's estate.

53 Marc Chagall. "Dance," 1920-21, oil on canvas. Tretyakov Gallery, Moscow.

54 Marc Chagall. Sketch for the mural for the Jewish Theatre, detail, 1920-21. Artist's estate.

55 Photograph of the ceiling of the Mohilev Synagogue, cat. 173$_2$.

56 El Lissitzky. Cover illustration for K. Bolshakov's *The Spent Sun*, 1916. Pen and wash. George Costakis Collection.

57 El Lissitzky. Cover page illustration for M. Broderzon's *Legend of Prague*, cat. 73.

58 El Lissitzky. Illustration no. 3 for *Had Gadya*, 1917, watercolor. Tretyakov Gallery, Moscow.

59 El Lissitzky. Illustration no. 4 for *Had Gadya*, 1917, watercolor. Tretyakov Gallery, Moscow.

60 El Lissitzky. Illustration no. 7 for *Had Gadya*, 1917, watercolor. Tretyakov Gallery, Moscow.

61 El Lissitzky. Illustration no. 10 for *Had Gadya*, 1917, watercolor. Tretyakov Gallery, Moscow.

62 El Lissitzky. Vitebsk synagogue, cat. 75.

63 El Lissitzky. Emblem of "Yidish Ferlag," cat. 78.

64  El Lissitzky. Illustration for "Shlomo Hamelekh," cat. 77.

65  El Lissitzky. Illustration for *Yingl Tsingl Khvat* (The Mischievous Boy), cat. 79.

66  El Lissitzky. Last illustration in *Hob Ikh Mir a Lidele* (I Have a Little Song), Warsaw: Kultur Lige, 1922. Chimen Abramsky Collection.

67  El Lissitzky. Illustration for sheet music, cat. 82.

68  El Lissitzky. Emblem of Yidisher Folks Farlag, cat. 79.

69  El Lissitzky. Emblem of Yidisher Folks Farlag.

70  El Lissitzky. Emblem of Kiever Farlag, cat. 81.

71  El Lissitzky. Illustration no. 1 for *Had Gadya*, 1918-19, cat. 87.

72  El Lissitzky. Illustration no. 1 for *Had Gadya*, c. 1918, cat. 86.

73  El Lissitzky. Illustration no. 10 for *Had Gadya*, 1919, cat. 89.

74  El Lissitzky. Dustjacket for *Had Gadya* (inside), 1919, color lithograph. Private collection.

75  El Lissitzky. Dustjacket for *Had Gadya* (outside), 1919, color lithograph. Private collection.

76  El Lissitzky. Cover illustration for *Di Hun Vos Hot Gevolt Hoben a Kam* (The Hen That Wanted a Comb), cat. 95.

77  El Lissitzky. "The Flying Ship," cat. 98.

78  Photograph of drawing of ship by Lissitzky, from the Mohilev Synagogue, cat. 173.

79  El Lissitzky. Front-to-back cover illustration for *Vaysrusishe Folkmayses* (White Russian Folktales), cat. 108.

80  El Lissitzky. Front-to-back cover illustration for Ukraynishe Folkmayses (Ukrainian Folktales), cat. 103.

81  El Lissitzky. Title page (1922) for *Yingl Tsingl Khvat* (The Mishievous Boy), cat. 104.

82  Marc Chagall. Introduction to the Jewish Theatre, 1920-21, oil on canvas. Tretyakov Gallery, Moscow.

83  Marc Chagall. Sketch for stage design of Shalom Aleichem's *The Agents*, Jewish Chamber Theatre, 1920, pencil and watercolor on paper. Artist's estate.

84  Marc Chagall. Photo showing stage set for Shalom Aleichem's *The Agents*, Jewish Chamber Theatre.

85  Marc Chagall. Sketch for stage design of Shalom Aleichem's *Mazeltov*, Jewish Chamber Theatre, 1920, oil on cardboard. Artist's estate.

86  Natan Altman. Stage design for S. An-Sky's *The Dybbuk*, Habimah, cat. 19.

87  Natan Altman. Photo showing stage set for S. An-Sky's *The Dybbuk*, Act III, Habimah, 1922.

88  Natan Altman. Costume design for S. An-Sky's *The Dybbuk*, Habimah, cat. 26.

89  Natan Altman. Costume design for S. An-Sky's *The Dybbuk*, Habimah, cat. 25.

90  Natan Altman. Stage set for Carl Gutzkov's *Uriel Accosta*, Jewish Chamber Theatre, 1922.

91  Isaac Rabinovich. Stage set for Abraham Goldfaden's *The Sorceress*, Jewish Chamber Theatre, 1922.

92  Isaac Rabinovich. Photo showing stage set for Abraham Goldfaden's *The Sorceress*, Jewish Chamber Theatre, 1922.

93  Isaac Rabitchev. Photo showing stage set for tailor's workshop, for the musical comedy *200,000*, Jewish Chamber Theatre, 1923.

94  Robert Falk. Photo showing stage set for Y. L. Peretz's *Night in the Old Market*, Jewish State Theatre (GOSET), 1925.

95  Robert Falk. Sketch for Y. L. Peretz's *Night in the Old Market*, Jewish State Theatre (GOSET), 1925.

96   Abram Efros, 1920s. Photo reproduced in M.V. Tolmachev (ed.), *A. M. Efros*, Moscow: Sovetskii Khudozhnik, 1979, p. 5.

97   Page from Abram Efros (translator), *Song of Songs*, St. Petersburg: Pantheon, 1909.

98   Planche X from *L'Ornement Hébreu*, cat. 159.

99   Vladimir Favorsky. Frontispiece and title page for *The Book of Ruth* (in Russian), Moscow: Sabashnikov, 1925.

100  Yakov Tugendkhold, c. 1925. Photo reproduced in Ya. Tugendkhold: *The Art of the October Epoch* (in Russian), Leningrad: Academy, 1930.

# Bibliography

Abramsky, Chimen. "Eliezer Lissitzky (1890-1941)." *Jewish Quarterly*, vol. 9, no. 1 (1962).
—. "El Lissitzky as Jewish Illuminator and Typographer." *Studio International*, vol. 172, no. 882 (October 1966).
—. "The Rise and Fall of Soviet Yiddish Literature." *Soviet Jewish Affairs*, vol. 12, no. 3 (1982).
—. "Russian Jews." *Midstream* (1978).
Altman, Nathan. "Das Plastische Element in der Theater Dekoration, Des Staatlichen Jüdischen Kammerspiel Theater, Moscow." *Kunstchronik und Kunstmarkt* (Leipzig), vol. 58 (December 1922).
—. *Evreiskaia grafika*. Berlin: Petropolis, 1923.
—. *Jüdische Graphik*. Berlin: Razum-Verlag, 1923.
Amishai, Ziva. "Chagall's Jerusalem Windows: Iconography and Sources." *Scripta Hierosolymitana, Studies in Art*, (Jerusalem), vol. 24 (1972).
Amishai-Maisels, Ziva. "Chagall's Jewish In-Jokes." *Journal of Jewish Art*, vol. 5 (1978).
. "The Jewish Jesus." *Journal of Jewish Art*, vol. 9, (1982)
—. *Gauguin's Religious Themes*. New York: Garland, 1985.
Anderson, Troels. *Moderne Russisk Kunst 1910-1930*. Copenhagen: Borgen, 1967.
Andreev, Leonid, Maxim Gorky, and Fedor Sologub. *Shchit*. Moscow, 1915.
    (Two numbers of literary miscellany.)
An-Sky, S. *Dos Yidishe Etnografishe Program*. St. Petersburg, 1914.
—. "Evreiskoe nardnoe tvorchestvo." *Perezhitoe* (St. Petersburg), vol. 1 (1909).
Antokolsky, Lev. "Jurij Paen." *Novyi voskhod*, no. 38 (1912).
—. "Jurij Paen." *Ost und West*, vol. 12 (August 1912).
—. *Maliarnoe delo*. Moscow: VZITO, 1933.
—. *Novyi voskhod*. (St. Petersburg), no. 16 (April 1914).
—. "O rabotakh etnograficheskoi ekspeditsii." *Evreiskaia starina*, vol. 8 (St. Petersburg?), (1915).
—. *Programma kruzhkov po izucheniiu maliarnykh rabot*. Moscow: Central Committee of the Union of Construction Works, 1928.
—. *Spravochnik po maliarnym rabotam*. Moscow and Leningrad: Gosstzouzdat, 1933.
Apter-Gabriel, Ruth. "A Drawing Comes to Light: The Ceiling of the Mohilev Synagogue by Ryback." *Israel Museum News* (Jerusalem), vol. 6 (1987).
Arkin, David Efimovich. "Falk i moskovskaia zhivopis." *Russkoe iskusstvo* (Moscow and St. Petersburg), no. 2-3 (1923).
—. *Iskusstvo bytovoi veshchi*. Moscow: Izogiz, 1932.
—. *Keramika Frikh-Khara*. Moscow: Gizlegpzom, 1934.
—. *Obrazy skulptury*. Moscow: Iskusstvo, 1961.
Aronson, Boris. *Marc Chagall*. Berlin: Razum, 1924.
—. *Sovremyennaya Evreiskaya Grafika*. Berlin, 1924.
Aronson, Khil. "Bilder un geshtalth fun Montparnasse." Paris, 1963.
Aronson, N. Discussion of the Jewish artist. Manuscript owned by his widow, Mrs. Naum Aronson of New York City.
Arvatov, B. *Nathan Altman*. Berlin, 1924.
Aster, Howard. *Jewish-Ukrainian Relations: Two Solitudes*. Oakville, Ontario: Mosaic Press, 1983.
S. B. "Die 'Hagade'." *Ost und West*, vol. 1 (April 1901).
Bakst, Leo. "Puti Klassitzizma v Iskusstv." *Apollon*, no. 3 (1909).
Balaban, B. "Evreiskie istoricheskie pamiatniki v Polishe." *Evreiskaia starina* (St. Petersburg), vol. 1 (1909).
Ben-Ari, Raikin. *Habima*. New York, 1957.
Benois, A. "Po povodu 'Evreiskoi vystavki'." *Rech* (Petrograd), no. 109 (April 1916).
Bergelson, David. "Dikhtung un Gezelshaftlikhkayt." *Bikher-Velt* (Kiev), 4-5 (1919).
Beskin, E. "Altman, Shagal, Shterenberg." *Izvestiia VTsIK i Mossoveta* (Moscow), no. 115 (May 1922).
Bialik, Chaim Nachman and Max Osborn. *L. Pasternak*. Berlin: Stybel, 1924.
Billington, James. *The Icon and the Axe*. New York: Vintage Books, 1970 (originally published in 1966).
Birnholz, Alan. "El Lissitzky." Yale University Ph.D. dissertation 1973. Ann Arbor: University Microfilms, 1974.
—. "El Lissitzky and the Jewish Tradition." *Studio International* (London), vol. 186, no. 959 (October 1973).
Bowlt, John. "A Child's Topography of Typography." *Art News* (New York), vol. 81, no. 7 (September 1982).
—. *Russian Art of the Avant-Garde: Theory and Criticism 1902-1934*. New York: Viking, 1976.
—. *The Silver Age: Russian Art of the Early Twentieth Century and the "World of Art" Group*. Massachusetts: Oriental Research Partners, 1979.
Braun, Joachim. *Jews and Jewish Elements in Soviet Music*. Tel Aviv: Israeli Music Publications, 1978.
Brazer, G. "Yehuda Pen." *Shtern* (Minsk), no. 4 (1937).
Bredius, A., and H. Gerson. *Rembrandt Paintings*. London: Phaidon, 1971.
Breunig, Leroy C., ed. *Apollinaire on Art: Essays and Reviews, 1902-1918*. London: Thames and Hudson, 1972.
Brieger-Wasservogel, Lothar. "Elias Jacowlewitsch Guenzburg." *Ost und West*, vol. 4 (March 1904).
Brodsky, V. and A. Zemtsova. *Solomon Borisovich Yudovin*. Leningrad: Khudozhnik RSFSR, 1962.
Burko, Faina. "The Soviet Yiddish Theatre in the Twenties." Ph.D. dissertation, Southern Illinois University at Carbondale, 1978.
Butorin, ed. *Vystarki Sovetskogo Isobrazitel'nogo iskuysstva spravocnik*. Moscow: Sovetskii Khudozhnik, 1965.
Carr, E. H. *The Bolshevik Revolution, 1917-1923* (3 vols.). London, 1950-53.
Chagall, Bella. *Nerot Dolkim*. Tel Aviv: Dvir, 1970.
Chagall, Marc. *Bilderbuecher*. Berlin, 1923.

—. "Blettlach." *Shtrom*, no. 1, 1922 (reprinted with minor changes in "Eygns." *Die Zukunft*, June 1925).

—. "Eygns." *Vitebsk Amol*, ed. Gregor Aronson. New York, 1956.

—. "Mein Arbet in Moskver Yidishen Kamer-theater." *Die Yidishe Velt*, no. 2 (May 1928). Reprinted in *Die Geldene Keit*, no. 43 (1962).

—. "Moi pervie uchitelya." *Rassviet* (Paris), no. 4 (1927).

—. "My First Teacher. For the Jubilee of the Artist Y. Pen." *Shtern* (in Yiddish) (Minsk) no. 3, (1927).

—. *My Life*. New York: Orion Press, 1960.

—. "O Vitebskom narodnom khudozhestvennom uchilishche." *Shkola i revoliutsiia* (Vitebsk), no. 24-25 (1919).

—. "Pamiati Ya. A. Tugendkholda." *Iskusstvo* (1928).

—. "Pamyat: M. M. Vinavera." *Rassviet* (Paris), no. 43 (1923).

Chamot, Mary. *Goncharova, Stage Designs and Paintings*. London: Oresko, 1979.

Cherikov, I. *Istoriia obshchestva dlia rasprostzaneniia mezhdu evreiami v Rossii 1963-1913*. St. Petersburg: Fleishman, 1913 (vol. 1, [no others published]).

Cogniat, R. *I. Ryback*. Paris, 1935.

Compton, Susan. *Chagall*. London: Royal Academy of Arts, 1985.

—. *The Russian Background in Chagall*. London: Royal Academy of Arts, 1985.

—. *The World Backwards. Russian Futurist Books, 1912-1916*. London: British Library, 1978.

Davidovitch, David. *Tziyurai Kir B'vatai Knesset B'Polyn*. Jerusalem: Bialik Institute, 1968.

Dawidowicz, Lucy, ed. *The Golden Tradition*. Boston: Beacon Press, 1967.

Deich, A. "Krakh proletarskogo iskusstva." *Teatralnaia zhizn* (Kiev), no. 18 (1918).

—. *Maski evreiskogo teatra*. Moscow: Russkoe teatralnoe obshchestvo, 1927.

Der Nister. *Hanazir V'Hag'diya*. Jerusalem: Bialik Institute, 1963.

Diebold, Bernhard. *Habima Hebraeisches Theater*. Berlin, 1922.

Dobrushin, Yeheskiel. "Kunst-primitiv un kunst-bukh far kinder." *Bikher-Velt* (Kiev), no. 4-5 (August 1919).

Dubnov, Simon. *History of the Jews*. New York: Thomas Yoseloff, 1973.

Edvabnyi, F. "Zametki dilletanta. Evreiskii teatr i Klara Yung." *Teatr i kino* (Odessa), no. 6 (1917).

Efros, A. "Almanakh molodykh pisateli Khmel, Kn. I." *Utro Rossii* (Moscow), no. 243 (October 1911).

—. "Bibleiskaia lirika." Vostok (book 2) (Leningrad–Moscow) (1923).

—. "D. Kokovtsov: Vechnyi potok. Vtoraia kniga stikhov." *Utro Rossii* (Moscow), no. 243 (October 1911).

—. "Izrael Zangvill. Komedii Getto. Mechtateli i Fantazery Getoo." *Utro Rossii* (Moscow), no. 5 (January 1911).

—. "Khudozhniki teatra Granovskogo." *Iskusstvo* (books 1-2) (Moscow) (1928).

—. *Kniga Ruf. (Graviury V. Favorskogo)*. Moscow: Sabashnikovy, 1925 (translator and author of postface).

—. "Lampa Aladina." *Evreiskii mir Literaturnye sborniki* (*Ereiskaia starina*) (book 1) (Moscow) (1918).

—. "Leon Perets. Sobranie sochinenii, T. I. Iz ust naroda." *Utro Rossii* (Moscow), no. 237 (October 1911).

—. "Les fresques de V. Favorsky." *Le Journal de Moscou* (Moscow), no. 39.

—. "Pavel Geize. Deti veka. Sobranie sochinenii." *Utro Rossii* (Moscow), no. 110 (May 1911).

—. *Portret Natana Altmana*. Moscow: Shipovnik, 1922.

—. *Profili*. Moscow: Federatsiia, 1930.

—. "Sholom Aleikhem: Sobranie sochineno. T. V. Neunyvaiushchie." *Utro Rossii* (Moscow), no. 86 (April 1911).

—. "V. Favorsky i sovremennaia ksilografiia." *Russkoe iskusstvo*. no. 1 (1923) (partially republished in Yu. Molok, Kinga).

—. "Zametki ob iskusstve." *Novyi put* (Moscow), no. 48-49 (1916).

—. "Zhizn iskusstva." *Russkie vedemosti* (Moscow), no. 84 (April 1917).

Efros, A. (translation and commentary), and V. Rosanov, (preface). *Pesn pesnei Solomona*. St. Petersburg: Pantheon, 1909. (Second edition appeared in 1910.)

Efros, A. and Ya. Tugendkhold. *Iskusstvo Marka Shagala*. Moscow: Gelikon, 1918.

Efros, A und J. Tugendkhold. *Die Kunst Marc Chagals*. Berlin-Potsdam: Kiepenheuer, 1921 (translation from the 1918 Russian edition).

Ehrenburg, Ilya (translated by Tatonia Shebunina). *Memoirs 1921-1941*. Cleveland and New York: The World Publishing Company, 1963.

Emgal. "Syn 'Cherty'." *Novyi put*, no. 15 (1916).

Erben, Walter. *Marc Chagall*. New York: Frederick A. Praeger, 1957.

Etkind, Mark Gregorievich. *Nathan Altman* (in Russian). Moscow: Sovetskii Khudozhnik, 1971.

—. *Nathan Altman*. Dresden: VEB Verlag der Kunst, 1984 (based on the 1971 Russian edition).

Ettinger, Shmuel. "The Position of Jews in Soviet Culture. A Historical Survey." In *Jews in Soviet Culture*, ed. Jack Miller. London, 1984.

—. "The Jews in Russia at the Outbreak of the Revolution." In *The Jews in Soviet Russia since 1917*, ed. Lionel Kochan. Oxford, 1970.

Fabian, Max. "Emigrants of 1902." *Ost und West*, vol. 4 (June 1904).

Frankl, Giza. *Migzerot Niyar*. Givataim: Massada, 1983.

Frenkel, Borvine. *Mit Yidishe Kinstler*. Paris: Yidisher Kultur-Kongres in Frankraykh, 1963.

Friedberg, Haia. "Lissitzky's Had Gadîa." Jewish Art (formerly, *Journal of Jewish Art*) (Jerusalem), vol. 12/13 (1986-87), pp. 293-303.

Frost, Matthew. "Marc Chagall and the Jewish State Chamber Theater." *Russian History*, vol. 8, pt. 1-2 (1981). Furman, ed. *Vitebsk v gravjnri S*. Yudovina. Vitebsk, 1926.

George, W. *Boris Aronson et l'art du théâtre*. Paris, 1928.

Georges, W., and I. Ehrenburg. *Nathan Altman*. Paris, 1933.

Gessen, Yu. *Istoriia evreev v Rossii*. St. Petersburg: Pravo, 1906.

Gilula, Debora. "Natan Altman – Tzayar 'Hadybbuk'". *Bamah*, nos. 101-2 (1985).

Ginsburg, Saul. *Amoike Petersburg*. New York: Cyco Farlag, 1944.

Gintsburg, I. A letter to M. Antokolski. Central State Archive of Literature and Art. Moscow (F. 698, op. I, ed. khr. 7, 11. 1-9).

—. *Iz moei zhizni*. St. Petersburg: Trud, 1908.

—. *Iz proshlogo*. Leningrad: Gosizdat, 1924.
—. "Tolstoi i evrei." *Novyi voskhod* (St. Petersburg), no. 34 (1910).
—. Untitled note on Savelii Zeidenberg. *Novyi voskhod* (St. Petersburg), no. 9 (1910).
—. Untitled note on the synagogue in St. Petersburg. *Novyi voskhod* (St. Petersburg), no. 10 (1910).
Ginzburg, G., ed. *Evreiskii vestnik*. Leningrad: Society for the Dissemination of Enlightenment Among Jews, 1928.
Girtovich. Manual on Hebrew Calligraphy. Vilnius: Tegudiia, 1914.
Gitelman, Zvi Y. *Jewish Nationality and Soviet Politics*. Princeton: Princeton University Press, 1972.
Goldelman, Salomon. *Jewish National Autonomy in Ukraine, 1917-1920*. Chicago: Ukrainian Research Information Institute, 1968.
Goldschmidt, Alfons. "Das Jüdische Theater in Moskau." *Das Moskauer Jüdische Akademische Theater* (Berlin) (1928).
Gollerbakh, E., and L. Ioffe. *S. Yudovin, Gravjuri na dereve*. Leningrad: Academy of Arts, 1928.
Golomstock, Igor. "Jews in Soviet Art." In *Jews in Soviet Culture*, ed. Jack Miller. London, 1984.
Gorchakov, Nikolai. *The Theater in Soviet Russia*. New York, 1957.
Gordon, Donald E. *Modern Art Exhibitions, 1900-1916*. Munchen: Prestel-Verlag, 1974.
Granovsky, Alexander. "Dos Yidishe Kamer Teater." *Yidishe Teatrale Gesellshaft*. Petrograd, 1919.
Gray, Camilla. *The Great Experiment: Russian Art, 1863-1922*. London: Thames and Hudson, 1962 (published in New York: Harry N. Abrams, 1971).
Grunwald, Max. "Portugiesengraeber auf Deutscher Erde." *Ost und West*, vol. 2 (1902).
Guerman, Mikhail, ed. *Art of the October Revolution*. Leningrad-London, 1979.
Guinzberg, I. Article on Jewish national art. *Ost und West*, vol. 5 (October-December 1905).
Haftmann, Werner. *Marc Chagall*. New York: Harry N. Abrams, 1972.
Ioffe, Ieremii Isaevich. *Sinteticheskaia istoriia iskusstva*. Leningrad: Ogiz-Izogiz, 1933.
—. *Krizis sovremennogo iskusstva*. Leningrad: Priboi, 1925.
Ivask, U. *Evreiskaia periodicheskaia pechat v Rossii*. Tallin: Society of Friends of the Yiddish Scientific Institute, 1935.
Jacobs, Monty. "200,000 Im Theater Des Westens." *Vossische Zeitung* (Berlin), 4-12 (1928).
Kamensky, A. "Skazochno-groteskovye motivy v tvorchestve Marka Shagala." In *Primitiv iego mesto v khudozhestvennom kulture novogo i noveishego vremeni*. ed. V. Prokofiev. Moscow: Nauka, 1983.
Kampf, Avram. *Jewish Experience in the Art of the Twentieth Century*. Massachusetts: Bergin and Garvey, 1984.
—. "In Quest of Jewish Style in the Era of the Russian Revolution." *Journal of Jewish Art* (Jerusalem), vol. 5 (1978).
Karshan, Donald. *Malevich, The Graphic Work: 1913-1930*. Jerusalem: Israel Museum, 1975.
Kerr, Alfred. "The Jewish Academic Theatre of Moscow." *Berliner Tageblatt* (April 1928).
Khlebnikov, V. *Sobranie sochinenii*. Leningrad: Sovetskii pisatel, 1930.
Khodasevich, Vladislav and L. B. Yaffe, eds., Mikhail Gershenzon (Introduction). *Evreiskaia antologiia. Sbornik molodi poezii*. Moscow: Safrut, 1918.
Kirichenko, E. *Arkhitekturnye teorii XIX veka v Rossii*. Moscow: Iskusstvo, 1986.
Koenig, Leo. *Folk un Literatur*. London, 1947.
—. Manuscript in the Archives of the Jewish National and University Library, Jerusalem (no. 4°1269/173).
Kogan, P. S. "Gosudarstvennaia Akademiia Khudozhestvennykh Nauk." *Pechat i Revoliutsiia* (Moscow), no 7 (1927).
—. "Kniga na vystavke iskusstva narodov SSSR." *Pechat i Revoliutsiia*, (Moscow) (1927).
Kondratiev, A. I. "Rossiiskaia Akademiia Khudozhestvennykh Nauk." *Iskusstvo* (Moscow), no. 1 (1923).
Kornfeld, Eberhard W. *Verzeichnis der Kupferstiche, Radierungen und Holzschitte von Marc Chagall*. Berne: Kornfeld und Klipstein, 1970 (vol. 1).
Kutna, G. "Jozef Israels." *Ost und West*, vol. 2 (August-September 1911).
Kuzmin, E. "Laborantskoe iskusstvo." *Iskusstvo* (Kiev), no. 5 (1922).
Lavrsky, Nikolai. *Iskusstvo i evrei*. Moscow: Zhizn, 1915.
Lebedev, A., ed. Skulptor Ilia Gintsburg. *Vospominaiia. Stati Pisma*. Leningrad: Khudozhnik RSFSR, 1964.
Levitin, E., ed. *Ob iskusstve, o knige, o graviure*. Moscow: Kniga, 1986.
Lichtenshtein, Yitzhak. "Vitebsker Kinstler." In *Vitebsk Amol*, ed. Gregor Aronson. New York, 1956.
Lissitzky, El. "Novaia kultura." *Shkola i revoliutsiia* (Vitebsk), no. 24-25 (1919).
—. "Memoirs Concerning the Mohilev Synagogue." *Milgroim* (in Yiddish) and Rimon (in Hebrew) (Berlin), no. 3, (1923).
—. *Victory Over the Sun*. Hanover, 1923.
Lissitzky-Küppers, Sophie. *El Lissitzky*. London: Thames and Hudson, 1968 (1980 edition).
—. *El Lissitzky – Maler Architect Typograf Fotograf*. Dresden, 1967.
Litvakov, Moshe. *Finf yor Melukhisher Yidisher Kamer Teater, 1919-1925*. Moscow, 1924.
Lodder, Christina. *Russian Constructivism*. New Haven and London: Yale University Press, 1983.
Lozowick, Louis. "The Art of Nathan Altman." *Menorah Journal*, no. 12 (1966).
—. "Moscow Theatre 1920." In *Russian History*, vol. 8, pt. 1-2, 1981.
Malevich, Kasimir. *Supermatizm*. Vitebsk, 1920.
—. *Essays on Art, 1915-1928* (2 vols.). Copenhagen, 1971.
Malkin, M., and S. Yudovin. *Yidishe Folks-Ornament*. Vitebsk: Y. L. Peretz Society, 1920.
Marcadé, Jean-Claude. "Le contexte russe de l'oeuvre de Chagall." *Marc Chagall*. Paris: Centre Georges Pompidou, 1984.
—. "Chronologie du futurisme russe." *Europe*, vol. 53 (April 1975).
Marek, P. *Ocherbi po istorii prosvesncheniia evreev v Rossii*. Moscow: Society for the Dissemination of Correct Information on Jews, 1909.
Markov, P. A. *The Soviet Theater*. London, 1934.
Meyer, Franz. *Marc Chagall, Life and Work*. Cologne: Verlag M. Dumont Schauberg, 1961 (in German), Paris: Flammarion, 1961 (in French). New York: Harry N. Abrams, 1963 (in English).
Milner, John. *Vladimir Tatlin and the Russian Avant-Garde*. New Haven and London: Yale University Press, 1983.

Molok, Yu. *Kniga. Vladimire Favorskom*. Moscow: Progress, 1967.

Nakov, Andrei. *Avant-garde russe*. Paris, 1986.

Niger, Shmuel. "Lirishe Siluetn." *Tsukunft* (New York), vol. 25, no. 8 (1920).

Norman, Yitzhak, ed. *Bereishit Habima. Nahum Zemach Meyased Habima Bahazon U'Be'ma'as*. Jerusalem, 1967.

Nossig, Alfred. "Austellung Jüdischer Künstler." *Ost und West*, vol. 7 (December 1907).

Nusenbaum, Sh. B. *Evreyski nagrobine goroda lyublina* (XVI-XIX centuries). St. Petersburg: Lire, 1913.

Olkhovsky, Yuri. *Vladimir Stassov and Russian National Culture*. Ann Arbor, Michigan: UMI Research Press, 1983.

Osborne, Max. *Jüdische Graphik*. Petropolis: Reiner, 1923.

Patai, Fr. Dr. "Der Maler der jüdischen Mutter." *Aus alter und neuer Zeit* (January 1931).

Picon-Vallin, Beatrice. *Le théâtre juif soviétique pendant les années vingt*. Lausanne: La Cité-L'Age d'Or, 1973.

Pilichowski, L. "Jozef Israels." *Ost und West*, vol. 2 (August-September 1911).

Pozharskaya, M. *Nisson Abramovich Shifrin*. Moscow: Sovetskii Khudozhnik, 1971.

Prokofiev, V., ed. *Primitiv iego mesto v khudozhestvennom kulture novogo i noveishego vremeni*. Moscow: Nauka, 1983.

Rabinovich. Letter to Shifrin dated 19 April. Central State Archive of Literature and Art. Moscow: Fund 2422,
    opus 1, ed. khr. 311, 1. 5.

Rakitin, V. "El Lissitzky 1890-1941." In *O. A. Shvidkovsky, Building in the USSR, 1917-1932*. New York: Praeger, 1971.

Rapoport, S. "Religioznoe i svetskoe vospitanie." *Novyi voskhod*, no. 19 (1910).

Rejzen, Zalman. *Leksikon fun der Yiddishel Literatur Presse un Filologie* (4 vols.). Wilno, 1928-30.

Rokhlin, L. *Mestechko Krasnopolie Mogilevskoi gub*. St. Petersburg: Sever, 1909

Romm, A. *Di Roite Velt* (Moscow) nos. 5-6 (on Falk) and 10 (on Tchaikov) (1926).

Roth, Joseph. *Das Moskauer Jüdische Akademische Theater*. Berlin, 1928.

Rudenstine, Angelica Zander, ed. *The George Costakis Collection. Russian Avant-Garde Art*. New York: Harry N. Abrams, 1981.

Ryback, I., and B. Aronson. "Di Vegn fun der Yidisher maleray." *Oyfgang* (Kiev), first collection, (1919).

S. M. (untitled) in *Novyi voskhod*, no. 28 (October 1910).

Saminsky, L. *Ob evreiskoi muzyke*. St. Petersburg, 1914.

Samuel, Ben. "Synagogale Kunst." *Ost und West*, vol. 3 (June 1903).

"Samuel Hirszenberg." *Ost und West*, vol. 4 (October 1904).

Sarabjanow, Dimitri. *Robert Falk*. Dresden, 1974.

Schwartz, Marek. "The National Element in Jewish Art." *Literarishe Bleter* (Warsaw) vol. 1, no. 48 (April 1925).

Segal, Binjamin. "Synagogale Kunst." *Ost und West*, vol. 1 (April 1909).

Shachar, Yeshayahu. *Osef Feuchtwanger: Massoret V'Omanut Yehudit*. Jerusalem: Israel Museum, 1971.

Shargorodskaia, F. "O nasledii An-skogo." *Evreiskaia starina* (St. Petersburg[?]), vol. 2 (1924).

Sheyn, Yosef. *Arum Moskver Yidishn Teater*. Paris: Les Editions Polyglottes, 1964.

Shmeruk, Chone, ed. *Jewish Publications in the Soviet Union, 1917-1960, Hapirsumim Be'Yiddish*. Jerusalem, 1961.

—. "Yiddish Literature in the U.S.S.R." In *The Jews in the Soviet Russian Since 1917*, ed. L. Kochan. Oxford, 1970.

—. ed. *A Shpigel oyf a Shtein*. Tel Aviv, 1965.

Shmidt, I. *Iosif Chaikov*. Moscow: Izd. Sovetskii Khudozhnik, 1977.

Shmidt, O., ed. *Bolshaia sovetskaia entsiklopediia*. Moscow: Ogiz, 1934.

Sidney, Alexander. *Marc Chagall*. London: Cassell, 1978.

Silver, Kenneth. *The Circle of Montparnasse: Jewish Artists in Paris, 1905-1945*. New York: Universe Books, 1985.

Slonim, Marc. *Russian Theater*. New York, 1961.

Sokolov, B."Ya. A. Tugendkhold i iskusstvo narodov SSSR." *Iskusstvo* (Moscow) (1928).

Sorlier, Charles, ed. *Chagall by Chagall*. Tel Aviv: Steimatzky, 1979.

Stassof, V. "Evreiskoe plemia v sozdaniiakh evropeiskogo iskusstva." *Evreiskaia biblioteka* (St. Petersburg), vol. 3 (1873), vol. 5
    (1875), vol. 6 (1878).

Stassof, V. and D. Gunzburg. *Drevne-evreiskii ornament po rukopisiam*. St. Petersburg, 1886.

—. *L'Ornement Hébreu*. Berlin: S. Calvary Co., 1905.

Sternin, G. "Yakov Alexandrovich Tugendkhold." *Sovetskoe iskusstvoznanie* (Moscow) (1978).

Syrkin, M. "Doklad o evreiskom iskusstve v Evreisko – Istoriko – Etnograficheskom Obshchestve." *Novyi voskhod* (St. Petersburg),
    no. 2 (1911).

—. "Drevinie derviannye sinagogi v Polshe i Litve." *Novyi voskhod* (St. Petersburg), no. 11 (1910).

—. "Iskusstvo i evrei." *Evreiskaia nedelia* (Moscow), nos. 25, 26 (1916).

—. "Mark Shagal." *Evreiskaia nedelia* (Moscow), no. 20 (1916).

—. "Vystavki." *Novyi voskhod* (St. Petersburg), no. 10 (1911).

Syrkina, F. *Alexander Grigorievich Tyshler* Moscow: Sovetskii Khudozhnik, 1966.

—. *Issaak Rabinovich*. Moscow: Sovetskii Khudozhnik, 1972.

Tarabukin, N. "Altman, Shagal, Shterenberg." *Vestnik iskusstva* (Moscow), no. 5 (1922).

Tolmachev, M., ed. *A. M. Efros. Dva veka russkogo iskusstva*. Moscow: Iskusstvo, 1969.

—. *A. M. Efros. Mastera raznykh epoch*. Moscow: Sovetskii Khudozhnik, 1979.

Trunk, Isaiah. "Historians of Russian Jewry." In *Russian Jewry*, eds. J. Frumkin, Gregor Aronson, and Alexis Goldenweiser. New
    York: Thomas Yoseloff, 1966.

Tchaikov, Joseph. *Skulptur*. Kiev: Metukhe Farlag, 1921.

Tugendkhold, Yakov Alexandrovich. "Iskusstvo narodov SSSR." *Pechat i revoliutsiia* (Moscow) (1927).

—. *Iskusstvo oktiabrskoi epokhi*. Moscow: Akademiia, 1930.

—. "Iskusstvo SSSR i natsionalyi element." *Novyi mir* (Moscow), no. 8 (1925).

—. "K proizvedeniiam R. Falka." *Krasnaia niva* (Moscow), no. 17 (1924).

—. "Mark Shagal." *Apollon* (Petrograd), no. 2 (1916).

Venturi, Lionello. *Chagall.* Geneva: Albert Skira, 1956.

Vinaver, Maxim. *Nedavnee. Vospominaniia i kharakteristiki.* Petrograd: Yakor, 1917.

Voronova, O. *V. I. Mukhina.* Moscow: Iskusstvo, 1976.

Waldemar, George. *Larionov.* Paris: Bibliothèque des Arts, 1966.

Waldmann, Mojzesc. *Maurycy Gottlieb* (in Polish). Cracow: Narodowa, 1932.

Weissenberg, S. Jüdische Kunst und Jüdisches Kultur-und Hausgeraet." *Ost und West,*vol. 3 (March 1903).

Williams, Robert C. *Artists in Revolution.* Bloomington: Indiana University Press, 1977.

Winternitz, Josef. "Der alte Prager Jüdische Friedhof." *Ost und West,* vol. 4. (February 1904).

Wischnitzer, Rachel. *The Architecture of the European Synagogue.* Philadelphia: Jewish Publication Society of America, 1964.

——. "Umschau: Jüdische Kunst in Kiev and Petrograd (1918-1920)." *Der Jude* (Berlin), vol. 5 (1920-21).

——. "The Wise Men of Worms." *Reconstructionist,* vol. 25, no. 9 (June 1959).

With, Karl. *Marc Chagall.* Leipzig: Klinkhanrdt and Biermann, 1923.

Wolfe, Bertram D. *The Russian Revolution.* Ann Arbor, 1961.

Wolitz, Seth L. "The Kiev-Grupe, 1918-1920, Debates the Function of Literature." *Modern Jewish Studies, Annual Two* (New York) (1978).

Yashunskii, I. *Evreiskaia periodicheskaia pechat v 1917 i 1918.* Petrograd: Vestnik, 1918.

Zadkine, Ossip. *Le maillet et le ciseau: souvenirs de ma vie.* Paris: Editions Albin Michel, 1968.

Zhadova, Larissa A. *Malevich: Suprematism and Revolution in Russian Art 1910-1930.* London: Thames and Hudson, 1982.

Zlocisti, Theodor. "Die Haggadah von Mantua (1560)." *Ost und West,* vol. 4 (April 1904).

Zuskin, Benjamin. "Wi Mir Hoben Gearbet Oyf Perez's *Bei Nacht Oyfn Altn Mark.*" *Literarische Blatter* (Warsaw) (1928).

Author unknown. *Evreiskii narodnyi universitet. Ocennii semestr 1920-21 (III akademicheskii god).* Moscow: Narkompros (People's Commissariat for Enlightenment), 1921.

## Miscellaneous Periodical Entries

*Der Emes.* Moscow, 11 August and 20 October 1918.

*Der Freytog.* Berlin, no. 2, August 1, 1919.

*Der iskusstva.* Vilna, 1914.

*Der Yidisher Artist* (cultural review). Kharkov, 1918.

*Di Yidishe Velt.* St. Petersburg, no. 1, 1912.

*Evreiskaia nedelia.* Nos. 6, 21, 13, and 51, 1916; nos. 47-48 1917.

*Evreiskaia starina.* Supplement to: vol. 8, 1915: vol. 9, 1916, vol. 10, 1918, and vol. 11, 1924,

*Evreiskaia starina voskhod.* St. Petersburg, 1881-1906.

*Germes.* Kiev, 1919.

*Kultur un Bildung (cultural review).* Moscow: Cultural-Enlightenment Section of the Jewish Commissariat, nos. 3-4, 6 September 1918; no. 1 (24), 1920.

*Kultur Lige Bulletin 2.* Kiev, June-July 1920.

*Kultur Lige Zamlung.* Kiev, November 1919.

*Mir iskusstva.* St. Petersburg, 1898-1905.

*Novyi put.* No. 28, 1911; and nos. 9, 13-14 (23 April), 18, 36-37, and 50, 1916.

*Novyi voskhod.* St. Petersburg, no. 10, 1910; nos. 16, 27, 33, and 51, 1911; and nos. 10-11, 1915.

*Ost und West.* vol. 1, 1901; vol. 2, 1902; vol. 3, 1903; vol. 4, July 1904; and vol. 5, 1905.

*Oyf der Vakh.* Kiev, 12 July 1918, no. 9; 24 May 1918; 7 June, 1918, no. 6.

*Rabochii zhurnal.* Kiev, no. 1 1919.

*Safrut (3 collections).* Moscow, 1917, 1918 (front covers by Altman and back covers by Lissitzky).

*Teatr i Kino.* Odessa, 1915 (regarding Joel Engel's lecture "At the Source of the Jewish Song").

*Utro Rossii.* Moscow, January 1917.

*Vestnik evreiskogo prosveshcheniia.* St. Petersburg, 1910-16.

*Velt Am Abend.* Berlin, 4-12, 1928.

*Zolotoe Runo.* Moscow, 1906, 1910.

## Miscellaneous Exhibition Catalogs

*Art in Revolution. Soviet Art and Design Since 1917* (especially "Constructivism in the Theatre" by Edward Brown.) London: Hayward Gallery, 1971.

*Austellung Jüdischer Künstler.* Berlin: Galerie Jür alte und neue Kunst, 1907.

*Bezalel 1906-1929* by Nurit Shilo-Cohen. Jerusalem: Israel Museum, 1983.

*Boris Aronson – From His Theatre Work.* Vincent Astor Gallery, New York Public Library at Lincoln Center, 1981.

Catalog for an exhibition by Nathan Altman, Marc Chagall, and David Shterenberg (in Russian). Moscow: Kultur Lige, 1922.

*El Lissitzky* (especially "Einführung" by J. Leering and "El Lissitzky in Warschau" by Henry Berlewi). Eindhoven: Stedelijk van Abbemuseum, and Hanover: Kestner-Gesellschaft, 1965.

*El Lissitzky 1890-1941.* Oxford: Museum of Modern Art, 1977.

*El Lissitzky* (especially "Information on the work of the Book Artist" by El Lissitzky). Cologne: Galerie Gmurzynska, 1976.

*El Lissitsky.* Eindhoven: Stedelijk van Abbemuseum, 1965-66.

*Evrei v tsarkoi Rossii v SSSR.* Leningrad: State Museum of Ethnography, 1939.

*Jewish Exhibition of Sculpture, Graphics and Drawings.* Kiev, 1920.

*Kandinsky: Russian and Bauhaus Years, 1915-1933.* New York: Solomon R. Guggenheim Museum, 1983.

*Malevich* by Troels Andersen. Amsterdam: Stedelijk Museum, 1970.

*Malevitch. Architectures Peintures Dessins.* Paris: Centre Georges Pompidou, 1980.

Marc Chagall. *Oeuvre sur papier*. Paris: Centre Georges Pompidou, 1984.

*Pablo Picasso, A Retrospective*. New York: Museum of Modern Art, 1980.

*Russian Stage Design* by John Bowlt. Mississippi Museum of Art, 1982.

*Sieg über die Sonne*. Berlin: Academie der Künste, 1983.

*Unovis: Art as Process* by Sarah Bodine. New York: Leonard Hutton Galleries, 1979.

*Vystavka kartin i skulptury khudozhnikov evreev* (cover designed by El Lissitzky). Moscow: Jewish Society for the Encouragement of the Arts, 1917.

*Solomon Borisovich Yudovin 1892-1958* by N. H. Vilenskoia and A. M. Zemtsova. Leningrad, 1956.

*Yubileinaia vystavka iskusstva narodov SSSR*. Moscow: GAKHN, 1927.

## Illustrated Books, (listed by artist)

Altman, Nathan. *Shtam/Azkore* by David Hofstein, and Aron Kushnirov. Moscow: Shtrom, 1922.

—. *Zverushki. Stikhi malenkim* by Natan Vengrov. Moscow-Petrograd, 1923.

Bernstein-Wischnitzer, Rachel. *Istoriia evreiskogo naroda* ed. M. Wischnitzer Moscow, 1914.

Chagall, Marc. *A Mayse mit a Hon* by Der Nister. [Petrograd]: Vilner Farlag B. A. Kletskin House, 1917. Vilna: B. A. Kletskin, 1917 (printed in Petrograd).

—. *Dos Tsigele* by Der Nister. [Petrograd]: Vilner Farlag B. A. Kletzkin House, 1917.

—. *The Magician* by Y. L. Peretz, [Petrograd]: Vilner Farlag B. A. Kletzkin House, 1917.

—. *Shtrom*. Moscow, 1922.

—. *Troyer* by David Hofstein. Kiev: Kultur Lige, 1922.

Lilien, E. M. *Evreiskii almanakh*. Kiev, 1908.

Lissitzky, El. *Dem Zeydns Kloles* by Tzadok Dolgopolski. Moscow: Tsentraln Yidishn Komisariat, 1919.

—. *Der Ber.* by Ben Zion Raskin. Kiev: Yidisher Folks Farlag, 1919.

—. *Der Milner, di Milnerin un di Milsteyner* by Ben Zion Raskin. Kiev-St. Petersburg: Yidisher Folks Farlag, 1919.

—. *Di Hon Vos Hot Gevolt Hoben a Kam* by Ben Zion Raskin. Kiev-St. Petersburg: Yidishe Folks Farlag, 1919.

—. *Di Weisse Tsig* by Alphonse Daudet. Kiev: Kiever Farlag, 1918.

—. *Hatochen Hatochenet Veavnei Hareichaim* by Ben Zion Raskin. Warsaw: Tarbut, 1923.

—. *Hob Ich Mir a Liedele.* Warsaw: Kultur Lige, 1922.

—. *Had Gadya.* Kiev: Yidisher Folks Farlag, 1919. Kiev: Kultur Lige, 1919.

—. *Kinder Gortn* (series) by Ben Zion Raskin. Kiev: Yidisher Folks Farlag, 1919-20.

—. *Andersen's Mayselekh* by Hans Christian Andersen (translated into Yiddish by Der Nister). Kiev: Kiever Farlag, 1919.

—. Sheet music by Joel Engel. Moscow: Society for Jewish Folk Music, 1919.

—. *Rabbi* by Olga Forsch. Berlin: Skythen, 1922.

—. *Shabbes in Vald* by Jacob Fichman. Kiev: Kiever Farlag, 1919.

—. *Sikhes Kholin* by Moshe Broderzon. Moscow: (Nashe Iskusstvo) Shamir, 1917.

—. *Six Stories with Easy Endings* by Ilya Ehrenberg. Moscow-Berlin: Helikon, 1922.

—. *The Spent Sun* by K. Bolshakov. 1916.

—. *U rek vavilonskikh.* Moscow: Safrut, 1917.

—. *Ukraynishe Folkmayses* by Leib Kvitko. Moscow: Der Yidisher Sektsie Bam Komisariat Far Folksbildung, 1922.

—. *Vaysrusishe Folkmayses* by Leib Kvitko. Moscow: Der Yidisher Sektsie Bam Kommissariat Far Folksbildung, 1923.

—. *Yingl Tsingl Khvat* by Mani Leib. Kiev-St.Petersburg: Yidisher Folks Farlag, 1919, Warsaw: Kultur Lige, 1922.

Maimon, Moisei. *Nashim Detiam* eds. M. G. Aizenshtadt and M. I. Daikhes. St. Petersburg, 1911-12.

Pasternak, Leonid. *Yiddish Folk Songs* by Joel Engel.

Ryback Issachar Ber. *Foyglen* by Leib Kvitko. Berlin: Shveln [1922].

—. *Gringroz* by Leib Kvitko. Berlin: Yidisher Literarisher Farlag, 1922.

—. *In Vald* by Leib Kvitko. Berlin.

—. *Pioneer Bichl* by Leib Kvitko. Kharkov: Knihaspilka, [1927].

—. *Vinter-Mayses* Kiev: Kultur Lige, 1919.

Shifrin, N. *Dos Pantofele* by Itzik Kipnis. Kiev: Kultur Lige, 1923.

—. *Dos Tsigayner.* by Itzik Kipnis. Kiev: Kultur Lige, 1923.

Shor, Chasia. *A Ber is Geloifn* by Itzik Kipnis. Kiev: Kultur Lige, 1924.

—. *Mayselekh* by Itzik Kipnis. Kiev: Soravkop, 1924.

—. *Russische Mayselekh* by Itzik Kipnis. Kiev: Soravkop, 1924.

Tchaikov, Joseph. *Baginen*. Kiev: All-Ukrainian Literary Committee Jewish Section, 1919.

—. *Bereishit by Abraham Krivoruchko (A. Kariv).* Berlin, 1925.

—. *Der Galaganer Hon* by Peretz Markish. Berlin, 1922.

—. *Dos Kelbel* by Mendele Mokher Seforim. Warsaw: Kultur Lige, 1921.

—. *Finf Arbeslakh* by Leib Kvitko. Kiev: Anhoyb Farlag, 1919.

—. *Kinder* by Aharon Reuveni. Kiev: Kiever Farlag, 1918.

—. *Lemel Nasher* by Leib Kvitko. Kiev: Kiever Farlag, 1919.

—. *Temerl* by Moshe Broderzon. Moscow: Farlag Khaver, 1917.

Tyshler, Alexander. Petukh by Natan Vengrov. Kiev, 1918.

Yudovin, Solomon. *Khozhdenie ba vostok venitseiskogo gostia Marko Polo prozvannogo millionshchikom* by P. Guber. Leningrad: Brokgauz-efron, 1929.

—. *Rasskazy o semi getto* by E. Kish. Leningrad: Khudozhestvennaia literatura, 1927.

—. *Starinnaia pavest* by S. Rozenfeld. Leningrad: Izdatelstvo pisatelei, 1934.

# Index

*Italicized page numbers refer to illustrations.*

צוויטן פֿרעמדע

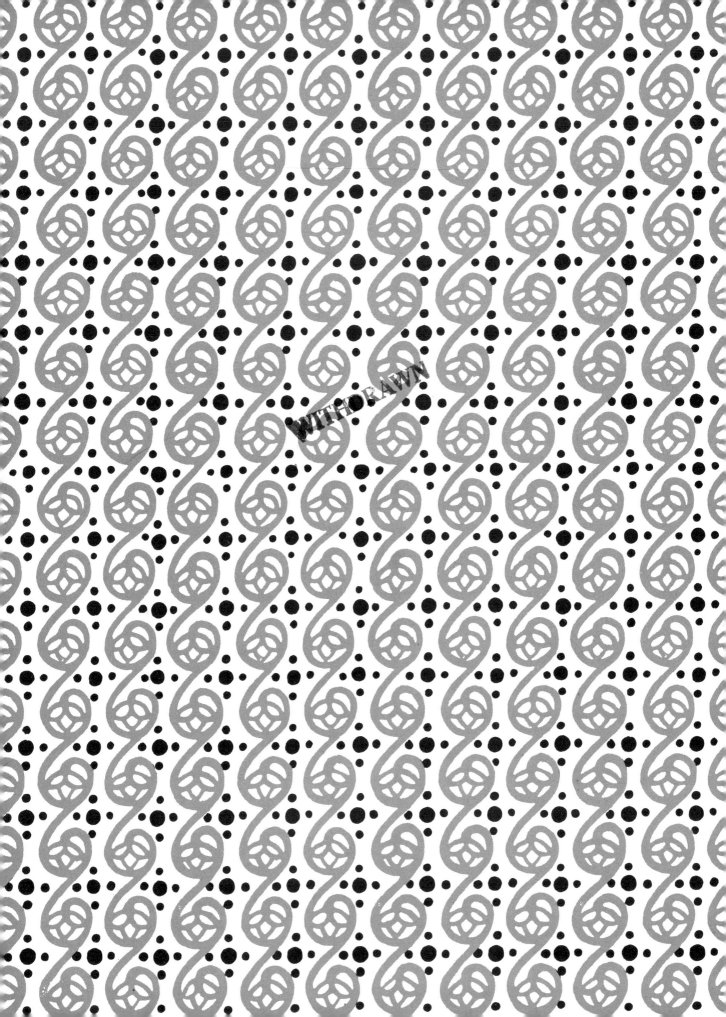